JOHN HENRY NEWMAN AND JOSEPH RATZINGER

JOHN HENRY NEWMAN AND JOSEPH RATZINGER

A THEOLOGICAL ENCOUNTER

EDITED BY **EMERY DE GAÁL** AND **MATTHEW LEVERING**

THE CATHOLIC UNIVERSITY OF AMERICA PRESS
WASHINGTON, D.C.

Copyright © 2025
The Catholic University of America Press
All rights reserved
The paper used in this publication meets the minimum requirements
of American National Standards for Information Science—
Permanence of Paper for Printed Library Materials, ANSI Z39.48–1992.

Cataloging-in-Publication Data is available from the Library of Congress

ISBN (cloth): 978-0-8132-3896-8
ISBN (ebook): 978-0-8132-3897-5

Book design by Burt&Burt
Interior set in Meta Serif Pro and Rift Soft

CONTENTS

Acknowledgments. vii

Introduction by Matthew Levering. 1

1 Seven Shared Hallmarks of the Theology of Newman,
Söhngen, and Ratzinger, *Tracey Rowland* 7

2 Newman and Ratzinger and the Development of Dogma,
Guy Mansini, OSB 35

3 Newman and Pope Benedict (Ratzinger)
on Faith and Reason, *Frederick D. Aquino* 55

4 Newman and Ratzinger on the Ecclesiastical
Scope of Scripture, *Aaron Pidel, SJ* 75

5 "Light and Darkness, Bless the Lord!" (Dn 3:72):
John Henry Newman and Joseph Ratzinger
on God's Mystery, *Marial Corona* 97

6 The Material Consonances between Scripture, Ancient Thought,
Newman, and Ratzinger on Conscience, *Emery de Gaál* 115

CONTENTS

7 The "Signs of the Times" in Newman
and Twentieth-Century Catholic Theology,
Andrew Meszaros 145

8 Approaching Ratzinger's Interculturality
through Newman's Power of Assimilation,
Jacob Phillips 189

9 Conceptions of the Ecclesia:
Mystical Body Imagery in John Henry Newman
and Joseph Ratzinger, *Elizabeth A. Huddleston* 211

10 Newman and Ratzinger on Ecclesial Authority,
Ryan Marr 233

11 "A Larger Idea of Divine Skill": Newman, Ratzinger, and
the Theory of Evolution, *Matthew J. Ramage* 255

12 Deification in the Work of Newman and Ratzinger:
A Comparative Analysis, *Jeremy Pilch* 282

Bibliography... 309

Index... 347

ACKNOWLEDGMENTS

It is our privilege to thank the superb contributors to this volume, which arose from a conference held at Mundelein Seminary in the Fall of 2022. The conference was cosponsored by the Center for Scriptural Exegesis, Philosophy, and Doctrine at Mundelein Seminary and by the National Institute for Newman Studies. We are very grateful for this support, and we especially wish to thank Jim and Molly Perry, who committed the necessary resources to the Center for Scriptural Exegesis, Philosophy, and Doctrine. The Perrys' generous financial grant also assisted us in readying the manuscript to be submitted to The Catholic University of America Press, a task in which we were aided by the estimable copyeditor Bob Banning. Here at Mundelein, we owe thanks to those who helped to make the conference a success, including Mary Bertram and Elaine LaMarre. Our gratitude also goes to the seminary's rector, John Kartje, and to the faculty of the seminary who have enhanced our lives and work. Matthew Levering's wife Joy is a constant source of support; may God bless her for all that she does! Last but not least, we are greatly indebted to John Martino and the team at CUA Press for steadfast encouragement of Catholic theology and for publishing this book.

This volume is dedicated to the memory of two beloved Catholics: Joseph Ratzinger/Pope Benedict XVI and Anne de Gaál.

INTRODUCTION

Matthew Levering

Catholicism over the past two centuries, beginning with the publication of the young Johann Adam Möhler's *Unity in the Church* in 1825, has arguably been shaped more than anything else by German Catholic theology. For example, the Tübingen School, founded by Möhler's teacher Johann Sebastian von Drey, has had an extraordinary impact. One also thinks of the German Jesuit scholars of the Roman School who contriuted much to the First Vatican Council, including Johann Baptist Franzelin and Josef Kleutgen. Then there are the contributions of perhaps the greatest theologian of his era, the Rome-trained German priest Matthias Joseph Scheeben.

In the twentieth century, in the decades prior to the Second Vatican Council, some of the brightest lights among Catholic theologians wrote in German: Erich Przywara, Hans Urs von Balthasar, Romano Guardini, and Karl Adam, just to name a few. After the Council, the impact of German-speaking theology has, if anything, been even more pronounced. One thinks of the worldwide spread of the theology of Karl Rahner along with the prominence earned by many other German theologians such as Johann Baptist Metz and Walter Kasper. However, Joseph Ratzinger surely merits a certain pride of place among all these thinkers, not only for his theology but also for his service and magisterial teachings as Pope Benedict XVI.

Arguably, too, of the above-named theologians, Ratzinger is the one whose writings and personality are most similar to those of John Henry

Newman. Yet, the contemporary German theologian Michael Seewald has sharply contrasted the two thinkers. Seewald argues that Newman, at least in the first edition of his *Essay on the Development of Christian Doctrine*, is representative of "*objectively regulated* theories, which claim to provide 'tests' that function as unambiguous indicators of a legitimate development."[1] In Seewald's view, Ratzinger's perspective on doctrinal development is quite different. Seewald describes Ratzinger as an exponent of "the *dynamic* type, which does not presuppose a static deposit of revelation, but postulates instead that revelation always occurs anew in the space of the Church."[2]

But this is a misreading of Ratzinger, since Ratzinger, with *Dei Verbum*, affirms a deposit of revealed truth as found in the Church's biblically grounded dogmatic teaching, which, for Ratzinger (as for Newman), does not allow for rupture or reversal.[3] Much depends, of course, upon what Seewald means by "static"—since both Ratzinger and Newman are well aware that the doctrinal reception of this deposit in the church is anything but "static," given that it dynamically develops and, in a sense, occurs anew in every generation. Seewald recognizes that in the final edition of his *Essay on the Development of Christian Doctrine*, Newman "downgraded the criteria that he described in the first edition," so that they become "notes" that "distinguish developments, but are themselves not given the character of a strict criteriological test."[4] Newman, like Ratzinger, rejects mechanical or solely logical understandings of doctrinal development.

Seewald, however, puts the matter more forcefully. He states, "The failure of attempts to identify rules and tests as unambiguous indicators of authentic development shows that doctrinal development is not a mechanical process, and that we cannot draw on methods from the natural sciences to discover

---

1 Michael Seewald, *Theories of Doctrinal Development in the Catholic Church*, trans. David West (Cambridge: Cambridge University Press, 2023), 176.

2 Seewald, *Theories of Doctrinal Development in the Catholic Church*, 176.

3 In his *Revelation, Hermeneutics, and Doctrinal Development in Joseph Ratzinger* (Steubenville, OH: Emmaus Academic, 2024), Mauro Gagliardi observes: "*Ratzinger . . . specifies that once approved councils have positively established doctrine, nobody, not even the pope, can contradict them.* If the episcopal body expressed itself definitively in communion with the pope, and the latter confirmed these decisions, then the doctrinal development manifested remains forever, as the inalienable patrimony of the Ecclesial Community. The pope cannot nullify defined doctrines or even doctrines that, although not defined, have always been proposed by the universal ordinary magisterium and, for that reason, are held by the Church as infallibly taught" (145–46).

4 Seewald, *Theories of Doctrinal Development in the Catholic Church*, 184.

INTRODUCTION

and present as formulas the laws according to which this mechanism works."[5] I do not think that Newman would accept the notion that the "notes" *fail*, given his understanding of converging probabilities in demonstration, and given his consistent insistence that if the church has contradicted a doctrine that it has previously solemnly taught (as part of the deposit of faith), then the Catholic Church has corrupted the deposit, and no theory of "development" can mask the presence of doctrinal corruption.

Newman is a relatively marginal figure in Seewald's *Theories of Doctrinal Development in the Catholic Church*—he is one nineteenth-century voice among many, and certainly not a guiding voice. The generation of German theologians who were Ratzinger's teachers, by contrast, found in Newman a particularly powerful and important voice, and the great English theologian and saint was a notable source of wisdom for the young Ratzinger. Emery de Gaál remarked about Ratzinger's seminary formation in the immediate aftermath of World War II, "Turning to the texts of the Church fathers, the Tübingen School of Theology, and John Henry Cardinal Newman had a liberating effect on young Ratzinger."[6] As Rowland and de Gaál observe in their essays in this volume, the prefect of studies at Ratzinger's seminary, Alfred Läpple, wrote his doctoral dissertation on Newman on conscience and introduced Ratzinger to this subject.[7]

In their study of "The Roman Catholic Reception of the *Essay on Development*," Kenneth Parker and Michael Shea noted that in the early 1960s, "Young theologians like Joseph Ratzinger embraced the need for a historicized [though, I would add, not historicist] understanding of tradition."[8] Parker and Shea make clear that over the course of his career, Ratzinger held to a consistently Newmanian account of doctrinal development. As Pope Benedict XVI, he presided over Newman's beatification in 2010. Traveling to England for the occasion, Benedict visited the Birmingham Oratory founded by Newman. He praised *The Idea of a University* as a model of true academic formation and also

---

5 Seewald, *Theories of Doctrinal Development in the Catholic Church*, 184.

6 Emery de Gaál, *The Theology of Pope Benedict XVI: The Christocentric Shift* (New York: Palgrave Macmillan, 2010), 24.

7 See de Gaál, *Theology of Pope Benedict XVI*, 25, as well as the essays by Tracey Rowland and Emery de Gaál below.

8 Kenneth L. Parker and C. Michael Shea, "The Roman Catholic Reception of the *Essay on Development*," in *Receptions of Newman*, ed. Frederick D. Aquino and Benjamin J. King (Oxford: Oxford University Press, 2015), 48.

INTRODUCTION

paid tribute to Newman's *The Present Position of Catholics in England.* Twenty years earlier, on the centenary of Newman's death, Ratzinger had delivered an address in Rome in which he recalled that in his Bavarian seminary, "Newman was always present."[9]

Claus Arnold has systematically examined the reception of Newman in Germany, and he points out that for the great German Jesuit scholar Erich Przywara in the interwar period, Newman was not to be set in opposition to Thomas Aquinas. Rather, in a "catholic polarity" typical of Przywara's thought, Newman's thought complements Aquinas's—much as Reinhard Hütter has argued in our day.[10] In 1922, Przywara published a multivolume collection of Newman's writings titled *Kardinal Newman. Christentum,* which included passages from Newman's Anglican letters and diaries translated by Edith Stein. Similarly, in the first decade of the twentieth century, Wilhelm Koch (later an ardent opponent of Nazism), guided Romano Guardini toward Newman and stimulated Maria Knoepfler's translations of a variety of Newman's works. Guardini's range of interests and personalist outlook reflect a strongly Newmanian spirit, even if he never published a book on Newman. For his part, Matthias Laros led a branch of liberal German Catholic thought sympathetic to Newman. Laros's associates included a diverse set of scholars, including the eminent figure Theodor Haecker, who converted from Protestantism due to his encounter with Newman's writings and who during the late 1930s translated many works by Newman.

In the aftermath of World War II, German Catholic enthusiasm for Newman's writings reached its apex. Numerous conferences and publications were organized, and important ecclesiastical figures became involved. During this time, the two German Catholic schools of reception of Newman—Przywara's and Laros's—both thrived. Of the two, Arnold concludes that "Ratzinger comes closer to Przywara's reception."[11] This makes sense given that Ratzinger's *Doktorvater* Gottlieb Söhngen was a major influence on the young Ratzinger's appreciation for Newman, as Rowland shows in her essay in this volume. Like

---

9 "Presentation of His Eminence Cardinal Josef Ratzinger on the Occasion of the First Centenary of the Death of Cardinal John Henry Newman," April 28, 1990, cited in Colin Barr, "Historical (Mis) understandings of *The Idea of a University,*" in *Receptions of Newman,* 116.

10 Claus Arnold, "Newman's Reception in Germany: From Döllinger to Ratzinger," *Newman Studies Journal* 18 (2021): 15. See Reinhard Hütter, *John Henry Newman on Truth and Its Counterfeits: A Guide for Our Times* (Washington, DC: The Catholic University of America Press, 2020).

11 Arnold, "Newman's Reception in Germany," 22.

INTRODUCTION

Przywara, though in his own way, Söhngen was a broadly Thomistic thinker who admired Newman and who developed an understanding of the *analogia entis* in critical dialogue with Karl Barth.

After Vatican II, Newman became much less important for German Catholic thought. For example, whereas the preconciliar Karl Rahner had written on doctrinal development in a strongly Newmanian way, Rahner's postconciliar writings explicitly break with Newman's perspective. Rahner argues that the era of "an evolutive explication and systematizing differentiation of the basic substance of faith"—taken for granted by Newman—is now over.[12] Today, relatively few German theologians follow Newman on doctrinal development or, for that matter, on much else.[13] As Arnold says, "the 'Ratzinger generation' of German Catholic theologians was the last one to be more or less uniformly and directly influenced by Newman's thought."[14]

The Anglican theologian Katherine Sonderegger has aptly described Newman as "a favorite of Ratzinger's youth."[15] Sonderegger recognizes that on issues such as Magisterium, doctrinal development, and conscience, Ratzinger has remained consistently in accord with Newman's perspective. At the same time, the mature Ratzinger only rarely wrote directly about Newman. To bring Ratzinger into dialogue with Newman, therefore, one cannot rely upon an extensive body of writings in which Ratzinger engages with Newman's main works.

Perhaps for this reason, Ratzinger and Newman have never been explicitly studied together, as the present book sets out to do. Our rationale for undertaking this project is that on topic after topic—doctrinal development, conscience, papacy, Magisterium, scripture, Mary, the university, and so on—Ratzinger's thought and Newman's are often deeply consonant and, in our view, mutually enriching. Both thinkers clearly have much to offer to

---

12 See Karl Rahner, SJ, "Yesterday's History of Dogma and Theology for Tomorrow," in *Theological Investigations*, vol. 18, *God and Revelation*, trans. Edward Quinn (New York: Crossroad, 1983), 3–34. See also the deeply un-Newmanian ecumenical proposal of Heinrich Fries and Karl Rahner, *Unity of the Churches: An Actual Possibility*, trans. Ruth C. L. Gritsch and Eric W. Gritsch (New York: Paulist Press, 1985).

13 One who consciously does is Gerhard Müller, former prefect of the Congregation for the Doctrine of the Faith and previously a professor of theology at Ludwig Maximilian University of Munich. See for example his *John Henry Newman begegnen* (Augsburg: Sankt Ulrich Verlag, 2000), as well as his *The Power of Truth* (San Francisco: Ignatius Press, 2019).

14 Arnold, "Newman's Reception in Germany," 23.

15 Katherine Sonderegger, "Writing Theology in a Secular Age: Joseph Ratzinger on Theological Method," in *The Theology of Benedict XVI: A Protestant Appreciation*, ed. Tim Perry (Bellingham, WA: Lexham, 2019), 39.

INTRODUCTION

contemporary theology. For Newman's part, he was in dialogue with some of the most influential German thinkers of his day. As an Anglican, he read Möhler, and as a Catholic, he engaged in a crucial debate about history and dogma with Ignaz von Döllinger, the great German Church historian and theologian who, on historical grounds connected with his insistence that only dogmas known to the church fathers can be true, could not accept the dogma of papal infallibility as pertaining to the apostolic deposit of faith, and who chose to die as an excommicant.[16]

The present volume begins with Tracey Rowland's examination of Söhngen's mediation of Newman to the young Ratzinger, emphasizing that the two thinkers (Newman and Ratzinger) exhibit seven shared "hallmarks." On this foundation in Ratzinger's formative encounter with Newman, the next six essays have to do with fundamental theology: Guy Mansini, OSB, on dogmatic development; Frederick D. Aquino on faith and reason; Aaron Pidel, SJ, on biblical inspiration; Marial Corona on mystery; Emery de Gaál on conscience; and Andrew Meszaros on the "signs of the times" in theological hermeneutics. Then come four essays broadly related to ecclesiology: Jacob Phillips investigates "interculturality"; Elizabeth A. Huddleston explores the imagery of the Mystical Body; Ryan Marr discusses how to understand ecclesial authority; and Matthew Ramage shows how Newman and Ratzinger offer constructive responses to Darwinian evolutionary theory, which illuminates the range of the Church's authority. Lastly, as seems fitting, the final word goes to deification—treated by Jeremy Pilch.

✳ ✳ ✳ ✳ ✳

Although both Emery de Gaál and I teach at Mundelein Seminary, he is a priest incardinated in the diocese of Eichstätt, Germany. We thus unite German and American streams of thought. It is our hope, therefore, that this book will not only stimulate the ongoing English-language interest in the thought of the great German Catholic Ratzinger/Benedict but will also help to stimulate a desperately needed renewal of German theological and philosophical interest in the thought of the great English Catholic Newman. Wherever one of these two thinkers is valued, the other will be too.

---

16 For further discussion, in the context of Pope Pius IX's *Tuas Libenter* (1863) and the rise of German nationalism, see chapter 5 of my *Newman on Doctrinal Corruption* (Park Ridge, IL: Word on Fire Academic, 2022).

SEVEN SHARED HALLMARKS OF THE THEOLOGY OF NEWMAN, SÖHNGEN, AND RATZINGER

Tracey Rowland

In a speech delivered on April 28, 1990, to mark the centenary of the death of Newman, Joseph Ratzinger wrote: "When I continued my studies in Munich in 1947, I found a well read and enthusiastic follower of Newman in the fundamental theologian, Gottlieb Söhngen, who was my true teacher in theology.[1] He opened up the *Grammar of Assent* to us and in doing so, the special manner and form of certainty in religious knowledge."[2] Of Newman he wrote: "He had placed the key in our hand to build historical thought into theology, or much

---

1 From 1947 until his retirement in 1958, Gottlieb Söhngen held the Chair of Fundamental Theology and Philosophical Propaedeutics in the Catholic Theological Faculty at the Ludwig Maximilian University in Munich. The faculty is associated with a seminary known as the *Herzögliches Georgianum,* the second oldest seminary in the world. Ratzinger's student years overlapped with Söhngen's decade in Munich. Söhngen became Joseph Ratzinger's *Doktorvater* and the supervisor of his *Habilitationsschrift.* During this period, Ratzinger's prefect of studies was Alfred Läpple, who gained his doctorate in 1951 with a thesis on the "Fundamental Features of a Theology of the Individual in John Henry Newman." Thus, the young Joseph Ratzinger had both a prefect of studies and eventually a *Doktorvater* who were interested in Newman.

2 Joseph Ratzinger, "Presentation of His Eminence Joseph Cardinal Ratzinger on the Occasion of the First Centenary of the Death of Cardinal John Henry Newman," Rome, April 28, 1990).

more, he taught us to think historically in theology and so to recognize the identity of faith in all developments."[3]

In 1946, Söhngen published a monograph titled *Kardinal Newman: Sein Gottesgedanke und seine Denkergestalt—Cardinal Newman: His idea of God and the Form of his Thought*—in which he described Newman as an "original theological thinker of great magnitude."[4] In the foreword, Söhngen also spoke of Newman as "the great English cardinal who has also become ours."[5] He declared that just as Shakespeare was adopted by the German people, so also Newman became "a thinker who inspired us Germans as if he were one of our own and as if he had written especially for us, without this interrupting his significance for the Christianity of England and the rest of the world."[6] This judgement concurs with that of Erich Przywara, SJ, who in a paper written in 1948 stated that "Newman was the name under which German Catholicism saw its own religious renewal after the [First] World War: it was the Catholic form of what Kierkegaard said was needed for general religious renewal."[7] Przywara further described this Kierkegaardian "renewal" as a triple confrontation with the crisis of the Reformation, the crisis of the conflict between Idealism and Romanticism, and the crisis of modernity in general.

The two main sections of Söhngen's book on Newman were originally delivered as a lecture during what was called "Newman Week" from October 7 to October 13, 1945, held at the University of Cologne to celebrate the 100th anniversary of Newman's reception into the Catholic Church on October 9, 1845. The entire book was later presented in three parts at a Newman Day organized by the two theological colleges in Bonn, the Collegium Albertinum and the Collegium Leoninum, on the first Sunday of Advent in 1945.

The following essay addresses seven themes covered in this work that highlight theological hallmarks shared by Newman, Söhngen, and Ratzinger. This is not to argue that these seven hallmarks were all first held by Newman, then transmitted to Söhngen, and subsequently mediated to Ratzinger. Such a thesis would require a doctoral-level analysis of the intellectual formation

---

3 Ratzinger, "Presentation of His Eminence Joseph Cardinal Ratzinger."

4 Gottlieb Söhngen, *Kardinal Newman: Sein Gottesgedanke und seine Denkergestalt* (Bonn: Verlag Götz Schwippert, 1946), 29.

5 Söhngen, *Kardinal Newman*, first page of the foreword, not numbered in the original text.

6 Söhngen, *Kardinal Newman*, first page of the foreword, not numbered in the original text.

7 Erich Przywara, "Kierkegaard-Newman," *Newman Studien* 1 (1948): 88.

of both Söhngen and Ratzinger in order to determine precisely what they *owed* to Newman and what they *merely shared* with Newman. This essay has a narrower scope of simply highlighting shared hallmarks or intellectual affinites, leaving the study of their genesis and precise mode of reception to others. In some areas, however, it is possible to declare a direct influence of Newman on Ratzinger via Söhngen because Ratzinger explicitly referred to the influence in one of his occasional lectures, as in the above-mentioned April 1990 speech.

CHRISTIAN HUMANIST GENTLEMEN

The first hallmark is the humanist disposition of Newman, his urbanity and openness to the best that classical culture has to offer. Söhngen was attracted to scholars with this disposition. In several of his publications, he praised his former supervisor Arnold Rademacher (1873–1939) for his interest in the unity of noble humanity with Christian holiness.[8] This notion of "noble humanity" was also called "Adventist Humanism" by Theodor Haecker, a public intellectual who converted to the Catholic faith after translating Newman's *Grammar of Assent* into German. Haecker used the expression "Adventist Humanism" to describe the humanism of Virgil, whose ideas represented the very highest expression of Roman culture on the brink, or "advent," of the Christian era. Newman, Haecker, Rademacher, and Söhngen all shared this interest in the synthesis of the classical *Humanitas* with Christian holiness. John Henry Newman spoke of this synthesis in his autobigraphical memoir of 1874, saying:

> One additional feature in Mr Newman's mind shall be noticed, which seemed to intimate from the first that the ethical character of Evangelical Religion could not lastingly be imprinted upon it. This was his great attraction to what he called the literature of Religion, whether the writings of [the] Classics, or the works of the Fathers. As to the Greek and Latin authors, poets and philosophers, Aeschylus, Pindar, Herodotus, Virgil and Horace, or again Aristotle and Cicero, he had

---

8 Gottlieb Söhngen, *Humanität und Christentum* (Essen: Verlagsgesellschaft Augustin Wibbelt, 1946), 7. Rademacher was a Professor of Fundamental Theology at the Friedrich Wilhelms University in Bonn.

from the first made much of them, as the Holy Fathers did, as being in a certain sense inspired moralists and prophets greater than they knew.[9]

In his *The Idea of a University*, Newman referred to Homer as the "first apostle of civilisation." He also noted that St. Charles Borromeo promoted the reading of Cicero, Ovid, Virgil, and Horace, and he proudly quoted a contemporary historian of Pope St. Gregory the Great as saying that Gregory supported the hall of the Apostolic See upon the columns of the Seven Liberal Arts. In their work *John Henry Newman*, Guy Nicholls and James Arthur commented:

> The Greek Fathers articulated a unique kind of pedagogy, or *paideia*: a much broader term than "moral education." *Paideia* implies more than a purely intellectual grasp of morality, by including a thorough training in its practice. Although it is a word that has been lost to modern educational vocabulary, *paideia* was central to Newman's thought, embracing the total development of the human person: body, mind, heart, will, senses, passion, judgements and instincts, aiming at *arete*, excellence in living. It is this concept of *paideia* that Newman took from the classical philosophers and Greek Fathers of the early Church and it runs through all his works.[10]

In the introductory section of this monograph on Newman, Söhngen drew attention to the contrast between the characters of Cardinal Newman and Cardinal Manning, noting that while both were Englishmen, both had lives that filled almost the entire nineteenth century, and both left the Anglican Church for Rome, one, Manning, "had the tangible consistency of the ecclesiastical man made for discipline," while the other, Newman, "had the delicacy of the *homo religiosus* with his reverence for all personality as the image of God."[11] It does not require too much imagination to identify Ratzinger with Newman in this distinction and to classify Ratzinger as a gentleman-scholar and eventual gentleman-pope who shared the interest of Newman, Haecker, Rademacher, and Söhngen in affirming the best of the tradition of "noble humanity" or

---

9 John Henry Newman, *Autobiographical Writings* (London: Sheed & Ward, 1956), 82–83. The author is indebted to Fr. Guy Nicholls for this reference.

10 James Arthur and Guy Nicholls, *John Henry Newman* (London: Bloomsbury, 2007), 90.

11 Söhngen, *Kardinal Newman*, 17.

"Adventist humanism" and absorbing it into an account of the humanism of the Incarnation.[12]

A secondary school report shows that the young Ratzinger studied eight subjects: German, Greek, Latin, mathematics, biology, physics, history, and geography.[13] His secondary school was what in Germany is called a "Humanistic Gymnasium." Söhngen had also attended one of these in Cologne, which at one time in its history gloried in the name of the "Tricoranatum," or "three crowns" school, a reference to the relics of the Magi—Balthasar, Melchior, and Kasper—said to be buried in Cologne cathedral. In his book of memoirs titled *Milestones*, Ratzinger recalled the education of his youth and said that it seemed to him, in retrospect, "that an education in Greek and Latin antiquity created a mental attitude that resisted seduction by a totalitarian ideology."[14] He noted that those of his teachers who had received such an education were not so easily manipulated as those who had missed out on this formation.

Throughout his career, Ratzinger constantly opposed movements to de-Hellenise the faith. In his Regensburg Address, he declared that the "inner *rapprochement* between biblical faith and Greek philosophical inquiry was an event of decisive importance not only from the standpoint of the history of religions, but also from that of world history."[15] He declared that this "convergence, with the subsequent addition of the Roman heritage, created Europe and remains the foundation of what can rightly be called Europe."[16]

In his General Audience Address of August 27, 2008, on the life of St. Paul, we have another example of Ratzinger/Benedict's appreciation of classical culture. In this context he wrote:

> Paul was born in Tarsus, Cilicia (cf. Acts 23:3). The town was the administrative capital of the region and in 51 B.C. it had had as Proconsul

---

12 The phrase "humanism of the incarnation" refers to the humanism built upon the notion, found in the conciliar document *Gaudium et Spes*, 1965, no. 22, among other places, that Jesus Christ reveals humanity to itself and makes it purpose clear (https://www.vatican.va/archive/hist_councils/ii_vatican_council/documents/vat-ii_const_19651207_gaudium-et-spes_en.html). In other words, Christ is the model of a perfected humanity. See also Tracey Rowland, *The Culture of the Incarnation: Essays in Catholic Theology* (Steubenville, OH: Emmaus Academic, 2017).

13 Derek Scally, "Roots in Traumatic German History," *Irish Times*, April 21, 2005.

14 Joseph Ratzinger, *Milestones: Memoirs, 1927–1977* (San Francisco: Ignatius Press, 1998), 23–24.

15 Benedict XVI, "Regensburg Address," appendix 2 in Tracey Rowland, *Ratzinger's Faith: The Theology of Pope Benedict XVI* (Oxford: Oxford University Press, 2008), 166–74.

16 Benedict XVI, "Regensburg Address."

no less than Marcus Tullius Cicero himself, while 10 years later, in 41 B.C., Tarsus was the place where Mark Antony and Cleopatra met for the first time.[17]

It is hard to imagine an "ecclesial man made for discipline" getting excited about a link between St. Paul and Mark Antony and Cleopatra or thinking that the faithful might be interested to know that Cicero was once the Proconsul of St. Paul's home town. For Ratzinger/Benedict, however, these elements of St. Paul's biography, along with the facts that he was a Jew from the Diaspora who had a name of Latin origin but spoke Greek and was a Roman citizen, giving him credentials in the three great cultures of the time—Roman, Greek, and Jewish—were not random accidents of history but acts of Providence that disposed St. Paul for "fruitful universalistic openness, for a mediation between cultures, for true universality."[18] For Ratzinger, the fact that St. Paul had a dream in which a Macedonian begged him to come to Europe was a sign that the culture of Greece was fertile soil for the reception of the Gospel. It meant that the meeting of Christianity with Greek culture was nothing less than a matter of divine providence.

Numerous other examples could be given of Ratzinger's knowledge of classical culture and sensitivity to its significance for Christianity. Suffice it to say that the kind of education that Newman received in English public schools and in Oxford, and that Söhngen and Ratzinger received in their respective "Humanistic Gymnasia," does foster what Söhngen called the "delicacy of the *homo religiosus* with his reverence for all personality as the image of God." Newman's sketch of the character of a gentleman in his *The Idea of a University* is his own account of that delicacy.

We do not have an essay by Ratzinger analogous to Newman's account of the nature of a gentleman, but we do have Ratzinger's own personality. When the Archbishop of Granada, Don Javier Martinez, himself a distinguished scholar of patristic works, was asked to comment on his meetings with Pope Benedict, he remarked that what left the strongest impression on him was Benedict's "exquisite manners."[19] Pope Benedict's speech announcing his

---

17 Benedict XVI, "General Audience Address," August 27, 2008.

18 Benedict XVI, "General Audience Address."

19 Javier Martinez, "Address to the Youth of the Archdiocese of Melbourne," May 12, 2014, in response to a question from the student audience.

intention to become a pope emeritus, delivered in Latin, epitomized this gentleman-scholar character.

Thus, the first of the shared hallmarks of Newman, Söhngen, and Ratzinger is that they are all classically educated gentleman scholars interested in the integration of the best of noble humanity—the humanism of classical Greece and Rome—with the humanism of the Incarnation.

THEOLOGICAL ANTHROPOLOGY

From this primary characteristic there flows a second, that is, a general interest in theological anthropology, especially in the relationship between faith and reason. We find this across all of their works, but with Newman, this subject is especially strong in his *Grammar of Assent*, while with Söhngen, it is central to his *Humanität und Christentum*, his doctorate on Kantian epistemology, and his *Habilitationsschrift* on human participation in divine knowledge. The theme also appears in Söhngen's 1947 publication *Der Geist des Glaubens und der Geist der Wissenschaft* (*The Spirit of Belief and the Spirit of Science*). With Ratzinger, the theme is especially strong in his *Introduction to Christianity*, his essay on the human person in *Gaudium et Spes,* his Regensburg Address, and the encyclical *Lumen Fidei*, which he drafted, even though it was promulgated in the name of Francis.[20]

Söhngen emphasized that for Newman, the image of the human person and of the world he inhabits is not an abstract-metaphysical concept but something historical and concrete. Newman did not view the human person through the lens of Aristotelian physics and metaphysics but with "biblical and Augustinian eyes"—he never regarded man, his nature or being, his abilities or powers in a way abstracted from the salvation-historical context of his fallen condition, otherwise known as the *status naturae lapsae*.[21] Another way to express this point is to say that Newman did not operate within a "duplex ordo" universe defined by a "pure nature" topped up by grace, as others of a more scholastic bent were inclined to do in his era. Söhngen argued that in the world of the English thinker, "who avoids abstract and metaphysical

---

20 For works addressing this dimension of Ratzinger's thought, see Maurice Ashley Agbaw-Ebai, *Light of Reason, Light of Faith: Joseph Ratzinger and the German Enlightenment* (South Bend, IN: St. Augustine's Press, 2021); Pablo Blanco Sarto, "Fe, razon y amor: Los discursos de Ratisbona," *Scripta Theologia* 39, no. 3 (2007): 767–82.

21 Söhngen, *Kardinal Newman*, 32.

concepts like ghosts, the metaphysical order of essence and property almost completely recedes before the ethical state and the order of its operations."[22] In contrast to metaphysical conceptions, Newman's vision of the human person is focused on the operation of the voice of God in the human conscience, and the conscience is always burdened with the guilt of sin. Söhngen regards Newman's assessment of the human predicament as "tragic," sharing qualities with Shakespearian tragedies, where the world, the human person, and nature are all out of joint.[23]

While Söhngen reads Newman as more Augustinian than scholastic and thus more Platonic than Aristotelian, he does note that Newman makes positive reference to Aristotle's *Nicomachean ethics*, and he suggests that it is significant that Newman appealed to Aristotle's ethics, not his metaphysics or a metaphysical piece of Aristotelian ethics. In so doing, Söhngen regarded Newman as quintessentially English and wrote that the "practical basic feature of English philosophy is written on [Newman's] forehead."[24] In other words, Söhngen seems to be suggesting that while a German scholar might get bogged down in abstractions and systems of concepts, not so an Englishman.[25]

While Ratzinger cannot be described as a practical Englishman, he does share with Newman and Söhngen an approach to the human person that begins with the person's actual place in post-lapsarian salvation history. All three authors accept that human nature is fallen, and this is a theological judgement at the center of their understanding of what is means to be human. In other words, their conception of what it means to be "human" is post-lapsarian, not a free-floating ahistorical "pure nature" of baroque scholasticism. In his *Apologia Pro Vita Sua*, published some six years before Vatican I's *Dei Filius*, Newman wrote:

---

22 Söhngen, *Kardinal Newman*, 32.

23 Söhngen, *Kardinal Newman*, 33.

24 Söhngen, *Kardinal Newman*, 37.

25 For other accounts of the place of Aristotle and Plato in the thought of Newman, see Scott Goins, "Newman: A Student and Tutor of Classics," in *A Guide to John Henry Newman: His Life and Thought*, ed. Juan R. Vélez (Washington, DC: The Catholic University of America Press, 2022), 140–57; Angelo Bottone, *The Philosophical Habit of Mind: Rhetoric and Person in John Henry Newman's Dublin Writings* (Bucharest: Zeta Books, 2010); Paul Shrimpton, *The Making of Men: The Idea and Reality of Newman's University in Oxford and Dublin* (Leominster: Gracewing, 2011); Johnathan J. Sanford, "Newman and the Virtue of Philosophy," *Expositions* 9, no. 1 (2015): 41–55; and D. J. Pratt Morris-Chapman, "The Philosophical Legacy of John Henry Newman: A Neglected Chapter in Newman Research," *New Blackfriars* 98 (November 2017): 722–50.

I have no intention at all to deny, that truth is the real object of our reason, and that, if it does not attain to truth, either the premise or the process is in fault; but I am not speaking (here) of right reason, but of reason as it acts in fact and concretely in fallen man. I know that even the unaided reason, when correctly exercised, leads to a belief in God, in the immortality of the soul, and in a future retribution; but I am considering it actually and historically; and in this point of view, I do not think I am wrong in saying that its tendency is towards a simple unbelief in matters of religion.[26]

This particular passage of Newman is evocative of Ratzinger's opening to his *Introduction to Christianity* in which he describes the situation of the believer as being like that of a person fastened to the plank of a shipwreck suspended over an abyss, an image he borrowed from Paul Claudel's *The Satin Slipper*. There is nothing in this image that suggests that all will be well if one simply adopts the correct philosophical method, that one can, as it were, reason one's way across the abyss with a textbook on logic.

Consistent with this more personalist approach to the act of faith the trio (Newman, Söhngen, and Ratzinger) also eschew an approach to the question of the *humanum*, which begins with a dissection of the human person into separate philosophical and theological categories. This comes across strongly in Ratzinger's criticisms of the document *Gaudium et Spes*. He spoke of the attitude of theologians from German-speaking countries, with which he clearly concurred, that in *Gaudium et Spes* there was not a "radical enough rejection of the doctrine of man divided into philosophy and theology."[27] These unnamed German-speaking theologians were "convinced that fundamentally the text was still based on a schematic representation of nature and the supernatural viewed far too much as merely juxtaposed."[28] In one of the most critical passages in the entire long essay, Ratzinger said that in the minds of the German-speaking theologians, *Gaudium et Spes* "took as its starting-point the fiction that it is possible to construct a rational philosophical picture of man intelligible to all

---

26 John Henry Newman, *Apologia Pro Vita Sua* (Melbourne: E. W. Cole, 1920), 335–36.

27 Joseph Ratzinger, "The Dignity of the Human Person," in *Commentary on the Documents of Vatican II*, ed. Herbert Vorgrimler (New York: Herder & Herder, 1968), 119.

28 Ratzinger, "Dignity of the Human Person," 119.

and on which all men of goodwill can agree, the actual Christian doctrines being added to this as a sort of crowing conclusion."[29]

The idea of finding philosophical unanimity among all "men of good will" was itself an extraordinary presumption in 1964 after almost a century of philosophical debate about the *humanum* and horrendous experiments with alternative atheistic humanisms. Leaving aside the merit of the presumption, Ratzinger remarked that the presentation of the human person from separate philosophical and theological angles makes the theological *imago Dei* concept "appear as a sort of special possession of Christians, which others ought not to make a bone of contention, but which at bottom can be ignored."[30] If agreement can be found on the plane of philosophy, then the theological explanations are for non-Christians, "an unintelligible addition to a picture that was already quite complete in itself."[31] It was for this reason that both Ratzinger and his papal predecessor, Karol Wojtyła, preferred to read *Gaudium et Spes* through the lens of its Article 22, which argues that the human person can only be fully understood if one begins from the principle that "the Adam-figure and the doctrine of man as the image of God are transferred to Christ as the definitive Adam."[32] In other words, the conclusion of Article 22 of *Gaudium et Spes* is that Christology is necessary for any adequate anthropology. Söhngen reached the same conclusion about the need for a theological account of the human person in his statement: "humanism has its great limit, this limit is exposed by Christianity and Christianity alone is capable of filling out this place where humanism fails, and thus of purifying humanism."[33] This notion of Christ as a pattern of a new or perfected humanity can also be found in Newman's appropriation of Alexandrian Christology.[34]

In Ratzinger's theological anthropology, the noble humanism of the Greco-Roman heritage is purified by way of the theological virtues and the gifts of the Holy Spirit. For Ratzinger, the act of faith is "a process that frees both the reason and the existence of the individual from the bonds that restrict them; it is the introduction of the isolated and fragmented reason of the individual

---

29 Ratzinger, "Dignity of the Human Person," 119.

30 Ratzinger, "Dignity of the Human Person," 119.

31 Ratzinger, "Dignity of the Human Person," 120.

32 Ratzinger, "Dignity of the Human Person," 121.

33 Söhngen, *Humanität und Christentum*, 76.

34 Roderick Strange, *Newman and the Gospel of Christ* (Oxford: Oxford University Press, 1981), 53–54.

into the realm of Him who is the *logos*, the reason and the rational ground of all things and all persons."[35] Moreover, Ratzinger observes that in St. Paul's *Letter to the Romans* the act of faith is defined as "the process by which an individual submits himself to one particular creed and, in doing so, performs an act of obedience that comes from his heart, that is, from the center of his whole being."[36] Here, the affinities between Newman and Ratzinger are palpably strong. Ratzinger subordinates philosophy to theology and insists that the two work together. In his *Apologia*, Newman says that the church's infallibility is a "provision, adapted by the mercy of the Creator, to preserve religion in the world, and to retrain that freedom of thought, which of course in itself is one of the greatest of our natural gifts, and to rescue it from its own suicidal excesses."[37] In his *Principles of Catholic Theology*, Ratzinger refers to the tradition of the church as a "ground station" in the sense in which the expression is used to refer to flight paths.[38] Without a ground station, flights would never reach their proper destination.

CONSCIENCE

The single most important element of Newman's theological anthropology of interest to the Germans was his account of the human conscience as laid out across his works, especially in the fifth chapter of the *Grammar of Assent*, his *Apologia Pro Vita Sua*, and in his various homilies. Newman's idea of conscience was widely discussed in German Christian intellectual circles during the Nazi era. In 1933, for example, Romano Guardini published a small monograph consisting of three lectures around the subject of conscience. It was originally titled *Das Gute, das Gewissen und die Sammlung* (*The Good, the Conscience and Inner Composure*). Newman's ideas were clearly the seedbed for this work. More well known, however, is the fact that the White Rose martyrs, the students at the University of Munich who wrote anti-Nazi pamphlets, had

---

35 Joseph Ratzinger, *Principles of Catholic Theology: Building Stones for a Fundamental Theology* (San Francisco: Ignatius Press, 1989), 328–29.

36 Ratzinger, *Principles of Catholic Theology*, 328–29.

37 Newman, *Apologia Pro Vita Sua*, 337.

38 Ratzinger, *Principles of Catholic Theology*, 101.

been introduced to Newman's idea of conscience by Theodor Haecker and that they discussed Newman in their meetings.[39]

Newman wrote that the conscience has both a critical and judicial office.[40] As a judicial office, it is "an authoritative monitor bearing upon the details of conduct' not something that supplies the person with 'the elements of morals, such as may be developed by the intellect into an ethical code."[41] It is not a "rule of right conduct" but a "sanction of right conduct."[42] It is the "connecting principle between the creature and his Creator."[43] Söhngen described Newman's concept of the conscience as the spiritual place where truth and reality meet.[44] He noted that for Newman, "a right conscience is both a gift and a task."[45] If the conscience, which is a divine gift given at the creation of man, is acting correctly, the voice of conscience will speak of a supernatural legislator and judge. The conscience can, however, shut itself off from this voice and its graces. In this case, when "people do not hear the law and the voice of a higher legislator in their conscience and do not even become aware of their guilt before God and their distance from God, then the Pauline saying applies that they are inexcusable (Rom 1:20)."[46] Newman's doctrine of conscience is informed by both St. Paul's *Letter to the Romans*, including the notion that the law of God is written on the human heart (Rom 2:15) and that God reveals himself in his creation (Rom 1:18–25).[47] Söhngen concluded:

> No power in the world, no matter how spiritual, can relieve the conscience of its responsibility; even God cannot do this without denying

---

39 The leading German authority on the White Rose movement is Jakob Knab. See Jakob Knab, *Ich schweige nicht: Hans Scholl und die Weisse Rose* (Darmstadt: WBG Theiss, 2018); Alexander Lloyd and Jakob Knab, eds., *The White Rose: Reading, Writing, Resistance* (Oxford: Taylor Institution Library, 2019). See also Paul Shrimpton, *Conscience before Conformity: Hans and Sophie Scholl and the White Rose Resistance in Nazi Germany* (Leominster: Gracewing, 2018); Romano Guardini, *La Rosa Bianca* (Brescia: Morcelliana, 2007).

40 John Henry Newman, *A Grammar of Assent* (London: Longmans, Green, and Co., 1891), 106.

41 Newman, *Grammar of Assent*, 106.

42 Newman, *Grammar of Assent*, 106.

43 Newman, *Grammar of Assent*, 117.

44 Söhngen, *Kardinal Newman*, 60.

45 Söhngen, *Kardinal Newman*, 65.

46 Söhngen, *Kardinal Newman*, 66.

47 John Henry Newman, "Sermon 17: The Testimony of Conscience," *Newman Reader*, https://www.newmanreader.org/works/parochial/volume5/sermon17.html. See also Malachy Carroll, *The Mind and Heart of St. Paul: A Newman Anthology on St. Paul* (London: St. Paul Publications, 1959).

his creation of man as a self-responsible personality. According to Newman, this self-responsibility of the human spirit extends into the rational, intellectual and scientific achievements. I am responsible for my sense of inference and the sanctions it gives to inferences and probabilities. The right foundation of belief . . . does not only take place in the necessary sequence of logical functions, but also in the personal decisions of my conscience.[48]

Newman therefore anticipated the twentieth-century movement toward the philosophy of Personalism and an accompanying theological anthropology that views the conscience as the focal point of the entire personality.[49]

Newman's ideas on conscience were still very much in the air at the University of Munich in the immediate postwar period when Ratzinger was a seminarian, though they did not play any part in his major pieces of research at the time. The treatment of the topic of conscience tends to occur in the fields of moral theology and theological anthropology, while Ratzinger's earliest pieces of research were in the fields of ecclesiology and fundamental theology. By the later 1960s, however, the issue of the role of conscience became central to the moral theology debates that followed the promulgation of the encyclical *Humanae Vitae* (1968). In his commentary on the theological anthropology of *Gaudium et Spes*, published in 1969, Ratzinger weighed into the debate against those who proffered a theory of conscience designed to undermine the teaching of *Humane Vitae*, writing:

> We must note here that the thesis emphatically asserted by J. B. Metz in particular, that Aquinas was the first definitively to teach the obligatory force of an erroneous conscience, is historically and objectively the case only to a certain extent and with considerable qualifications. Historically speaking, Aquinas is here following Aristotelian intellectualism, according to which only what is presented to the will by reason can be its object; and the will is always in the wrong if it deviates from

---

48 Söhngen, *Kardinal Newman*, 67.

49 For a developed account of this, see John Crosby, *The Personalism of John Henry Newman* (Washington, DC: The Catholic University of America Press, 2014); Walter E. Conn, "Newman on Conscience," *Newman Studies* 6, no. 2 (Fall 2009): 15–26; Donald Graham, *From Eastertide to Ecclesia: John Henry Newman, the Holy Spirit and the Church* (Milwaukee: Marquette University Press, 2012); and Florence Abala Kabala, "Conscience as the Capacity for the Truth of Love: A Comparative Analysis between John Henry Newman and Joseph Ratzinger" (STL Thesis, Pontifical Lateran University, Rome, 2013).

reason. It cannot once again control the reason, it has to follow it; it is consequently bad if it contradicts reason, even if reason is in error. In reality, Aquinas's thesis is nullified by the fact that he is convinced that error is culpable. Consequently guilt lies not so much in the will which has to carry out the precept laid upon it by reason, but in reason itself, which must know about God's law. The doctrine of the binding force of an erroneous conscience in the form in which it is propounded nowadays, belongs entirely to the thought of modern times.[50]

This reading of conscience follows Newman in holding that while one must always follow one's conscience, not every judgement of the conscience is accurate, and thus one can still be in an objectively sinful state even if one is subjectively blissfully unaware of one's real condition.[51] As Ratzinger wrote: "the guilt lies then in a different place, much deeper—not in the present act, not in the present judgement of conscience, but in the neglect of my being that made me deaf to the internal promptings of truth."[52] Ratzinger asserts that for Newman, "the middle term—which establishes the connection between authority and subjectivity—is truth."[53] He also observed that it seemed to him that it was characteristic of Newman to emphasize the priority of truth over goodness in the order of virtues, and thus that for Newman, truth is always a higher good than consensus.[54]

In various publications, Ratzinger affirmed Newman's comments in the *Letter to the Duke of Norfolk* to the effect that he would happily drink a toast to the pope but only after a toast to conscience, since the holder of the Petrine Office is himself held to account by his conscience. As he wrote: "the pope cannot impose commandments on faithful Catholics because he wants to or finds it expedient. Such a modern, voluntaristic concept of authority can only distort the true theological meaning of the papacy." [55] In contrast:

---

50 Joseph Ratzinger, "Dignity of the Human Person," 136.

51 See, for example, Newman's comments on hypocrisy in "Sermon 17: The Testimony of Conscience."

52 Ratzinger, *On Conscience* (San Francisco: Ignatius Press, 2007), 38.

53 Ratzinger, *On Conscience*, 24.

54 Ratzinger, *On Conscience*, 25.

55 Ratzinger, *On Conscience*, 34.

The true sense of the teaching authority of the pope consists in his being the advocate of the Christian memory. . . . All power that the papacy has is the power of conscience. It is service to the double memory on which the faith is based—and which again and again must be purified, expanded, and defended against the destruction of memory that is threatened by a subjectivity forgetful of its own foundation, as well as by the pressures of social and cultural conformity.[56]

In following the trajectory that flows from Newman to Söhngen and others in the generation of German Catholic scholars of the Weimar and Nazi periods, Ratzinger ended up in a very different position, both in terms of his ecclesiology and his moral theology, from those who constructed theories, and the casuistry they fostered, that were to be the object of so much criticism in St. John Paul II's encyclical *Veritatis Splendor* (1993).[57]

THE TREATMENT OF ATHEISM

Söhngen suggested that if one analyses Newman's passages on conscience, especially in his *Apologia pro vita sua,* one can find two basic ideas that behave like a thesis and antithesis. The thesis is: "God my creator, testifies clearly in the personal voice of my conscience, and this inner witness is, because it is clear, the rule by which the two outer testimonies, the universal voice of humanity and the course of the world, are to be interpreted." The antithesis is: "The situation of the world is in conflict with the God in the voice of men's conscience. For this God is a God of the moral order; but the world is in a state of horrible moral disorder." From these, it follows that there are two alternatives. The first is: "Either there is no Creation, or our Creator and Lord is, in particular, a silent, hidden God, who has withdrawn from His creation; the human race is out of His sight and must be entangled in a primal guilt." The second is: "Either there is no salvation from atheism, or God Himself has made an event by a special revelation to secure the belief in God, and for that purpose has set up in the world a teaching power that has infallibility in matters of religion.

---

56 Ratzinger, *On Conscience*, 36.

57 For an extensive account of the different theories of the role of conscience produced by moral theologians in the past century, see Matthew Levering, *The Abuse of Conscience: A Century of Catholic Moral Theology* (Grand Rapids, MI: Eerdmans, 2021).

Either Catholicism or atheism!"[58] Söhngen concludes this summary with the statement: "There is no middle ground, no via media. Outside the Catholic Church one is either halfway to Catholicism like the right-wing Anglicanism that Newman sought to highlight in the Oxford treatises; or one is halfway to skepticism and atheism like religious liberalism, whose dominant power Newman sought to banish in the 1833 Oxford Movement."[59]

Söhngen went on to write a whole section in his book on Newman on the thesis that the only true pair of alternatives is Catholicism or atheism. He praises Newman for taking atheism seriously and having the capacity to see that contemporary atheism is a *form of religion*. He thought that whatever may be the case with English Protestantism, however, a subject Söhngen did not see himself as having any authority or expertise on which to comment, Newman's outlook was "bitterly unfair" to German Protestantism. Söhngen declared that "confessional Protestantism" of the German variety was neither a half-way house to atheism nor a half-way house to Catholicism.[60] In his *Vier Predigten* über *das Abendland* (*Four Sermons on the West*), published in 1948, Erich Przywara does offer something of a genealogical account of the slippery slope from Luther to Nietzsche, but Söhngen is a little more irenic. He was quite heavily involved in interdenominational discussions, especially around the thought of Karl Barth and Emil Brunner, and the theological debates over the *analogia entis* and *analogia fidei*. Ratzinger is similarly irenic in his remarks about the Lutheran tradition and later famously brokered the deal with the Lutheran leaders known as the *Joint Declaration on the Doctrine of Justification*.[61] However, he says little about Calvinism apart from academic nods here and there to Karl Barth's seminal contributions to the antiliberal trajectory, or more positively, the Christocentric trajectory, of twentieth-century Protestant theology.

---

58 Söhngen, *Kardinal Newman*, 29.

59 Söhngen, *Kardinal Newman*, 26.

60 Söhngen, *Kardinal Newman*, 46.

61 For an overview of Ratzinger's engagement with Luther, see James Corkery, SJ, "Luther and the Theology of Pope Emeritus Benedict XVI," in *Remembering the Reformation: Martin Luther and Catholic Theology*, ed. Declan Marmion, Salvador Ryan, and Gesa E. Thiessen (Minneapolis: Fortress, 2017), 125–41. See also Mickey L. Mattox, "The Luther the Cardinal Did Not Know: Occasional Notes on the Luther of Recent Research," in *Joseph Ratzinger and the Healing of the Reformation-Era Divisions*, ed. Emery de Gaál and Matthew Levering (Steubenville, OH: Emmaus Academic, 2019), 169–91; Emil Anton, "Ratzinger and Reformation Ruptures," forthcoming in *Oxford Handbook on Ratzinger*, ed. Francesca Murphy and Tracey Rowland (Oxford: Oxford University Press).

While Newman's criticisms of Protestantism seem not to have left deep marks on Ratzinger's work, Ratzinger strongly echoes Söhngen's positive assessment of Newman's insights about contemporary atheism. Söhngen wrote that Newman was not "satisfied with the cheap argument of some apologists for Christianity, that there are no atheists out of conviction; that at the bottom of their soul those who call themselves godless also worship some idol."[62] Instead, "Newman has guessed that the only serious antagonist of Christianity will be a serious atheism that is, an atheism, so to speak, as a matter of conscience" or what "Newman understands as a dogma, a lived reality of which one is convinced and for which one is willing to die."[63] Friedrich's Nietzsche's indictment of Christianity on the charge of being a crime against life itself is an example of such an atheism as a matter of conscience, and Ratzinger is well aware of the social influence of this judgement. His moral theology lecturer, Theodore Steinbüchel, published an entire work on the subject in 1946.[64] Speaking of his time in the seminary at Freising, Ratzinger remarked: "I read Steinbüchel's two volumes on the philosophical foundations of moral theology, which had just appeared in a new edition, and in them I found a first-rate introduction to the thought of Heidegger and Jaspers as well as to the philosophies of Nietzsche, Klages, and Bergson."[65]

Ratzinger therefore affirmed the treatment of atheism as it appeared in Article 19 of *Gaudium et Spes,* saying that this section makes it clear that atheism does not "simply express a metaphysical failure or a breakdown in epistemology, but draws its inspiration from an authentic desire for a true humanism."[66] Nonetheless, he thought that Article 21 of the same document missed the opportunity to explore the deeper causes of atheism, writing:

> [The Council] took no account of Augustine's epistemology, which is much deeper than that of Aquinas, for it is well aware that the organ by which God can be seen cannot be a non-historical *"ratio naturalis"*

---

62 Söhngen, *Kardinal Newman,* 46.

63 Söhngen, *Kardinal Newman,* 46–47.

64 Theodor Steinbüchel, *Friedrich Nietzsche: Eine christliche Besinnung* (Stuttgart: Deutsche Verlags-Anstalt, 1946). For an English summary of Steinbüchel's work on Nietzsche, see Tracey Rowland, *Beyond Kant and Nietzsche: The Munich Defence of Christian Humanism* (London: Bloomsbury, 2021), 69–77.

65 Ratzinger, *Milestones,* 44.

66 Ratzinger, "Dignity of the Human Person," 146.

which just does not exist, but only the *ratio pura*, i.e. *purificata* or, as Augustine expresses it echoing the gospel, the *cor purum* ("Blessed are the pure in heart, for they shall see God"). Augustine also knows that the necessary purification of sight takes place through faith (Acts 15:9) and through love, at all events not as a result of reflection alone and not at all by man's own power."[67]

Ratzinger concluded that "the real answer to atheism is the life of the Church, which must manifest the face of God by showing its own face of unity and love' and he added that knowing God 'is not a question of pure reason alone."[68] For Ratzinger, it is axiomatic that without love, the work of the intellect will be severely limited and even disordered.

Following St. Basil, Ratzinger speaks of a "spark of divine love which has been hidden in us" that gives the person "a basic understanding of the good."[69] Conceptions of "pure reason" narrow the scope of reason by bracketing out the assistance of revelation and pouring water over the spark of divine love. Both Ratzinger and Newman stand in a line of tradition reaching back to St. Augustine that emphasizes the epistemic importance of the heart. This places them both in a very different position from scholars associated with the movement of Leonine Thomism that was focused on defeating the problems of contemporary atheism and relativism by reference to philosophical arguments. The mere mention of the word "heart," notwithstanding its biblical provenance, can raise fears of subjectivism from those with a strong training in Leonine Thomism. Ratzinger's position has been one of a mutual affirmation of love and reason, which he has declared to be the "twin pillars" of all reality.[70]

In taking a stance against the concept of pure reason, Ratzinger placed himself in a position outside the tradition of German Idealism and outside the school of Kant and all of his followers. In taking this stance against a sharp separation of faith and reason, and by implication, love and reason and hope and reason, Ratzinger again follows Newman. Söhngen observed that Newman judged the various historical forms of religion by the standard of their moral seriousness, namely, how strongly the sense of guilt manifests itself in

---

67 Ratzinger, "Dignity of the Human Person," 155.

68 Ratzinger, "Dignity of the Human Person," 157.

69 Ratzinger, *On Conscience*, 31–32.

70 Joseph Ratzinger, *Truth and Tolerance: Christian Belief and World Religions* (San Francisco: Ignatius Press, 2003), 183.

them. Hence, "on account of its 'dark and severe seriousness' Newman gives the religious 'need and tradition of barbarian times' the decided preference over the 'so-called religion of civilization and philosophy'; this educational religion of the one-sidedly educated and thus enlightened intellect is no longer a 'natural' but an 'artificial religion,' in short, a great farce."[71]

SCHOLASTICISM NOT THEIR "BEER"

Söhngen also drew attention to the fact that Newman was not a scholastic. He noted that on the title page of the *Grammar of Assent* is found the saying of St. Ambrose: *Non in dialectica complacuit Deo salvum facere populum suum*—God did not accomplish the salvation of his people through dialectics. He also quoted a series of now famous passages from the *Grammar of Assent* in which Newman wrote:

> The heart is commonly reached, not by reason, but through the imagination, by means of direct impressions, by the testimony of facts and events, by history, by description. People influence us, voices melt us, looks subdue us, deeds inflame us. Many a person will live and die upon a dogma; no man will be a martyr for a conclusion.[72]
>
> After all, man is *not* a reasoning animal: he is a seeing, feeling, contemplating, acting animal.... Life is not long enough for a religion of implications; we will never have done beginning if we determine to begin with proof.[73]

Moreover, in the *Apologia*, Newman confessed:

> I had a great dislike of paper logic. For myself, it was not logic that carried me on; as well might one say that the quicksilver in the barometer changes the weather. It is the concrete being that reasons; pass a number of years, and I find my mind in a new place; how? The whole man moves; paper logic is but the record of it. All the logic in the world would not have made me move faster towards Rome that I did.... And a greater trouble still than these logical mazes, was the introduction

---

71 Söhngen, *Kardinal Newman*, 33.

72 Newman, *Grammar of Assent*, 92–93.

73 Newman, *Grammar of Assent*, 94–95, cited in Söhngen, *Kardinal Newman*, 38.

of logic into every subject whatever, so far, that is, as this was done. Before I was at Oriel, I recollect an acquaintance saying to me that "the Oriel Common Room stank of Logic."[74]

Söhngen concluded that for Newman, "the art of syllogistic thinking is to starve every expression until it becomes the ghost of itself and sufficiently tame and bandy to exist as a mere definition."[75]

Nonetheless, Newman also wrote in his *Apologia*:

> I consider that gradually, and in the course of ages, Catholic inquiry has taken certain definite shapes, and has thrown itself into the form of a science, with a method and a phraseology of its own, under the intellectual handling of great minds, such as St. Athanasius, St. Augustine, and St. Thomas; and I feel no temptation at all to break to pieces the great legacy of thoughts thus committed to us for these latter days.[76]

His methodology may have been different from that of the Leonine Thomism of the late nineteenth and early twentieth century and his theological anthropology more variegated, less focused on the faculty of the intellect, but he was not iconoclastic.

Here again, there is strong affinity between Ratzinger and Newman. Alfred Läpple, the young Ratzinger's Prefect of Studies, is now well-known for his statement that the seminarian Ratzinger was not much impressed by a "*summum bonum* who does not need a mother." Läpple wrote:

> He [Ratzinger] didn't feel at ease with neo-scholastic definitions that seemed to him like ramparts, whereby what is inside the definition is the truth, and what is outside is all mistaken. But if God is everywhere—he would say—I certainly can't be the one to put up barriers and say: God is here only. And if Christ himself said he was the way, the truth and the life, then the truth is a You that loves you from beforehand. According to him, God is not recognized because He is a *summum bonum* that is able to be grasped and demonstrated with exact formulas, but because He is a You that comes forward and gets Himself recognized. The

---

74 Newman, *Apologia Pro Vita Sua*, 264–65, cited in Söhngen, *Kardinal Newman*, 39.

75 Söhngen, *Kardinal Newman*, 39.

76 Newman, *Apologia Pro Vita Sua*, 343.

intelligence can try to build concepts that define true contents. But this, according to Ratzinger, is a theology that claims to dissect the mystery, not a theology that kneels. And such theology already didn't interest him then. In the dialect of Bavaria we would say: it wasn't his beer.[77]

In the idiom of Newman, one might say that Ratzinger was more interested in the illative sense, in the certitude that follows from a personal encounter with God. As Vincent Twomey, one of Ratzinger's former doctoral students, remarked: Ratzinger's works are "filled with brilliant insights into almost every subject of theology and yet it is not a fixed system."[78] Of Newman, Söhngen remarked: "this distinction between concrete-real religion and abstract-conceptual theology is not meant in the sense of an irrationalism, a pure philosophy of experience and feeling, such as in England was found in evangelical piety."[79] Newman himself in the *Grammar of Assent* declared: "Theology may stand as a substantive science, though it be without the life of religion; but religion cannot maintain its ground at all without theology. Sentiment, whether imaginative or emotional, falls back upon the intellect for its stay, when sense cannot be called into exercise; and it is in this way that devotions fall back upon dogma."[80] Söhngen's overall assessment of Newman's theological methodology was:

> It is not a division of religion and theology, but their union into a theology of experience, that is Newman's great concern: a theology of realizing, that is, the image of religious reality through the living and efficient comprehension and assertion of the content of the faith. With that, Newman finds himself in the lineage of St. Augustine, the theologian whose heart enters the writing hand. But here, too, the difference should not be overlooked: Augustine combines deep psychological insight with metaphysical profundity and thus becomes the master of speculation on the psychological Trinity; Newman, on the other hand, remains as it were in the prolegomena to dogma. He is far more a philosopher of religion and a fundamental theologian than a

---

77 Alfred Läpple, "That New Beginning That Bloomed among the Ruins," *30 Days*, February 1, 2006, 1.

78 Vincent Twomey, Interview by Carl Olsen, *Ignatius Insight*, June 7, 2007.

79 Söhngen, *Kardinal Newman*, 40.

80 Newman, *Apologia Pro Vita Sua*, 121.

dogmatist.... [As he himself wrote] "It is not easy, humanly speaking, to elevate an Englishman to the level of a dogmatic religion."[81]

In Newman's own words from his Sermon 12:

> What, then, is the safeguard, if Reason is not? I shall give an answer, which may seem at once common-place and paradoxical, yet I believe is the true one. The safeguard of Faith is a right state of heart. This it is that gives it birth; it also disciplines it. This is what protects it from bigotry, credulity, and fanaticism. It is holiness, or dutifulness, or the new creation, or the spiritual mind, however we word it, which is the quickening and illuminating principle of true faith, giving it eyes, hands, and feet. It is love which forms it out of the rude chaos into an image of Christ; or, in scholastic language, justifying Faith, whether in Pagan, Jew, or Christian, is *fides formata caritate*.[82]

In this context, Söhngen has noted the significance of the second chapter of the *First Letter of St Paul to the Corinthians* for Newman's anthropology.[83]

BOURGEOIS PELAGIANISM

A strong theme toward the end of Söhngen's book is that Newman was not in favor of bourgeois Christianity. The expression "bourgeois Christianity" can frequently be found in German theological publications in the era between the two world wars, and the use of the expression is always pejorative. It signifies a form of Christian commitment that is about an outward conformance to the Christian moral code but without any real interior intellectual or affective engagement with the Persons of the Trinity. Söhngen wrote:

> What is heralded in Newman's concept of God, and what renders Newman seminal as a religious thinker, is his de-bourgeoisation of a bourgeois Christianity; the unsettling of a settled, bourgeois Christianity and of a settled, Christian bourgeoisie. Only a Christian God disassociated from middle-class attitudes and a majority disassociated

---

[81] Söhngen, *Kardinal Newman*, 41–42.

[82] John Henry Newman, "Sermon 12: Love the Safeguard against Superstition," *Newman Reader*, https://www.newmanreader.org/works/oxford/sermon12.html, §16.

[83] Söhngen, *Kardinal Newman*, 43.

from the middle-class are able to genuinely complement one another. Yet how deeply enmeshed the Christian churches remain within a middle-class Christian milieu, even after all the revolutions that have occurred; a middle-class Christian milieu from which they wish to depart just as little as the first Christians wished to depart from their Lord Jesus![84]

European sociologists often use the adjective "bourgeois" to refer to a mentality that is about conformism to social norms and the adjective "aristocratic" to refer to a mentality that is about a quest for the excellent. Those with an aristocratic disposition are idealists, wanting the best, while those with a bourgeois mentality are the pragmatists, wanting to satisfy the minimum standards required for social acceptance and upward social mobility. If this is how the terms bourgeois and aristocratic are understood, then Newman was certainly an aristocrat and antibourgeois. This sociological fact was emphasized by Frank O'Malley in an essay on Newman published in *The Review of Politics* in 1959. O'Malley wrote:

> Because he was what he was, Newman could not abide the Philistine, the creature who is, in Arnold's terms, vulgar in beauty and taste, course in morals and feelings, and dull in mind and spirit. He could not comprehend the bourgeois mind, the enemy of light and the children of light. His spirit was hierarchical and aristocratic in the finest way, that is, he was antimediocre, hostile not to the people but to mob-judgments and mob-standards, hostile to the complacency, the pharisaism, the traps of routine and the spirit of dead-levelling, the lack of order and distinction in modern civilisation. . . . Newman says of small souls: "They who are ever taking aim, make no hits; they who never venture, never gain; to be ever safe is to be ever feeble." And he advises against bourgeois prudence: "Calculation never made a hero"; "Every great change is effected by the few, not the many; by the resolute, undaunted, zealous few," that is to say, by those who are not mediocre, not tepid, who are willing, right in the spirit of Christ, to give themselves for others.[85]

---

84 Söhngen, *Kardinal Newman*, 51.

85 Frank O'Malley, "The Thinker in the Church: The Spirit of Newman," *Review of Politics* 21, no. 1 (1959): 5–23.

Although Ratzinger does not juxtapose bourgeois Christianity with aristocratic Christianity, he does criticize two forms of Pelagianism. He calls these "Pious Pelagianism" and "Bourgeois Pelagianism." Ratzinger uses the expression Pious Pelagianism to refer to the mentality that if one performs certain actions and refrains from others, then one is "owed" salvation. Pious Pelagianism is about a contractual relationship with God, not an affective relationship. He further uses the expression "bourgeois Pelagianism" to refer to the mentality that so long as a person is in line with general community standards, God cannot expect anything higher of them. As Ratzinger explains the mentality: "if God really does exist and if he does in fact bother about people he cannot be so fearfully demanding as is described by the faith of the Church. Moreover, I'm no worse than the others: I do my duty, and the minor human weaknesses cannot really be as dangerous as all that."[86] Ratzinger regards the two forms of Pelagianism as symptomatic of one of two spiritual pathologies: the Pious Pelagians are guilty of the sin of presumption, and the Bourgeois Pelagians are guilty of the sin of despair. Neither, in the words of Friedrich Nietzsche, "look redeemed," and neither showcase the humanism of the Incarnation. Both lend themselves to the kinds of criticisms of Christianity found in the works of Feuerbach and Nietzsche. When in a famous radio interview in 1969 Ratzinger spoke of the church of the future being smaller but more faithful, he appeared to be suggesting that these deformed versions of Christianity will inevitably implode from a *de facto* or constructive atheism into a *de jure* or self-conscious atheism.[87] One could argue that such an implosion has gathered momentum over the past half century. What is called secularization is the logical development of these two forms of Pelagianism. In neither case is there any strong sense that the Christian meaning of life is about sanctification, or what the Eastern Churches call deification. In the words of Newman in his *Parochial and Plain Sermons*, Sermon 20, we must "venture something for the faith," and it is precisely in taking such risks and

---

86 Joseph Ratzinger, *The Yes of Jesus Christ: Spiritual Exercises in Faith, Hope and Love* (New York: Crossroad, 1991), 81.

87 For direct quotations from the radio interview, see Tod Worner, "When Father Ratzinger Predicted the Future of the Church," *Aleteia*, 13, June 2016, https://aleteia.org/2016/06/13/when-cardinal-joseph-ratzinger-predicted-the-future-of-the-church/.

enduring dangers, anxieties, and uncertainty that we find the "excellence and nobleness of faith."[88]

Given the reluctance of many to undertake risks and dangers and the concomitant bourgeois desire for comfort and security and the spiritual malaise these dispositions foster, Söhngen rhetorically asked: "where are the beginnings of ecclesiastical movements that promise to be for our 20th century and the social arrangements taking place in it, that the mendicant Orders were for the 13th century and the emerging bourgeoisie?"[89] Both Newman and Söhngen understood the problem of a mere bourgeois Christianity and anticipated the need for what Ratzinger was later to call a new evangelization.[90]

THE IMPORTANCE OF SACRAMENTALITY

Central to a life of sanctification or deification is the work of the sacraments. Sacramentality is the major point of difference between Calvinism and Catholicism and thus was an issue in the Oxford movement's revival of elements of Catholic theology. In his *Apologia*, Newman wrote:

> The *Christian Year* made its appearance in 1827. It is not necessary, and scarcely becoming, to praise a book which has already become one of the classics of the language. When the general tone of religious literature was so nerveless and impotent, as it was at that time, Keble struck an original note and woke up in the hearts of thousands a new music, the music of a school, long unknown in England. Nor can I pretend to analyse, in my own instance, the effect of religious teaching so deep, so pure, so beautiful. I have never till now tried to do so; yet I think I am not wrong in saying, that the two main intellectual truths which it brought home to me, were the same two, which I had learned from Butler, though recast in the creative mind of my new master. The first of these was what may be called, in a large sense of the word, the Sacramental system; that is, the doctrine that material phenomena are

---

88 John Henry Newman, "The Ventures of Faith," §295, *Parochial and Plain Sermons*, Sermon 20, *Newman Reader*, https://www.newmanreader.org/works/parochial/volume4/sermon20.html.

89 Newman, *Apologia Pro Vita Sua*, chap. 1.

90 Ratzinger recognized the need for a new evangelization prior to the Second Vatican Council. See his essay "The New Pagans and the Church," first published as "Die neuen Heiden und die Kirche," *Hochland* 51 (1958–59): 1–11. The English translation by Fr. Kenneth Baker, SJ, is available on the *Homiletic and Pastoral Review* website, accessed January 30, 2017.

both the types and the instruments of real things unseen—a doctrine, which embraces in its fullness, not only what Anglicans, as well as Catholics, believe about Sacraments properly so called; but also the article of "the Communion of Saints;" and likewise the Mysteries of the faith.[91]

The subject of sacramentality and the mysteries of the faith are treated by Söhngen in his 1937 monograph, *Symbol und Wirklichkeit im Kultmysterium*. In it, he declared:

> Christianity is a religion of the mysteries, and the Christian mysteries are not primarily a teaching but a cult, that is, mysterious acts in which the salvation of Christ becomes a real presence under the veil of symbols or signs. To speak in Newman's language: the Christian mysteries, the healing deeds and teachings of salvation of the God-man are first present by the living faith with a real or pictorial real comprehension for the purpose of the cult. The conceptual doctrinal recording of the Christ mystery follows in second place for the purpose of teaching and teaching development. . . . On the other hand, however, the figurative real grasp, the cultic anticipation, loses direction without the conceptual grasp, without clear and unambiguous teaching terms. We heard how much Newman cares about both.[92]

Toward the end of this work, Söhngen warns against trying to understand the notion of sacramentality with reference to Aristotelian or Platonic philosophy, writing that "both modes of thought have their own dangers":

> The application of Platonic thought leads to an attempted hypostatization of the (inner) sacramental simulacrum, as though this exists apart from the sacramental effectiveness and that this were somehow inherent. A unilateral employment of Aristotelian modes of thought leads to conceiving of the recollection of the salvific works of Christ within the sacramental action in a purely symbolic way, as purely external images, and to deeming the inner imitation of Christ that takes place within man as the external end of the sacramental effect, towards which the effect or grace is directed. We must attempt to

91 Newman, *Apologia Pro Vita Sua*, chap. 1.
92 Söhngen, *Kardinal Newman*, 53–54.

understand the sacrament within the mysterious symbolism that is particular to it alone.[93]

Joseph Ratzinger followed a similar path in his 1987 lecture, "The Meaning of Sacrament." He began by observing that the reality of sacramentality "is central for Christian consciousness but marginal for the normal awareness of everyday life today."[94] He then went on to emphasize that if we want to understand sacraments, we need to understand symbolism and the notion of mysterium. Much of the essay is taken up with a refutation of Eberhard Jüngel's judgement that Catholic conceptions of sacramentality are wrong because they rely on ideas borrowed from the Greek mystery cults. Ratzinger argues that while St. Paul adopts the terminology of the Greek mystery religions, "from a Christian point of view, [he] virtually turns them into the opposite."[95] Ratzinger recommends a reading of sacramentality as a blending together of "mystery" and "type." It is a very Pauline approach rather than an Aristotelian or Platonic approach. As Timothy P. O'Malley has argued, for Ratzinger, the sacramental economy is not "a neo-Platonic escape into some transcendent reality outside of time and space." It is instead "the recognition that all that is material will be transfigured not through an abstract divine reality but the sacrificial love of Jesus Christ."[96]

CONCLUSION

According to Alfred Läpple, Söhngen once drew an analogy between his relationship to Joseph Ratzinger and the relationship between St. Albert the Great and St. Thomas Aquinas. Like St. Albert, Söhngen recognized that he had a student who was destined to become much more renowned than himself. If Ratzinger comes to be regarded as a Doctor of the Church, along with Thomas and Albert, then at least one part of the back-story to the intellectual formation of the young seminarian Ratzinger is Gottlieb Söhngen's work on Newman and the wider interest in Newman within Catholic intellectual circles in interwar Germany. The young Ratzinger shared the Victorian English enthusiasm for

---

93 Gottlieb Söhngen, *Symbol und Wirklichkeit im Kultmysterium* (Bonn: Peter Hanstein, 1937), 95.

94 Joseph Ratzinger, "The Meaning of Sacrament," *FCS Quarterly* (Spring 2011): 28.

95 Ratzinger, "Meaning of Sacrament," 30.

96 Timothy P. O'Malley, "Joseph Ratzinger Is Not a Platonist," *Church Life Journal* 16 (October 2018), https://churchlifejournal.nd.edu/articles/joseph-ratzinger-is-not-a-platonist/.

noble or Adventist Humanism, for the Greco-Roman legacy, as did Söhngen. He also shared Newman and Söhngen's personalist approach to moral theology, their Pauline approach to conscience and sacramentality, and their preference for the patristic mode of doing theology over the neoscholastic emphasis on conceptual system building. He also understood, with both Newman and Söhngen, that the new atheism is itself a form of humanism and a religion. This is not, however, to argue for a straight theory of reception from Newman to Söhngen, then Söhngen to Ratzinger. In some cases, a straight theory of reception may well be demonstrable, but in others, there may have been more than one intermediary between Newman and Ratzinger. For example, Alfred Läpple, the young Ratzinger's Prefect of Studies, and Theodor Haecker, the journalist and translator described by Ratzinger as one of the heroes of his youth, were also significant figures in the German reception of Newman. For those who wish to understand Ratzinger's position in the world of Catholic letters of the past century and a half, however, it helps to be able to identify significant hallmarks he shared with Newman and Söhngen. This stream of Catholic theology flowed into the debates of the Second Vatican Council, and it remains at the core of the fundamental theology of scholars associated with the journal *Communio*, founded by Ratzinger, among others, in 1972.

2

NEWMAN AND RATZINGER AND THE DEVELOPMENT OF DOGMA

Guy Mansini, OSB

In December of 1965, a week after the close of the Second Vatican Council, Joseph Ratzinger delivered a lecture that addressed "The Problem of the History of Dogma from a Catholic Viewpoint."[1] In it, he speaks of the history of dogma rather than development of dogma, since the history includes both progress and decline.[2] An understanding of both, however, is required as an integral element of any future Catholic dogmatics. It was the point of the lecture to show this.

Ratzinger was well set up to deliver just such an argument in 1965. His *Habilitationsshrift* of 1955 on St. Bonaventure, afterall, included a careful consideration of the nature of revelation and the theology of history.[3] At the Second Vatican Council, he provided Cardinal Frings with a critical evaluation

---

[1] Joseph Ratzinger, *Das Problem der Dogmengeschichte in der Sicht der katholischen Theologie* (Cologne: Westdeutscher Verlag, 1966). This lecture was first given under the auspices of the Arbeitsgemeinschaft für Forschung des Landes Nordrhein-Westfalen in Düsseldorf on December 15, 1965.

[2] Ratzinger, *Das Problem der Dogmengeschichte*, 12n9.

[3] Joseph Ratzinger, *Das Offenbarungsverständnis und die Geschichtstheologie Bonaventuras: Habilitationsschrift und Bonaventura-Studien*, in *Joseph Ratzinger: Gesammelte Schriften*, vol. 2, ed. Gerhard Ludwig Müller (Freiburg: Herder, 2009). The second half of this study was published in English in Joseph Ratzinger, *The Theology of History in St. Bonaventure*, trans. Zachary Hayes, OFM (Chicago: Franciscan Herald Press, 1971).

of the proposed schema *De fontibus revelationis*, later expanded in a lecture for German-speaking bishops in October of 1962, the most important point of which is that revelation is prior to the witnesses to it, scripture and tradition.[4] In view of the council's work, he had also proposed a synthetic treatment, *De voluntate Dei erga hominem*, which formed a compact treatment of revelation and the witnesses to it, its purpose, and its Christological nature.[5] During the council, he wrote on the notion of tradition at the Council of Trent.[6]

In what follows, there is first an extended summary of the content and argument of "The Problem of the History of Dogma." Second, the standards that his account implies must be met by any Catholic account of the development or history of dogma are articulated. The third section of this essay asks whether John Henry Newman's *Essay on the Development of Christian Doctrine* meets these standards. Doubtless, Ratzinger's thinking on the history and historicity of dogma are influenced by his reading of Newman, but it will be more illuminating for us in our own theological moment to read backward from Ratzinger to Newman than to read forward from Newman to Ratzinger. That is because there is a development from Newman to Ratzinger, and developments are most easily understood from their later moments, just as a stream is clearer to us, as someone has said, when its bed is deep and broad and full than at its spring.

"THE PROBLEM OF THE HISTORY OF DOGMA FROM A CATHOLIC VIEWPOINT"

"The Problem of the History of Dogma" is nicely arranged and executed. First, it considers *past* "histories" of dogma, Catholic and Protestant; second, it indicates our *present* access to the history of Christian faith and theology;

---

4 Joseph Ratzinger, "Evaluation of the First Draft Texts for Vatican II, prepared for Cardinal Frings,"; Joseph Ratzinger, "Observations on the Schema *De fontibus revelationis*," in Jared Wicks, SJ, "Six Texts by Prof. Ratzinger as *Peritus* before and during Vatican Council II," *Gregorianum* 89 (2008): 233–311.

5 Joseph Ratzinger, "The Will of God regarding Human Beings," in Jared Wicks, SJ, "Another Text by Joseph Ratzinger as *Peritus* at Vatican II," *Gregorianum* 101 (2020): 233–49.

6 Joseph Ratzinger, "The Question of the Concept of Tradition: A Provisional Response," in *God's Word: Scripture—Tradition—Office*, trans. Henry Taylor, ed. Peter Hünermann and Thomas Söding (San Francisco: Ignatius Press, 2008), 41–89. This study first appeared in 1965.

and third, it delimits the historical challenge Catholic theology must face in the *future*.

In a "Preliminary Reflection" that serves to introduce the lecture, however, Ratzinger contrasts the modern and the medieval minds: "as the Middles Ages had undertaken a *reductio in theologiam* for the whole range of knowledge, so now an equally all-encompassing *reductio in historiam* is carried out."[7] We are to think of St. Bonaventure's *De reductione artium in theologiam*. Ratzinger does not contest the legitimacy of the call for such a reduction to history, the call to consider things in their becoming, the call to acknowledge the historical character of all phenomena. He grants that Christian faith and theology do not escape this call, even though it seems to put faith in question as possessing the absolute and immutable truth of God: "The final stage of the [modern] movement of thought was no longer the return of historical change to the abiding truth of God, but the return of the apparently abiding to the creative process of historical changes."[8] If he does not dismiss the call for leading all things, including Christian things, back to history, however, neither does he reject the call to lead all things and all truths back to God, which would include historical truth—the truth history discovers about whatever it is that it considers.[9] He notes the two calls, the two reductions. If we may put it this way, the problem the lecture addresses is how to think about the relation of both of these calls to one another given that their most intimate encounter is in the history of Christian things and Christian dogma.

---

7 Ratzinger, *Das Problem der Dogmengeschichte*, 7.

8 Ratzinger, *Das Problem der Dogmengeschichte*, 8.

9 Of course, there is nothing named "history" that is led back to theology in St. Bonaventure's *De reductione artium*. But this is deceptive. The history of Israel is led to theological intelligibility according to Bonaventure by the word of God delivered by the prophets, and the entire saving history of the world and its truth will at the end of time be led to Christ. See Ratzinger, *Theology of History*, 75–84, esp. 82–84. On the other hand, summarizing Bonaventure, Ratzinger says, "Only he who knows its [Scripture's] *history* knows its [theological] meaning" (83, emphasis added). Richard DeClue Jr., *Joseph Ratzinger's Theology of Divine Revelation* (Washington, DC: The Catholic University of America Press, 2021), 187, summarizes Ratzinger's understanding of Bonaventure's theology of the Word as follows: the Word as pattern of creation is the center of metaphysics; the Word as incarnate is the center of history; and the Word as both human and divine, declaring the truth of both God and man, is the center of dogma. DeClue's dissertation is available at https://cuislandora.wrlc.org/islandora/object/cuislandora%3A223939/datastream/PDF/view. For the threefold consideration of the Word as Son, the metaphysical pattern of creation, and as incarnate, see Ratzinger, *Das Offenbarungsvertändnis und die Geschichtstheologie Bonaventuras*, 132–34; relative to the emanation of things from God and their return to him, see 136, and for Christ as center of history, see 242–44.

Part 1 of the lecture addresses itself to past considerations of the history, or what passed for the history of dogma, Catholic and Protestant. First, however, he addresses two magisterial constraints that hampered Catholic historical endeavors. In the fourth chapter of *Dei Filius*, the First Vatican Council taught in 1870 that once defined, dogma is immutable and, contrary to the position of Anton Günther, not perfectible in the way that some philosophical discovery of human reason is perfectible. The council cites Vincent of Lérins, according to whom there is progress in achieving insight into the same dogma, and this, Ratzinger says, opens the door to a recognition of the historicity of dogmatic statements and their reception. But in fact, it was rather the Vincentian canon, according to which only what has been held in faith *semper, ubique, et ab omnibus*, that controlled Catholic thought on tradition and its history and therefore precluded any genuine history of dogmas.

The second magisterial constraint was imposed by Pius X in the decree *Lamentabili* of 1907, which provided the first magisterial formulation of the principle that revelation is closed with the death of the last apostle (no. 21; DH 3420) and rejected the rejection of the idea that dogma is "a truth fallen from heaven" and is instead merely "a certain interpretation of religious facts that the human mind has acquired by laborious effort" (no. 22; DH 3422). Is it the laborious and historically conditioned effort of formulation that is reproved, or the denial of the divine authority of dogma, or both? However *Lamentabili* is to be interpreted, it discourages coming to terms with the historicity of the path to the formulation of dogma, just as does Vatican I's emphasis on the immutability of a dogma once formulated hinders a consideration of its history *after* it is formulated.

Ratzinger then turns to a characterization of Catholic and Protestant thinking on the history of dogma, where Catholic thought was controlled by the idea of unwritten traditions that enabled it to assert an "identity theology" such that there really is no history of Christian faith and teaching to be discerned since all of it was explicit from the beginning, and where Protestant thought was controlled by the idea of a fall into Catholicism, which includes not just a recognition of history but a history of ever-increasing Catholic corruptions of the gospel, not a history of genuinely and holy Christian things:

> While the post-Tridentine Catholic acceptance of tradition [i. e., of the postulation of unwritten traditions] forced a loss of history, the Protestant criticism of tradition led equally to a critique of history which

THE DEVELOPMENT OF DOGMA

it rejected as *Christian* history, and therewith demanded a history-less concept of Christianity in another way.[10]

Nor, for Ratzinger, do the more modern Protestant histories of dogma, for example, those of Adolf von Harnack or Reinhold Seeberg, escape from the project of detailing a fall from Christian things rather than presenting a proper history of a Christian reality that remains truly Christian. And modern Catholic histories, such as A. Landgraf's history of early scholasticism, only modify the standard Catholic approach and do not reconstruct it.

Ratzinger then turns in part 2 to providing contemporary points of departure for recognizing the historicity of Christianity. Each way of access itself depends on a careful deployment of historical research and illustrates its power in the service of theological thinking. The second and third, from the idea of revelation and the idea of tradition, evidently belong to fundamental theology, as is appropriate. The first, too, belongs equally to fundamental theology, although it is more expressly Christologically focused. Faith, Ratzinger observes, bears not simply on a past Christ but also on the present and coming Christ, since faith is foundationally faith in his resurrection. This means that when the believer hears again the words of Christ recorded in the scriptures, he is not activating a past voice, as we do when we recite the Gettysburg Address or Lincoln's Second Inaugural, but rather is hearing Christ speaking to him now.[11] This means that Christ's speaking is speaking into our situation, our circumstances, and so will be heard now perhaps in a new way. The historicity of Christian faith is therefore written into how faith in Christ, and so revelation itself, is actualized by Christians across the centuries.

Ratzinger appeals for this understanding to Günther Bornkamm, a distinguished proponent of the "Second Quest" for the historical Jesus, then at the height of his influence. This understanding reflects the original experience of the first Christians recollecting and hearing again the logia of a living Jesus, and it is the very reason why we have the sayings in more than one form.[12]

---

10 Ratzinger, *Das Problem der Dogmengeschichte*, 14.

11 Ratzinger, *Das Problem der Dogmengeschichte*, 16. Ratzinger made the same point just before the opening of the Second Vatican Council in a speech to the German bishops on October 10, 1962, criticizing the draft schema on the sources of revelation. See "Observations on the Schema *De fontibus revelationis*," in Wicks, "Six Texts by Prof. Joseph Ratzinger," 282.

12 Günther Bornkamm, *Jesus of Nazareth*, trans. Irene and Fraser McLuskey with James M. Robinson (New York: Harper & Row, 1960 [German, 1956]), 20–21.

Faith in the presence of Jesus is thus something theologically prior to the formulation of his sayings as preserved by the church, the first stage of what we may call "the history of dogma." It follows first that the core of Christ's teaching cannot consist in one or another formulation in human words but calls instead for "new appropriations" and translations.[13] It follows as well that Christianity is not turned exclusively to the past, but also to the future: "The course of Christianity is not finished with the originating event, even if it receives from it its authoritative and abiding norms."[14] The "originating event" does not unfold itself and realize all its possibilities except in its encounter with humanity over the course of time. This way of thinking is very much like Newman's way of conceiving how an "idea" is realized in history—realized in the minds of men who in different places and across time in turn encounter, consider, explore, compare, interpret it.

Ratzinger closes this section by pointing out the evident need for a critical historical control of what does and does not constitute a genuine encounter of the core, or its origins, with what follows, and the expressions thereof. He has also adverted to the need for some transcendent guarantee of what is and is not genuine adaptation and appropriation. The thoughtful reader could already put two and two together at his point and say that these two controls must work together and in harmony and within each other.

The second point of access to the historicity of revelation and faith, dogma and theology, is provided by the idea of revelation itself. There has already been at work in the appeal to the Christology of the first Christians an understanding that revelation does not occur unless someone receives it: there is no showing unless someone sees; there is no speaking unless someone hears. This insight, central to his *Habilitationsschrift* on St. Bonaventure, comes into play more expressly in this section.[15]

Concordant with Ratzinger's insistence on the dialogical nature of revelation just adverted to—nothing shown unless it is seen—is Ratzinger's characterization of revelation as an event. It is not to be conceived of as a summa of propositions, and indeed, a collection abstracted from the intended hearer of the word and so existing in a sort of no man's land between God and

---

13 Ratzinger, *Das Problem der Dogmengeschichte*, 16.

14 Ratzinger, *Das Problem der Dogmengeschichte*, 17.

15 Ratzinger, *Das Offenbarungsverständnis*, 91–92, 101–2, 221, 239–41; Ratzinger, "Question of the Concept of Tradition," 52; and DeClue, *Joseph Ratzinger's Theology of Divine Revelation*, 183–85.

THE DEVELOPMENT OF DOGMA

man, but rather as an event.[16] Two things are to be noted. First, Ratzinger here continues the effort of the *Habilitationsschrift* to pry the notion of revelation out of the grip of a neoscholasticism that since F. Suarez has narrowed revelation to its propositional articulation.[17] Second, although he does not mention Karl Barth here as helping open up the idea of revelation to include more than its propositional articulation, he does so in his commentary on *Dei Verbum*, which is practically coeval with "Das Problem."[18] "Revelation in the biblical realm," Ratzinger summarizes in "Das Problem," "is not grasped as a system of propositions but as the occurring and in faith always still occurring event of a new relation between God and man."[19]

Ratzinger's exposition of this point of access to the historicity of dogma importantly includes his frontal attack on a too-simplistic notion of the closure of revelation with the death of the last apostle. The closure axiom cannot be an original datum of Christian consciousness for two reasons. First, the fathers regularly spoke of ecumenical councils as inspired of the Holy Spirit. Second, the Middle Ages also recognized a continuing inspiration of the Holy Spirit giving the church access to new understandings of the revelation of Christ.[20] So revelation cannot therefore be conceived as a collection of propositions finished with the closure of the New Testament canon, and to do so would contradict scripture itself, according to which St. Paul finds a sufficient ground of the articulation of Christian faith in Christ's resurrection.[21]

The upshot of this point of access to the historicity of dogma is once again a recognition of the secondary and dependent character of the dogmatic formulas of faith. They "are no longer properly revelation itself but just its

---

16 A revelational proposition unheard by man would indeed exist in a no man's land since God does not think in propositions—that is, it would not exist. See Thomas Aquinas, *Summa theologiae* I, q. 14, a. 7, "Utrum scientia Dei sit discursiva."

17 DeClue, *Joseph Ratzinger's Theology of Divine Revelation*, 29–30, 339. For Suarez, see also Jean-Luc Marion, "The Epistemological Interpretation of Revelation," chap. 1 of *Givenness and Revelation*, trans. Stephen E. Lewis (Oxford: Oxford University Press, 2016), esp. 20–25.

18 Joseph Ratzinger, "Commentary on Chapter I, Revelation Itself," in *Commentary on the Documents of Vatican II*, vol. 3, ed. Herbert Vorgrimler (New York: Herder & Herder, 1969), 170. The German publication date is 1967. See Karl Barth, *Church Dogmatics* I, Part I, *The Doctrine of the Word of God*, trans. G. T. Thomson (Edinburgh: T. & T. Clark, 1936), 162–64 (in 5.3), 368–69 (in 8.2).

19 Ratzinger, *Das Problem der Dogmengeschichte*, 19

20 Ratzinger, *Das Problem der Dogmengeschichte*, 18. For both points, see the collection of citations in Yves Congar, OP, *Tradition and Traditions*, trans. Michael Naseby and Thomas Rainborough (New York: Macmillan, 1967), 120–37.

21 Ratzinger, *Das Problem der Dogmengeschichte*, 18.

explication within human speech."[22] Revelation maintains itself in history by coming to completion in new appropriations and linguistic articulations of it. This does not mean there are no normative statements of faith. Rather, it means that normative expressions of faith proceed within a history that has not come to an end.

The third point of access to the historicity of dogma is the understanding of tradition, another topic well investigated by Ratzinger, not only in St. Bonaventure but also in the fathers of the Council of Trent in his work on the drafting of *Dei Verbum*.[23] We are led astray in thinking about tradition by the notion of "unwritten traditions," a notion that belongs rather to Gnosticism and not to Christianity.[24] The true notion of tradition emerges from the "doubling" of scripture that the New Testament establishes. The teaching of the New Testament is the original tradition within which Christians first understood the Old Testament. When this tradition is written out and added to the Old Testament as the second part of scripture, then the creed, itself extracted from the scriptures, becomes the framework for reading the New Testament—the canon of the creed is the measure for reading the canon of scripture, and is the first form of dogma.[25] Tradition, then, "is here understood as the explication of the Christian event witnessed to in Scripture in the history of the faith of the Church."[26]

The theologian here sees that just because the scriptures need an ongoing interpretation, faith is "always more than a mere formula"—the dogmatic articulation of traditioned faith does not of itself produce a summa of *propositions* that exhaustively state Christian reality.[27] And the historian sees that Christian believers recognize a transcendent principle that guarantees

---

22 Ratzinger, *Das Problem der Dogmengeschichte*, 19.

23 Ratzinger, "Question of the Concept of Tradition," 67–89. See his earlier speech to the German bishops on the draft schema on the sources of revelation, "Observations on the Schema *De fontibus revelationis*," in Wicks, "Six Texts by Prof. Ratzinger," 275.

24 Ratzinger, *Das Problem der Dogmengeschichte*, 20. This is repeated in his "Commentary on Chapter II" of *Dei Verbum*, in Vorgrimler, *Commentary on the Documents of Vatican II*, 182.

25 Ratzinger, *Das Problem der Dogmengeschichte*, 20. This argument is found at greater length in "Question of the Concept of Tradition," 58–64, which reminds us that what is originally handed over—*traditum*—to the church is Christ himself; tradition then exists subsequently in faith, in the authority of the church, and in the rule of faith (63–64). Thus, tradition relative to scripture is the "extra" (not materially but formally) that "distinguishes dogmatics from biblical theology" (61).

26 Ratzinger, *Das Problem der Dogmengeschichte*, 21.

27 Ratzinger, *Das Problem der Dogmengeschichte*, 20.

THE DEVELOPMENT OF DOGMA

the maintenance of the church in faith, namely, the continuing presence of Christ in the Spirit.[28] The theologian recognizes, theologically, a *reductio in historiam*; the historian recognizes, historically, a *reductio in theologiam*. The practice of the one calls for the practice of the other. This is in short form the solution of the problem the "Preliminary Reflection" poses.

If we today have access to discerning the historicity of Christian faith and dogma, what does this mean for the future? Ratzinger spells out three things in part 3 of the lecture. First, there is a necessity to integrate the history of a dogma up to its formulation into dogmatic theology. Second, there should be a recognition that even once formulated, dogmas have a history ahead of them. I hazard to say that this is the most contentious part of the lecture. Third, there is the question of whether history can be "pure" and whether it can be carried out hermetically sealed off from faith.

If Christological faith is not exclusively turned to the past, if the ongoing appropriation of this faith is a constitutive moment of revelation, and if this faithful reception of revelation is not maintained without a never-finished interpretative chain called "tradition," then change has been recognized as providing the conditions of the maintenance of an identity through time. But an identity so maintained by change is the very definition of a real history of that identity.[29] The Catholic investment in an always-already-possessed reality in a form perfect for every age, and the Protestant investment in such change only as corrupting the gospel in time, must both yield to a recognition of a real history of Christian things—of Christian faith, of Christian dogma, of Christian theology. How can the cultivation of the witnesses to and monuments of that history not serve to understand the identity—the Christian thing—better, or at least to aid a contemporary, newly conditioned understanding today? And how could the neglect of such cultivation not be a derogation of theological duty?

The two trajectories of any history that really remains a history of one thing—rise and fall, progress and decline, enrichment and bankruptcy—will be verified in the history of Christian doctrine, too, but not such that the believer supposes the history could really cease to be a history of the genuine Christian thing genuinely maintained in the world.[30] In order to prevent decline and fall, the theologian's duty is always to lead back whatever interpretation is

28 Ratzinger, *Das Problem der Dogmengeschichte*, 21.
29 Ratzinger, *Das Problem der Dogmengeschichte*, 22.
30 Ratzinger, *Das Problem der Dogmengeschichte*, 23.

proposed as installing the gospel in a new age to the Christian source—every new incarnation of Christian truth in time must always be led back to the crucifixion and resurrection of the Incarnate Lord.[31]

What history establishes, its own utility for theological understanding, is moreover according to Ratzinger also confirmed by the Second Vatican Council in its decree on the education of priests (no. 16): dogmatic theology is to begin with the biblical theme, proceed to the understanding of the relevant individual truths by the fathers, and then press on to the further history of dogma.

Ratzinger concludes this section, then, by noting that the historian of dogma, aware of the hazards of human history, alerts us to the necessity of "a recollective reduction" of what we want to say to the source of Christian faith. The second thing we learn is that we grasp faith in the history of faith, and "not in the form of some completed system that must cover up the historical nature of its own statements."[32] We are thus warned again about the pretensions of neoscholasticism.

After the question of some dogma and its prehistory, Ratzinger next turns to the question of the posthistory, as we may call it, of an already formulated dogma. For there must be such a history since dogma is necessarily subject to two deficiencies. There is first of all its distance from the reality it seeks to express: "the word remains a human word ever behindhand and back of the reality," and this is especially so when the reality is a divine reality. Second, there is its historical relativity, for it necessarily assumes some historical point of view into itself at the moment of its formulation.[33] Because of the insufficiency of words in this twofold way, there will necessarily be history of a formulated dogma going forward.[34]

Second, Ratzinger takes up the question of the immutability of dogma. He sees the foundation of this, with St. Augustine, in an authoritative interpretation

---

31 Ratzinger, *Das Problem der Dogmengeschichte*, 23–24.

32 Ratzinger, *Das Problem der Dogmengeschichte*, 24.

33 Ratzinger, *Das Problem der Dogmengeschichte*, 25. We may recall here Ambroise Gardeil's observation of what he calls the twofold relativity of dogma, its metaphysical and its historical relativity; see *Le donné révélé et la théologie*, 2nd ed. (Paris: Cerf, 1932), 116.

34 Ratzinger enlists Karl Rahner for this view in K. Rahner and K. Lehmann, "Geschichtlichkeit der Vermittlung," 727–87, *Mysterium Salutis* I, at 731, as well as Walter Kasper, *Dogma unter dem Wort Gottes* (Mainz: Matthias-Grünewald, 1965). The historicity of dogma in this sense will subsequently lead Karl Rahner to deny we ever really know what dogma authoritatively affirms and what it does not; see his "Yesterday's History of Dogma and Theology for Tomorrow," 10–16.

of scripture which uses scripture itself as its interpretive guide.[35] It is the case, however, that the immutability has historically been extended "not only to the subject or content of dogma but also directly to the dogma as a formula."[36] This, Ratzinger insinuates, is a mistake: while dogma lifts the deliverances of scripture expressed in figures and metaphors into the abstraction of a concept, concepts are not as transhistorically constant as are the figures and images which they summarize, for they invite their own interpretative history, which then threatens to cover over the communicative ability of the dogmatic formula. Thus, not only is there need of a history of dogma to stay on top of this forward going interpretive history, but there is need to return again and again to the scriptural source and origin in a never-ending circle of interpretation, from scripture to dogma and from dogma back to scripture.[37]

This section of the lecture is contentious because it obliquely calls in question another proposal for accounting for the identity of dogmatic formula across time, a proposal not founded primarily in an ongoing interpretative commentary but on the transcultural and transhistorical communicative power of such basic concepts as nature and human nature, person, freedom, life, and substance.[38] The distance between word and reality that Ratzinger assumes, moreover, where the word is, as it were, a substitute for the thing, also elicits questions.[39]

Finally, Ratzinger takes up the relation of science—historical *Wissenschaft*—and faith. Do we think that the scholarly and learned history of Christianity can be successfully pursued independent of faith, and is such independence even a necessary condition of the possibility of a successful

---

35 Ratzinger, *Das Problem der Dogmengeschichte*, 26. The reference is to Augustine, *De doctrina christiana* 3.2.2.

36 Ratzinger, *Das Problem der Dogmengeschichte*, 27.

37 Ratzinger, *Das Problem der Dogmengeschichte*, 27. For this point, he enlists Magnus Löhrer, "Überlegungen zur Interpretation Lehramtlicher Aussagen als Frage des ökumenischen Gesprächs," 499–523, in *Gott in Welt* II [Festschrift K. Rahner] (Freiburg: Herder, 1964), 510–11.

38 For which, see Réginald Garrigou-Lagrange, OP, *Thomistic Common Sense*, trans. Matthew Minerd (Steubenville, OH: Emmaus Academic, 2021). This is a translation of the 1936 French edition. See also Guy Mansini, "The Historicity of Dogma and Common Sense," *Nova et Vetera* 18 (2020): 111–38. Ratzinger recognizes the self-transcending character of Greek *culture*, however, in "Faith, Truth, and Culture: Reflections Prompted by the Encyclical *Fides et Ratio*," in *Truth and Tolerance: Christian Belief and World Religions*, trans. Henry Taylor (San Francisco: Ignatius Press, 2004), 200.

39 See, for example, the relation between word and reality in Robert Sokolowski, "God's Word and Human Speech," *Nova et Vetera* 11 (2013): 187–210; George Steiner, *Real Presences* (London: Faber and Faber, 1989), 87–94.

history? The answer is that a successful history of Christian things is rather absolutely dependent on faith. Ratzinger the Augustinian steps forward. We know things accordingly as we love them, and therefore without loving faith, we will gain no accurate access, no successful access, to realities whose only access is by such faith. He quotes Heinrich Schlier to the same effect:

> Whoever interprets the New Testament with all the means of philological-historical scholarship and does not submit himself thereby to the fundamental experience out of which the New Testament itself speaks, namely, faith, will never recognize what reality is brought to speech in the New Testament.[40]

QUESTIONS AND CLAIMS

According to the taxonomy of Avery Dulles, theories of dogmatic development are logical-propositional, or organic-intuitionist (where dogma progresses partly by way of assimilation), or historical-situational (where doctrine is translated and retranslated in different times and places).[41] We are to think respectively of the neoscholastics of the twentieth century (e. g., F. Marín-Sola), Newman, and Dulles himself. Should we try to shoehorn Ratzinger into one of these boxes? Ratzinger mentions only once the attempt to connect doctrine to the sources by way of logic,[42] and as we have seen, he is not altogether confident of the power of the "concept" to make sense of the history of dogma. If he instead privileges attention to the historicity of human thought, shall we classify him as historical-situationist? It may be doubted, however, whether this would sufficiently capture the idiosyncratic contribution he makes to thinking about "development."

Ratzinger gives an account of the historicity of dogma and a call for the history of dogma that is itself both historically situated and theological. As historically situated, it is itself subject to *a reductio in historiam*, and, of course, Ratzinger knows this. He knows he is writing in a context that tended to focus exclusively on the words, the propositional articulation of dogma.

---

40 Ratzinger, *Das Problem der Dogmengeschichte*, 29, quoting Heinrich Schlier, *Besinnung auf das Neue Testament* (Freiburg: Herder, 1964), 11–12.

41 Avery Dulles, *The Resilient Church* (Garden City, NY: Doubleday, 1977), 46.

42 Ratzinger, *Das Problem der Dogmengeschichte*, 25.

Ratzinger is so fully aware of what else is required to makes sense of revelation, namely faith itself, the interior illumination and the interior grace of the Holy Spirit, the community of the church, personal obedience to God, and he is so anxious to move beyond a scholastic narrowness of focus, that he can be thought too greatly to subjectivize revelation.[43] This is a mistaken criticism, although we might find more satisfactory the way Heinrich Schlier himself conceives things, according to which the word, the formula, is more interior to the event of revelation, including the Lord's resurrection, than some of Ratzinger's formulations indicate.[44]

Perhaps we can capture Ratzinger's contribution by asking two questions that are raised in "Das Problem der Dogmengeschichte." The recognition of the validity of these questions, and the successful execution of the claims they imply would, I think, vindicate Ratzinger's view of things. They might also give us a new way to appreciate Newman. The questions are generated by the distinction between the modern *reductio in historiam* and the medieval *reductio in theologiam* and have been already anticipated. First, does Ratzinger think a dogma's *reductio in historiam* will call also for its *reductio in theologiam*? Second, does Ratzinger think such a *reductio in theologiam* will in turn call for a *reductio in historiam*? If these questions are answered by Newman on behalf of his own account of development, as I suppose Ratzinger must answer them as to *his* account of the necessity for a history of dogma, then they have the same historical *and* theological account of the historicity or development of dogma, call it what you will.

Does Ratzinger think a dogma's *reductio in historiam* will call for its *reductio in theologiam*? It does call for it, and he knows it. There are at least three ways to show this.

First, his account calls for such a *reductio*, and we know this from the two arguments he makes for the necessity of leading dogma back to the origin of Christianity and from the fact that a grasp of this origin occurs only by

---

43 See the discussion in DeClue, *Joseph Ratzinger's Theology of Divine Revelation*, 346–47, 359–64. This, of course, was one of Michael Schmaus's problems with the *Habilitationsschrift*. Ratzinger does not, it is fair to say, take anything back; see Ratzinger, *Milestones*, 108–9. On the other hand, as Matthew Levering has pointed out, when Ratzinger comments on the newly published *Catechism of the Catholic Church* in 1992, he, so to speak, rehabilitates the importance of the proposition he had paid no attention to earlier in the Herder commentary on *Dei Verbum*. See Matthew Levering, *An Introduction to Vatican II as an Ongoing Theological Event* (Washington, DC: The Catholic University of America Press, 2027), 20–23. Much had changed in only fifteen years.

44 See Heinrich Schlier, "Kerygma und Sophia: Zur Neutestamentlichen Grundlegung des Dogmas," in *Die Zeit der Kirche: Exegetische Aufsätze und Vorträge* (Freiburg: Herder, 1966), 215–16.

faith. So at the end of the first section of the third part of the lecture, he says: "the history of dogma therefore must always embrace a double movement: it needs on the one side the movement of unfolding, but it needs on the other at the same time again and again the movement of reduction."[45] The reduction is Christological—back to the cross and resurrection of the Lord. But the resurrection is accessible only to believers, only to faith. Second, at the end of the next section of Part 3 of the lecture, he introduces the circle of interpretation formulated by Magnus Löhrer: dogma interprets scripture and scripture interprets dogma, and this second interpretive task must be express and explicit. The interpretation of the scriptures, however, is at this point not merely historical-critical but also theological—done with and in faith.[46] Or we might say it is just one historico-theological reduction. Ratzinger, we should recall, was uniquely gifted in seeing how things we might think separable are not only inseparable but are interior to one another.

Second, there is the argument of Heinrich Schlier that Ratzinger adduces at the end of the lecture.[47] It is the argument that historical-critical methods will understand the scriptures *historically* only if the object disclosed therein is loved. But this love is the love of faith. In other words, the historical reduction calls for, or perhaps better said, is coincident with, a *theological* reduction.

Third, there is an argument from outside the text of the lecture but from a text of Ratzinger from the time of the council, a short piece of a proposed schema he drafted in October of 1962 as a replacement for the introductory paragraphs of the schema *De fontibus revelationis* entitled *De voluntate Dei erga hominem*. In paragraph 4, we read *"ubi ipse [Christus] est, ubi in eum creditur et ex eo vivitur, nihil veritatis generi humano umquam datae perditur, sed in plenam lucem adducitur*/where he [Christ] is and one believes in him and lives from him, no part of all the truth ever given to humanity is lost, but instead it is led into full light."[48] Whatever truth there is that is given to humanity of whatever order is led back to Christ. As Jared Wicks remarks, we should see here an anticipation of *Gaudium et Spes* no. 22, in which only Christ fully reveals the truth of man, and a recollection of St. Bonaventure's *De reductione artium in theologiam*.[49]

---

45 Ratzinger, *Das Problem der Dogmengeschichte*, 23.

46 Ratzinger, *Das Problem der Dogmengeschichte*, 27.

47 Ratzinger, *Das Problem der Dogmengeschichte*, 29.

48 Ratzinger, "Will of God regarding Human Beings," 239. The translation is Wicks's.

49 Wicks, "Another Text," 243–44.

Second, does Ratzinger think such a *reductio in theologiam* of a dogma will in turn call for a *reductio in historiam*? The answer to this question is perhaps so obvious that the question need not be asked. The call for *a reductio in historiam* follows from the truth of the Incarnation, from the fact that God's Word is spoken in a temporally conditioned humanity, that God's word is spoken in men's words. In one way, this call is nothing but the idea of revelation that lies behind Ratzinger's idea of tradition. Thus, in the essay on "The Question of the Concept of Tradition" of 1965, he argues vigorously for the unity of "word, reality, and history"—that is, of the word of God, the reality it brings about, and third, the intelligently moved and intelligible history the unity of word and event bring about.[50] Combining a response to our two questions, he writes:

> Certainly, texts [the Scriptures] have to be referred back to their historical setting and interpreted in their historical context. Then, however, in a second process of interpretation, they must also be seen from the perspective of the movement of history as a whole and of Christ as the central event. Only harmony between the two methods results in understanding the Bible.[51]

There is, then, a sort of circumincession of history and theology, of historically understood text and dogmatic interpretation thereof.[52]

JOHN HENRY NEWMAN AND THE RATZINGERIAN EXIGENCIES

Ratzinger mentions Newman once in "Das Problem der Dogmengeschichte" as having initiated a more historically minded understanding of dogma.[53] The most evident point of similarity between them, perhaps, is the Christocentrism of

---

50 Ratzinger, "Question of the Concept of Tradition," 120.

51 Ratzinger, "Question of the Concept of Tradition," 121.

52 Perhaps it is worth nothing that Ratzinger addresses the same problematic in *Biblical Interpretation in Crisis: The Ratzinger Conference on Bible and Church* (Grand Rapids, MI: Eerdmans, 1989). For a different reading of Ratzinger's lecture than the one I have given, see Michael Seewald, *Theories of Doctrinal Development in the Catholic Church*, trans. David West (Cambridge: Cambridge University Press, 2023), 154–64.

53 Ratzinger, *Das Problem der Dogmengeschichte*, 12. In the same breath, he mentions Maurice Blondel and the Tübingen theologians of the nineteenth century.

dogma that they share with Henri de Lubac.[54] But it would be surprising if there were not deeper and more fundamental principles of fundamental theology itself that they have in common.[55] All the while, of course, Newman's own account of the history (or development) of dogma is certainly itself subject to a *reductio in historiam*, of which he is well aware. This awareness is indicated for one thing by the fact of the double edition of the *Essay on Development*. Writing as a Catholic for Catholics is different from writing as an Anglican for Anglicans—the knowledge of the historicity of his own thought is inscribed therein.[56]

But let us ask the questions formulated for Ratzinger expressly of Newman. Does Newman think the subjection of a dogma to a *reductio in historiam* will also call for its *reductio in theologiam*? This is the nub of the matter.

In the first place, there is Newman's *a priori* argument in chapter 2 of the *Essay*, the argument from the antecedent probability of an infallible authority for the discrimination of doctrinal developments from doctrinal corruptions. The constant emergence of purported re-articulations and further interpretations of the apostolic deposit, an emergence investigated by and known by history, poses a theological question: how is the believer to know the difference between the authentic and the inauthentic?[57] An historically driven question demands a theological answer. The notes of an authentic development explored in part 2 of the 1878 edition of the *Essay*, from maintenance of type to continuity of principles to logical sequence and so on, do not suffice here, for "they are of a scientific and controversial, not of a practical character."[58] For a practical question, a practically available answer must be possible.

Newman lays out a thoroughly theological argument for such a practical solution. First, the original revelation and the developments thereof are one

---

54 For de Lubac, see Nicholas Healy, "Henri de Lubac on the Development of Doctrine," in *Ressourcement after Vatican II: Essays in Honor of Joseph Fessio, S.J.*, ed. Nicholas J. Healy and Matthew Levering (San Francisco: Ignatius Press, 2029), 348, 356. For Newman, see *An Essay on the Development of Christian Doctrine*, foreword by Ian Ker (Notre Dame, IN: University of Notre Dame Press, 1989), 93–94. All subsequent references to the *Essay* are to this edition. For Ratzinger, see *Das Problem der Dogmengeschichte*, 23–24.

55 For Newman's view of revelation and the reception thereof, see William J. Abraham, "Reception of Newman on Divine Revelation," in Aquino and King, *Receptions of Newman*, 197–213.

56 See James Tolhurst, editor's introduction to John Henry Cardinal Newman, *An Essay on the Development of Christian Doctrine* (Leominster, England: Gracewing, 2018), li–lv. The same shift can be observed in the third edition of *The Prophetical Office*, its preface and notes, brought out after Newman's reception into the Catholic Church.

57 Newman, *Essay on the Development*, 75–76.

58 Newman, *Essay on the Development*, 78.

THE DEVELOPMENT OF DOGMA

whole thing, since developments are just distinct explications of it. Second, if the original revelation meets us as revelation and so as guaranteed to be true, the developments must meet us with like claim and authority. Third, the believer must therefore take some standard of measurement (and take it in reasonably warranted faith), whether Bible or council or pope.[59]

This, however, is not quite the reduction Ratzinger would have us think of, which is a reduction of the history to the theological origin or source of Christian faith. In other words, it must be a reduction to Christ, to the apostolic deposit. This Newman provides in chapter 4, section 3, "The Papal Supremacy." The argument is as follows. The fourth and fifth centuries' instances of the exercise of the supremacy and contemporaneous recognitions of its legitimacy so clearly show the fulfillment of the antecedent probability of the divine and providential provision of such an authority, which is external to the process of development but which alone can guarantee it, that they can be taken to be the key to the interpretation of the pre-Nicene hints and obscure intimations of such an external and supreme authority in the pregnant but hardly conclusive phrases of Ignatius and Clement and Irenaeus. But after providing that key to hints and clues within hailing distance of apostolic times, they reasonably can be taken to bespeak their own anchoring in apostolic presumption and witness, and so bring the discernment of Petrine authority home to a dominical intention not to leave his church widowed and without the protection of his continuing spousal care.[60]

Newman has given here an instance of the kind of argument he proposes generally in the first section of chapter 3. The "method of proof" that Roman doctrines are providentially intended developments of apostolic witness consists in confirming the antecedent probability thereof by so-called ordinary sign enthymemes. I paraphrase Newman's grand argument: If Catholic doctrines are genuine developments, we should expect them, even if late, to be called apostolic; but they are so called; therefore, they are genuine; again, if Catholic doctrines are genuine, they will have some warrant, even if slight, in Scripture; but they do; therefore, they are genuine; again, if they are genuine, they will form a coherent whole; but they do form a coherent whole; therefore, etc.; and so on. Now strictly logically, nothing at all follows the "therefore" in each case. But if there are many such ordinary sign arguments, then the

---

59 Newman, *Essay on the Development*, 79–80.
60 I am here summarizing the upshot of Newman, *Essay on the Development*, 154–55.

51

probability of the truth of the apodosis grows very strong.[61] Each argument alone is a wire that would not support one's weight, but many wires make a cable such that one confidently embarks on the Brooklyn Bridge to cross in safety over the East River.[62] Collectively, they argue the apostolic character of all Catholic doctrines.[63] The history leads us back to the divine deposit.

This argument taken most simply is nothing but an application of Newman's observation that we see the stream more easily in its wide bed, deep and full, than we do at the tiny spring of its origin.[64] From the easily recognized and broadly exfoliated doctrine of the church, we are led back by historically plausible arguments and connections to a theological reality, the foundation of the church by Christ.

It is not just the history of Christian doctrine that is ineluctably theological, however. All the disciplines lead back to theology for Newman, whose spontaneous articulation of this is in terms of what he calls the unity of knowledge, the idea that all human knowledge makes one coherent whole. This he pursues in *The Idea of a University*, the third and fourth discourses that treat the relation of theology to the other disciplines and the relation of the other disciplines to theology.[65] He addresses it most directly, however, in Discourse V of 1852, "General Knowledge Viewed as One Philosophy," and the 1852 appendix to the Discourses, in which he adduces authorities for the theses defended therein. Section four of the appendix concerns the unity of knowledge: "The Branches of Knowledge form one whole." Here, he brings forward Hugh of St. Victor, the Sacred Congregation of Studies under Pope Leo XII, and Lord Bacon. He brings forward St. Bonaventure, too, whom he cites as follows: "From God, the Fontal Light, all illumination descends to man. The Divine Light, from which as from its source, all human science emanates, is of four kinds."[66] The quotation is from the *De reductione artium ad theologiam*.

---

61 For this kind of argumentation in Newman, see Andrew Meszaros, *The Prophetic Church: History and Doctrinal Development in John Henry Newman and Yves Congar* (Oxford: Oxford University Press, 2016), 74–80.

62 The cable analogy is Newman's own; see Meszaros, *Prophetic Church*, 76–77.

63 For the entire list, see Newman, *Essay on the Development*, 99–100.

64 Newman, *Essay on the Development*, 40.

65 John Henry Newman, *The Idea of a University Defined and Illustrated*, ed. I. T. Ker (Oxford: Clarendon, 1976).

66 Newman, *The Idea of a University*, 448.

The arts and sciences for Newman are not accidentally one but one because all truth is one in God.

To the second question—does Newman think a dogma's *reductio in theologiam* in turn calls for a *reductio in historiam*? This call follows from the truth of the dogma of dogmas, the dogma of the Incarnation. It follows from the fact that God's word is spoken in human words and from the fact that human words are historically conditioned words. In a lapidary phrase in *The Idea of a University*, he says: "Let the doctrine of the Incarnation be true: is it not at once of the nature of an historical fact, and of a metaphysical?"[67] He is at once both historical and—let us say—theological. He says also in these lectures that "the existing documentary testimony to Catholicism and Christianity may be so unduly valued as to be made the absolute measure of Revelation," and he resists a sort of historical positivism according to which no part of theological teaching can be true "which cannot bring its express text . . . from Scripture, and authorities from the Fathers or profane writers." A *reductio in historiam* does not make the divine thing that is brought back to the historicity of human faith and formulation disappear.[68] The presence of theology in history and the presence of history in theology, their circumincession, does not lead to the abandonment of either one: rather, there is a mutual upbuilding if indeed the Incarnation is at once historical and metaphysical.

CONCLUSION

If the two questions are answered the same way by Newman and Ratzinger, then both have discerned the same identity in a manifold: the identity is the gospel, the word of God, the faith of the Church, and the manifold is composed by the differences of its manifestation and interpretation and appropriation in history.

But they have also discerned it *in the same way*, although the historical circumstances of their discernment of the same thing are of course not the same. We can then put things as follows: the identity they both discern is the

---

67 Newman, *The Idea of a University*, 38. See the contrast between theological historicity and historicist historicity in Reinhard Hütter, "Progress, Not Alteration of the Faith: Beyond Antiquarianism and Presentism; John Henry Newman, Vincent of Lérins, and the Criterion of Identity of the Development of Doctrine," *Nova et Vetera* 19 (2021): 362–66.

68 Newman, *The Idea of a University*, 90. For Newman on history, see Matthew Levering, *Newman on Doctrinal Corruption* (Park Ridge, IL: Word on Fire Academic, 2022), 69–93.

historicity of God's word, of the event of revelation, of the church's reception of the divine word by faith, of the church's traditioning of that faithfully received word, of the church's normative articulation in doctrine of that traditioned word. The manifold in which this identity is discerned by Newman is constituted by the different accounts that first as an Anglican and then as a Catholic he gives to the location of what extant ecclesial communion is the heir of the church of the fathers, while for Ratzinger the manifold is composed by the different histories of dogma produced by Catholics and Protestants, in which a genuine history of Christian things shows up indeed but shows up as in fact *absent* in each case.

Both Newman and Ratzinger resist abstractions. To think something truly is also to think of its relations to other things. All the arts are to be led back to the expression in time of the Incarnate Word. This is the historical reduction, the reduction to salvation history. And every truth is to be led back to the Word that is expressed in the Incarnation, which is the theological, metaphysical reduction. Both reductions are reductions of faith seeking understanding.

3

NEWMAN AND POPE BENEDICT (RATZINGER) ON FAITH AND REASON

Frederick D. Aquino

Though separated historically and culturally, there are some fascinating connections between John Henry Newman and Pope Benedict (Ratzinger) on faith and reason.[1] The similarity, as I hope to show, is in their mutual rejection of narrowly construed accounts of faith and reason (e.g., fideism, hard rationalism, positivism) and in their attempt to carve out a broader and more plausible alternative.[2] Toward this end, I will focus primarily on the philosophical aspects of their understanding of faith and reason, though

---

[1] In this chapter, I will cover the writings of Ratzinger and Benedict; henceforth, I will use the name Benedict when discussing his account of faith and reason.

[2] David J. Bonagura Jr., "The Relation of Revelation and Tradition in the Theology of John Henry Newman and Joseph Ratzinger," *New Blackfriars* 101, no. 1091 (2020): 67, points out that in Ratzinger's memoirs, he "describes the energy with which Newman's work on conscience, history, and on the development of doctrine was read and discussed in his seminary days. Yet, in terms of Ratzinger's own work on history, tradition, and revelation, he makes almost no direct mention of Newman in his writings over his long theological career." See also Joseph Ratzinger, *Milestones: Memoirs, 1927–1977*, trans. Erasmo Leiva-Merikakis (San Francisco: Ignatius Press, 1998), 109–10; cf. 43, 56. On some overlapping themes and sources (e.g., the Augustinian notion of *cor ad cor loquitor*—heart speaks to heart, conscience, and the development of doctrine), see Joseph Ratzinger, "Presentation by His Eminence Cardinal Joseph Ratzinger on the Occasion of the First Centenary of the Death of Cardinal John Henry Newman," April 28, 1990, www.vatican.va/roman_curia/congregations/cfaith/documents/rc_con_cfaith_doc_19900428_ratzinger-newman_en.html; Tracey Rowland, *Ratzinger's Faith: The Theology of Pope Benedict XVI* (Oxford: Oxford University Press,

with some theological implications in mind. I will begin by spelling out how Newman and Benedict construe the relationship between faith and reason and how they seek to advance a broader account. In addition to the aim of broadening the horizons of rationality, I will then highlight two (related) constructive points of contact: the passional nature of reason and the importance of a regulative approach to philosophical and theological inquiry. In reading Newman and Benedict philosophically, the aim is to do justice to their thought while drawing attention to some constructive points of contact.

NEWMAN ON FAITH AND REASON

One of the main philosophical concerns for Newman involved examining existing accounts of faith and reason. More specifically, he sought to clarify the conditions under which Christian belief (belief in God or, for that matter, any belief) can be considered rational (e.g., is it rational to assent to propositions for which a person lacks full understanding and demonstrative proof? Is reason reducible to an explicit or formal mode?). The aim was to attend carefully, closely, and critically to the ways in which people employ terms like faith and reason and thus attempt to clarify their relationship. He also drew attention to how reason works within real-world environments and in other domains of inquiry.

Newman, for example, challenges two claims. The first is that faith is simply a "moral quality," "feeling," or "sentiment" that depends on and follows "a distinct act of Reason beforehand." Reason warrants, on the "ground of evidence, both ample and carefully examined, that the Gospel comes from God, and *then*" faith embraces it.[3] Understood in this way, reason secures the epistemic credentials, for example, by showing how the "apostolic testimony is trustworthy" or how the "purported revelation" is "warranted by the evidence

---

2007), 3, 7–9, 81–83; and Emery de Gaál, *O Lord, I Seek Your Guidance: Explorations and Discoveries in Pope Benedict XVI's Theology* (Steubenville, OH: Emmaus Academic, 2018), 5, 67–68, 91, 217.

3 John Henry Newman, *Fifteen Sermons Preached before the University of Oxford: Between A.D. 1826 and 1843*, ed. James David Earnest and Gerard Tracey (Oxford: Clarendon, 2006), 130, 143, preface 6, hereafter cited as *US*. See also *US* 132–33, 155–58, and John Henry Newman, *The Idea of a University Defined and Illustrated*, ed. I. T. Ker (Oxford: Clarendon, 1976), 39, hereafter cited as *Idea*. For discussion of the background and reception of Newman's philosophical thought, see the chapters on Whately, Butler, evangelicalism, divine revelation, the British Naturalist tradition, and epistemology in *The Oxford Handbook of John Henry Newman* and the chapters on the philosophical and theological receptions of the *Grammar of Assent* in *Receptions of Newman*.

of a miraculous nature."[4] Faith, according to this view, relies on an explicit kind of reasoning and the resultant evidential support.

The depiction of faith as a "mere sentiment," Newman contends, is "a dream and a mockery."[5] It fails to recognize the intellectual aspect of faith and, as a result, misunderstands the nature and scope of faith and reason. Moreover, Newman challenges the second claim that reason is reducible to an explicit or formal mode because such a view fails to grasp or make a basic distinction between reasoning and arguing. In other words, our "professed grounds are no sufficient measures of their real ones."[6] A "person may reason well, without knowing the rules of Reason, or being able to put into shape or into words the process which he goes through. Reason may be implicit, and yet be as truly Reason as if it were drawn out into explicit form."[7]

Newman consequently offers an alternative construal of faith and reason. In the broadest sense, reason is a natural faculty that draws conclusions from premises.[8] The senses give us direct knowledge or immediate awareness of the material world, whereas knowledge by reason is "attained beyond the range of sense," and thus "indirectly." In terms of the indirect mode of knowledge, inference plays a crucial role. Reason proceeds "from things that are perceived to things which are not; the existence of which it certifies to us on the hypothesis of something else being known to exist, in other words, being assumed to be true."[9] If reason is understood in this way, faith may be construed as a process of reasoning in which we accept "things as real, which the senses do not convey, upon certain previous grounds; it is an instrument of indirect knowledge concerning things external to us."[10]

Faith is therefore not divorced from reason but, like most of our beliefs, involves an implicit process of reasoning. Moreover, such a construal of

---

4 Geertjan Zuijdwegt, "Richard Whately's Influence on John Henry Newman's Oxford University Sermons on Faith and Reason (1839–1840)," *Newman Studies Journal* 10, no. 1 (2013): 88.

5 John Henry Newman, *Apologia Pro Vita Sua*, ed. Martin Svaglic (Oxford: Clarendon, 1967), 54, hereafter cited as *Apo*.

6 Newman, *US*, 149.

7 Appendix B: "Newman's 'Rough Draft of Matter for Preface to French Translation of Univ. Sermons: Afterwords Written for Dalgairns in Latin (1847),'" in *US*, 246.

8 Newman, *US*, 155; see also Appendix B, 238.

9 Newman, *US*, 145–46.

10 Newman, *US*, 146.

reasoning, as Newman points out, is in accordance with the natural state of things.[11] That is, faith is not incompatible with "the state in which we find ourselves by nature with reference to the acquisition of knowledge generally,—a state in which we must assume something to prove anything, and can gain nothing without a venture."[12] This kind of reasoning, then, is not unique to faith. Newman highlights the ways in which such reasoning factors in the formation of religious and nonreligious beliefs. There is ample empirical evidence that most people operate on the level of implicit reasoning until "antecedent probabilities fail."[13] They dispense with the need for demonstrative proof and follow the dictum that probability is the way of life in everyday affairs. Reliance upon antecedent probabilities (i.e., our expectations given all we have observed in the past) typically ensures a reliable process of belief-formation in everyday life. Therefore, faith is "not the only exercise of Reason, which, when critically examined, would be called unreasonable, and *yet is not so*."[14]

The crucial distinction is between the origin and justification of faith, and failing to make this distinction is equivalent to misunderstanding the difference between a "creative" and "critical" power.[15] That is, Newman distinguishes between the evidential considerations in the formation of faith and

---

11 In the *Grammar of Assent*, Newman likewise seeks to show that his account of assent is in accordance with nature and thus is a natural mental state.

12 Newman, *US*, 151.

13 Newman, *US*, 135; see also *US*, 150. In a letter to J. D. Dalgairns, Newman summarizes the aim of the second series of sermons (10–15) on faith and reason in the *University Sermons*: "These sermons take in the *two* principles which are so prominent in the Essay [*An Essay on the Development of Christian Doctrine*], that no real idea can be comprehended in all its bearings at once—that the main instrument of proof in matters of life is 'antecedent probability'" (*LD* xii.5). In a document that he wrote in advance of the French translation of the *University Sermons*, Newman describes faith as a mode of "reasoning on antecedent probabilities . . . this kind of reasoning is *the highest*, as being used by the highest minds, and in the highest discoveries" (Appendix A: "Newman's Memorandum in Diary Appendix, Planning the Preface to the Proposed Translation of the *University Sermons*," in *US*, 236).

14 Newman, *US*, 147, emphasis added. Newman is offering a parity argument to show that faith is a kind of reasoning distinct from formal argumentation. For different interpretations of Newman's parity argument, see Basil Mitchell, "Newman as a Philosopher," in *Newman after a Hundred Years*, ed. Ian T. Ker and Alan G. Hill (Oxford: Clarendon, 1990), 228–29; Duncan Pritchard, "Wittgenstein on Faith and Reason: The Influence of Newman," in *God, Truth, and Other Enigmas*, ed. Miroslaw Szatkowski (Berlin: de Gruyter, 2015), 197–216; Frederick D. Aquino, "Epistemology," in *The Oxford Handbook of John Henry Newman*, ed. Frederick D. Aquino and Benjamin J. King (Oxford: Clarendon, 2018), 375–94; and Frederick D. Aquino and Logan P. Gage, "Newman the Quasi-fideist: A Reply to Duncan Pritchard," *Heythrop Journal* 64, no. 5 (2023): 695–706.

15 Newman, *US*, 131.

the articulation of them in a publicly accessible manner.[16] Explicit reasoning may "be the judge, without being the origin, of Faith; and that Faith may be justified" by this mode of reasoning, "without making use of it."[17] The difference is between faith having grounds and articulating the grounds or providing an argument for our beliefs. In other words, the operation of the mind is not reducible to the capacity to formalize one's reasoning, and not all grounds are reducible to a publicly available (or formal mode of) presentation. As a result, faith is "not an illogical process, because it is not exhibited in logical form. The analysis of reason does not make reason good, but proves it to be so; it was good before the analysis, and the analysis does but test it by critical rules."[18]

Nevertheless, the distinction between a creative and critical power does not mean that faith is impervious to critical reflection. In fact, Newman thinks that it is problematic to exempt faith from rational analysis. Though faith is the "simple lifting of the mind to the Unseen God, without conscious reasoning or formal argument, still the mind may be allowably, nay, religiously engaged, in reflecting upon its own Faith; investigating the grounds and the Object of it, bringing it out into words, whether to defend, or recommend, or teach it to others."[19] It is clear that Newman does not think that everyone needs to be engaged in this kind of critical thinking, but to rule it out is to "discard the science of theology from the service of Religion."[20] In many ways, Newman presumes that people largely employ implicit reasoning and most likely defer to (trust) those who are capable of rendering apt judgments concerning the subject at hand.[21]

A comparable distinction is made in the *Grammar of Assent*. Simple assent (SA) is "exercised unconsciously," that is, propositions "pass before us and receive our assent without our consciousness" or without a "recognition"

---

16 See John Henry Newman, *The Theological Papers of John Henry Newman on Faith and Certainty*, ed. Derek Holmes (Oxford: Clarendon, 1976), 84–86, 121, hereafter cited as *TP* i; *US*, 178; *GA*, 249; John Henry Newman, *Parochial and Plain Sermons* (San Francisco: Ignatius Press, 1987), vi/23: 339; and Zuijdwegt, "Richard Whately's Influence," 89.

17 Newman, *US*, 132.

18 Appendix B, 247.

19 Newman, *US*, 174.

20 Newman, *US*, 174. On Newman's distinction between religion and theology, see John Henry Newman, *An Essay in Aid of a Grammar of Assent*, ed. Ian T. Ker (Oxford: Clarendon, 1985), esp. chap. 5, hereafter cited as *GA*.

21 For the role that epistemic dependence plays in the formation and sustenance of faith, see Newman, *TP* i.26; Frederick D. Aquino, *Communities of Informed Judgment: Newman's Illative Sense and Accounts of Rationality* (Washington, DC: The Catholic University of America Press, 2004), esp. chap. 4.

of an assent or of its "grounds."[22] Complex assent (CA) entails a reflexive endorsement of the grounds for an assent. It is "an assent, not only to a given proposition, but to the claim of that proposition on our assent as true."[23] So, Newman recognizes that not every SA is necessarily true.[24] Some may be "merely expressions of our personal likings, tastes, principles, motives, and opinions."[25] In this sense, CA determines the validity or justification of SA: "All this I am accustomed to take for granted without a thought; but, were the need to arise, I should not find much difficulty in drawing out from my own mental resources reasons sufficient to justify me in these beliefs."[26]

As a result, Newman's account of faith and reason does not reject the importance of reasoning or, more exactly, a reflexive component; rather, he emphasizes the extent to which intuitive judgments or an implicit process of reasoning factor in the formation of both our religious and nonreligious beliefs. The distinction is between the implicit process of reasoning and the capacity to explain or translate this process of reasoning on paper (or reflexively endorse the grounds for a belief).[27] Contrary to narrowly construed views of faith and reason, most of our reasoning is implicit rather than explicit; its grounds are not typically publicly available and are only presented to others in syllogistic form with much difficulty. We engage in this explicit process of reasoning, Newman recognizes, only when we examine our reasons at a metalevel and think about whether they would be the kind of reasons that others might accept.[28] The implicit reasoning of faith is not some special process (or special pleading) in which only believers engage but rather the very process by which we form most of our beliefs.

Thus, Newman's dissatisfaction with some accounts of faith and reason is that they fail to consider the ways in which the whole character of the

---

22 Newman, *GA*, 124.

23 Newman, *GA*, 128.

24 On Newman and the grounds of faith, see Frederick D. Aquino, "Newman on the Grounds of Faith," *Quaestiones Disputatae* 8, no. 2 (2018): 5–18. Newman also thinks it is important to assess the implicit process of reasoning. In both the *University Sermons* and the *Grammar of Assent*, Newman makes it clear that not all grounds are necessarily adequate or truth-conducive. For a contemporary account of adequate grounds, see William P. Alston, *Beyond "Justification": Dimensions of Epistemic Evaluation* (Ithaca, NY: Cornell University Press, 2005), esp. chap. 5.

25 Newman, *GA*, 124; see also 138.

26 Newman, *GA*, 139; see also 127.

27 See Newman, *GA*, 216.

28 Newman, *US*, 177.

person factors in the evaluation of evidence, and they restrict the rationality of religious belief to those who are intellectually capable of following the relevant arguments (e.g., hard rationalism). He also shows that faith as an implicit mode of reasoning is not reducible to an explicit mode of reasoning, and this is the case in other domains of inquiry. The comparison is between demonstrative and non-demonstrative modes of reasoning, not between grounded and groundless commitments or beliefs (unless grounds are restricted to what can be professed or put on paper). If restricted to an explicit or demonstrative kind of reasoning, most fail to meet the bar of reason. If broadened to include implicit reasoning, however, faith (or religious belief) is not unique. The process is still rational, though to be distinguished from a more explicit or formal one.

What Newman rejects out of hand, then, is the claim that faith requires or is synonymous with the operation of an explicit or demonstrative kind of reasoning. Though reason plays an important role in evaluating the process of belief-formation, it does not follow that faith springs from a formal account, nor does it follow that reason is reducible to an explicit kind of reasoning and that faith is dependent upon this kind of reasoning. Being aware of how reason operates, then, is not a precondition to having rationally acceptable beliefs. Faith, as a tacit or implicit kind of reasoning, is "independent of and distinct from what are called philosophical inquiries, intellectual systems, courses of argument, and the like."[29] However, faith is not groundless. It is "independent not of objects or grounds . . . but of perceptible, recognized, producible objects and grounds." As a result, faith "admits, but does not require, the exercise" of explicit reasoning.[30] In other words, the reasoning of faith includes but is not reducible to explicit reasoning.

POPE BENEDICT (RATZINGER) ON FAITH AND REASON

Benedict, like Newman, seeks to lay out a broader construal of the relationship between faith and reason.[31] He believes a proposal to "'widen the horizons of rationality' . . . must not simply be counted among the new lines of theological

---

29 Newman, *US*, 149; see also *US*, 146, 155.

30 Newman, *US*, 175.

31 See Joseph Cardinal Ratzinger, *Truth and Tolerance: Christian Belief and World Religions* (San Francisco: Ignatius Press, 2003), 158; Thomas V. Gourlay, "The Nuptial Character of the Relationship between Faith and Reason in the Thought of Joseph Ratzinger/Benedict XVI," *Heythrop Journal*

and philosophical thought, but it must be understood as the requisite for a *new opening* onto the reality" that humanity in its "uni-totality is, rising above ancient prejudices and reductionisms, to open [itself] also to the way toward a true understanding of modernity."[32] However, Benedict identifies some roadblocks to that end. The first reduces reason to a particular mode of inquiry (e.g., scientific reasoning). He agrees that the aim of seeing the world in rational (intelligible) terms and empirical verification is "necessary and right."[33] Yet, there is a basic kind of rationality that is prior to specific instantiations. If a narrowly construed rationality is

> declared to be the absolute and unsurpassable form of human thought, then the basis of science itself becomes contradictory; for it is both pro-claiming and denying the power of reason. But above all, a self-limiting reason of that kind is an amputated reason. If man cannot use his reason to ask about the essential things in his life, where he comes from and where he is going, about what he should do and may do, about living and dying, but has to leave these decisive questions to feeling, divorced from reason, then he is not elevating reason but dishonoring it.[34]

In other words, a narrow construal equates reason with a particular appropriation of it. One of the obstacles to the goal of broadening horizons, then, is traceable to the "self-limitation of reason." The "laws of method" that brought a particular mode of reasoning its "success have, though being generalized, become its prison."[35]

It is equally problematic to reduce faith to a practical kind of reasoning. For example, according to Benedict, Kant grounds faith "exclusively in practical reason," believing that in order to make room for faith, it is necessary to "set thinking aside." As a result, the reasoning of faith is denied "access to

---

59 (2018): 265; and Daniel P. Maher, "Pope Benedict XVI on Faith and Reason," *Nova et Vetera* 7, no. 3 (2009): 627.

32 Benedict XVI, *A Reason Open to God: On Universities, Education, and Culture* (Washington, DC: The Catholic University of America Press, 2013), 31–32. Benedict adds, "The truth of revelation does not superimpose the truth achieved by reason; rather, it purifies and exalts reason, thereby enabling it to broaden its horizons to enter into a field of research as unfathomably expansive as mystery itself" (35).

33 Ratzinger, *Truth and Tolerance*, 157.

34 Ratzinger, *Truth and Tolerance*, 157–58.

35 Ratzinger, *Truth and Tolerance*, 156.

reality as a whole."[36] Such a move excludes theology from a meaning-making inquiry and disconnects it from the (broader or basic) rational structure of the world. A different but related move is to claim that divine transcendence rules out any connection or analogy between the divine and the human. Benedict certainly acknowledges the transcendence of the divine. God is "infinitely greater than all our concepts and all our images and names."[37] Yet God does not "become more divine when we push him away from us in a sheer, impenetrable voluntarism; rather, the truly divine God is the God who has revealed himself as *logos* and, as *logos*, has acted and continues to act lovingly on our behalf."[38] In other words, divine transcendence does not render human reason void or meaningless.

Benedict's construal of faith and reason navigates between the views that locate God above and contrary to reason. He affirms the importance of critically examining or probing the "legitimacy of inquiry into God as a proper exercise of human reason, over against those who view all speech about God as belonging to myth."[39] If, for example, theology "arrives at all kinds of absurdities and tries, not only to excuse them, but even where possible to canonize them by pointing to the mystery, then we are confronted with a misuse of the idea of 'mystery,' the purpose of which is not to destroy reason but rather to render belief possible *as* understanding."[40] Faith, therefore, is not a "blind surrender to the irrational," nor is it an invitation to insulate one's beliefs from critical examination.[41] Instead, "it is a movement toward the *logos*, the *ratio*, toward meaning and so toward truth itself, for in the final analysis the ground on which man takes his stand cannot possibly be anything else but the truth revealing itself."[42] The God who is "*logos* guarantees the intelligibility of the world, the intelligibility of our existence, the aptitude of reason to know God

---

36 Benedict XVI, "The Regensburg Lecture," in James Schall, *The Regensburg Lecture* (South Bend, IN: St. Augustine's Press, 2007), 139–40.

37 Joseph Ratzinger, *Introduction to Christianity*, 2nd ed. (San Francisco: Ignatius Press, 2004), 25.

38 Benedict XVI, "Regensburg Lecture," 138.

39 Maher, "Pope Benedict XVI on Faith and Reason," 632.

40 Ratzinger, *Introduction to Christianity*, 77.

41 Ratzinger, *Introduction to Christianity*, 75.

42 Ratzinger, *Introduction to Christianity*, 75; see also 139.

and the reasonableness of God, even though his understanding infinitely surpasses ours and to us may so often appear to be darkness."[43]

A broadened account of faith and reason presumes that people from different perspectives and disciplines have a common source in reason. The appeal is to a common rationality that precedes science and other domains of inquiry and to "the right use of reason."[44] Humans share the general capacity to reason with one another and grow in understanding, even in light of their different starting points. More exactly, rationality is domain specific in terms of particular forms of inquiry (e.g., scientific reasoning) and general in terms of a more fundamental sense of being able to make sense of things. Thus, humans are "rational not only when they engage in scientific research; we are rational also in the pre-scientific and ordinary use of reason."[45]

In addition, Benedict's account of faith and reason is philosophically and theologically framed and developed, that is, religion and reason must be interrelated "without confusion and without separation."[46] Without confusion means that both must preserve their distinctive identity and goals. Though distinctive in terms of aim and scope, religion and reason also need to undergo a mutual process of purification. Accordingly, Benedict speaks of a "necessary relatedness between reason and religion, which are called to purify and help one another. They need each other, and they must acknowledge this mutual need."[47] So, without separation means that philosophy, for example, "does not

---

43 Ratzinger, *Introduction to Christianity*, 26. Aidan Nichols, *The Conversation of Faith and Reason: Modern Catholic Thought from Hermes to Benedict XVI* (Chicago: Hillenbrand Books, 2009), 194, says that Ratzinger connects the ontological (e.g., the intelligibility of the world) and the epistemological (the aptitude of reason to know God).

44 Benedict XVI, "Regensburg Lecture," 131.

45 Maher, "Pope Benedict XVI on Faith and Reason," 630–31. Jeremy Morris, "Pope Benedict XVI on Faith and Reason in Western Europe," *Pro Ecclesia* 17, no. 3 (2008): 331, rightly points out that granting "absolute value to rational inquiry and science," according to Benedict, "constitutes first and foremost an epistemological error. Science, he argues, operates 'within the limits of certain categories, within which it is strictly valid; but to maintain that it is only within these categories that men can know anything at all is an unfounded presupposition, which in any case is shown by experience to be untrue'" (see also Ratzinger, *Truth and Tolerance*, 31).

46 Benedict XVI, *Reason Open to God*, 27.

47 Ratzinger, "That Which Holds the World Together: The Pre-political Moral Foundations of a Free State," in *The Dialectics of Secularization: On Reason and Religion*, by Jürgen Habermas and Joseph Ratzinger (San Francisco: Ignatius Press, 2005), 78. Ratzinger acknowledges that there are "*pathologies in religion* that are extremely dangerous and that make it necessary to see the divine light of reason as a 'controlling organ.' Religion must continually allow itself to be purified and structured by reason. . . . However, we have also seen in the course of our reflections that there are also *pathologies of reason*, although mankind in general is not as conscious of this fact today"

start again from zero with every thinking subject in total isolation, but takes its place within the great dialogue of historical wisdom, which it continually accepts and develops in a manner both critical and docile."[48] Theologically speaking, a religious posture that refuses to act "in accordance with reason is contrary to God's nature."[49] Construed in these terms, thinking and inquiring reasonably can legitimately be seen as a proper employment of our divinely given capacities. We ought to learn how to employ our cognitive powers rightly in order to acquire true (rather than false) beliefs and greater understanding. Given that God desires not only that we form beliefs but also that they be true rather than false, our belief-forming faculties must be trained and developed properly. The key to a harmonious or integrative relationship is to combine faith and reason in "their reciprocal relationship, while also respecting the sphere of autonomy of each."[50]

Faith does not, therefore, "obviate or excuse the free exercise of rationality, but—on the contrary—it requires and reinforces it."[51] In essence, Benedict grounds his account of faith and reason in the eternal Logos. This is what makes intelligible his broader construal of reason that includes faith and other modes of inquiry. His proposal respects the integrity and particularity of different modes of inquiry while showing how the inability to recognize the limits of a particular mode of inquiry and the need for purification can have disastrous consequences.

CONSTRUCTIVE POINTS OF CONTACT

Newman and Benedict, as we have seen, reject narrowly construed accounts of faith and reason and attempt to broaden horizons.[52] They make a distinction

---

(77). See also Benedict XVI, *Deus Caritas Est*, especially sections 5–8, 10, 17. Benedict's emphasis on the mutual process of purification finds some resonance in Newman's *University Sermons*, especially sermons 11–14, and in Newman's 1877 *Preface to the Third Edition of the Via Media*.

48 Benedict XVI, *Reason Open to God*, 27.

49 Benedict XVI, "Regensburg Lecture," 134.

50 Benedict XVI, *Reason Open to God*, 33.

51 Pablo Blanco Sarto, "*Logos* and *Dia-Logos*: Faith, Reason, (and Love) According to Joseph Ratzinger," *Anglican Theological Review* 92, no. 3 (2010): 501.

52 Benedict XVI, *Reason Open to God*, 81, says that Newman's "insights into the relationship between faith and reason, into the vital place of revealed religion in civilized society, and into the need for a broadly based and wide-ranging approach to education were not only of profound importance for Victorian England, but continue today to inspire and enlighten many all over the world."

between a basic sense of rationality and domain-specific modes of inquiry. They accordingly challenge the claim that human rationality originates in or is reducible to one of field of knowledge or discipline. In addition, they draw attention to the problem of reducing reason to a particular mode. A form of reason "so closed in on itself cannot avoid creating a world in its own image in isolation." In such a world, individuals and societies become "bunkers without windows."[53] Conversely, an enlarged scope of reason involves coming out of "the prison we built for ourselves and [recognizing] other forms of ascertaining things, forms in which" the whole human person "comes into play."[54] We know what it is like when people are unwilling to open up their own views to critical reflection—and when they refuse to glean insights from others. Insulating claims from public scrutiny also cuts against the grain of wisdom. Thus, we must make every effort to "operate in the open, and not wildly, in the dark."[55]

Narrowness of perspective in due course takes a deep hold on those who try to make "their particular craft usurp and occupy the universe."[56] People shaped in this way deem their own mode of reflection as the "centre of all truth, and view every part or the chief parts of knowledge as if developed from it, and determined by its principles." They feel compelled to say something about "every subject; habit, fashion, the public require it of them: and, if so, they can give sentence according to their knowledge."[57] Contracted pursuits of this sort, however, actually get in the way of gaining greater levels of understanding of the subject at hand. They turn out to be nothing more than obstacles to perceiving and assessing things beyond domain-specific commitments.

With this emphasis on broadening horizons in mind, I want to highlight two (related) constructive points of contact. The first focuses on the passional nature of reason. Newman and Benedict are deeply drawn to the notion that

---

53 Wael Farouq, "The Windows of Benedict XVI: Reason, Revelation, and Law," in *Pope Benedict XVI's Legal Thought: A Dialogue on the Foundation of Law*, ed. Marta Cartabia and Andrea Simoncini (Cambridge: Cambridge University Press, 2015), 57.

54 Benedict XVI, *Truth and Tolerance*, 159.

55 Isaiah Berlin, *The Power of Ideas*, ed. Henry Hardy (Princeton, NJ: Princeton University Press, 2000), 35.

56 Newman, *Idea*, 63.

57 Newman, *Idea*, 76, 81.

the heart has its reasons.[58] Such an emphasis, however, is not an invitation to superstition, fanaticism, and enthusiasm,[59] nor does it replace reason with an emotion like love. Rather, what seems to be in mind here is the right relationship to the object of faith. Benedict, for example, sees an integral relationship between the intellectual, volitional, and affective dimensions of Christian faith.[60] As he points out, love and reason are the "twin pillars of all reality: the true reason is love, and love is the true reason. They are in their unity the true basis and the goal of all reality."[61] The "ethos of Christianity must consist in love and reason converging with one another as the essential foundation pillars of reality."[62] Consequently, faith "is not merely intellectual, or merely volitional, or merely emotional activity—it is all of these things together. It is an act of the whole self, of the whole person in his concentrated unity."[63]

---

58 Rowland, *Ratzinger's Faith*, 3, 149–50. See also Benedict, *Reason Open to God*, 47, 80. Like Newman, Benedict XVI, *Deus Caritas Est*, section 17, rejects the claim that love is simply a "sentiment." On Newman, see William J. Wainwright, *Reason and the Heart: A Prolegomenon to a Critique of Passional Reason* (Ithaca, NY: Cornell University Press, 1995); Frederick D. Aquino and Logan P. Gage, "On the Epistemic Role of Our Passional Nature," *Newman Studies Journal* 17, no. 2 (2020): 41–58.

59 Newman in fact says that he concurs with Locke's criticism of enthusiasm; see, for example, *GA*, 107.

60 Benedict XVI, *Deus Caritas Est*, 17, also says that a characteristic of "mature love" is that it "engages the whole man" (e.g., the volitional, intellectual, and emotional aspects of human selfhood). On the constructive relevance of Newman's emphasis on the integral relationship of love and reason, see Pope Benedict XVI, "Mass with the Beatification of Venerable Cardinal John Henry Newman," www.vatican.va/content/benedict-xvi/en/homilies/2010/documents/hf_ben-xvi_hom_20100919_beatif-newman.html.

61 Ratzinger, *Truth and Tolerance*, 183. Nichols, *Conversation of Faith and Reason*, 193, says that the "central feature" of Benedict's account of faith and reason is the "convergence of the (mainly philosophical) disclosure of logos and the (chiefly theological) revelation of love." See also Ratzinger, *Introduction to Christianity*, 26; Pope Benedict XVI, *Deus Caritas Est*; and Sarto, "*Logos* and *Dia-Logos*," 505.

62 Rowland, *Ratzinger's Faith*, 64.

63 Benedict XVI, "On the Meaning of Faith," in *Essential Pope Benedict XVI*, 212. A question along these lines is whether Benedict affirms the cognitive function of emotions. He clearly thinks that the contours of the faith require an integration of the intellectual and the emotional. For example, he says in *A Reason Open to God*, 182, that the human person is not "only reason and intelligence, although they are constitutive elements. He bears within himself, written in the most profound depths of his being, the need for love, to be loved and in turn to love." For a discussion of the cognitive function of the emotions, see Robert Solomon, *The Passions: Emotions and the Meaning of Life* (Indianapolis, IN: Hackett, 1993); Martha Nussbaum, *Upheavals of Thoughts: The Intelligence of Emotions* (Cambridge: Cambridge University Press, 2001); Robert C. Roberts, *Emotions: An Essay in Aid of Moral Psychology* (Cambridge: Cambridge University Press, 2003); Ronald de Sousa, *Emotional Truth* (Oxford: Oxford University Press, 2011); Peter Goldie, "Emotion, Feeling, and Knowledge of the World," in *Thinking about Feeling: Contemporary Philosophers on*

Newman likewise says that it is the whole person that reasons.[64] He recognizes that our background beliefs, wishes, and desires can certainly get in the way of deciphering things correctly. As a result, faith must be constrained by the object or the facts. Both the moral and intellectual aspects of our existence "require and admit of discipline; and, as it is no disproof of the authority of conscience that false consciences abound, neither does it destroy the importance and the uses of certitude, because even educated minds, who are earnest in their inquiries after the truth, in many cases remain under the power of prejudice or delusion."[65] Our perspective must be expanded, deepened, and completed "by means of education, social intercourse, experience, and literature."[66]

Properly formed faith involves "reasoning upon holy, devout, and enlightened presumptions," namely, "deliberately, seriously, soberly, piously, and humbly, counting the cost and delighting in the sacrifice."[67] However, Newman's understanding of the role that the passional nature plays in the evidential considerations of faith is complex and multifaceted. On the one hand, he rejects, as we have seen, the claim that faith is "but a feeling, an emotion, an affection, an appetency," and, as a result, the connection of "faith with Truth and Knowledge is more and more either forgotten or denied."[68] On the other hand, Newman thinks that the passional nature can be epistemically beneficial. A properly disposed mind can put one in a place to perceive things correctly or even to perceive something that otherwise would not be perceived at all.[69] What matters is whether a particular kind of commitment or a properly disposed mind puts one in a better epistemic position.

Emotions, ed. Robert C. Solomon (Oxford: Oxford University Press, 2004), 91–106; and Peter Goldie, *The Emotions: A Philosophical Exploration* (Oxford: Clarendon, 2000).

64 Newman, *Apo.*, 155.

65 Newman, *GA*, 153.

66 Newman, *GA*, 80. For further reflection on this point and related issues, see Frederick D. Aquino, "An Educated Conscience: Perception and Reason in Newman's Account of Conscience," *Studies in the Literary Imagination* 49, no. 2 (2018): 63–80; Mark Wynn, "The Relationship of Religion and Ethics: A Comparison of Newman and Contemporary Philosophy of Religion," *Heythrop Journal* 46, no. 4 (2005): 435–49; and Wainwright, *Reason and the Heart*; and William Wainwright, *Religion and Morality* (Aldershot: Ashgate, 2005).

67 Newman, *US*, 165.

68 Newman, *Idea*, 39–40. See also *Idea*, 43, 161; *US*, 130, 143, preface 6.

69 See H. H. Price, *Belief* (London: George Allen & Unwin, 1969), 471–72.

Newman, for example, makes a connection between love and the acquisition of particular epistemic goods. That is, he insists on the importance of a properly formed mind or the possession of an abiding disposition. "The divinely-enlightened mind sees in Christ the very Object whom it desires to love and worship,—the Object correlative of its own *affections*; and it trusts Him, or believes, from loving Him."[70] In this respect, love, far from distorting our outlook, is an abiding disposition for knowledge of God. "To say that 'love is the parent of faith' is true, if by 'love' is meant . . . that desire for the knowledge and drawing towards the service of our Maker." Moreover, this abiding disposition does not "stand in antagonism or in contrast to Reason, but is a sovereign condition without which Reason cannot be brought to bear upon the great work in hand."[71]

Accordingly, a properly disposed mind creates and disciplines faith while guarding it from deficiencies such as superstition, fanaticism, and dogmatism. Love is "the eye of Faith, the discriminating principle which keeps it from fastening on unworthy objects, and degenerating into enthusiasm or superstition."[72] The distinction here is between an improperly and properly formed heart and mind. Thus, Newman does not divorce reason from love as a safeguard of faith but rather suggests that love properly construes and responds to the object of faith. Love is a vital part of our cognitive apparatus whereby we come to perceive things divine, ruling out inappropriate depictions of the divine.

Another constructive point of contact involves the importance of a regulative approach to philosophical and theological inquiry. Both Newman and Benedict see an integral relationship between intellectual, as well as spiritual, formation and the pursuit of goods such as truth, knowledge, understanding, and wisdom. Recent work on the regulative aspect of epistemology focuses principally on the questions of how intellectual and social practices guide and shape the formation of cognitive agents and the process of inquiry. For example, drawing from Nicholas Wolterstorff's work on Locke, Roberts and Wood note the distinction between "rule-oriented" (e.g., Descartes) and

---

70 Newman, *US*, 164.

71 John Henry Newman, *Discussions and Arguments on Various Subjects* (New York: Longman, Greens, and Co., 1907), 252. See also Mary Katherine Tillman, "The Two-Fold Logos of Newman and Pascal," in *John Henry Newman: Man of Letters* (Milwaukee: Marquette University Press, 2015), esp. 67–73.

72 Newman, *US*, 165; see also 162, 166.

"habit-oriented" (e.g., Locke) versions of regulative epistemology. The former concentrates on the "procedural directions for acquiring knowledge, avoiding error, and conducting oneself rationally," while the latter focuses on the "habits of mind of the epistemically rational person" or on the process of "training that nurtures people in the right intellectual dispositions."[73] Notwithstanding the different emphases here, the common ground lies in the attempt to provide an apt "response to perceived deficiencies in people's intellectual conduct" and therefore to "generate guidance for epistemic practice."[74]

Along these lines, an important theme in Newman's writings is the importance of forming a stable, properly oriented, and discerning habit of mind. For example, Newman's notion of a connected view (the result of a philosophical habit of mind) is congenial to Locke's notion of a comprehensive view. Locke contrasts the enlargement of mind with the kind of narrow perspective that seeks full comprehension of issues through a single glance or perspective. People who occupy such a narrow perspective become "muffled up in the zeal and infallibility of [their] own sect, and will not touch a book or enter into debate with a person that will question any of those things which to [them] are sacred."[75] They interact with "only one sort of people," "read only one sort of books," and consider only "one sort of notions." They create for themselves a little island in the "intellectual world, where light shines, and, as they conclude, day blesses them; but the rest of that vast [intellectual world] they give up to night and darkness, and avoid coming near it."[76]

Newman's says comparable things in the *Idea of a University* and the fourteenth *University Sermon* (on wisdom). For example, some people may "hear a thousand lectures," "read a thousand volumes," and yet understand things very much as they did at the beginning of their inquiry.[77] In this sense, they "embrace in their minds a vast multitude of ideas, but with little

---

73 Robert C. Roberts and W. Jay Wood, *Intellectual Virtues: An Essay in Regulative Epistemology* (Oxford: Clarendon, 2007), 21–22. See also Nicholas Wolterstorff, *John Locke and The Ethics of Belief* (Cambridge: Cambridge University Press, 1996).

74 Roberts and Wood, *Intellectual Virtues*, 21.

75 John Locke, *"Some Thoughts concerning Education" and "Of the Conduct of the Understanding,"* ed. Ruth W. Grant and Nathan Tarcov (Indianapolis, IN: Hackett, 1996), 172 (henceforth cited as *Thoughts* and *Conduct*).

76 Locke, *Thoughts* and *Conduct*, 170.

77 Newman, *Idea*, 393–94.

sensibility about their real relations towards each other."[78] They are satisfied with acquiring and regurgitating large amounts of information, but they fail to decipher and understand "the respective relations which exist between their acquisitions" and thereby fall short of forming a connected view of the relevant issues at hand.[79]

Newman made these comments about the formation of a philosophical habit of mind in the context of framing his vision of university education. Such an emphasis coheres with his claim that it is the whole person that reasons. Some may be tempted to interpret his notion of a philosophical habit of mind as strictly limited to his philosophy of education, but this would be a mistake. He said something similar about the evaluative process, for example, in the *Essay on the Development of Christian Doctrine*:

> It is characteristic of our minds, that they cannot take an object in, which is submitted to them simply and integrally . . . whole objects do not create in the intellect whole ideas, but are, to use a mathematical phrase, thrown into series, into a number of statements, strengthening, interpreting, correcting each other, and with more or less exactness approximating, as they accumulate, to a perfect image . . . we cannot teach except by aspects or views, which are not identical with the thing itself which we are teaching.[80]

It would, then, be a mistake to restrict his emphasis on this integrative though complex capacity to one field of knowledge or one kind of philosophical reading. Newman was deeply interested in the formative practices and habits that enable people to develop their cognitive capacities and enlarge their intellectual horizons (e.g., his focus on wisdom, pace narrow-mindedness, in the *University Sermons* and on the cultivated illative sense in the *Grammar of Assent*). He saw the danger of isolating fields of knowledge and of ignoring both their limitations and their connections.[81]

Benedict as well highlights the challenges of employing an "amputated" and unpurified employment of religion and reason. He envisions a shared space of inquiry in which people, from different points of view, promote, and

---

78 Newman, *Idea*, 121.

79 Newman, *US*, 197.

80 Newman, *Essay*, 55 (2.1.1).

81 See Newman, *Idea*, 101, 162–63.

do not obstruct, the requisite avenues for obtaining truth, emphasizing the importance of readiness or a properly disposed habit of mind for engaging, for example, in theological and philosophical inquiry. The process of inquiring requires the cultivation and exercise "intellectual charity," "humility," a "readiness to seek the truth," "inner openness," attentiveness, and so on.[82] Benedict seems to be drawing on the great masters of spirituality (e.g., Gregory the Great) in which the subject engages in the "inner climb," which entails the capacity to "grow and broaden out."[83] Such a process is deeply relevant to the challenge of cutting through the "noise" and acquiring an attentive and discerning mind. In this sense, the self seeks to be liberated from false desires and thoughts. Love of wisdom means the "readiness to seek the truth and also the humility to let ourselves be found,"[84] and figuring out whether what we believe and think tracks with the world outside of our thoughts and desires. We need practices and guidance to help us see things for what they really are, not what we want them to be.[85]

The point here is not to resolve the relevant disputes in regulative approaches to epistemology but to highlight the importance of practices and virtues for forming people intellectually and thereby regulating inquiry.[86] Cultivating a shared space of inquiry demands a host of interlocutors and thus presupposes the capacity to extend our personal judgment to social spheres of discourse. As Benedict and Newman point out, intellectual as well as spiritual formation takes into account the complex dynamic between implicit and explicit processes of belief-and-agent-formation. Undergirding this emphasis is the importance of practice and disciplined reflection within various social settings (e.g., church, society, university). A constructive project along these lines draws attention to the ways in which the process of intellectual and spiritual formation shapes theological and philosophical inquiry.[87]

---

82 Ratzinger, *Truth and Tolerance*, 159; see also Benedict XVI, *Reason Open to God*, 83.

83 Ratzinger, *Truth and Tolerance*, 160–61.

84 Ratzinger, *Truth and Tolerance*, 159.

85 See Farouq, "Windows of Benedict XVI," 57.

86 For a discussion of the landscape and the relevant issues in regulative epistemology, see Roberts and Wood, *Intellectual Virtues*; Jason Baehr, *The Inquiring Mind: On Intellectual Virtues and Virtue Epistemology* (Oxford: Oxford University Press, 2011); and Nathan Ballantyne, *Knowing Our Limits* (Oxford: Oxford University Press, 2019).

87 For discussion of the connection between intellectual (and spiritual) formation and the pursuit of epistemic goods, see Harriet Harris, "Does Analytical Philosophy Clip our Wings? Reformed Epistemology as a Test Case," in *Faith and Philosophical Analysis: The Impact of Analytical*

CONCLUSION

In this essay, I have briefly spelled out the understanding of faith and reason in the thought of Newman and Benedict. Both reject a kind of hyper-rationalism that reduces reason to a mode of inquiry (or to a formal mode of reasoning) and a kind of fideism that insulates faith from criticism. Instead, they propose a broader construal of faith and reason in which the former includes an implicit and basic mode of reasoning as well as a reflective mode of reasoning. In addition, they see an integral relationship between the affective and cognitive aspects of Christian faith and highlight the importance of a regulative approach to philosophical and theological inquiry. The constructive points of contact are preliminary in nature; I hope they provoke further attention, work, and development.

Philosophy on the Philosophy of Religion, ed. Harriet A. Harris and Christopher J. Insole (Aldershot: Ashgate, 2005), 100–118; Frederick D. Aquino, "Spiritual Formation, Authority, and Discernment," in *The Oxford Handbook of the Epistemology of Theology*, ed. Frederick D. Aquino and William J. Abraham (Oxford: Clarendon, 2017), 157–72; Sarah Coakley, "Dark Contemplation and Epistemic Transformation: The Analytic Theologian Re-Meets Teresa of Ávila," in *Analytic Theology: New Essays in the Philosophy of Theology*, ed. Oliver D. Crisp and Michael C. Rea (Oxford: Oxford University Press, 2009), 280–312; John Cottingham, *The Spiritual Dimension: Religion, Philosophy, and Human Value* (Cambridge: Cambridge University Press, 2005); John Cottingham, *Philosophy of Religion: Towards A More Humane Approach* (New York: Cambridge University Press, 2014); Paul Moser, *The Severity of God: Religion and Philosophy Reconceived* (Cambridge: Cambridge University Press, 2013); Paul Moser, "Philosophy and Spiritual Formation: From Christian Faith to Christian Philosophy," *Journal of Spiritual Formation and Soul Care* 7 (2014): 258–69; Steve Porter, "Philosophy and Spiritual Formation: A Call to Philosophy and Spiritual Formation," *Journal of Spiritual Formation and Soul Care* 7 (2014): 248–57; and Brandon L. Rickabaugh, "Eternal Life as Knowledge of God: An Epistemology of Knowledge by Acquaintance and Spiritual Formation," *Journal of Spiritual Formation and Soul Care* 6 (2013): 204–28.

4

NEWMAN AND RATZINGER ON THE ECCLESIASTICAL SCOPE OF SCRIPTURE

Aaron Pidel, SJ

Despite being born more than a century and a quarter apart, St. John Henry Newman and Joseph Ratzinger, later Benedict XVI, share in many respects a common theology of scripture. Each in his own day considered it an urgent pastoral need to square the doctrine of biblical inspiration with the changing state of human knowledge. It was during Newman's time that the so-called "higher criticism" of the German universities first began to penetrate Oxford,[1] and that Darwin's *Origin of the Species* (1859) began to cast doubt on the picture of human origins painted by Genesis. Sensing a growing disquiet among educated Catholics in the early 1860s, Newman indicated in unpublished writings his desire to do his part in "destroying the feverishness and nervousness which is abroad, the vague apprehensions of some coming discoveries hostile to faith, that spontaneous unwelcome rising of questionings and perplexities in the secret heart, which cut at the root of devotion, and dry up the founts of love, homage, loyalty, admiration, joy, peace and all the other best and

---

1 Newman's friend Edward Pusey (1800–1882), who studied at the University of Göttingen, led the way. See Stephen Thomas, *Newman and Heresy* (Cambridge: Cambridge University Press, 1991), 42.

noblest attributes of religion."[2] Newman evidently anticipated that Catholic theology would have its hands full assimilating the deliverances of history and natural science.

By Ratzinger's day, of course, historical criticism and Darwinian cosmology had already grown from discomfiting hypotheses into dominant cultural paradigms. Unsurprisingly, Ratzinger shows a similar pastoral solicitude for their potentially chilling effect on faith and devotion. Though many well-meaning exegetes have long looked to science to determine just how much of the creation account could be "literally" maintained, Ratzinger observes in *In the Beginning*, "such an operation often ends up by putting faith itself in doubt, by raising the question of the honesty of those who are interpreting it and of whether anything at all there is enduring."[3] In a similar way, the many quests to reconstruct a "historical" Jesus very different from the Jesus of the Gospels have created a disconcerting impression: "Intimate friendship with Jesus, on which everything depends, is in danger of clutching into thin air."[4] Like Newman, then, Ratzinger indicates the need for a renewed theology of biblical inspiration, a theory that would ideally minimize the field of potential conflict between faith and reason without undermining the stability of Revelation on which faith and devotion depend.

This shared *desideratum*, I would argue, led Newman and Ratzinger in turn to a common strategy. Each in his own way ends up recovering the premodern idea of scripture's "scope" (σκοπός). This is the overarching sense or "grain" that polarizes the biblical text into foreground and background elements, allowing the interpreter to distinguish what scripture properly intends to affirm from the accidental vehicles of that affirmation.

---

2 Newman, "Essay on the Inspiration of Holy Scripture (1861–1863)," in Jaak Seynaeve, *Cardinal Newman's Doctrine on Holy Scripture according to His Published Works and Unedited Manuscripts*, Universitas Catholica Lovaniensis Series II, tomus 5 (Leuven: Publications Universitaires de Louvain, 1953), 60*–144*, here 70*. The asterisked numbers refer to the pagination of Seynaeve's appendices, which would otherwise be indistinguishable from the pagination of his own work. The same writings can also be found collected and better transcribed in J. Derek Holmes, ed., *The Theological Papers of John Henry Newman on Biblical Inspiration and Infallibility* (Oxford: Clarendon, 1979), 36. I will cite both, putting Seynaeve's pagination before the virgule, Holmes's after—for example, "Essay on the Inspiration of Holy Scripture (1861–1863)," 70*/36. In cases of discrepancy, I have favored Holmes's transcription.

3 Joseph Ratzinger, *In the Beginning . . . A Catholic Understanding of the Story of Creation and the Fall* (Grand Rapids, MI: Eerdmans, 1995), 7.

4 Joseph Ratzinger, *Jesus of Nazareth*, vol. 1, *From the Baptism in the Jordan to the Transfiguration*, trans. Adrian Walker (San Francisco: Ignatius Press, 2007), xii, hereafter cited as JN 1:xii.

Though Newman and Ratzinger retrieve a similar reading strategy, they arrive at it by different means and with different degrees of integration. Whereas Newman seems to owe the greatest intellectual debt to Athanasius, Ratzinger owes his to Bonaventure; and because Ratzinger draws on Bonaventure's more developed theory of inspiration, he can give his readerly assumptions a sharper Christological focus and a more thorough metaphysical grounding. One might say that Ratzinger brings to fruition the seeds that Newman had planted but which had lain fallow in an unfavorable theological climate.

Showing how Newman and Ratzinger independently recover the "scope" of scripture requires a layered argument. It will begin by describing how Athanasius deploys the *skopos* of scripture in his *Orations against the Arians* and then show how Newman adapts this reading strategy in his own attempts to resolve the conflict between the givens of biblical faith and the findings of human reason. The second part of the chapter will describe how Ratzinger repurposes Bonaventure's understanding of inspiration for similar ends, assigning to the transhistorical People of God scripture's governing intention, the only means by which one can distinguish scripture's revealed affirmations from its historically conditioned assumptions.

NEWMAN'S RETRIEVAL OF ATHANASIUS

In classical Greek, the word σκοπός means literally the "mark or object on which one fixes the eye" and, in an extended sense, any "aim, end, object."[5] But Athanasius gives this general idea a central and distinctive meaning in course of his exegetical debates with the Arians. Indeed, as the Jesuit patrologist Hermann-Josef Sieben points out, no other patristic author except perhaps Origen makes *skopos* such a focal principle of biblical interpretation; and even he uses this principle rather differently, that is, to designate certain "ineffable mysteries regarding human affairs."[6] These include the nature of the Son, the motive of the Incarnation, rational beings and their fall, the differences among souls and their causes: in short, everything that the Spirit has veiled

---

5 Henry Liddell, Robert Scott, and Henry Stuart Jones, *A Greek-English Lexicon*, 9th ed. (Oxford: Oxford University Press, 1940), s.v., σκόπος.

6 ὁ σκοπὸς . . . ἦν προηγουμένως μὲν ὁ περὶ τῶν ἀπορρήτων μυστηρίων τῶν κατὰ τοὺς ἀνθρώπους πραγμάτων. See Origen, *De principiis* 4.2.7. Greek text: H. Görgemanns and H. Karpp, Origenes vier Bücher von den Prinzipien (Darmstadt: Wissenschaftliche Buchgesellschaft, 1976).

behind the literal narrative.[7] For Origen, therefore, the Spirit's primary *skopos* turns out to be a heterogeneous catalogue of spiritual senses rather than an overarching literal sense.

Athanasius, by contrast, gives biblical *skopos* a more definite ecclesial reference and a sharper Christological focus. This becomes especially clear in the third of his *Discourses against the Arians*, which Newman himself translated in 1844 and retranslated in the late 1870s. In it, Athanasius attempts to reconcile the Word's full divinity with the Arians' favorite proof texts, those biblical passages that seem to portray the Word's creaturely weakness or temporal origination. He counters that we cannot understand such passages correctly by reading them in isolation: we can do so only—according to Newman's 1844 translation—"if we now consider the drift (σκοπὸν) of that faith which we Christians hold, and using it as a rule (κανόνι), apply ourselves, as the Apostle teaches, to the reading of inspired Scripture."[8] At the end of the exegetical section, Athanasius returns to the importance of scripture's *skopos* for squaring Christ's weakness and passibility with his divinity: "Had Christ's enemies thus dwelt on these thoughts, and recognised the ecclesiastical scope (τόν τε σκοπὸν τὸν ἐκκλησιαστικὸν) as an anchor for the faith, they would not have of the faith made shipwreck, nor been so shameless as to resist those who would fain recover them from their fall, and to deem those as enemies who are admonishing them to be religious."[9] Whereas Origen characterized the *skopos* of scripture primarily as a material content, that is, the hidden mysteries intended by the Spirit, Athanasius adds a formal aspect, making the church's faith the *Gestalt* or pattern for correctly interpreting each individual text.

But this not to say that that for Athanasius scripture's *skopos* is merely a formal rule about reading parts in light of the whole. In an important passage, he also identifies the Bible's *skopos* with a central content:

---

7 See Hermann-Josef Sieben, "Hermeneutik der dogmatischen Schriftauslegung des Athanasius von Alexandrien," in *Manna in deserto: Studien zum Schriftgebrauch der Kirchenväter*, Edition Cardo 92 (Cologne: Koinonia-Oriens, 2002), 52.

8 *Orationes contra Arianos* 3.28.6. I have used Newman's own 1842 translation for the Library of the Fathers Series, *Select Treatises of St. Athanasius*, available with a later reprint's internal pagination from the *Newman Reader*, https://www.newmanreader.org/works/athanasius/original/index.html. For the Greek text, I have used the critical edition of K. Metzler and K. Savvidis, incorporated into *Traités contre les ariens*, 2 vols., introduction and notes Lucian Dîncă, trans. Charles Kannengiesser and Adriana Bara, Sources chrétiennes, 598–99 (Paris: Cerf, 2019).

9 *Orationes contra Arianos* 3.58.3.

ECCLESIASTICAL SCOPE OF SCRIPTURE

> Now the drift (σκόπος) and character (χαρακτὴρ) of holy Scripture, as we have often said, is this, it contains a double account of the Saviour; that He was ever God, and is the Son, being the Father's Word and Radiance and Wisdom; and that afterwards for us He took flesh of a Virgin, Mary Mother of God, and was made man. And this scope is to be found throughout inspired Scripture, as the Lord Himself has said, *Search the Scriptures, for they are they which testify of Me* (John 5:39).[10]

Athanasius thus understands the *skopos* of scripture to be not just hidden mysteries in general but the mystery of Christ in particular, of whom all scripture speaks, whether openly or hiddenly, literally or spiritually.[11]

A couple distinctives of Athanasius's understanding of *skopos* and of Newman's handling of the term bear mentioning at this point. First, Athanasius understands the faith of the church to bear the *skopos* of scripture, and Christ to fill it with content. Second, Newman's work as translator suggests that he attached a particular importance to this Athanasian idea and deliberately avoids standard dictionary definitions, rendering *skopos* either by the English barbarism "scope" or by the idiosyncratic term "drift." Newman also comments on it extensively in his annotations. In the note attached to Athanasius's appeal to scripture's "ecclesiastical scope," for example, Newman enters on a lengthy disquisition:

> Thus ends the exposition of texts, which forms the body of these Orations. It is remarkable that [Athanasius] ends as he began, with reference to the ecclesiastical scope, or Regula Fidei, which has so often come under our notice, vid. p. 328, note L. p. 341, note I. as if distinctly to tell us, that Scripture did not so force its meaning on the individual as to dispense with an interpreter, and as if his own deductions were not to be viewed merely in their own logical power, great as that power often is, but as under the authority of the Catholic doctrines which they subserve. Vid. p. 426, n. 14 fin. It is hardly a paradox to say that

---

10 *Orationes contra Arianos* 3.29.1.

11 For the Athanasian *skopos* of scripture as its Christological unity, see James D. Ernest, "Athanasius of Alexandria: The Scope of Scripture in Polemical and Pastoral Context," *Vigiliae Christianae* 47 (1993): 342. Khaled Anatolios draws attention to the broader "Trinitarian hermeneutics" of the *Discourses against the Arians* as a whole. See his *Retrieving Nicaea: The Development and Meaning of Trinitarian Doctrine* (Grand Rapids, MI: Baker Academic, 2011), 108–9.

in patristical works of controversy the conclusion in a certain sense proves the premisses.[12]

The fact that Athanasius "ends as he began," namely, with scripture's "ecclesiastical scope," furnishes Newman with a key literary-critical ground for considering the first three *Discourses against the Arians* a rounded literary unit and the fourth an accidental appendage. He argues as much, at least, in his 1847 essay *De quarta oratione s. Athanasii contra Arianos*.[13] One can say, in sum, that Athanasius turned the idea of the biblical *skopos* into a term of art and that Newman recognized this fact.

One can trace the influence of this idea on Newman's own theology of inspiration, moving both backward and forward. Looking backward, one can see how Newman's early *Arians of the Fourth Century* (1833) presents Arian exegesis as the photo negative of Athanasius's method. According to Rowan Williams, the originality of *Arians* lay in attributing the rise of Arianism not to the influence of Neoplatonic philosophy but to the exegetical poverty of the Antiochene School. Newman presents the difference between Antiochene and Alexandrian exegesis as a difference of intellectual and spiritual dispositions, with the Antiochene exhibiting a more humanitarian and dialectical temper and the Alexandrian school exhibiting a more spiritual and allegorical inclination.[14]

Though contemporary scholars recognize *Arians* as the beginning of modern critical scholarship on Arianism,[15] many nevertheless suggest that Newman's contrasting portrait of Antiochene and Alexandrian exegesis serves more as a projection screen for the spiritual and ecclesial ideals of the nineteenth-century Oxford Movement than as an account of the fourth-century

---

12 See Newman, *Select Treatises of St. Athanasius* {482}, note F.

13 "Incipit autem, procedit, et terminatur scopo ecclesiastico, seu canone fidei, proponendo, ut divinorum oraculorum justo interprete. At in hac accurata rerum dispositione nullum plane sedem sibi vindicare potest quartus ille liber seu Oratio Maurinorum" (*Tracts Theological and Ecclesiastical*, {11–12}). See the *Newman Reader*, https://www.newmanreader.org/works/tracts/dissertations/dissertation1.html. Contemporary scholars agree with Newman's conclusion, except that they tend to ascribe the Fourth Oration not only to a different occasion than the first three but to a different author. See J. T. Lienhard, SJ, "From Gwatkin Onwards: A Guide through a Century and a Quarter of Studies on Arianism," *Augustinian Studies* 44, no. 2 (2013): 277.

14 See Rowan Williams, *Arius: Heresy and Tradition*, 2nd ed. (London: SCM, 2001), 3. Benjamin King notes that Newman's Anglican forebears had presented Alexandrian philosophy as the precursor to Arianism. See also *Newman and the Alexandrian Fathers: Shaping Doctrine in Nineteenth-Century England*, Changing Paradigms in Historical and Systematic Theology (Oxford: Oxford University Press, 2009), 71.

15 Williams, *Arius*, 3.

dispute on its own terms.[16] Stephen Thomas shows convincingly that *Arians* represents Newman's polemical contribution to the "Church-State crisis of 1829–1832," which turned on the suitability of requiring assent to Anglican doctrines as a condition for full participation in English public life.[17] Newman took pains to help his reader connect Arian opposition to *homoousion* with "Latitudinarian" opposition to such credal tests.[18] Benjamin King draws attention to Newman's efforts to link Arius's allegedly materialistic exegesis with his low spiritual ideals, "his opposition to the bishop Alexander, and his unethical living."[19] Referring to the psychologizing aspects of *Arians*, Stephen Thomas dubs it "Newman's first novel."[20] Rowan Williams characterizes it as a brilliant polemic built on "complacent bigotry and historical fantasy."[21]

Despite the many criticisms leveled against *Arians*, one aspect of Newman's account has survived largely unscathed. According to Maurice Wiles, Newman was right to see that the heart of the dispute between the Arians and Catholics was the "understanding of 'the sense of Scripture' 'viewed as a whole.'"[22] Newman charges the Arians repeatedly with lacking an integrated overview and, therefore, a certain spiritual depth. "The Arians did not neglect to support their case from such detached portions of the Inspired Volume as suited their purpose," he argues in *Arians*, but they did fail to temper their deductive syllogisms by a "profound respect for the sacred text, a cautious adherence to the whole of the doctrine therein contained, and a regard for those received statements, which, though not given to us as inspired, probably are derived from inspired teachers."[23] Indeed, the whole point of extrabiblical, credal language (such as *homoousion*) for Newman is "piously and cautiously to collect the sense of Scripture, and solemnly to promulgate it in such form as is best suited, as far is it goes, to exclude the pride and unbelief of the world."[24]

---

16 Wiles, *Archetypal Heresy: Arianism through the Ages* (Oxford: Clarendon, 1996), 158.

17 Thomas, *Newman and Heresy*, 36.

18 See *Arians of the Fourth Century*, {133}, the *Newman Reader*, https://www.newmanreader.org/works/arians/index.html.

19 King, *Newman and the Alexandrian Fathers*, 80.

20 Thomas, *Newman and Heresy*, 43.

21 Williams, *Arius*, 5.

22 Wiles, *Archetypal Heresy*, 171. Cf. Williams, *Arius*, 249.

23 Newman, *Arians of the Fourth Century*, {219, 220}.

24 Newman, *Arians of the Fourth Century*, {148}.

Even before he translated Athanasius's *Discourses against the Arians*, in other words, he had traced the origin of the Arian heresy back to a exegetical method devoid of an "ecclesiastical scope."[25] He would carry this insight forward into other works of his Anglican period, such as "Holy Scripture in its relation to the Catholic Creed" (1838)[26] and the *Oxford University Sermons* (1843).[27]

During the whole time Newman was writing about the Arian controversy, the English professoriate remained largely unaware of theology on the continent. All this began to change in the 1850s when scholars began publishing commentaries on scripture more in keeping with German university exegesis.[28] Newman had by this time converted to Catholicism and naturally sought to square these and other findings with the Catholic dogmatic tradition on inspiration. The fruits of these efforts can be found in a series of papers that Newman began writing from 1861 to 1863 but that he ultimately deemed too inconclusive and too adventurous for publication in the tense ecclesial climate of his time.[29]

Even in this intermediate state of development, however, Newman reveals the ongoing influence of the Athanasian concept of the "scope" of scripture. At one point, he admits that the most satisfactory way to avoid the impression of conflict between faith and reason would be to reformulate inspiration in such a way as to change the unit of analysis from the individual oracle, narrative, or even book to that of the whole of scripture. "Though a portion of [Scripture] is in its first instance <origin> the word of man, as the speeches introduced into

---

25 For King, too, Newman's complaint against the Arians boils down to a matter of improper *skopos*. See *Newman and the Alexandrian Fathers*, 80.

26 See especially "Difficulties in the Scripture Proof of the Catholic Creed," in *Discussions and Arguments*, {109–25}, the *Newman Reader*, https://www.newmanreader.org/works/arguments/scripture/lecture1.html.

27 In his sermon "Implicit and Explicit Reason," Newman lists among the holistic principles of biblical interpretation "the question of mystical interpretation, the theory of the double sense, the doctrine of types, the phraseology of prophecy, the *drift* and *aim* of the several books of Scripture" (emphasis added). In his sermon "On the Development of Doctrine," Newman observes, "The great Object of Faith on which [the Fathers] lived both enabled them to appropriate to itself particular passages of Scripture, and became to them a safeguard against heretical deductions from them." See *Oxford University Sermons* {264, 334}, *Newman Reader*, https://www.newmanreader.org/works/oxford/sermon13.html.

28 Jaak Seynaeve mentions the publication of Jowett and Stanley's historical-critical commentaries on Paul in 1855 and the 1860 volume *Essays and Reviews*, which challenged the traditional doctrine of inspiration. See *Cardinal Newman's Doctrine on Holy Scripture*, 9–10.

29 For the historical background to the 1861–1863 papers, see Seynaeve, *Cardinal Newman's Doctrine on Holy Scripture*, 66–69.

the historical and other portions, yet He has, as it were, spoken the whole of it over again and made it His, even in those human parts, by the new sense or drift which he has put into them. This is the inspired sense."[30] The echoes of the Athanasian *skopos* are clear. Newman speaks of global sense that would relativize all regional senses as a criterion for identifying scripture's revealed content, and he calls this global sense a "drift," the same word by which he translated *skopos* in his *Select Treatises of St. Athanasius*.

Though Newman clearly remains to indebted Athanasius, he adapts the idea of the *skopos* to his own controversial purposes. Athanasius had identified the scope of scripture materially with the double generation of the Son, making it a rule for understanding how the passages of Christ's humility did not contradict his full divinity; but Newman broadens the concept to include religious truth in general. And he uses it not so much to identify how certain attributes are predicated of the Word—either with respect to his humanity or his divinity—as to distinguish which ideas in scripture enjoy divine authority. This line of thinking is already present in the 1861–1863 essays,[31] but several factors make his 1884 essays, "Inspiration in its Relation to Revelation" and "Further Illustrations," the best place to study this adaptation.[32] By 1881, Newman had already revised his translations of Athanasius, no doubt refreshing his knowledge of the Alexandrian doctor.[33] The crisis of critical historiography had by that time penetrated the Catholic Church as well. Newman found it especially disconcerting that the French exegete Ernest Renan renounced his faith on the grounds that the "Roman Catholic Church admits no compromise on questions of Biblical criticism and history."[34] Finally, Newman, having been created cardinal in 1879, was by then in a secure enough position to speak more forthrightly about what he saw as the limitations of biblical inerrancy.

---

30 Newman, "Essay on the Inspiration of Holy Scripture (1861–1863)," 129*/62.

31 "What that province is and that object of the inspiration of the Prophets and Apostles, is very determinate. It is religious truth." See "Essay on the Inspiration of Holy Scripture (1861–1863)," 123*/58.

32 These essays are cited, respectively, according to versions found in Derek Holmes and Robert Murray, SJ, eds., *On the Inspiration of Scripture: John Henry Newman*, introduction by Derek Holmes and Robert Murray (Washington, DC: Corpus Books, 1967), 101–31, 132–53.

33 King argues that Newman's revised translation, which he prepared during the 1870s, subtly conformed Athanasius to later Latin theology. See his chapter, "The Athanasius 'With Whom I End' (1864–81)," in *Newman and the Alexandrian Fathers*, 218–47.

34 Newman, "Inspiration in Its Relation to Revelation," §2, 102.

Newman argues in "Inspiration in its Relation to Revelation" that when the ecumenical councils solemnly affirm the reliability of revelation, they typically limit their affirmations to the domain of faith and morals. It hardly seems reasonable, then, to extend the inerrancy of scripture beyond this same domain, provided one accounts for the unique interwovenness of biblical faith with certain secular facts: "It seems unworthy of the Divine Greatness, that the Almighty should, in His revelation of Himself to us, undertake mere secular duties, and assume the office of narrator, as such, or an historian, or geographer, except so far as the secular matters bear directly upon revealed truth. The Councils of Trent and the Vatican . . . specify 'faith and moral conduct' as the drift of that teaching which has the guarantee of inspiration."[35] Here again the word "drift" resurfaces, now as the normative aspect of any statement sharing in divine authority.

In "Further Illustrations," a follow-up essay intended to address criticisms of the first, Newman makes the same point citing biblical authority and using different language for the object of inspiration. Here he observes that his first essay was simply affirming of inspiration what St. Paul affirms of all *gratiae gratis datae*, namely, "that they had a special scope and character and, in consequence, . . . were limited in their range of operation. I am not here affirming or denying that Scripture is inspired in matters of astronomy or chronology, as well as in faith and morals; but I certainly do not see that because Inspiration is given for the latter subjects, therefore it extends to the former."[36] The language of both "drift" and "scope" are familiar to us as Newman's own translations of the Athanasian *skopos*, and the pairing of "scope and character" echoes unmistakably Athanasius' identification of the twofold generation of the Savior as the "drift (σκόπος) and character (χαρακτὴρ) of holy Scripture." He has turned Athanasius's *skopos* into a general principle for identifying scripture's divinely inspired content, a content that, when properly determined, new scholarly discoveries would never contradict.

Though warmly welcomed by a few, Newman's conciliatory theory of inspiration remained largely unreceived for several reasons. Most importantly,

---

35 Newman, "Inspiration in Its Relation to Revelation," §11, 108.

36 Newman, "Further Illustrations," §31, 135–36. In another passage using the term "scope," Newman, having recalled certain chronological discrepancies in the Gospels, asks rhetorically, "Does this not teach us to fall back upon the decision of the Councils that 'faith and morals pertaining to the edification of Christian doctrine' are the scope, the true scope, of inspiration?" (Newman, "Inspiration in Its Relation to Revelation," §27, 127).

it was widely thought to have fallen under papal censure. Newman's later essays had reasoned that scripture, if it has a main point, may also contain ideas that are beside the point, or ideas that enjoy divine guarantee only so far as they bear upon the point. The purely beside-the-point ideas he called *"obiter dicta,"*[37] a term deriving from the hermeneutics of canon law,[38] but not long after Newman's death, Leo XIII's encyclical *Providentissimus Deus* (1893) censured those who "concede that divine inspiration regards the things of faith and morals, and nothing beyond."[39] The encyclical probably intended to intervene in a French debate sparked by the Assyriologist François Lenormant's restriction of inspiration to scripture's "supernatural teachings."[40] Though Newman had expressly—albeit ambiguously—denied that inspiration covered "nothing beyond" faith and morals,[41] some theologians understood Leo's admonition to implicate Newman as well. The English Cardinal sometimes appeared among the ranks of "adversaries" in manualist theology,[42] and theologians would understandably shy away from any solutions along Newman's lines for decades.

Another reason for the nonreception of Newman's theory was its weak metaphysical underpinning. Though Newman had retrieved and adapted a venerable reading strategy in the Athanasian *skopos*, he had not really provided the sort of philosophical justification for it that the neoscholastic theology of his day had come to expect. How exactly has God "spoken the whole of [Scripture] over again," imbuing it with a *skopos* that transcended the vision of his human instruments? How could this process be rendered in

---

37 Newman, "Inspiration in Its Relation to Revelation," §26, 125.

38 According to James T. Burtchaell, an *obiter dictum* is a statement "beside the matter in hand, and thus external to the authority, infallible or otherwise, of the enactment." See *Catholic Theories of Biblical Inspiration Since 1810: AR Review and Critique* (Cambridge: Cambridge University Press, 1969), 78n2.

39 Leo XIII, *Providentissimus Deus*, 1893, no. 20, https://www.vatican.va/content/leo-xiii/en/encyclicals/documents/hf_l-xiii_enc_18111893_providentissimus-deus.html.

40 Burtchaell, *Catholic Theories of Inspiration*, 64. Lenormant's posthumously published book, *Les origins de l'histoire d'après la Bible et les traditions des peuples orientaux* (Paris: Maisonneuve & Cie., 1880–84), was eventually placed on the *Index* (65).

41 Newman affirms the inerrancy of "matters of fact" so far as they "bear on faith." See "Further Illustrations," §33, 140.

42 See Robert Murray, introduction to Holmes and Murray, *On the Inspiration of Scripture*, 85–86. Still, writing in 1969, Burtchaell judges—incorrectly, in my opinion—that Newman divides scripture materially into inspired and uninspired passages: "In 1884 the Word had last become materially separable as those *portions* of the Book that treat of faith and morals" (*Catholic Theories of Biblical Inspiration*, 79).

causal categories or traced back to first principles? In a tantalizing passage from an 1868 letter to J. S. Flanagan on doctrinal development, Newman suggests that the church interprets scripture best because she is animated by the same Spirit that moved the apostles: "What the apostle is in his own person, that the Church is in her whole evolution of ages, per modum unius, a living, present treasury of the Mind of the Spirit of Christ."[43] Despite his insight into the church's transhistorical participation in the "Mind of the Spirit of Christ," it does not seem to occur to Newman to present the church's memory as the bearer of scripture's overarching "drift." Ratzinger, as will see, will do exactly this. In the process, he will belatedly "receive" Newman's theory, arguably providing the metaphysical integration it lacked and restoring Athanasius's Christocentric accent to the idea of *skopos*.

RATZINGER'S RETRIEVAL OF BONAVENTURE

Though Ratzinger reaches many of the same hermeneutical conclusions as Newman, he arrives at them by a Bonaventurian rather than an Athanasian path. In what follows, I will retrace this path, beginning with a couple key discoveries from Ratzinger's *Habilitationsschrift* on Bonaventure and moving to his elaboration of them into a full-fledged theory of biblical inspiration and normative interpretation. Though Ratzinger seldom mentions Athanasius, *skopos*, or Newman in this context, one might nevertheless fairly argue that he brings to fruition much that remains seminal in Athanasius's and Newman's hermeneutics of "ecclesiastical scope."

Ratzinger's early research on the *Offenbarungsverständnis und Geschichtstheologie Bonaventuras*, published in its original integrity only in 2008,[44] provided him with the central insights from which he would construct his own theory of inspiration. One such insight pertained to Bonaventure's *Offenbarungsverständnis*, in which Ratzinger found that Bonaventure did not

---

43 C. S. Dessain, "An Unpublished Paper by Cardinal Newman on the Development of Doctrine," *Journal of Theological Studies* 9 (1958): 332.

44 The integral *Habilitationsschrift* can now be found in Ratzinger, *Offenbarungsverständnis und Geschichtstheologie Bonaventuras: Habilitationsschrift und Bonaventura-Studien*, ed. Gerhard Ludwig Müller, vol. 2 of *Joseph Ratzinger Gesammelte Schriften* (Freiburg: Herder, 2008), hereafter cited as *JRGS* 2. One of the readers of Ratzinger's *Habilitation*, Michael Schmaus, strongly opposed Ratzinger's conclusions regarding Bonaventurian Revelation as excessively subjective, leading Ratzinger to submit only the part of it later translated into English as *The Theology of History in St. Bonaventure*, trans. Zachary Hayes, OFM (Chicago: Franciscan Herald Press, 1971).

use the terms *revelatio* and *inspiratio* as twentieth-century theology tended to use them, with *inspiratio* designating the divine assistance given to biblical authors and *revelatio* the objective results of this divine communication. The Seraphic doctor instead uses the words more interchangeably and less narrowly, with both referring to a kind of mystical vision enabling a subject to penetrate the veil of the sensible to the spiritual and intelligible world. This mystical vision always contains a surplus of meaning beyond what can be expressed in words: "The inspired writer cannot relate his *visio intellectualis* in its naked spirituality; he must wrap it in the swaddling clothes of the written word. This means that that which truly constitutes revelation is accessible in the word written by the hagiographer, but that it remains to a degree hidden behind the words and must be unveiled anew."[45] *Inspiratio* or *revelatio* turns out to be necessary not only for the biblical author but for the biblical interpreter, who needs constant divine assistance to see beyond the letter. This was the conclusion that Ratzinger's examiners found objectionable.[46] On Ratzinger's interpretation of Bonaventure, supernaturally elevated subjectivity entered into the very definition of revelation, such that there simply was no revelation without a subject to receive it.[47]

Does the "subject-relatedness" of Bonaventurian revelation really "destroy the objectivity of revelation in favor of a subjective actualism?"[48] Ratzinger answers this charge by noting that, for Bonaventure, the basic form of this mystical perception, without which scripture would remain simply a literary artifact, is the church's faith and creeds. "The understanding which elevates Scripture to the status of 'revelation' is not to be taken as an affair of the individual reader; but is realized only in the living understanding of Scripture in

---

45 Ratzinger, *Theology of History in St. Bonaventure*, 66. Ratzinger here cites Bonaventure's *Breviloquium* §4: "Ideo decebat [Christum] et eius doctrinam habere *humilitatem in sermone* cum *profunditate sententiae*, ut, sicut Christus fuit panniculis involutus, ita sapientia Dei in Scriptura figuris quibusdam humilibus involveretur." Bonaventura, *Opera omnia* (Quaracchi: Collegium S. Bonaventurae, 1891), 5:206.

46 For what Ratzinger calls the "drama of *Habilitation*," including Michael Schmaus's opposition to its allegedly modernist doctrine of revelation, see *Milestones: Memoirs, 1927–1977* (San Francisco: Ignatius Press, 1998), 103–14.

47 For a fuller exposition of these points, see Aaron Pidel, "*Christi Opera Proficiunt*: Ratzinger's Neo-Bonaventurian Model of Social Inspiration," *Nova et Vetera* 13, no. 3 (2015): 693–711, esp. 695–700; Aaron Pidel, *The Inspiration and Truth of Scripture: Testing the Ratzinger Paradigm* (Washington, DC: The Catholic University of America Press, 2023), 56–64.

48 Ratzinger, *Theology of History in St. Bonaventure*, 66–67.

the Church."[49] It is not scripture as textual object that constitutes Revelation, in other words, but scripture as understood and animated by the church. Nevertheless, because the church's perduring faith constantly enfolds the individual interpreter's subjectivity, Bonaventure's theory of inspiration is not reducible to a "subjective actualism." Through Bonaventure's position that the church's faith elevates scripture to the status of revelation, Ratzinger arrives at the "ecclesiastical" dimension of Athanasius's "ecclesiastical scope."

Though Ratzinger draws the ecclesiastical embeddedness of scripture from Bonaventure's *Offenbarungsverständnis*, he draws its Christological finality more from the Seraphic Doctor's *Geschichtstheologie*. Ratzinger identifies as distinctively Bonaventurian the tendency to fold logic, being, and salvation history together into common *reductio*, or "movement back" to origin. In the domain of logic, Bonaventure presupposes the Averroistic axiom that all the members of any genus are referred back to some highest instance of that genus as a standard.[50] He then transposes this logical principle into the realm of metaphysics, giving being itself the dynamic unity of *exitus* and *reditus*. As an example of such a transposition, Ratzinger cites Bonaventure's argument that intellect and will are powers of a single soul. Intellect and will cannot constitute separate substances *alongside* the soul, argues Bonaventure, because "the first power of acting, which is said to have its provenance (*egressum*) from the substance itself, is referred back (*reducitur*) to the same genus."[51] Just as a single genus can contain diverse members as long as they refer to a highest instance, so a single soul can contain diverse powers as long as they proceed from and resolve into the intellect and will as a "first power of acting." This notion of the soul as a unity of movement, a pattern of emanation and return, already goes well beyond the classical Aristotelian frame.

This notwithstanding, Ratzinger considers even more creative Bonaventure's bid to apply the conceptuality of *reductio* to salvation history. Bonaventure's *Sentence Commentary*, when explaining why it was fitting for the Son to

---

49 Ratzinger, *Theology of History in St. Bonaventure*, 66–67. Here Ratzinger cites, inter alia, Bonaventure, III *Sent* d 25, a 1, q 1: "Scientia scripturae fundatur super articulos fidei, qui sunt duodecim fundamenta civitatis" (Bonaventura, *Opera omnia*, 3:534).

50 "In quolibet genere est reperire unum primum, quo mensurantur omnia, quae sunt in illo genere." See II *Sent* d 3, p 1 a 1 q 2 f 2 (II 94a); cited in *JRGS* 2:411.

51 "Prima enim agenda potentia, quae egressum dicitur habere ab ipsa substantia, ad idem genus reducitur, quae non adeo elongatur ab ipsa substantia, ut dicat aliam essentiam completam." See II *Sent* d. 24, p. 1, a. 2, q. 1 ad 8 (II 562b–563); cited in *JRGS* 2:411.

become incarnate, compares Christ to a kind of highest instance in the genus of salvation-history: "If the lower has to be referred back (*reduci*) through what is first in the same genus, it was fitting that we become sons of God through him who is the natural Son."[52] Bonaventure thus includes not only logic and being but even history in the movement of Christological *reductio*. History no longer represents a static container for events but an intelligible pattern of movement: "The whole of reality, being, and history, are in the concept of *reductio* 'referred back' to a process of logic; the whole flowing stream of being is held together through the possibility of being referred back to God, who in the man Jesus graciously became a reality."[53] If Christ is the terminus of all salvation history, it follows that he will be the *skopos* of scripture as well.

Ratzinger wastes little time bringing these Bonaventurian insights to bear on the pre-conciliar controversies regarding scripture as source of Revelation. Invited by Cardinal Frings in October 1962 to give a theological assessment of *De fontibus revelationis*, the draft schema composed by the Preparatory Commission, Ratzinger took aim at what he considered the rather undifferentiated claims made on behalf of the Bible's inerrancy. After pointing out several errors of fact in the Bible's historical record that he considered undeniable, Ratzinger concludes, "*Scripture* is and remains inerrant and beyond doubt in everything that *it properly intends to affirm*, but this is not necessarily so in that which accompanies the affirmation and is not part of it. As a result, in agreement with what no. 13 says quite well, the inerrancy of Scripture has to be limited to its *vere enuntiata* [what is really affirmed]. Otherwise historical reason will be led into what is really an inescapable conflict."[54] Not unlike Newman, then, Ratzinger appeals to something like a *skopos* by which one could discriminate between scripture's inspired affirmations and its *obiter dicta*, or "accompaniments." Only by attentiveness to such a *skopos*, Ratzinger implies, can the church put to rest what Newman called the "vague apprehensions of some coming discoveries hostile to faith."

---

52 "Si ergo posterius per illud habet reduce, quod est prius in eodem genere, congruum fuit, ut filii Dei efficeremur per eum qui est Filius naturalis." See III *Sent* d. 1, a. 2, q. 3 c (III 30a); cited in *JRGS* 2:412.

53 Bonaventure, *JRGS* 2:412.

54 Jared Wicks, SJ, "Six Texts by Prof. Joseph Ratzinger as *Peritus* before and during Vatican Council II," *Gregorianum* 89, no. 2 (2008): 280. "No. 13" here refers to the paragraph of *De fontibus* entitled *Quomodo inerrantia diiudicanda sit*—"How inerrancy is to be discerned." See *Acta Synodalia Sacrosancti Concilii Oecumenici Vaticani II*, volumen I, pars 3: *Congregationes generales XIX-XXX* (Vatican City: Typis polyglottis Vaticanis, 1971), 18–19.

Though in this passage the connection between scripture's *skopos* and the church's faith is not explicit, it is nevertheless presumed, for Ratzinger does not speak of the inerrant intentions of scripture's authors taken separately. In his artfully constructed sentence, it is "scripture" that stands as grammatical subject, as the agent that "properly intends to affirm."[55] Those familiar with the conclusions of Ratzinger's *Habilitationsschrift* will realize that "scripture" here means not scripture as written document but rather scripture *qua* Revelation—that is, as understood and animated by the People of God. Before taking up the question of inerrancy, Ratzinger had already recalled this more comprehensive understanding of scripture: "Neither Bonaventure nor Thomas are scripturalists, since they both know well that revelation is always more than its material principle, the Scripture, namely, that it is life living on in the Church in a way that makes Scripture a living reality and illumines its hidden depths."[56] To use Newman's words, scripture receives its coherent "drift" from the one faith bywhich the church lives, "per modum unius."

What about the Christological character of the biblical *skopos*, the hallmark of Athanasius's thought, quietly dropped by Newman? Here we find Ratzinger committed to the view that all of scripture intends Christ and must be interpreted according to its various ways of relating to Christ: prophetic anticipation, direct testimony, retrospective interpretation. Ratzinger's mid-1962 draft schema, *De voluntate Dei erga hominem*, developed as an early alternative to *De fontibus revelationis*, emphasizes both of these points. Its fourth paragraph portrays Christ as the omega of Revelation: "In this man, Christ Jesus, the end toward which human history tends has already begun, for he is himself the kingdom of God, in whom 'God is all in all' (1 Cor 15:28)." Its fifth paragraph goes on both to distinguish and unite Revelation's various "layers" by reference to Christ: "The several revealed truths which are found [*leguntur*] in the Old and New Testaments and developed [*explicantur*] in Holy Mother Church's teaching and preaching, all lead back [*reducuntur*] to the one truth that is Jesus Christ."[57] Ratzinger construes Revelation here as a

---

55 Ratzinger makes scripture the intending subject more than once in his address: "According to a practically irrefutable consensus of historians there definitely are mistakes and errors in the Bible in profane matters of no relevance for what Scripture properly intends to affirm" (Wicks, "Six Texts by Prof. Joseph Ratzinger," 280).

56 Wicks, "Six Texts by Prof. Joseph Ratzinger," 276.

57 Jared Wicks, SJ, "Another Text by Joseph Ratzinger as *Peritus* at Vatican II," *Gregorianum* 101, no. 2 (2020): 238.

kind of hierarchically ordered, Bonaventurian genus, with Christ himself as the highest instance and all other members—Old Testament, New Testament, Church doctrine—emanating from him and being "referred back" to him. Ratzinger thus offers a Christologically concentrated, ecclesiastical scope with a thick metaphysical description.[58]

Having established in his early writings that the People of God intends Christ through the scriptures, Ratzinger can now adapt this broadly Bonaventurian framework for the purposes of discerning what falls within scripture's proper *skopos* and what belongs to its *obiter dicta*. Essentially, this requires the interpreter to retrace in thought the path of Bonaventurian *reductio*, referring the various layers of revelation—each corresponding to a different phase in journey of the People of God—back to their Christological center. Though Ratzinger performs such a noetic *reductio* on many occasions, the homilies on creation that he preached in 1981 at the Liebfrauenkirche in Munich, later collected and translated into English as *In the Beginning* (1985), might serve as a fitting illustration of his approach. For there we find Ratzinger, in a methodologically transparent way, circumscribing the true *skopos* of the creation narratives.

Ratzinger's way of engaging the creation narratives follows naturally from his Bonaventurian principles. After introducing the creation narrative of Genesis 1, with its solemn, hexameral structure, Ratzinger poses an inevitable question for the contemporary reader: "T[hese words] are beautiful and familiar, but are they also true?"[59] The apparent incompatibility of modern science with the biblical narrative as a natural-scientific account has given rise, he observes, to a new interpretive strategy: "One must distinguish between the form of the portrayal and the content that is portrayed."[60] One must differentiate between the images meaningful to an ancient culture, in other words, and the

---

58 It is worth noting that Dionysius, to whom Bonaventure is much indebted for his idea of a hierarchically structured *exitus* and *reditus*, describes hierarchy's "scope" as union with its "leader": "The goal (Σκοπὸς) of hierarchy, then, is to enable beings to be as like as possible to God and to be at one with him. A hierarchy has God as its leader (καθηγεμόνα) of all understanding and action" (*Celestial Hierarchy* 3.2). English translation: *Pseudo-Dionysius: The Complete Works*, trans. Colm Lubheid, foreword, notes, and translation collaboration by Paul Rorem, preface by René Roques, introduction by Jaroslav Pelikan, Jean Leclercq, and Karlfried Froehlich, Classics of Western Spirituality (New York: Paulist Press, 1987), 154; Greek text: *Corpus Dionysiacum*, vol. 2, *De coelesti hierarchia; De ecclesiastica hierarchia; De mystica theologia; Epistulae*, ed. Günter Heil and Adolf Martin Ritter, Patristische Texte und Studien 36 (Berlin: de Gruyter, 1991), 17.

59 Ratzinger, *In the Beginning*, 3.

60 Ratzinger, *In the Beginning*, 5.

enduring religious truths expressed through them. Ratzinger finds himself in basic agreement with this approach, but he points to the need for deeper reflection on the manner of drawing the line between form and content. "If theologians and even the church can shift the boundaries between image and intention, between what lies buried in the past and what is of enduring value, why can they not do it elsewhere—as, for instance, with respect to Jesus' miracles?"[61] He seeks criteria for identifying scripture's *skopos* that can admit the presence of historically conditioned ideas without reducing its revealed content to whatever the contemporary world readily accepts.

It is here that Ratzinger seeks to make his contribution, giving the Bonaventurian method of *reductio* a more historical cast. Determining the normative sense of scripture now means tracing a biblical theme along the course of its historically layered development to its culmination in Christ: "The Christian Old Testament represents, in its totality, an advance toward Christ; only when it attains to him does its real meaning, which was gradually hinted at, become clear. Thus every individual part derives its meaning from the whole, and the whole derives its meaning from its end—from Christ. Hence we only interpret an individual text theologically correctly (as the fathers of the church recognized and the faith of the church in every age has recognized) when we see it as a way that is leading us ever forward, when we see in the text where this way is tending and what its inner direction is."[62] Once determined, scripture's "inner direction" plays much the same role in Ratzinger's hermeneutics as scripture's "scope" or "drift" plays in Newman's.

But there is one difference: Ratzinger performs the prescribed historical *reductio* with an awareness of contemporary exegesis. Taking into account the picture of the Bible's composition painted by historical criticism, he traces the development of Genesis 1—albeit in broad strokes—through the course of salvation history to its term in Christ. *In the Beginning* begins by observing that the biblical account of creation contained in Genesis 1 is hardly the only one. Genesis 2–3 probably represents an older tradition. The Psalms and Wisdom

---

61 Ratzinger, *In the Beginning*, 7.

62 Ratzinger, *In the Beginning*, 9. In "Biblical Interpretation in Conflict" (1988), Ratzinger elsewhere advocates for a Christotelic view of scripture on Thomistic grounds. See Joseph Ratzinger, *God's Word: Scripture—Tradition—Office*, trans. Henry Taylor, ed. Peter Hünermann and Thomas Söding (San Francisco: Ignatius Press, 2008), 119–20.

ECCLESIASTICAL SCOPE OF SCRIPTURE

Literature carry biblical reflection on creation even further, entirely dispensing with the framework of seven days.[63] This Wisdom Literature forms, in turn, the

> final bridge on the long read that leads to Jesus Christ and the New Testament. Only there do we find the normative and conclusive scriptural creation account, which reads: "In the beginning was the Word, and the Word was with God, and the Word was God. . . . All things were made through him and without him was not anything made that was made" (Jn 1:1, 3). John quite consciously took up here once again the first words of the Bible and read the creation account anew, with Christ, in order to tell us definitively what the Word is which appears throughout the Bible and with which God desires to shake our hearts.[64]

Performing the layered *reductio* to Christ, argues Ratzinger, one soon sees that scripture does not intend to affirm the cosmology and hexameral timeline of the creation narrative as such. Rather, its principal affirmations concern the majesty of the creator, the order and goodness of creation, the special dignity of the human person as steward of creation, etc.[65]

This restriction of the normative content of Genesis 1 should not, according to Ratzinger, be seen as a rearguard action, or "some subsequently discovered trick" deployed only once science backed theologians into a corner.[66] Long before the rise of the scientific method, patristic and medieval interpreters were already reading Genesis 1 in much the same way, that is, in light of the whole and with reference to Christ. The creation narratives later became a theater for the conflict of faith and science not simply because science progressed but because biblical interpretation regressed. Imitating the methods of the natural sciences, exegetes began studying parts of scripture in isolation from the whole, thus ceasing to read texts forward and discerning their normative significance in light of Christ. Scholars instead started reading backwards, taking scripture's most primitive strands as decisive for its true meaning.[67] They lost sight, in short, of scripture's ecclesiastical and Christological *skopos*.

---

63 Ratzinger, *In the Beginning*, 14–15.

64 Ratzinger, *In the Beginning*, 15–16.

65 For Ratzinger on the "enduring significance of the symbolic elements in the text," see *In the Beginning*, 25–39.

66 Ratzinger, *In the Beginning*, 16–17.

67 Ratzinger, *In the Beginning*, 16–17.

CONCLUSION

In many ways, one can say that Ratzinger both revives and completes Newman's exploratory theology of inspiration. He acquires from Bonaventure what Newman acquired from Athanasius: the belief that the church's faith provides the hermeneutical key by which both to clarify scripture's ambiguities and to discern its proper intentions from its culturally conditioned modes of expression. Both point to such an "ecclesiastical scope" as the only way of reconciling the teaching of scripture with the demands of reason without, at the same time, giving the disconcerting impression that the Bible is shifting sand, its revealed content steadily retreating before the advances of the natural and human sciences.

Despite these points of notable convergence, Ratzinger's theology of inspiration represents more than an inadvertent repetition of Newman's. The seventy years that lay between Newman's last writings on inspiration and Ratzinger's first writings were a time of intense reflection on revelation in general and biblical inspiration in particular. This period of fruitful enquiry witnessed important attempts by Catholic theology to integrate historical and metaphysical perspectives into a unified theory of biblical inspiration and inerrancy. Having written his *Habilitation* just ten years before the promulgation of *Dei Verbum*, and having served on the drafting committee for this same Dogmatic Constitution, Ratzinger comes in some ways at the high-water mark of this conversation. He naturally noticed how Bonaventure's assumptions differed from those taken for granted by all parties in the twentieth-century debate, especially his "subject-related" understandings of *inspiratio-revelatio* and his application of metaphysical-logical *reductio* to salvation history. In Bonaventure, Ratzinger found not just a serviceable reading strategy but a theological and metaphysical grounding for it: one can read texts "forward" because thought, being, and history are all advancing toward Christ as the "highest instance" of the whole genus of salvation history. In identifying Christ as the term of this salvation-historical *reductio*, Ratzinger ends up in some ways closer to Athanasius's understanding of *skopos* than Newman himself.

Newman's and Ratzinger's independent retrievals of scripture's "ecclesiastical scope" offer an instructive lens, of course, through which to view *Dei Verbum*'s teaching on biblical inerrancy. Its central statement reads as follows: "Since everything asserted by the inspired authors or sacred writers must be held to be asserted by the Holy Spirit, it follows that the books of

Scripture must be acknowledged as teaching solidly, faithfully and without error that truth which God wanted put into sacred writings for the sake of salvation."[68] The statement's complex drafting history reveals its nature as a "compromise" document. More scholastically formed bishops and theologians wanted to locate the criterion for discerning revelation in the mind of the human authors, and their point of view finds expression in the supposition that "everything asserted by the inspired authors or sacred writers must be held to be asserted by the Holy Spirit." Bishops and theologians more aligned with the *ressourcement*, by contrast, tended to locate the criterion for identifying scripture's inspired meaning with the purpose of salvation history as a whole, and their perspective finds expression in the reminder that God consigned truth to scripture "for the sake of salvation" and the use of the "books of scripture" as the grammatical subject of "teaching." The council seems to have left the reconciliation of these author-centered and purpose-centered criteria to theologians of the next generation.[69]

The Newman-Ratzinger line perhaps provides the best theological synthesis available to date. In identifying the church as the bearer of scripture's *skopos*, Ratzinger finds a way of harmonizing the two active subjects of biblical teaching mentioned by *Dei Verbum*: the "inspired authors" who "assert" and the "books of scripture" themselves, which must "be acknowledged as teaching solidly, faithfully, and without error." Scripture as Revelation can be said to teach in a more-than-metaphorical way because the church belongs to its very definition. The church is the Bible's principal "inspired author," the subject without whose living understanding the Scripture would remain a dead letter. At the same time, Newman's idea that faith and morals constitute the "drift" of the Bible comes close to *Dei Verbum*'s purposive criterion, namely, that God give this truth "for the sake of salvation." Though Ratzinger's understanding of Christ himself as the omega of salvation history is certainly compatible, Newman's broader notion of "faith and morals" perhaps comes even closer to the conciliar formula. Both authors rule out any *a priori* restriction of inspiration and inerrancy to the domain of faith and morals, as well as any material restriction of inspiration to scripture's more "inspiring"

---

[68] Vatican II, *Dei Verbum*, 1965, no. 11, https://www.vatican.va/archive/hist_councils/ii_vatican_council/documents/vat-ii_const_19651118_dei-verbum_en.html.

[69] For more on the drafting history and its tensions, see Avery Dulles, SJ, "The Authority of Scripture: A Catholic Perspective," in *Scripture in the Jewish and Christian Traditions: Authority, Interpretation, Relevance*, ed. Frederick E. Greenspahn (Nashville: Abingdon, 1982), 14–40.

passages. Each nevertheless finds a way, whether by drawing on Athanasian "ecclesiastical scope" or Bonaventurian *reductio*, to affirm that biblical ideas in any domain—including science and history—enjoy divinely guaranteed reliability to the extent that they bear upon salvation in Christ.[70] This seems to me to be a model of inspiration and inerrancy capable of harmonizing faith and reason without either predestining scripture to constant retreat or cutting at the root of devotion.

---

[70] For a fuller exposition of Ratzinger in this point, see Aaron Pidel, "Joseph Ratzinger on Biblical Inerrancy," *Nova et Vetera* 12, no. 1 (2014): 307–30, esp. 322–24.

5

"LIGHT AND DARKNESS, BLESS THE LORD!" (DN 3:72)
JOHN HENRY NEWMAN AND JOSEPH RATZINGER ON GOD'S MYSTERY

Marial Corona

In the Canticle of the three Hebrew brothers who are about to suffer martyrdom in the hands of Nebuchadnezzar, we find one of the most beautiful and rich hymns of praise to God that sacred scripture offers us. While bringing to God's feet all of creation, sun and moon, dolphins and plains, dew and sleet, Shadrach, Meshach, and Abednego offer us a tremendous insight when they cry out: "Light and darkness, bless the Lord."[1] They recognize that both light and darkness *as such* can be manifestations of God's glory and bring him praise.[2] Darkness does not need to become light to give glory to God: it can do so as darkness.

---

1 While this prayer is not found in the Hebrew-Aramaic text of Daniel, it is found in the *Septuagint* and therefore forms parts of the Catholic canon. For an introduction to its history and theological significance, see David A. deSilva, "Prayer of Azariah and Song of the Three Jews," in *Introducing the Apocrypha: Message, Context, and Significance*, 2nd ed. (Grand Rapids, MI: Baker Academic, 2018), 292–99.

2 Isaiah 60:2 is another scripture verse that states that God's glory is revealed through darkness. Using this passage, Cyril of Alexandria illustrated the reality of the Incarnation and showed how the glory of Christ's divinity assumed the darkness of his humanity, and yet both remained. See

This essay explores the themes of light and darkness, as an expression of God's mystery, in the writings of John Henry Newman and Joseph Ratzinger. As the title suggests, the argumentation I offer moves in the lights and shadows of truth, where sparks of light are accompanied by patches of darkness, and as we advance, the mystery is not unraveled but deepened. I find Ratzinger and Newman to be particularly fitting guides for such undertaking: while they undoubtedly elucidated the truths of faith, they did not do so by eliminating darkness but were strong apologists of the fruitfulness of accepting mystery as such.[3]

In his final Christmas Address to the Roman Curia, which year to year provides an opportunity for the Holy Father to offer a balance of the year, not of his governance decisions but of that which occupies his heart and mind and that he finds most relevant for the mission of the Church, Benedict XVI stated:

> The Christian can afford to be supremely confident, yes, fundamentally certain that he can venture freely into the open sea of the truth, without having to fear for his Christian identity. To be sure, we do not possess the truth, the truth possesses us: Christ, who is the truth, has taken us by the hand, and we know that his hand is holding us securely on the path of our quest for knowledge. Being inwardly held by the hand of Christ makes us free and keeps us safe: free, because if we are held by him, we can enter openly and fearlessly into any dialogue [and] safe, because he does not let go of us.[4]

Pope Benedict's confidence can give us much courage as we venture into the open sea, not only the sea of quandaries and decisions that day-to-day life presents to us but those in our professional and academic endeavors as well:

Cyril of Alexandria, "The Glory of Zion," in *Isaiah 40–66*, ed. Mark W. Elliott and Thomas C. Oden, Ancient Christian Commentary on Scripture 11 (Downers Grove, IL: IVP Academic, 2007), 323. Additionally, Psalm 36:9 expresses that God's light enables us to see darkness as bright.

3 The luminosity of darkness is a common theme in spiritual theology. See, for example, Thomas à Kempis, "Lack of Consolation," in *The Imitation of Christ*, ed. Mary Lea Hill, trans. Mary Nazarene Prestofillipo (Boston: Pauline Books & Media, 2015), 111; John of the Cross, *Dark Night of the Soul*, ed. and trans. E. Allison Peers (New York: Image Books, 1959), 69–72; and Thérèse of Lisieux, *Story of a Soul*, trans. John Clarke (Washington, DC: ICS Publications, 1996), 198.

4 Benedict XVI, "Address on the Occasion of Christmas Greetings to the Roman Curia" (Clementine Hall, December 21, 2012). Commenting upon this address of the Holy Father, James Keating states that the pursuit of truth and surrendering to a relationship with the Word are closely related and builds on this assertion the proper methodology for theological studies. See James Keating, "Theology as Thinking in Prayer," *Chicago Studies* 53, no. 1 (2014): 79.

GOD'S MYSTERY

"The Christian can be supremely confident that he can venture freely into the open sea of the truth; to be sure, we do not possess the truth, the truth possesses us." In these uncertain times where many securities seem to shift repeatedly, from the most pragmatic to the most profound, Pope Benedict offers us a way to engage with confidence that which we do not fully grasp or comprehend.

While Benedict's assertion that "we do not possess the truth" may sound odd coming from him and could seem to be in opposition to the last homily he gave as a Cardinal seven years earlier, where he denounced the growing "dictatorship of relativism that does not recognize anything as definitive and whose ultimate goal consists solely of one's own ego and desires,"[5] this is not the case. We can attempt to reconcile both statements and better understand Benedict's mind by appealing to Newman's description of "an educated man": "If he has one cardinal maxim in his philosophy, it is, that truth cannot be contrary to truth; if he has a second, it is, that truth often seems contrary to truth; and, if a third, it is the practical conclusion, that we must be patient with such appearances, and not be hasty to pronounce them to be really of a more formidable character."[6]

Holding on to the conviction that truth cannot be contrary to truth, what then does Pope Benedict mean by stating that we do not possess it? It seems to me that he is saying that truth is not a property, a good, or a treasure that we can store, manipulate, or access at will.[7] With fear of stating the obvious, truth

---

5 Joseph Ratzinger, "Homily at the Mass *Pro Eligendo Romano Pontifice*" (Vatican Basilica, April 18, 2005). For a thoughtful analysis of relativism in Ratzinger's thought, see Daniel Cardó, "Relativism," in *What Does It Mean to Believe? Faith in the Thought of Joseph Ratzinger* (Steubenville, OH: Emmaus Academic, 2020), 30–34; for a critique of Ratzinger's position, see Richard Shusterman, "Fallibilism and Faith," in *A "Dictatorship of Relativism"? Symposium in Response to Cardinal Ratzinger's Last Homily*, ed. Jeffrey M. Perl (Durham, NC: Duke University Press, 2007), 379–84.

6 John Henry Newman, *The Idea of a University* (London: Longmans, Green, and Co., 1907), 461. Twenty-two years earlier, Newman had addressed the theme of apparent contradictions in a homily. After stating that the human soul "is in every part of the body; it is no where, yet every where," he explained: "I do not of course mean that there is any real contradiction in these opposite truths; indeed, we know there is not, and cannot be, because they are true, because human nature is a fact before us. But the state of the case is a contradiction when put into words; we cannot so express it as not to involve an apparent contradiction." See John Henry Newman, *Parochial and Plain Sermons* (London: Longmans, Green, and Co., 1907), iv, 286.

7 In the *Idea*, Newman explains: "When we inquire what is meant by truth, I suppose it is right to answer that truth means facts and their relations, [as knowledge is] the apprehension of these facts, whether in themselves, or in their mutual positions and bearings" (45). Reinhard Hütter connects truth and knowledge as follows: "The human intellect operates in a horizon of transcendent truth, indeed, of subsistent truth, first truth . . . , the pursuit of knowledge is a created participation in the divine perfection of knowledge." See Reinhard Hütter, *John Henry Newman on Truth and Its Counterfeits* (Washington, DC: The Catholic University of America Press, 2020), 200.

is greater than the individual, not subject to him. If truth is beyond us, how then can we avoid a precarious relativism and barren skepticism? What can be an epistemological source of freedom and safety as we navigate the open seas of our times? If truth is not something we possess, how can we relate to it?

Giving a definitive answer to these critical questions goes beyond the scope of this chapter. While I don't have a categorical solution, I have found some significant clues in the writings of John Henry Newman and Joseph Ratzinger, which have illumined and strengthened my own relationship with truth and have been fruitful in the lives of others when I bring them to their attention. Most of these clues revolve around Newman's and Ratzinger's understanding of mystery.[8]

MYSTERY AS AN EXPERIENTIAL REALITY FOR NEWMAN AND RATZINGER

While the nature of this collection of essays set the choice of authors for this discussion, both Newman and Ratzinger not only dealt with mystery, light, and darkness in their academic careers but revealed their existential grappling with them in their most personal writings. Rather than a scholarly production, their engagement with mystery was foremost a lived experience. The first lines of Newman's famous poem "The Pillar of the Cloud," which he wrote at the end of his pilgrimage to continental Europe when he was thirty-one years old, come to mind:

> Lead, Kindly Light, amidst th'encircling gloom, Lead Thou me on!
> The night is dark, and I am far from home, Lead Thou me on!
> Keep Thou my feet; I do not ask to see the distant scene; one step
>   enough for me.[9]

---

8 For an in-depth study of faith and reason in the thought of Newman and Ratzinger, see Bryce A. Evans, "Objective and Subjective Elements of Faith in John Henry Newman and Joseph Ratzinger" (MA thesis, University of St. Thomas, 2017). The section entitled "The Redemption of Reason," 154–60, is particularly relevant to this discussion.

9 John Henry Newman, *Verses on Various Occasions* (London: Longmans, Green, and Co., 1903), 156. An insightful introduction to the context of this poem can be found in Donald Capps, "A Biographical Footnote to Newman's *Lead, Kindly Light*," *Church History* 41, no. 4 (1972): 480–86; see also Ian Ker, *John Henry Newman: A Biography* (Oxford: Oxford University Press, 2010), 78–80.

GOD'S MYSTERY

In this poem, we can see that Newman chose to abandon himself to the light and darkness of the road that lay before him, a road which led him to set in motion the Oxford Movement and ask to be received into the Roman Catholic Church fourteen years later.

Looking into Ratzinger's works, one of his clearest assertions of how he engaged with light and darkness at a personal level is not an act of abandonment for the future but a view in retrospect. In his *Memoirs*, which he published when he was seventy-one years old, he wrote:

> I was born on Holy Saturday, April 16, 1927, in Marktl am Inn. The fact that my day of birth was the last day of Holy Week and the eve of Easter has always been noted in our family history. This was connected with the fact that I was baptized immediately on the morning of the day I was born with the water that had just been blessed. (At that time the solemn Easter Vigil was celebrated on the morning of Holy Saturday.) To be the first person baptized with the new water was seen as a significant act of Providence. I have always been filled with thanksgiving for having had my life immersed in this way in the Easter mystery, since this could only be a sign of blessing. To be sure, it was not Easter Sunday but Holy Saturday, but, the more I reflect on it, the more this seems to be fitting for the nature of our human life: we are still awaiting Easter; we are not yet standing in the full light but walking toward it full of trust.[10]

Ratzinger closed this reflection by alluding to walking a path. In this chapter, I set out to discuss mystery as a pathway to truth. Using the term pathway could imply that it is a temporary road that must be overcome, a road that will be ultimately left behind once we reach truth as our desired destination. This is not what I have in mind, however, nor I believe what Newman and Ratzinger had in mind when they discussed the notion of mystery. Perhaps it would be more precise to speak of mystery as a characteristic of truth that allows us

---

10 Joseph Ratzinger, *Milestones: Memoirs, 1927–1977* (San Francisco: Ignatius Press, 1998), 8. In his 1969 *Meditations on Holy Week*, Ratzinger expands on the mystery of light and darkness in the context of Easter: "The darkest mystery of faith is simultaneously the brightest sign of hope that is without limits. And one thing further: only through the failure of Good Friday, only through the deathly stillness of Holy Saturday could the disciples be led to grasp who Jesus really was and what his mission truly meant." See William Congdon and Joseph Ratzinger, *The Sabbath of History* (Washington, DC: WGC Foundation, 2006), 39–40, originally published as Joseph Ratzinger, *Meditationen Zur Karwoche* (Freising: Meitinger Kleinschriften, 1969).

to access it as finite creatures.[11] Ono Ekeh argues that Newman understood mystery as a hermeneutical problem, stating that for him, "mystery is not a restraint on one's intellect, but is rather recognition of human imperfection and inability to absorb truths superior to its capacity to receive."[12]

Neither Newman nor Ratzinger dealt with mystery as a theological or philosophical category in a systematic way. However, they alluded to this notion in some of their writings. Further, as we have seen, they understood and framed their lives within the context of mystery. For both, mystery was not a reality to overtake and eliminate but a personal invitation to ponder.[13] Newman often extended this invitation through his sermons. Speaking of his style as a preacher, Denis Robinson wrote that he

> carries the discourse forward by introducing a series of questions that he does not answer. In fact he admits that "these and many other questions admit of no satisfactory solution." The reality of Christ's mystery lies in the paradox, that is, in the suspension of solutions in favour of further relational enquiry. The satisfaction of "knowing" Christ comes in the mystery of connections. . . . Questions generate questions in Newman's homiletic economy. One question leads to another. . . . None of the questions is answered. Instead, in Newman's preaching, they have rather the cumulative effect of *drawing the enquirer deeper into the mysterious relationship.*[14]

---

11 For a philosophical approach to mystery see Richard Jones, *Mystery 101: An Introduction to the Big Questions and the Limits of Human Knowledge* (Albany: SUNY Press, 2018), 1–20. Jones sustains that "Descartes's search for certainty and clarity shaped the modern philosophical quest: since the Age of Enlightenment, a campaign to banish all mystery from the world has been waged in the West. The objective is to maximize our vision and minimize mystery. . . . [However] even if philosophy and science advance as far as is humanly possible, some genuine mysteries to reality still appear to remain—we cannot demystify reality totally no matter how hard we try" (Jones, *Mystery 101*, 10, 8).

12 Ono Ekeh, "John Henry Newman on Mystery as a Hermeneutical Problem," *New Blackfriars* 96, no. 1061 (2015): 82.

13 In one of his earlier sermons Newman denounced "the tendency of reasoning minds to get rid of mysteries" (Newman, *Sermons, 1824–1843*, iv, 215) and criticized how some scholars "instead of viewing . . . two distinct and complete truths distinctly and completely, . . . bring the Scripture statements containing them together, to mingle them with each other, to view them as modifying each other, and as neutralizing each other's force and exactness, and so at length to bring out both together some vague and general doctrine neither the one nor the other. This error, and this very form of it, is one which lies before us in this day, as an enemy in the way" (iv, 109–10).

14 Denis Robinson, "Preaching," in *The Cambridge Companion to John Henry Newman*, ed. Ian Ker and Terrence Merrigan (Cambridge: Cambridge University Press, 2009), 250 (emphasis added). For his part, Roderick Strange comments that "the concern for mystery and the wish for it to be

GOD'S MYSTERY

After explaining how I approach this chapter's topic, I will speak first of Ratzinger's engagement with mystery and then of Newman's. Although this approach is anachronistic, I am choosing to do so because it is how I started reflecting on mystery as a tool for understanding; a means for light where darkness is not a negative element to be overcome but rather a means of revelation to be welcomed and a pathway that does not lead to the possession of truth but to allowing ourselves to be possessed by the Truth Incarnate.

My discussion of Ratzinger's understanding of mystery will be limited to his work *Introduction to Christianity,* the collection of lectures he offered in the University of Tübingen in 1967 and published in 1968. Many have considered this volume the cornerstone of his five decades of theological work. As a point of access to Newman's thought on mystery, I will rely heavily on three pieces he wrote in 1836: Tract 73 and two posterior sermons.[15] I will also draw from the insights developed on two lectures that John Crosby gave in 1990 and 1991 in which he explored what he labeled the "coincidentia oppositorum" in Newman's intellectual character and personal spirituality,[16] and a lecture of Roderick Strange titled "Newman and the Mystery of Christ."

HOW I APPROACH THE SUBJECT

In the preface to the 2000 edition of *Introduction to Christianity,* Ratzinger explores how we encounter God and get to know him. He recognizes the dogmatic character of Christian revelation and ponders why dogmatic certainty seems to be less attractive to contemporary men and women, while eastern mysticism, which leads to a more vague and uncertain contact with the divine, often seems a better answer to our spiritual needs.[17]

---

received vividly and really by congregations and readers characterized the way [Newman] wrote." See Roderick Strange, "Newman and the Mystery of Christ," in *Newman after a Hundred Years,* ed. Ian Ker and Alan Hill (Oxford: Oxford University Press, 1990), 331.

15 The tract is from February 2; the sermons are from April 17 and May 8. Their bibliographic references are given in subsequent footnotes.

16 Nicholas of Cusa coined the term "coincidentia oppositorum" and applied it to God, holding that it was his "least imperfect name." This term has influenced the work of a number of Western scholars who consider the psyche of each individual to likewise be a coincidence of opposites. See Hillary S. Webb, "Coincidentia Oppositorum," in *Encyclopedia of Psychology and Religion,* ed. David A. Leeming, Kathryn Madden, and Stanton Marlan (Boston: Springer, 2010), 157–59.

17 In his book *Liturgical Mysticism,* David Fagerberg masterfully connects the sacramental action of the church with the mystical experience of the soul. He writes: "This source of life, this energy of love, this supernatural and sacred power has sustained the world as a divine liturgical economy

103

All through this work, and we can also say, all through his life, Ratzinger defended with courage and unambiguity the reality of the Incarnation as the central event in history. While he acknowledged that God has come to dwell in our midst in the Person of Jesus Christ, he went on to affirm that "in this way, his mystery has also become still greater. God is always infinitely greater than all our concepts and all our images and all our names."[18] That mystery is enlarged rather than dissipated in the face of the central event of God's self-revelation is a powerful insight.[19]

To show the basis upon which I build my argument and the direction I take, I want to mention an insight from John Crosby regarding Newman, which I found highly complementary to Ratzinger's thought. At a conference on the theme "John Henry Newman, Lover of Truth," Crosby's lecture was titled "Newman on Mystery and Dogma." He explained:

> The more I read and reread Newman, the more I find a union of apparent opposites in his thought. I find that the breadth and fullness of his teaching comes, at least in part, from his ability to hold fast to apparently opposed truths. A weaker mind plays such truths off against each other, and declares one of them to be an error, but Newman is distinguished by the comprehensiveness of his thought, that is, by his ability to find room for each of the apparently opposed truths, and this even when he cannot explain exactly *how* it is that they cohere.[20]

---

since its creation; it took prophetic and typological form in Israel's prophets, priests, and kings; it now has visible, sacerdotal, sacramental, fleshly form as the mystical body of Christ that is formed and fed by his Eucharistic body; and it still awaits its final consummation in the eschaton. . . . It's all one and the same mystery." See David W. Fagerberg, *Liturgical Mysticism* (Steubenville, OH: Emmaus Academic, 2019), xix–xx.

18 Joseph Ratzinger, *Introduction to Christianity* (San Francisco: Ignatius Press, 2004), 25.

19 Newman writes that it is our duty to attempt to enlarge rather than eliminate mysteries: "Upon all these we ought to dwell and enlarge, mindfully and thankfully. . . . Enlarge upon them we ought, even because they are few and partial, not slighting what is given us, because it is not all (like the servant who buried his lord's talent), but giving it what increase we can" (Newman, *Parochial and Plain Sermons*, iii, 159).

20 John Crosby, "Newman on Mystery and Dogma," in *John Henry Newman, Lover of Truth* (Rome: Pontificia Universitas Urbaniana, 1991), 37. Crosby discusses the union of opposite perfections in Newman's personality in his paper "Christliche Heiligkeit Als Einheit von scheinbaren Gegensätzen: Die Lehre und das Zeugnis John Henry Newmans," in *Newman-Studien* (Sigmaringendorf: Glock und Lutz, 1988), 207–18. Roderick Strange explains that Newman's "patience with ambiguity and desire to live deeply within the organic life of the Church gave him the confidence to respect their distinctiveness as the threshold of mystery" (Strange, "Newman and the Mystery of Christ," 335).

The two apparent opposites that Crosby singles out are Newman's commitment to the dogmatic principle and his equally strong commitment to subjective religious experience as a valid source of knowledge about God. He writes: "For all of his zeal for doctrinal truth, Newman was a great friend of religious experience and a sharp critic of the religious rationalism which expects too much from definition and demonstration."[21] Crosby built his essay upon Newman's longing for truth along with his recognition that it is not to be found in this world. In Crosby's words: "Newman has a particular strong sense of the limits of human knowledge, of the darkness in which we remain even after our best attempts at knowing, and of the mystery which encompasses us on all sides."[22] Roderick Strange locates the source of Newman's creativity in his struggle to simultaneously live out these two commitments.[23]

These glimpses into Ratzinger's and Newman's understanding of mystery point to the thesis that I hold throughout this essay: a mystery is a source of revelation, a source of light that encompasses darkness as darkness.

RATZINGER'S INSIGHTS ON MYSTERY IN *INTRODUCTION TO CHRISTIANITY*

In *Introduction to Christianity,* Ratzinger introduces the notion of mystery as he discusses several instances of God's self-revelation to Israel. He argues that mystery is not the antagonist of knowledge or faith but an essential characteristic in them, or, in his own words, the means we have "to render belief possible *as* understanding."[24] Mystery is a tool to aid understanding,

---

21 Crosby, "Newman on Mystery and Dogma," 42. In a similar vein, Scott Hahn writes about Ratzinger: "[He] believes, too, there are lessons to be learned from the fourth-century debate between the Church father, St. Gregory of Nyssa, and a rationalist interlocutor, Eunomius, who believed he could develop an accurate understanding of God by using exclusively rational and scientific means. Gregory demurred, charging that his opponent's scientific approach 'transforms each mystery into a 'thing.'" See Scott Hahn, "The Authority of Mystery: The Biblical Theology of Benedict XVI," *Letter & Spirit* 2 (2006): 98.

22 Crosby, "Newman on Mystery and Dogma," 43. Ekeh explains that for Newman, "mystery was a result of the human incapacity and inability to grasp the fullness of truth" (Ekeh, "John Henry Newman on Mystery," 74).

23 Strange, "Newman and the Mystery of Christ," 334.

24 Ratzinger, *Introduction to Christianity*, 77. For his part, Stephen Prickett argues that "ambiguity is not merely a concomitant of religious experience, but is actually characteristic of, and historically central to, man's experience of God. Elijah on Horeb, Moses and the Burning Bush, the Incarnation itself present events so baffling as to imply quite new ways of seeing the world." See

not an obstacle to understanding,[25] which allows us to express a divine truth "as fully and explicitly as it can be set forth in human words."[26]

Ratzinger begins his exploration of the biblical belief in God by asking, "What is the specifically new element expressed by the name 'Yahweh?'"[27] We recall that at the scene of the Burning Bush, God called himself Yahweh, "I am who I am" (Ex 3:14), and thus revealed himself as a God entirely different from the other gods of the ancient world.[28] Ratzinger explains that God's revelation as Yahweh

> effects a sort of withdrawal from the only too well known, which the name seems to be, into the unknown, the hidden. It dissolves the name into mystery, so that the familiarity and unfamiliarity of God, concealment and revelation, are indicated simultaneously. The name, a sign of acquaintance, becomes the cipher for the perpetually unknown and unnamed quality of God. Contrary to the view that God can here be grasped, so to speak, the persistence of an infinite distance is in this way made quite clear.[29]

Through his revelation as Yahweh, God simultaneously shows his familiarity and unfamiliarity, his concealment and revelation, and dissolves his name, which usually serves as an objective identifier, into the shadows of mystery. Then we can say that mystery and name, shadows and light, are like the two

---

Stephen Prickett, *Words and the Word: Language, Poetics, and Biblical Interpretation* (Cambridge: Cambridge University Press, 1986), 224.

25 In very similar terms, Thomas Sheridan explains how Newman pays recourse to mystery as an instrument to deepen God's revelation found in the scriptures and in the teaching of the Church. See Thomas L. Sheridan, "Justification," in *The Cambridge Companion to John Henry Newman*, ed. Ian Ker and Terrence Merrigan (Cambridge: Cambridge University Press, 2009), 111.

26 Newman, *Parochial and Plain Sermons*, iv, 283.

27 Ratzinger, *Introduction to Christianity*, 126–27.

28 Regarding other ancestral gods, and the uniqueness of the God of Israel, Thomas Römer writes: "The revelation of the divine name Yhwh is something new. In the original text, the deity presented itself as Moses' patriarchal God and Moses identifies this god with the ancestral deity of the Israelites. The fact that ancestral gods do not bear personal names is attested by texts from Ugarit that often mention an *'ilu 'ibi* ('god of the father'). The author of Exodus 3 wants to emphasize that this unknown god is in fact the deity Yhwh." See Thomas Römer, "The Revelation of the Divine Name to Moses and the Construction of a Memory about the Origins of the Encounter between Yhwh and Israel," in *Israel's Exodus in Transdisciplinary Perspective*, ed. Thomas Levy, Thomas Schneider, and William Propp (New York: Springer, 2015), 310.

29 Ratzinger, *Introduction to Christianity*, 128.

GOD'S MYSTERY

sides of the coin that allow us to come into close contact with God, and in him, with all of reality.[30]

A second instance in which Ratzinger introduces mystery as an epistemological tool with which to encounter and know God is a brief allusion he makes to the book of Job. After speaking of the evils of the totalitarian regimes of the twentieth century, Ratzinger asserts that when questioned about suffering, God's answer to Job "explains nothing; rather, it sets boundaries to our mania for judging everything and being able to say the final word on a subject, and it reminds us of our limitations. It admonishes us to trust the mystery of God in its incomprehensibility."[31]

Ratzinger's unambiguous description of our tendency to find and say the final word on any given subject as a mania to which God sets boundaries is quite telling. He goes on to say that while we recognize God's darkness, we must also emphasize his light. It seems to me that the point he wants to make is that one cannot cancel the other: light is not meant to cancel mystery, nor vice versa. We must learn to sit with both, because only within the tension they create can we grow in understanding.[32]

A third instance where Ratzinger introduces the notion of mystery is in Israel's journey through the wilderness as narrated in the book of Exodus. Speaking of the cloud that guided the Israelites, he says that it hides God's

---

30 Ekeh identifies the same arguments in Newman's thought. He writes: "The initial context for mysteries is the interplay between presence and absence. In an 1838 sermon, Newman noted how we speak differently about people in their presence and absence. In the presence of people, speech is guided by the knowledge that they are aware of what is being said about them and how they would react. In their absence, Newman noted that one assumes a different mode of speech . . . God's mysteriousness here is tied to a sense of God's presence which overcomes the existential sense of God's absence, thus pointing to certain characteristics of God that amaze the Christian. God's mysteriousness has roots in His invisibility, not *qua* invisibility, but invisibility as absence leading to greater sense of presence" (Ekeh, "John Henry Newman on Mystery," 75–76).

31 Ratzinger, *Introduction to Christianity*, 26. On a related note, Brian Daley writes that Newman understands that mysteries as "authoritatively articulated within a universal teaching Church." See Brian E. Daley, "The Church Fathers," in Ker and Merrigan, *Cambridge Companion to John Henry Newman*, 36.

32 Matthew Ramage writes: "Benedict looks to Job's desperate, even impious pleas to God as a model for how are we to relate to the divine mystery . . . to walk the path of faith is not primarily about receiving answers from the Lord but more about letting the Lord pose the question to us of how we are going to live our life in the light of his love and law." See Matthew J. Ramage, *The Experiment of Faith: Pope Benedict XVI on Living the Theological Virtues in a Secular Age* (Washington, DC: The Catholic University of America Press, 2020), 69–70.

107

glory while revealing his presence (Ex 40:34).[33] The fact that the same element, in this case, a cloud, revealed God's closeness while hiding it deeply touched me when I was a junior in college and read *Introduction to Christianity* for the first time. As a young woman who was discerning a possible call to consecrated life, the idea that one and the same thing could show me God's ways while keeping them from me was fascinating and allowed me to identify his action, not in what I perceived to be "blinding lights" as clear and distinct ideas or strong emotional experiences but in the pale lights and shadows of daily prayer and ordinary life.

Ratzinger goes on to say that just as the cloud concealed and revealed God's presence among the Israelites in the desert, Christ's humanity concealed and revealed God's presence to his contemporaries in Galilee and Jerusalem, and the Eucharist does the same for us: it conceals and reveals. We can continue with this line of thought and apply it to the church, pondering how it reveals God's presence through her beauty, while hiding him from view through her sin,[34] and hope and pray that the same is true in us: that our words and actions, with their light and shadows, while they conceal, also serve to reveal God's presence and love to others.

Revelation and concealment are central to Ratzinger's notion of mystery, and for him, both are positive and necessary elements in our knowledge of God. He clarifies "the true idea of 'mystery,' the purpose of which is not to destroy reason but rather to render belief possible *as* understanding . . . In *this* sense we can rightly speak of mystery as the ground that precedes us and always and ever goes beyond us, which can never be caught up or overtaken."[35] Once more, we see mystery as a pathway, not to be caught or overtaken but instead traveled in confidence.

---

33 See Ratzinger, *Introduction to Christianity*, 272–73. Charles Whitaker explains: "God's cloud, then, embodies a paradox. It can be a facility through which God reveals Himself, that is, a vehicle through which He communicates to mankind. Shortly before the Israelites entered the Promised Land, Moses reminds the people of the cloud's revelatory nature. It was God, he says, who for decades 'went in the way before you to search out a place for you to pitch your tents, to show you the way you should go, in the fire by night and in the cloud by day' (Dt 1:33)." See Charles Whitaker, "Clouds (Part One): A Really Special Cloud," *Forerunner Magazine* 30, no. 2 (2021).

34 Applying to the church the description of the bride from the Song of Songs, "I am black but beautiful" (Song 1:5), Ratzinger says that the paradoxical presence of holiness and sinfulness in the church is "typically characteristic" of Christian thought. See Joseph Ratzinger, "Soy Negra Pero Hermosa," in *El Nuevo Pueblo de Dios* (Barcelona: Herder, 1972), 285–90.

35 Ratzinger, *Introduction to Christianity*, 77–78.

Further along in his collection of lectures, Ratzinger refers to the destination of this pathway: Jesus Christ. He invites his readers to accept the mystery of darkness for the sake of the greater light that comes through it and explains that the Gospels depict God's self-revelation in Christ, "not with the object of eliminating that mystery, but precisely to confirm it."[36]

NEWMAN'S INSIGHTS ON MYSTERY AS "COINCIDENTIA OPPOSITORUM"

About ten years passed from the moment I began to ponder Ratzinger's notion of mystery to my discovery of John Crosby's essay where he speaks of dogma and mystery in Newman. While Ratzinger showed me the reality of mystery as a desirable revelation not to be overcome, Newman's insights helped me to understand how mystery can bring forth truth with even more clarity than "pure light."

Speaking within the context of Divine Revelation, Newman gives his most thorough exposition of what he understands by mystery in *Tract 73*:

> A Revelation is religious doctrine viewed on its illuminated side; a Mystery is the selfsame doctrine viewed on the side unilluminated. Thus revealed Truth is neither light nor darkness, but both together; it is like the dim view of a country seen in the twilight, with forms half extricated from the darkness, with broken lines, and isolated masses. Revelation, in this way of considering it, is not a revealed *system*, but consists of a number of detached and incomplete truths belonging to a vast system unrevealed, of doctrines and injunctions mysteriously connected together; that is, connected by unknown media, and bearing upon unknown portions of the system.[37]

"Truth is neither light nor darkness, but both together," Newman explains, saying that "the impossibility of our reconciling the two truths together, does not at all affect the intrinsic, independent, unchangeable reality of both the

---

36 Ratzinger, *Introduction to Christianity*, 271.

37 John Henry Newman, *Essays Critical and Historical* (London: Longmans, Green, and Co., 1907), i, 41–42. Commenting upon these words of Newman, David Brown concludes: "Mystery and doctrine I would suggest go together rather than in competition. There is plenty of support for such a perspective from within Scripture itself." See David Brown, *God and Mystery in Words: Experience through Metaphor and Drama* (Oxford: Oxford University Press, 2008), 4.

one doctrine and the other."[38] Newman's genius lies in the fact that when faced with apparently opposed truths, instead of affirming one at the expense of the other, he firmly adheres to both and allows the mystery to stand, which he recognizes to be beyond his current intellectual possibilities.[39] He expounds on this way of receiving the truths of Christianity in the first chapter of his *Essay on Development*, writing: "One aspect of Revelation must not be allowed to exclude or to obscure another . . . Christianity is dogmatical, devotional, practical all at once; it is esoteric and exoteric; it is indulgent and strict; it is light and dark; it is love, and it is fear."[40]

This recognition of the concurrence of dogma and experience, light and darkness, allows Newman to pierce the veil of the visible world and discern God's hidden and mysterious action within it. Since he acknowledges that what he can apprehend intellectually is intrinsically limited, his understanding of mystery does not detract from his defense of dogma but instead serves and perfects it, allowing it to be grasped through notional assent and stand in the face of contradiction.[41] He specifies that "the mystery lies as much in what

---

38 Newman, *Sermons, 1824–1843*, iv, 110.

39 See John Crosby, "The 'Coincidentia Oppositorum' in the Thought and in the Spirituality of John Henry Newman," *Anthropotes* 6, no. 2 (1990): 196. More recently, the editors of the *Oxford Handbook of John Henry Newman* ascertained: "Part of Newman's philosophical appeal is his ability to expand the intellectual horizons of his time and open up new constructive possibilities." See Frederick Aquino and Benjamin King, introduction, *The Oxford Handbook of John Henry Newman* (Oxford: Oxford University Press, 2018), 2. On the same vein, Roderick Strange concluded his lecture on "Newman and the Mystery of Christ" stating, "Sensitivity to mystery is indispensable for theologians. Whatever defects there may now appear to be in Newman's teaching . . . , these features of his thought—stereoscopic vision, patience with ambiguity, and a sense of the organic life of the Catholic Church—gave him an instinctive respect for mystery. There is a lesson to be learnt" (Strange, "Newman and the Mystery of Christ," 335).

40 John Henry Newman, *An Essay on the Development of Christian Doctrine* (London: Longmans, Green, and Co., 1909), 36.

41 John Henry Newman, *An Essay in Aid of a Grammar of Assent* (London: Longmans, Green, and Co., 1909), 46. He also writes: "No revelation can be complete and systematic, from the weakness of the human intellect; so far as it is not such, it is mysterious. When nothing is revealed, nothing is known, and there is nothing to contemplate or marvel at; but when something is revealed, and only something, for all cannot be, there are forthwith difficulties and perplexities" (Newman, *Essays Critical and Historical*, i, 41). Newman's epistemological work aimed to expand the modern understanding of reason: "Newman wants to show that the scope, range, and modalities of human cognition cover more territory than an ideal version of rationality (e.g. a formal kind of reasoning). Furthermore, he seeks to offer a deeper analysis of the natural workings of reason in concrete matters." See Frederick Aquino, "Epistemology," in *The Oxford Handbook of John Henry Newman*, 382. See also Crosby, "Coincidentia Oppositorum," 209; Crosby, "Newman on Mystery and Dogma," 53; and Strange, "Newman and the Mystery of Christ," 331.

we think we know, as in what we do not know."[42] Because he does not feel the need to tie together every loose end, Newman can keep a window open for our deeper understanding of God's continuous revelation and action. In a sermon for the feast of the Ascension, he invited his listeners not to neglect what they did not understand because they did not understand it but to hold it as a mystery and thus allow themselves to be transformed by its truth.[43]

He expressed a deep admiration for the first Christians precisely for their capacity to embrace the mysteries of the faith: "How different is the state of those who have been duly initiated into the mysteries of the kingdom of heaven! How different was the mind of the primitive Christians, who . . . felt that in saying that Christ was the Son of God, they were witnessing to a thousand marvellous and salutary truths, which they could not indeed understand, but by which they might gain life, and for which they could dare to die!"[44]

Twenty years later, when describing the imperial intellect in a lecture for the School of Science in the Catholic University of Dublin, Newman spoke of the educated man as someone who recognizes and allows mysteries to remain so. He said:

> His watchword is, Live and let live. He takes things as they are; he submits to them all, as far as they go; he recognizes the insuperable lines of demarcation which run between subject and subject; he observes how separate truths lie relatively to each other, where they concur, where they part company, and where, being carried too far, they cease to be truths at all. It is his office to determine how much can be known in each province of thought; when we must be contented not to know; in what direction inquiry is hopeless, or on the other hand full of promise; where it gathers into coils insoluble by reason, where it is absorbed in mysteries, or runs into the abyss. . . . If he has one cardinal maxim in his philosophy, it is, that truth cannot be contrary to truth; if he has a second, it is, that truth often *seems* contrary to

---

42 Newman, *Parochial and Plain Sermons*, iii, 157.

43 Newman, *Parochial and Plain Sermons*, ii, 211. Ekeh explains that for Newman, "the fact that we cannot fully articulate an experience does not mean that it is not valid. It simply makes the experience a mystery" (Ekeh, "John Henry Newman on Mystery," 80).

44 Newman, *Parochial and Plain Sermons*, iii, 161–62.

truth; and, if a third, it is the practical conclusion, that we must be patient with such appearances.[45]

While countless Christians throughout history have sought to explain the dogmas of our faith and develop a strong apologetic, and Newman himself did so in a myriad of instances, Crosby asserts that it was "more congenial to Newman's mind and his whole spirituality to stress what we do not know, and to warn us not to be too quickly satisfied."[46]

Newman not only incorporated mysteries into his theological understanding but found in them a sure foundation for worship. In relation to the Psalms, he wrote: "The inspired writer finds in the mysteries without and within him, a source of admiration and praise. . . . It awes his heart and imagination, to think that God sees him, wherever he is, yet without provoking or irritating his reason. . . . He does not submit his reason by an effort, but he bursts forth in exultation, to think that God is so mysterious."[47] Denis Robinson went as far as stating that "Newman not only displays the complexity of the engagement with the mystery, he revels in it."[48]

CONCLUSION

Though some Newman scholars might disagree with this assessment, it portrays well Newman's insatiable desire for truth.[49] Whether we believe that Newman stresses that which we do not know or that which we do know, I hope that these glimpses into his thought have succeeded in showing that, in Newman's mind, mysteries are not meant to be overcome but instead pondered and accepted as such, and that darkness, as darkness, is a bright source of light.

Let me conclude these brushstrokes with the invitation Newman made to his listeners in his 1834 sermon on the Ascension, which I have quoted before:

---

45 Newman, *The Idea of a University*, 461. For a discussion on this text and others in which Newman defends similar ideas, see Juan Vélez, "Christianity and Scientific Investigation," in *Holiness in a Secular Age: The Witness of Cardinal Newman* (New York: Scepter, 2017), 159–64.

46 Crosby, "Newman on Mystery and Dogma," 48.

47 Newman, *Parochial and Plain Sermons*, iv, 282.

48 Robinson, "Preaching," 249.

49 This is the topic of my dissertation, titled "The Pragmatism of John Henry Newman: His Contributions for a Commitment to Truth in Contemporary Times." A slightly edited version has been published as *John Henry Newman and Pragmatism: A Comparison* (Washington, DC: The Catholic University of America Press, 2023).

GOD'S MYSTERY

> We are allowed with the Angels to obtain a glimpse of the mysteries of Heaven, "to rejoice with trembling." So far from considering the Truths of the Gospel as a burden, because they are beyond our understanding, we shall rather welcome them and exult in them, and feel an antecedent stirring of heart towards them, for the very reason that they are above us.[50]

I began this chapter by bringing forth the question of how we are to relate to truth if it is not something we possess. I believe that Ratzinger and Newman offer us their understanding of mystery as a means of allowing the truth to take possession of our minds. Perhaps we can say that we hold the mystery and Truth holds us.

50 Newman, *Parochial and Plain Sermons*, ii, 207.

6

THE MATERIAL CONSONANCES BETWEEN SCRIPTURE, ANCIENT THOUGHT, NEWMAN, AND RATZINGER ON CONSCIENCE

Emery de Gaál

Two eminent minds of two separate centuries developed clear notions of the high dignity of conscience: St. John Henry Newman and Joseph Ratzinger, Pope Benedict XVI. Sometimes Newman is referred to as *Doctor Conscientiae,*[1] evoking associations with the *Doctor Angelicus* or the *Doctor Seraphicus* of the Middle Ages, while the Irish moral theologian Vincent Twomey calls Ratzinger *The Conscience of Our Age.*[2] And yet, ironically, both men are neither ethicists nor moral theologians in the strict sense. Certainly, neither left us with a systematic tractate on the nature and calling of conscience—that "inner tribunal," as Anton Boisen has labeled it. Their treatment of conscience is occasional and disparate; in Newman's case, it is far more germane to his *vita* and theology

[1] Thus, Thomas J. Norris, "The Role of Conscience in the Adventure of Holiness according to Blessed John Henry Newman," in *Conscience: The Path to Holiness; Walking with John Henry Newman*, ed. Edward Jeremy Miller (Newcastle: Cambridge Scholars, 2014), 30.

[2] D. Vincent Twomey, SVD, *Pope Benedict XVI, The Conscience of Our Age: A Theological Portrait* (San Francisco: Ignatius Press, 2007).

than in Ratzinger's. How is one to remedy this malcondition? Can one gain some appreciation for the assumptions and associations, at times perhaps subcutaneously operative, when these consequential thinkers express their views on conscience's role?

Perhaps the biblical message and the ancient philosophers' reflections on conscience are helpful in unlocking the common occidental heritage that had shaped their views on this important characteristic of the human person—and thus helpful in valorizing better their contributions. This approach is justified insofar as both were formed by a similar Christian and humanist education.

THE SHARED NARRATIVE

SCRIPTURE

Earlier than ancient *Hellas*, the Old Testament expresses a stable view of conscience, while—apart from borrowing circumscriptions such as *lev*—paradoxically lacking an actual term for it for quite some time. As a people chosen by God, Israel is posited within an inextricable responsoriality and thus responsibility to God (Amos 3:2). The individual Israelite is accountable for his transgressions, as Jeremiah 31:29f; Ezekiel 18, and the Psalm of Contrition (Ps 51) forcefully underscore. These passages provide color to and develop further the Adam-Eve narrative (Gen 3) and the decalogue (Ex 20:2–17; Dt 5:6–17). As the story of Jonah and Psalm 139 bear out, there is no escaping God's omniscience—"you know every detail of my conduct" (Ps 139:3b). Sapiential literature observes, "Wickedness is confessedly very cowardly, and it condemns itself; under pressure from conscience" (Wis 17:11). In this passage's Koiné Greek Septuagint rendition, we encounter for the first time in scripture the *terminus technicus* for conscience, namely συνειδεσις. Conscience troubles the sinner by reminding him of his misdeeds.

While the gospels do not use the term "conscience," it occurs thirty times in Paul, the letters to the Hebrews, and Peter. It designates a form of rationality that enables an individual person's conscious participation in divine life. As a wise voice, it reinforces good ideals. Such interiority is granted every human being at his birth—including the pagan (Rom 2:15). Impartially, *syneidesis* distributes censure and praise (1 Cor 10:28f; Tit 3:11) as a sovereign, truthful judge (2 Cor 1:12). Its authority is unquestionable, as its witness is vouched for by Christ (1 Cor 8:12), and it acts in collaboration with the Holy Spirit (Rom 9:1). Examination of conscience is incumbent upon every human being; especially on the Christian (1 Cor 11:28; Gal 6:4; 2 Cor 13:5). Only such honest soul-searching in front of God enables genuine love of neighbor to come about (1 Jn 1:8 and 3:20–23). To a previously unimaginable degree, Christianity brings the human being via his/her conscience into a personal relationship with God.

A "good" conscience (1 Tim 1:5) is illuminated by the supernatural virtue of faith and is directed toward serving God (Rom 12:2). In contrast, a bad and defiled conscience (Titus 1:15) is incapable of making morally correct resolutions (Titus 1:16) or putting these into practice. At baptism, the conscience is cleansed and, as it were, consecrated to God (Heb 10:22; 1 Pet 3:21). Therefore, conscience is intimately connected with worship (Heb 9:9.14; 10:2). Participation in the sacraments leads to brotherly love (1 Cor 10:23f.).

Through conscience, the objective will of God becomes a subjective rule for the human person. The Christian is good or evil according to whether he obeys the precepts of his theonomous conscience. The stone tablets of laws of the Old Testament are replaced by the autonomous order of the Christian, who lives in a sacramental relationship with the Triune God; the order is inscribed into the heart of the individual Christian through his love for God. The Dominican exegete Ceslas Spicq summarized: "This inward and personal norm of the concrete conduct of life is spirit not letter, something of the most beautiful that the New Covenant ascribes to the child of God, freedom, pride, rectitude and frankness. In this—on the level of ethics—the step is taken from the Old to the New Covenant: from the written law to the personal conscience."[3]

The personal model of good behavior, the Son of God Jesus Christ, forms the Christian's conscience. Now, Christians are emphatically dutybound to follow God's call, even against pressures from traditional Jewish customs (Acts 5:29; Gal 5:11). Paul interiorizes the Greek word συνείδεσις to mean that the Spirit-filled Christian's conscience is ultimately only accountable to and accessible by God (Rom 13:5; 1 Cor 4:3ff; parr.).

The Alexandrian Jewish-Hellenistic philosopher Philo considers conscience "a guardian angel, counsel and friend."[4] He holds that when the divine beam of light, the ἔλεγχος, enters our souls, it becomes "our priest," enabling us to recognize the impious thoughts in our souls.[5]

---

3 Ceslas Spicq, "Gewissen," in *Bibeltheologisches Wörterbuch*, ed. Johannes B. Bauer (n.p.: SMB, 2001), 245.

4 Philo, *De fuga et inventione* (Gen 16:6–14), 5f. 67. 211. Cf. Philo, *De Fuga et Inventione* (Paris: Cerf, 1970). The author supplies all translations from Greek or Latin.

5 Philo, *Quod Deus immutabilis sit* (Gen 6:4–12), 128–35. Cf. Richard T. Wallis, "The Idea of Conscience in Philo of Alexandria," *Studia Philonica* 3 (1973/1975): 27–40.

Both a community-forming element and a personal dimension constitute conscience. Together the two elements define the quality of our relationship with God according to the Judeo-Christian worldview.

ANCIENT PHILOSOPHY

The above-described divinely revealed understanding of conscience through scripture runs chronologically parallel to the Greco-Roman world's experience of gradually and rationally comprehending the nature and scope of conscience.[6] One encounters this early on in Aristophanes, Euripides, and Homer. The etymological root can reveal a word's content: in the case of conscience, it is first used in Greek by Xenophon in *Memorabilia* when explaining and defending Socrates's voluntary death for the sake of the immortality of the human soul. It is *suneidenai tini*, that is, "to know something along with someone else."[7] This word's etymology, along with Socrates's testimony, denies any autarkic or solipsistic definition of conscience. It possesses a relational (syn = with) dimension that is beyond human construction or choice. At about the same time, Democritus uses the term *suneidesis tes en tw bio kakoprageosune* ("awareness of one's evil life conduct").[8] The incontrovertible, anthropological reality of conscience assumes that moral precepts are not for humans to choose, invent, disregard, or discard.

The *locus classicus* is found in Plato's *Phaedros* in which Socrates feels compelled to follow his (*daimonion*).[9] It seems that only through reflecting on Socrates's witness does the term "conscience" come into being with Xenophon. As Plato's *Euthydemos* makes clear, it is an infallible sign of the deity's presence.[10] Conscious that his life-conduct was good, as it was always in accord

---

6 For Ratzinger's education in the classics of antiquity, see Joseph Ratzinger, *Milestones: Memoirs, 1927–1977* (San Francisco: Ignatius Press, 1998), 21–29. See also Werner Huber, *Das Denken Joseph Ratzingers* (Paderborn: Schöningh, 2006), 22–26; Emery de Gaál, *The Theology of Pope Benedict XVI: The Christocentric Shift* (New York: Palgrave Macmillan 2010), 21–32. For Newman, see Brian Martin, *John Henry Newman: His Life and Work* (New York: Oxford University Press, 1982), 9–16.

7 Xenophon, *Memorabilia* 2.7.1, https://archive.org/details/gri_33125007255181.

8 Democritus, *Vorsokratiker*, B 297, in *Die Fragmente der Vorsokratiker*, ed. Walther Diels and Herrmann Kranz (Hildesheim: Weidmann, 2004). Perhaps Democritus wrote earlier than Xenophon on conscience.

9 Plato, *Phaedros* 242, https://archive.org/details/gri_33125007255181 and https://archive.org/details/platonosphaidonp00platuoft.

10 Plato, *Euthydemos* 273e3, https://archive.org/details/smtlichedialog00platuoft.

CONSCIENCE

with the *daimonion*, Socrates calmly drinks the cup with fatal hemlock.[11]

The Stoa are aware of absolute and objective ethical values and of their divine origin. Whoever does not take to heart divine injunctions is troubled by his conscience. After committing a sin, the person is inconsolably torn into pieces, as the sin accuses him, according to the Roman thinkers Cicero and Lactantius.[12] Cicero is certain that conscience is "a part of God,"[13] for at creation, God endowed man with his own divine abilities,[14] so that the human person may distinguish between good and evil.[15] To that end, there is a *daemon* in man as "guard and admonisher" alike.[16] God is man's own witness. Cicero asks rhetorically: could the gods give man something more divine than a conscience—"deorum numina subiecta uniuscuiusque conscientia est"?[17] And he continues: "conscientia mentis suae . . . quam ab dis immortalibus accepimus, quae a nobis divelli non potest: quae si optimorum consiliorum . . . testis . . . nobis erit . . . summa cum honestate vivemus" ("conscience of mind . . . which we have received from the immortal gods, from which we cannot tear ourselves apart: if it becomes the witness of best resolves, we will live with highest honorableness"),[18] for "homines divini esse spiritus, partem ac veluti scintillas quasdam astrorum in terram desiluisse" ("human beings are of divine spirit, as like sparks, so to speak, sent forth from the stars unto earth").[19]

11 For an in-depth investigation of Ratzinger's debt to Plato and Socrates as regards the term "conscience," see Manuel Schlögl, "Platón: Dios, conciencia y verdad," in *Ratzinger y Los Filosofos: De Platón a Vattimo*, ed. Alejandro Sada, Tracey Rowland, y Rudy Albino de Assunção (Madrid: Encuentro, 2023), 29–40.

12 Cicero, *De re publica* 3, https://archive.org/search.php?query=Cicero%2C%20De%20re%20 publica; Lactantius, *Divine Institutes* 6, 8, 7, 9, https://archive.org/details/lactantiusdivine0000lact.

13 Cicero, *De legibus* 1, 24f. 59; fin. 2, 114, https://archive.org/search.php?query=Cicero%2C%20 De%20legibus; *Tusculanae disputationes* 5, 38; *Tusculanae disputationes*, ed. Max Pohlenz (Leipzig: Bibliotheca Teubneriana, 1918); and Cicero, *Epicteti dissertationes ab Arriano digestae* 1, 14, 6, https://archive.org/details/dissertationesa00epicgoog.

14 Cicero, *De natura deorum* 2, 78f; cf. https://archive.org/search.php?query=Cicero%2C%20 De%20Natura%20Deorum. Cf. Marcus Aurelius, *Meditationes* 5, 27.

15 Cicero, *Epicteti dissertationes* 2, 6, 9.

16 Cicero, *Epicteti dissertationes* 1, 14, 12.

17 Cicero, *Contra Rullum* I, 2, 3. Cf. Cicero, *De officiis* 3, 44. Cf. Cicero, *Vom rechten Handeln (De officiis)*, lat.-dt. hrsg. und übers. von Karl Büchner, 3rd ed. (München: Artemis und Winkler, 1987).

18 Cicero in his speech defending *Aulus Cluentio* 159, https://archive.org/details/ mtulliiciceroni14cicegoog.

19 Seneca, *De Otio* 5, 5, in Seneca, *De Otio, De Brevitate Vitae*, ed. G. D. Williams (Cambridge: Cambridge University Press, 2008).

Seneca develops *conscientia* more fully than Cicero had done. It is now clearly a pre-given, absolute category. Both human reason and conscience are divine elements implanted in the human person[20] enabling him to make infallible judgments removed from exterior pressure, such as the ephemeral and inconstant praise of a fickle crowd.[21] A wise life of happiness knows of only one sure recipe: to keep one's conscience pure.[22]

Though culturally unrelated and at first geographically distant from one another—one divinely inspired, the other philosophical in nature—to a surprising degree, there is remarkable consonance between what scripture and ancient philosophy hold regarding the human conscience. Conscience is divine in origin and speaks *personally* to every human being as something like God's unerring voice, since it is eminently relational between the celestial realm and the human being: indeed, it is *suneidesin theou*, "knowing about or with God" (1 Petr 2:19; cf. Heb 10:2).

Augustine elaborates: more acutely than their fellow Roman citizens, Christians know that they stand "coram Deo" and "in conspectu Dei." God knows of the "secreta," "arcana" or even "abyssus" "conscientiae."[23] For both Newman and Ratzinger, Scripture, ancient thought, and Augustine are life-long sure lodestars in all matters pertaining to conscience.[24]

ST. JOHN HENRY NEWMAN, THE *DOCTOR CONSCIENTIAE*, "HOLINESS BEFORE PEACE"

Although Newman employs a variety of literary genres on separate occasions, there is remarkable consistency and coherence to his thinking.[25] His use of

---

20 Seneca, *Epistolae* 31, 11; 73, 16; 120, 14, https://archive.org/details/ned-kbn-all-00003728–001.

21 Seneca, *Epistolae* 66, 31f; 71, 32.

22 Seneca, *De vita beata* 20, 4, https://archive.org/details/SenecaFritzHeinerMutschlerDeVitaBeata. VoBookFi.

23 Augustine, *Sermo* 47, 9, 11; Augustine, *Enarrationes in Psalmos* 7, 9, 18, 15; Augustine, *Sermo* 12, 6, *De utilitate ieiunii* 24, and *Confessiones* 10, 22, respectively. See Johannes Stelzenberger, *Conscientia bei Augustinus: Studie zur Geschichte der Moraltheologie* (Paderborn: Schöningh, 1959).

24 For the Augustine-Newman connection, cf. Richard Penaskovic, "Two Classical Western Theologians," in *Augustinian Studies* 13 (1982): 67–79. For Ratzinger's debt to Augustine, cf. n. 11.

25 Here is not the proper place to present the possible correlation of conscience with Newman's epistemology and the manner in which ecclesial faith and the individual Christian's conscience form a symbiotic union. See the section on Ratzinger.

CONSCIENCE

"conscience" is one of the terms that demonstrates this. His understanding of conscience is eminently biographical and, in fact, is *the* hermeneutic key to accessing all of his thinking.[26] Three revelatory events mark his life: a

26 Here is an an overview of sources: John Henry Cardinal Newman, *Apologia Pro Vita Sua* (Garden City, NY: Image Books, 1956); Newman, *An Essay in Aid of a Grammar of Assent*, intro. by Nicholas Lash (Notre Dame, IN: University of Notre Dame Press, 2001); Newman, *Newman's University Sermons* (London: SPCK, 1970); Newman, *Callista: A Tale of the Third Century* (London: Longmans, Green, and Co., 1890). For discussion, see Ian Ker, *John Henry Newman* (Oxford: Oxford University Press, 1995); Ronald Ledek, *The Nature of Conscience and Its Religious Significance with a special Reference to John Henry Newman* (Bethesda, MD: International Scholars Publications, 1995); Gerard J. Hughes, "Newman and the Particularity of Conscience," in *Newman and Faith*, ed. Ian Ker and Terrence Merrigan (Louvain: Peeters, 2004), 53–74; Reinhard Hütter, *John Henry Newman on Truth and Its Counterfeits: A Guide for Our Times* (Washington, DC: The Catholic University of America Press, 2020), esp. 21–89; Bernard Dive, *John Henry Newman and the Imagination* (London: T&T Clark, 2018), esp. 66–109; Herrmann Geißler, "Gewissen und Wahrheit in den Schriften des seligen John Henry Newman," *Forum Katholische Theologie* 28 (2012): 185–200; D. A. Drennan, *Privilege of Intellect: Conscience and Wisdom in Newman's Narrative* (Scranton, PA: University of Scranton Press, 2013); Ludwig Gerhard Müller, *John Henry Newman begegnen* (Augsburg: Sankt Ulrich Verlag, 2000); Luc Terlinden, "The Originality of Newman's Teaching on Conscience," *Irish Theological Quarterly* 73 (2008): 294–306; Walter E. Conn, *Conscience & Conversion in Newman: A Developmental Study of Self in John Henry Newman* (Milwaukee: Marquette University Press, 2010); Anthony Fisher, OP, "Conscience, Relativism, and Truth: The Witness of Saint John Henry Newman," *Nova et Vetera* 18 (2020): 337–53 (slightly revised in Anthony Fisher, OP, "Voice of God? Conscience, Relativism, and Truth," in *A Guide to John Henry Newman: His Life and Thought*, ed. Juan R. Vélez [Washington, DC: The Catholic University of America Press, 2022]), 337–51; Kevin Brendan Fagan, "A Toast to Conscience: Freedom of Conscience in John Henry Newman" (PhD diss., University of Dallas; University of Michigan, 1999); Charlotte Hansen, "Newman, Conscience and Authority," *New Blackfriars* 3, no. 92 (2011): 209–23; Fabio Attard, SDB, *Conscience in the "Parochial and Plain Sermons" of John Henry Newman* (Valetta, Malta: Midseabooks, 2008); Michel Durand, "Newman et la conscience dans son roman Callista et dans son sermon '"Ce qui dispose à la foi,"' *Cahiers victoriens et édourdiens* 70 (2009), https://journals.openedition.org/cve/4778; Frederick D. Aquino, "An Educated Conscience: Perception and Reason in Newman's Account of Conscience," *Studies in the Literary Imagination* 49 (2016): 63–80; Frank Mobbs, "Newman's Doctrine of Conscience," *Irish Theological Quarterly* 57 (1991): 311–16; F. James Kaiser, *The Concept of Conscience according to John Henry Newman* (Washington, DC: The Catholic University of America Press, 1958); Bernd Trocholepczy, "Gewissen: Befähigung und Herausforderung zur Conversio Continua," in *Sinnsuche und Lebenswenden: Gewissen als Praxis nach John Henry Newman*, ed. Günter Biemer, Lothar Kuld, and Roman Siebenrock (Bern: Lang, 1998), 51–64; Günter Biemer, "Autonomie und Kirchenbindung: Gewissensfreiheit und Lehramt nach J. H. Newman," in *Sinnsuche und Lebenswenden*, 174–93; Terrence Merrigan, "Conscience and Selfhood: Thomas More, John Henry Newman, and the Crisis of the Postmodern Subject," *Theological Studies* 73 (2012): 841–60; Philip C. Rule, SJ, *Coleridge and Newman: The Centrality of Conscience* (New York: Fordham University Press, 2004) (the quotations are sometimes not without error); Selwyn Grave, *Conscience in Newman's Thought* (Oxford: Clarendon, 1989); Jean Honoré, *Newman: La fidelité d'une conscience* (Chambray-lés-Tours: CLD, 1986); James Keating, "Newman: Conscience and Mission," *Irish Theological Quarterly* 67 (2002): 99–112; Erwin Bischofsberger, *Die sittlichen Voraussetzungen des Glaubens: Zur Fundamentalethik John Henry Newmans* (Mainz: Matthias Grünewald, 1974); Vincent Gallois, *Église et conscience chez John Henry Newman: Un commentaire de la Lettre au duc de Norfolk* (Paris: Artège, 2010); Hermann Geißler, *Gewissen und Wahrheit bei John Henry Kardinal Newman* (Bern: Lang, 1995); Hermann Geißler, "'Das Gewissen ist der ursprüngliche Statthalter Christi': Ein Blick auf Newmans Lehre über das Gewissen," *Internationale Zeitschrift Communio*

perhaps mystical experience in 1816 as a young gentleman, his preference for intellectual over spiritual achievements in 1828 while at Oriel College, and finally his entry into the Catholic Church in 1845.

Newman records, "When I was fifteen, (in the autumn of 1816) a great change of thought took place in me. I fell under the influences of a definitive Creed, and received into my intellect impressions of dogma, which, through God's mercy, have never been effaced or obscured" since.[27] He discovered a personal God addressing him as person, dignifying him as a moral agent. He experienced "two supremely and luminously self-evident beings, myself and my Creator."[28]

This incontrovertible reality so deeply moved him that he decided to remain unmarried, devoted to priestly and professorial tasks, for the rest of his life. He had been influenced by Thomas Scott (1747–1821), a serious and beloved contemporary Anglican preacher, who had written the hugely popular books *Commentary on the Whole Bible* (1788) and *The Force of Truth* (1779). Newman referred to Scott as "the writer who made a deeper impression on my mind than any other, and to whom (humanly speaking) I almost owe my soul—Thomas Scott of Aston Sandford." He also wrote that Scott's works "show him to be a true Englishman, and I deeply felt his influence; and for years I used almost as proverbs what I considered to be the scope and issue of his doctrine, 'Holiness before peace,' and 'Growth is the only evidence of life.'"[29] In Scott's writings, he found confirmation of his personal faith experience, leading to a personal and living God who speaks to every person through his conscience.

Moving from a metaphysical to a psychological explanation of conscience, the 18th century Anglican bishop and ethicist Joseph Butler had described conscience as "moral Reason, moral Sense, or divine Reason . . . a Sentiment

---

46, no. 5 (2017): 466–80; Charles Morerod, OP, "La conscience, voie vers Dieu et l'Église selon John Henry Newman," *Nova et Vetera* 86 (2011): 29–57 ; Jouett Lynn Powell, "Cardinal Newman on Faith and Doubt: The Role of Conscience," *Downside Review* 99 (1981): 137–48; Francesco Maceri, *La Formazione della Coscienza del Credente: Una Proposta educativa alla Luce dei Parochial and Plain Sermons di John Henry Newman* (Rome: Gregorian University Press, 2002); Miguel Rumayor, "Notas sobre la Formacíon de la Conciencia en John Henry Newman," *Scripta Theologica* 51 (2019): 801–23; and *Cambridge Companion to John Henry Newman*.

27 Newman, *Apologia Pro Vita Sua*, 127.

28 Newman, *Apologia Pro Vita Sua*, 127.

29 Newman, *Apologia Pro Vita Sua*, 128, for this and the preceding quotation.

CONSCIENCE

of the understanding, or a perception of the Heart"[30] that allows an action to be judged by moral principles. It is God speaking to the human being in his conscience. As Levering summarizes, "For Butler conscience stands as an interior proof of God's existence."[31] Butler greatly influenced Newman and his generation.[32]

Newman was acutely cognizant that his religion was not a mere feeling, dream, or illusion but rather sure personal and objective truth, crystallized in dogma. Scripture, conscience, and religious precepts—as echoes of God, especially God the Holy Spirit—form one noncontradictory, mutually enriching whole for him.[33] Since God is ever accessible to Newman, Newman in turn strove to be personally accessible as vicar to both the poor church folk of St. Clement as well as to the prosperous parishioners of St. Mary in Oxford. In addition, he was a friend and loyal fellow wayfarer to countless students at Oriel College. Conscience as a personal reality obligated him to encounter in fellow human beings *persons*—much like God does—and to entertain authentic friendships. This explains the large corpus of letters he wrote. This stance is grounded in the insight that truth is not a cerebral idea but "the closest friend."[34] Hence, he writes much later in the *Grammar of Assent*: "Conscience is nearer to me than any other means of knowledge. . . . it provides for the mind a real image of Him [God]; as a medium of worship."[35]

Newman similarly observes that God "is more intimately connected with the nature of the human mind itself than any thing else."[36] In his *Philosophical Notebook,* Newman, echoing at first glance Descartes, but more to the point, Augustine, writes "conscientiam habeo, ergo sum" followed by "conscientiam

---

30 Joseph Butler, *Three Sermons upon Human Nature and a Dissertation on Virtue* (London: S. Bell and Sons, 1914), §1.

31 Matthew Levering, *The Abuse of Conscience: A Century of Catholic Moral Theology* (Grand Rapids, MI: Eerdmans, 2021), 72.

32 Joseph Butler, "Of the Nature of Virtue," in *The Analogy of Religion, Natural and Revealed, the Constitution and Course of Nature,* 2nd ed. (Oxford: Knapton, 1736), no. 1. See also Ker, *John Henry Newman,* 113–15; Newman, *Apologia Pro Vita Sua,* 12.

33 Also for Newman, of course, scripture and conscience are materially separate and distinct but also mutually reinforcing.

34 John Henry Newman, *The Via Media of the Anglican Church* I (Westminster, MD: Christian Classics, 1978), XIIf.

35 Newman, *Grammar of Assent,* part 2, chap. 10, sec. 1.

36 Newman, *Philosophical Notebook,* 2:43.

habeo, ergo Deus."[37] Prior to the exterior realms, there are two undeniable realities: the self and God.

Although he did pen *Essay on the Development of Christian Doctrine*, his conversion to the Catholic faith was marked by his confession—using conscience—to the blessed Passionist priest Dominic Barberi. The three years spent in almost monastic seclusion in Littlemore were not so much dedicated to studies as to allowing his conscience to speak in a more articulate form to him. In consequence, he first revoked all accusations he had levelled against Catholicism and then with a heavy heart laid down his prestigious positions as Oxford professor and Vicar of St. Mary's in 1843—following the clear and unambiguous voice of his conscience. He parted ways with longtime friends and relatives, honor, and career, but he was now at peace with his conscience and God—echoing Seneca, Butler, and Scott.[38]

Amid the visibly successful ideas of rationalism and deism, amid Malthus and Manchester liberalism, which propelled England to the forefront of the industrial revolution, Newman poses the "Romantic," that is, holistic, question of how can there be something that grounds the individual person and gives him unity, indeed grants access to the whole of being beyond the merely immediate and pragmatic? This approach must be unlike those that gave rise to the impersonal things so very celebrated around him, such as steam engines and steel mills. It cannot be that the same criterion of objective verifiability can be applied to both these exterior things and to matters of the human mind, such as culture and religion. In this regard he asks: "How can we gain an image of God and give real assent to the proposition that He exists?": he responds, "we have by nature a conscience." This becomes for him a "first principle" that does not deny the value of the positive sciences but denies them control of the definition of the human person.[39] Conscience is an invisible, personal, and relational organ, so to speak, that determines an action either "worthy of praise or blame."[40] This invisible organ is not subject to the criterion of objective, "noetic" verifiability, and yet is as real as sunshine. Unlike H_2O,

---

37 Newman, *Philosophical Notebook*, 2:59.

38 Newman, *Apologia Pro Vita Sua*, 313ff.

39 Newman, *Grammar of Assent*, 105, for this and the two preceding quotations.

40 Edward Sillem, ed., *The Philosophical Notebook of John Henry Newman* (Leuven: Nauwelaerts, 1969f), 2:47.

God cannot be facilely proved—and this is an opportunity for both God and us! We can discover the personal Thou of an absolute being.

The smashing successes brought about by the positive sciences and economic liberalism fascinated the nineteenty century, but these achievements deceive many to automatically assume the STEM principles can be applied to all areas of the humanities as well. This unwittingly peremptorial attitude Newman calls "doctrinal liberalism,"[41] and it commits the sin of counterfeiting the interior presence of God in the human conscience, asserting in final analysis "the right of self-will."[42] Without acknowledging conscience as the divine organ within us, a depressive, "all-corroding, all-dissolving skepticism of the intellect in religious matters" may hold sway over us, completely depersonalizing us.[43] Would Newman argue that contemporary postmodern *ennui* is the direct result? For him conscience is the voice of Christ. The gladdening experience of a good conscience places one into a healthy relationship with the Thou of God—thus occasioning a horizontal sociability that goes beyond the superficial *fraternité* of the supposedly ultrademocratic, but actually tyrannical, *sans culottes* of the French Revolution.

The following memorable lines of *Gaudium et Spes* 16 could have been penned by St. Newman:

> In the depths of his conscience, man detects a law which he does not impose upon himself, but which holds him to obedience. Always summoning him to love good and avoid evil, the voice of conscience when necessary speaks to his heart: do this, shun that. For man has in his heart a law written by God: to obey it is the very dignity of man; according to it he will be judged. Conscience is the most secret core and sanctuary of a man. There he is alone with God, Whose voice echoes in his depths. In a wonderful manner conscience reveals that law which is fulfilled by love of God and neighbor.[44]

---

41 For Newman and liberalism, see Keith Beaumont, "The Connection between Theology, Spirituality, and Morality," in Vélez, *Guide to John Henry Newman*, 393–413, esp. 407–11; David P. Delio, "Liberalism: Personal and Social Aspects in His Thoughts," in Vélez, *Guide to John Henry Newman*, 489–508.

42 For this and previous quotation, see Newman, *Apologia Pro Vita Sua*, 285–97; cf. the opening paragraphs of this book. See also Ian Ker, *On Being a Christian* (London: Harper Collins, 1992), 101.

43 Newman, *Apologia Pro Vita Sua*, 167.

44 On "Newman's Council," see Eamon Duffy, *John Henry Newman* (London: SPCK, 2019), 3.

Such fidelity to one's personal conscience profoundly unites and bonds humankind and permits global solidarity to grow, the council continues, as the one God created all consciences.

Newman preached to his congregations that the fulfillment and perfection of every religion is found in the logical consecution of the call of one's conscience. Though this organ is anthropologically the same everywhere, the Christian, more precisely the Catholic, conscience is one of an altogether different quality, as it is the perfection in supernatural grace every natural conscience in its natural state strives toward. The indwelling entelechy of every conscience is primordially tuned to ultimately reveal Christ in every human being. Thus, secular society's immanentist reconfigurations of conscience à la Bacon, Locke, Hobbes, etc. to something unrelated to a kind, self-communicating numinous volition undergirding it, amounts to the very denial of personhood and thereby to society's dissolution.

How can real apprehension of God be achieved? In his conscience, every human being experiences him- or herself as *a priori* addressed. It establishes a pure relationality and a responsoriality that is uniquely gladdening for every person and obligatory at the same time. The unavoidable givenness of a relationality between God and the human person cannot be denied, and yet its quality depends on both God and me, created in the image and likeness of God (Gen 1:26). This occurs quite separately and distinctly from the abstract, impersonal principles of the positive sciences, which made Newman witness unprecedented civilizational advances in his day. It is proper to the classic mindset of Plato, Cicero, and Newman to detect something everlasting and constant amid the inconstant flux of history. There is a theonomous dimension to conscience that allows the individual human person to become a codeterminant of the quality of a divine-human relationship! How very thrilling. Human beings are beckoned to listen to and obey this voice. Conscience elevates us "out of ourselves, and beyond ourselves, to go and seek for him in the height and depth, whose voice it is,"[45] Newman preaches. This invisible and yet ever present organ is objective in conveying the faithful image "of a Supreme Governor, a Judge, holy, just, powerful, all-seeing, retributive, and is the creative principle of religion as . . . the principle of ethics,"[46] to which

---

[45] John Henry Newman, *Fifteen Sermons Preached before the University of Oxford between AD 1826 and 1843* (Oxford: Oxford University Press, 2006), 65.

[46] Newman, *Grammar of Assent*, 110.

we owe out of a sense of honor "a dutiful obedience to what claims to be a divine voice, speaking within us," as he elaborates in his celebrated *Letter to the Duke of Norfolk*.[47] This reality is incontrovertible, however much removed from the purely exterior realm it might be, and is for Newman a strong proof for God's existence:

> If I looked into a mirror, and did not see my face, I should have the sort of feeling which actually comes upon me, when I look into this living busy world, and see no reflexion of its Creator. . . . Were it not for this voice, speaking so clearly in my conscience and my heart, I should be an atheist, or a pantheist, or a polytheist when I looked into the world. I am speaking for myself only; and I am far from denying the real force of the arguments in proof of a God, drawn from the general facts of human society and the course of history, but these do not warm me or enlighten me; they do not take away the winter of my desolation, or make the buds unfold and the leaves grow within me, and my moral being rejoice.[48]

The human being is more than logical deductions, numbers—or an accumulation of molecules—he is the bearer of an infinite dream of much more than the sum total of material needs. He is essentially intellect, mind, and spirit that grow or wither depending on how the human person relates to his conscience and thereby to God. Conscience is the proof of this "Romantic," or holistic, understanding of the universe, the human person, and the existence of God. In his core, the human being does not become more human by such exterior forms of progress that technology or the positive sciences can afford. The STEM disciplines may contribute to an increase in *the standard of living*. However, the degree to which a good conscience is cultivated amidst the ever-present alternative between good and evil defines *the quality of life*.

Alas, it always holds true: "For I do not do the good I want, but I do the evil I do not want" as St. Paul in the *Letter to the Romans* memorably writes (Rom 7:19). This realization requires a high degree of existential veracity. A conscience poorly formed may remain closed to words of reconciliation,

---

47 John Henry Newman, "Letter to the Duke of Norfolk," in *Certain Difficulties Felt by Anglicans in Catholic Teaching* (London: Burns and Oates, 1879), 2:255.

48 John Henry Newman, *The Heart of Newman's Apologia, Arranged by Margaret R. Grennan* (Toronto: Longmans, Green, and Co., 1934), 165.

mercy, and grace. In the *Grammar*, this thought is formulated in the words: "those who know nothing of the wounds of the soul, are not led to deal with the question . . . but when our attention is aroused, then the more steadily we dwell upon it, the more probable does it seem that a revelation has been or will be given to us."[49]

Addressing past thinkers such as Hobbes, Locke, Bacon, and Kant, but equally contemporary Darwinism and utilitarianism—who *cum grano salis* deny the religious dimension of conscience—Newman wrote in *Certain Difficulties*:

> The rule and measure of duty is not utility, nor expedience, nor the happiness of the greatest number, nor State convenience, nor fitness, order and the *pulchrum*. Conscience is not a long-sighted selfishness, nor a desire to be consistent with oneself, but a messenger from Him, who, both in nature and in grace, speaks to us be hind a veil. . . . Noble buildings have been reared as fortresses against that spiritual, invisible influence which is too subtle for science and too profound for literature. Chairs in universities have been made the seats of an antagonist tradition."[50]

The discoverer of Newman for the German-speaking countries, the Jesuit priest Erich Przywara, considers him "the great synthesizer of [Christian] interiority and the Church."[51] How can this be? Only if there is an identity between the God who creates this world and the one who redeems it in Christ. Only if this God speaks with one voice to both individual human beings and to the Church (cf. Gal 6:15; 2 Cor 5:17). In this divinely willed, creational, salvation-historical consonance, "conscience . . . [is] the aboriginal Vicar of Christ, a prophet in its informations, a monarch in its peremptoriness, a priest in its blessings and anathemas,"[52] as Newman famously wrote. The Gospel

---

49 Newman, *Grammar of Assent*, 423.

50 Newman, *Certain Difficulties*, 2:248–49.

51 Erich Przywara, "Newman möglicher Heiliger und Kirchenlehrer der neuen Zeit?," *Newman Studien* 3 (1957): 3. Newman influenced the *White Rose* resistance movement in Germany. One of its members, Sophie Scholl, had given Newman's sermons to her boyfriend Fritz Hartnagel, when he departed to serve in the German army on the eastern front (Fisher, "Conscience, Relativism, and Truth," 348).

52 Newman, *Certain Difficulties*, 2:248. The larger quotation is worthwhile reading as well: "When He became Creator, He implanted this Law, which is Himself, in the intelligence of all His rational creatures. The Divine Law, then, is the rule of ethical truth, the standard of right and wrong, a sovereign, irreversible, absolute authority in the presence of men and Angels. 'The eternal law,'

complements this.[53] In a most comprehensive sense, revelation is the interplay of conscience, scripture, and ecclesial, sacramental life: the "Presence of Persons—to know Christ and through him, the Father."[54]

Already in Newman's first sermon as an Anglican, "Holiness necessary for future Blessedness,"[55] the French Oratorian Louis Bouyer detects that Newman "wants us to hear the Word of God ... as it should be understood and accepted ... as the voice of our Lord and Saviour, who calls out to us in order to draw us away from the paths of sin and death, in order to bring us to the one way of life, in holiness."[56] Thomas Norris emphasizes that for Newman, "our most

---

says St. Augustine, 'is the Divine reason or Will of God, commanding the observance, forbidding the disturbance, of the natural order of things.' 'The natural law,' says St. Thomas 'is an impression of the Divine Light in us, a participation of the eternal law in the rational creature'. . . . This law, as apprehended in the minds of individual men is called 'conscience,' and though it may suffer refraction in passing into the intellectual medium of each, it is not therefore so affected as to lose its character of being the Divine Law, but still has, as such, the prerogative of commanding obedience."

This law of conscience, I know, is very different from that ordinarily taken of it, both by the science and literature, and by the public opinion, of this day. It is founded on the doctrine that conscience is the voice of God, whereas it is fashionable on all hands now to consider it in one way or another a creation of man. Of course, there are great and broad exceptions to this statement. It is not true of many or most religious bodies of men; especially not of their teachers and ministers. . . . They mean what we mean, the voice of God in the nature and heart of man, as distinct from the voice of Revelation. They speak of a principle planted within us, before we have had any training, although training and experience are necessary for its strength, growth, and due formation. They consider it a constituent element of the mind, as our perception of other ideas may be, as our powers of reasoning, as our sense of order and the beautiful, and our other intellectual endowments. They consider it, as Catholics consider it, to be the internal witness of both the existence and the law of God. They think it holds of God, and not of man, as an Angel walking on the earth would be no citizen or dependent of the Civil Power. . . .

. . . The rule and measure of duty is not utility, now expedience, nor the happiness of the greatest number, nor State convenience, not fitness, order and the *pulchrum*. Conscience is not a longsighted selfishness, nor a desire to be consistent with oneself; but it is a messenger from Him, who, both in nature and in grace speaks to us behind a veil, and teaches and rules us by His representatives. Conscience is the aboriginal Vicar of Christ, a prophet in its informations, a monarch in its peremptoriness, a priest in its blessings and anathemas, and, even though the eternal priesthood throughout the Church could cease to be, in it the sacerdotal principle would remain and would have a swa" (Newman, *Certain Difficulties*, 2:246–49). This section with the famous phrase "Conscience is the aboriginal Vicar of Christ" is quoted in *The Catechism of the Catholic Church*, 2nd ed. (Vatican City: Libreria Editrice Vaticana, 1997), §1778. The full quotation is, "Conscience is a law of the mind; yet Christians would not grant it is nothing more; I mean that it was not a dictate, nor conveyed the notion of responsibility, of duty, of a threat and a promise. . . . Conscience is a messenger of him, who, both in nature and in grace, speaks to us behind a veil, and teaches and rules us by his representatives. Conscience is the aboriginal Vicar of Christ."

53 John Henry Newman, *Plain and Parochial Sermons* (London: Longmans, Green, and Co, 1889), 2:155.

54 Norris, "Role of Conscience," 26.

55 Newman, *Plain and Parochial Sermons*, 1:1–14.

56 Louis Bouyer, CO, *Newman's Vision of Faith* (San Francisco: Ignatius Press, 1986), 17.

'real' and 'imaginative' grasp of moral and revealed truth comes through conscience in its imperative dimension."[57] Hütter eloquently summarizes his research on Newman's valorization of conscience in the following words: "any proper understanding of conscience must first and foremost articulate the *theonomic nature of conscience*, that is, its grounding in the divine law. Conscience is not simply a human faculty. It is constituted by the eternal law, the divine wisdom communicated to the human intellect."[58]

Perhaps Newman never expresses more succinctly his teaching on conscience than in his novel *Callista*, in the dialogue of the heroine with Polemo:

> Well," she said, "I feel that God within my heart. I feel myself in His presence. He says to me, 'Do this: don't do that.' You may tell me that this dictate is a mere law of my nature, as is to joy or, to grieve. I cannot understand this. No, it is the echo of a person speaking to me. Nothing shall persuade me that it does not ultimately proceed from a person external to me. It carries with it its proof of its divine origin. My nature feels towards it as towards a person. When I obey it, I feel satisfaction; when I disobey, a soreness—just like that which I feel in pleasing or offending some, revered friend. So you see, Polemo, I believe in what is more than a mere 'something.' I believe in what is more real to me than sun, moon, stars, and the fair earth, and the voice of friends. You will say, Who is He? Has He ever told you anything about Himself? Alas! no!—the more's a pity! But I will not give up what I have, because I have not more [sublime]. An echo implies a voice, a speaker. That speaker I love and I fear.[59]

JOSEPH RATZINGER AND CONSCIENCE

After the harrowing experiences of World War II, Joseph Ratzinger was introduced to Newman while a young seminarian through the Freising Seminary's prefect of studies, Alfred Läpple.[60] At the centenary of the British cardinal's

---

57 Norris, "Role of Conscience," 30.

58 Hütter, *John Henry Newman on Truth and Its Counterfeits*, 24–25.

59 Newman, *Callista*, 314–15.

60 Ratzinger, *Milestones*, 43. See also Alfred Läpple, *Der Einzelne in der Kirche: Wesenszüge einer Theologie des Einzelnen nach John Henry Kardinal Newman* (Munich: Zink, 1952), which was Father Läpple's doctoral dissertation. For Ratzinger's understanding of conscience, see Joseph Ratzinger

death, Ratzinger stated in 1990, "Newman's teaching on conscience became an important foundation for theological personalism" and continued "conscience in its true sense is the bedrock of papal authority."[61] In this way, Ratzinger addressed the positive, tension-filled relationship between ecclesial authority and the individual's conscience that neither Newman nor Vatican II had satisfactorily described.

Primarily through four little known texts, I will attempt in this chapter to unfold Ratzinger's approximations toward the nature of conscience: 1. a lecture he delivered 1972 at the *Reinhold Schneider Gesellschaft* titled "Conscience in its Time";[62] 2. the *Instruction on Christian Freedom and Liberation*, issued 1986 by the Congregation for the Doctrine of Faith under its prefect Cardinal Ratzinger;[63] 3. Ratzinger's as yet untranslated reflections on this instruction, published in *Communio* under the heading "Freiheit und Befreiung. Die anthropologische Vision der Instruktion '*Libertatis Conscientia*'" (Freedom and Liberation. The

---

[Benedikt XVI], *Priester aus innerstem Herzen* (Munich: Klerusblatt, 2007), 149–54; 162–67; Joseph Ratzinger, *Vom Wiederauffinden der Mitte: Grundorientierungen* (Freiburg i. Br.: Herder, 1997); Joseph Cardinal Ratzinger, *God Is near Us; The Eucharist; The Heart of the World* (San Francisco: Ignatius Press, 2003); Lieven Boeve and Gerard Mannion, eds. *The Ratzinger Reader* (London: T&T Clark, 2010); Joseph Ratzinger, "Freiheit und Befreiung: Die anthropologische Vision der Instruktion '*Libertatis conscientiae*,'" *Communio* [German] 15 (1986): 409–24; Joseph Ratzinger, *On Conscience: Two Essays* (San Francisco: Ignatius Press, 2007); Joseph Cardinal Ratzinger, "Conscience and Truth," https://www.ewtn.com/catholicism/library/conscience-and-truth-2468; Joseph Ratzinger, *Truth and Tolerance: Christian Belief and World Religions* (San Francisco: Ignatius Press, 2004); Joseph Cardinal Ratzinger, *Values in a Time of Upheaval* (San Francisco: Ignatius Press, 2006); Joseph Ratzinger, *Church, Ecumenism and Politics* (San Francisco: Ignatius Press, 2008); Idahosa Amadasu, "Conscience and Holiness: Joseph Ratzinger/Pope Benedict XVI's Reception of John Henry Newman," in *Conscience, the Path to Holiness: Walking with Newman* (Newcastle upon Tyne: Cambridge Scholars, 2014), 97–111; Michael E. Alsopp, "Conscience, the Church and the Moral Truth: John Henry Newman, Vatican II, Today," *Irish Theological Quarterly* 3 (1992): 192–208; and Jacob Phillips, "My Enemy's Enemy Is My Friend: Martin Luther and Joseph Ratzinger on the Bi-Dimensionality of Conscience," *Heythrop Journal* 61 (2020): 317–26. Matthew Levering supplies a lucid summary of Ratzinger's views on conscience in *Abuse of Conscience*, 184–90.

61 Hansen, "Newman, Conscience and Authority," 209–10.

62 Ratzinger, *Church, Ecumenism and Politics*, 160–72.

63 Congregation for the Doctrine of the Faith, *Instruction on Christian Freedom and Liberation*, Instruction on Christian Freedom and Liberation (vatican.va). The authoritative Latin text begins with "Libertas conscientiae." While the official French, Italian, Portuguese, and Spanish translations contain the expression "freedom of conscience," the German and English versions do not. This may explain the document's weak public reception.

Anthropological Vision of the Instruction *Libertatis Conscientia*) in 1986;[64] and 4. the book *Vom Wiederauffinden der Mitte,* in large part untranslated.[65]

REINHOLD SCHNEIDER

Reinhold Schneider (1903–1958) was an uncompromising opponent to the Nazi regime and stood as literary figure in some proximity to the *renouveau catholique.* On account of his dissident writings, Germans honored him after World War II as *"das Gewissen der Nation"* ("the German nation's conscience").[66] Ratzinger begins:

> In his memoirs *Conversations with Hitler,* Herrmann Rauschning, who served in 1933–1934 as president of the senate of the Free City of Danzig, reports the following remark made by the dictator to him: "I liberate man from the coercion of a mind that has become an end in itself, from the dirty and degrading self-inflicted torments of a chimera called conscience and morality and from the demands of a freedom and personal autonomy to which only a very few can ever measure up."[67]

Ratzinger does not believe that totalitarianism's threat to freedom of conscience has disappeared. It merely takes on different forms: well-nigh fifty years later, we might add now Critical Theory, consulting firms, political correctness, Chinese-Marxist ideology, etc. as reductive threats to conscience.[68] Like the fragile Indian Lucayan maiden experiencing the atrocities committed by the sixteenth-century Spanish *conquistadores* in Schneider's historical novel

---

64 Joseph Ratzinger, "Conscience in Time," trans. W. J. O'Hara, in *Anthropology and Culture*, ed. David Schindler and Nicholas J. Healy, vol. 2 of *Joseph Ratzinger in Communio* (Grand Rapids, MI: Eerdmans, 2013), 17–27.

65 Ratzinger, *Vom Wiederauffinden der Mitte*; there: "Wenn Du den Frieden willst, achte das Gewissen eines jeden Menschen"; and see 266–87. I follow the original German and supply sometimes an English translation when I believe the original is more felicitous. For the English, see Peter Jennings, ed., *Benedict XVI and Cardinal Newman* (Oxford: Family Publications, 2005), 41–52; Ratzinger, *On Conscience*, 12–41.

66 Hans Urs von Balthasar, *Nochmals Reinhold Schneider* (Einsiedeln: Johannes, 1991), 12; Cordula Koepcke, *Reinhold Schneider: Eine Biographie* (Würzburg: Echter, 1993).

67 Ratzinger, "Conscience in Its Time: A Lecture Given to the Reinhold Schneider Society," in *Church, Ecumenism and Politics*, 160.

68 Tracey Rowland, "Karl Marx y el marxismo: El problema de la primacía de la praxis," in Sada, Rowland, and Albino de Assunção, *Ratzinger y Los Filosofos*, 191–209.

Las Casas, "so conscience stands in the world to this day," Ratzinger notes.[69] Nowadays, it also seems a humanitarian gesture "to relieve" people of their conscience, just as a demonically benighted Hitler attempted to do almost a century earlier. The result is a cold, nonrelational world in which efficiency and pragmatism rule unchecked and the uniqueness of personhood is forgotten, since conscience as a divinely created reality is denied. Conscience is no longer apprehended as "the voice of God" speaking personally to each one.[70] Again, as during the Third Reich, it is a "worrisome" reality for not few: the "voluntary suffering of those who remain true to their conscience and thereby authentically witness" to the dignity of the human person. The hypothesis of a conscience gifted with divine presence is an annoying proposition, thus Ratzinger.[71] The scandal of the suffering servant of God, the crucified Lord, is witness to the dignity of the conscience. Ratzinger emphasizes that both the innocent suffering of the enslaved Ibero-American indigenous people in "the power of the Crucified" and the conversion of las Casas confronted with his guilty conscience served to advance humanizing Spanish legislation in the form of the *Leyes Nuevas* in 1542.[72]

In Ratzinger's view, Schneider describes very well the decisive dialogue between the Spanish King Charles I and the Dominican friar Bartolomé de las Casas leading to the *New Laws:* men "can ask their conscience for advice, and if they do so without hatred or rancor, their conscience will help them."[73] Even the absolute power of a monarch is under the control of the sovereign conscience, which is above man. Conscience, thus perceived, functions "as a check over tyranny by affirming the equal human dignity of all people."[74] The admission of conscience's creatureliness permits the human being to treat everyone as *"Zweck an sich selbst"* ("end in himself")—to quote Kant.[75]

---

69 Ratzinger, "Conscience in Its Time," 163.

70 Ratzinger, "Conscience in Its Time," 164.

71 Ratzinger, "Conscience in Its Time," 165.

72 Ratzinger, "Conscience in Its Time," 167; there had already been the Leyes de Burgos (1512) of Queen Isabella declaring all Indians free subjects of the crown. It had gone unheeded.

73 Ratzinger, "Conscience in Its Time," 170.

74 Levering, *Abuse of Conscience*, 185.

75 Immanuel Kant, *Groundwork to the Metaphysics of Morals*, trans. Allen Wood (New Haven, CT: Yale University Press, 2018), GMS AA 04:428.

A VATICAN INSTRUCTION

In the Vatican instruction *Libertatis Conscientiae* of 1986, issued by the Congregation for the Doctrine of the Faith under its prefect Ratzinger, the word "conscience" occurs thirteen times in the Latin original and eight times in the English translation. Every conscience obligates man in every state, be he a believer of some kind or a nonbeliever, to seek the truth—ultimately "the truth of the Gospel."[76] The document perceives inherent dynamics in the interplay of personal conscience and objective truth and a qualified mutual interdependence of both. In seeking to follow one's conscience, one finds deeper truth, which in turn enriches conscience: "By obeying the divine law inscribed in his conscience and received as an impulse of the Holy Spirit, man exercises true mastery over himself and thus realizes his royal vocation as a child of God. 'By the service of God, he reigns.'"[77] Genuine freedom is considered a theonomous gift. Becoming cognizant of this is a way "of recognizing every human being's character as a person responsible for himself and his transcendent destiny, as well as the inviolability of his conscience."[78]

Not following divine law and one's conscience, every relationship with God must appear onerous, in fact, as "intolerable slavery." Arguing indirectly against the then (as now) unchallenged regnant Critical Theory and its popularizing epigons, the document calls to mind that God's precepts are not "forms of alienation" but serve to realize genuine freedom as relationality. By denying God, one also rejects both a special relationship (which grounds all other relationships) and the objectivity of sin. In fact, now following Gotthold Lessing, the foolish claim is made that doing what may appear as sin to some is necessary for a human being to become truly "adult and free."[79]

The instruction agrees with liberation theology that every Christian conscience formed by the Gospel must be aroused "by the inequities and oppression of every kind."[80] Not abstract norms, nor inexorable economic or social laws, but the Lord Jesus enlightens consciences. More precisely a thus

---

[76] Congregation for the Doctrine of the Faith, *Instruction Libertatis Conscientiae*, no. 4.

[77] Congregation for the Doctrine of the Faith, *Instruction Libertatis Conscientiae*, no. 30. Misspelling in the Vatican English translation.

[78] Congregation for the Doctrine of the Faith, *Instruction Libertatis Conscientiae*, no. 32.

[79] Congregation for the Doctrine of the Faith, *Instruction Libertatis Conscientiae*, no. 41. This reference applies to all quotations in this paragraph.

[80] Congregation for the Doctrine of the Faith, *Instruction Libertatis Conscientiae*, no. 57.

properly Christian-formed conscience is the church's liberating tool of divine love in the world (cf. Rom 2:1–16). By allowing the Holy Spirit, "the source of freedom," to dwell in them, Christians "bring forth fruits of justice and peace"[81] and human integrity. Not in solipsistic certitude and self-righteous vainglory, but in a committed relationship to Christ, the human being matures to an instrument of genuine peace and justice in society, the document argues.

THE *COMMUNIO* ARTICLE

In the *Communio* essay, Ratzinger warns of compromising the individual's ethical freedom for the sake of "economic and social laws of nature," calling these the laws of an immanent "history."[82] It is naïve, in fact "a myth," to assume with Hegel and Marx man can "engineer history" and morality and thereby find fulfillment. Such a relegation of morality into the merely horizontal produces a being incapable of bonding and commitment—of maturing by acknowledging the inherently tragic nature of postlapsarian existence. *De facto* depriving the human being of the dignity of a personal conscience leads invariably to a dictatorial government, "a lording of people over people."[83]

In this context, Ratzinger reminds the reader that according to both the third-century church father Origen and the ninth-century *Codex Koridethianus* record of Matthew 27:16,[84] Christ and the political revolutionary Barabbas had the same first name: Jesus. It is, however, exclusively Jesus Christ who liberates human beings to relationships vertically with the Blessed Trinity and thereby horizontally with one another, liberating us from the impersonal and reifying *do ut des*. The human conscience is purified through the cross. Ironically and beguilingly "the other Jesus," Barabbas, stands for political liberation, which will never lead to genuine freedom as it cannot cancel out the divine construction of the cosmos and of the human heart, which is oriented toward God. Ratzinger states, "Merely promoting [technical] abilities while neglecting the conscience renders man easily deceived, humiliating him facilely to an ideal tool for a dictatorship. The formation of conscience, however, grants the individual person his human center: then [technical] abilities provide an area

---

81 Congregation for the Doctrine of the Faith, *Instruction Libertatis Conscientiae*, no. 61.

82 Ratzinger, "Freiheit und Befreiung," 409.

83 Ratzinger, "Freiheit und Befreiung," 412.

84 In the Armenian and Syriac variants. Ratzinger, "Freiheit und Befreiung," 413 and n. 3.

of [genuine] independence and rights, allowing [communitarian] togetherness in freedom to come about."[85]

An autarkic understanding of freedom outside a theonomous conscience is a blueprint for anarchy—the very denial of freedom. The dignity of the human person and the quality of his life rest primarily on his relationship with God, not on the quality of material goods or conditions.

The Exodus narrative does not relate *au fond* to the Israelites' horizontal, political, or social liberation as much as to their liberation to worship and sacrifice for the true God. This brings human beings into the proper position toward their Creator and toward the creation. The restoration of a covenantal relationship is of overriding importance. What the Exodus narrative provided for the ancient Israelites, the incarnation of God expands to all of human-kind—via the Church and her sacraments. Christ is the redemption of human beings to relate to and imitate "self-commitment [*Selbstbindung*] in triune love and thus [realize] pure freedom."[86] Mentioning in this context Hegel, Marx, and Adorno, Ratzinger argues again against the then as now regnant Critical Theory: every effort toward autarky and autonomy apart from God ultimately condemns people to social isolation, lack of friendships and relationships, and an arbitrary lifestyle.

In an *encomium* honoring the Bavarian politician and minister president Alfons Goppel (1905–1991), Ratzinger mentions both Plato and Aristotle and then Romano Guardini: politics becomes pernicious when it severs ties to the God-given conscience, as "the non-believer cannot properly manage the world."[87] The salutary possibilities lie in a conscience united with a living God. He praises Goppel for applying a conscience formed by the Gospel to his remarkably successful policies.

When preaching in 1979 in his titular church *Santa Maria Consolatrice* in Rome on the Eucharistic Lord, Ratzinger said:

> The true law of God is not an external matter. It dwells within us. It is the inner direction of our lives, which is brought into being and established by the will of God. It speaks to us in our conscience. The conscience is the inner aspect of the Lord's presence, which alone can

---

85 Ratzinger, "Freiheit und Befreiung," 415.

86 Ratzinger, "Freiheit und Befreiung," 424.

87 Ratzinger, *Priester aus innerstem Herzen*, 154.

render us capable of receiving the eucharistic presence. . . . The Lord is near us in our conscience, in his word, in his personal presence in the Eucharist: this constitutes the dignity of the Christian and is the reason for his joy.[88]

REDISCOVERING THE CENTER

Ratzinger mentions in a chapter of *Vom Auffinden der Mitte* that some claim that trust in an authority for moral guidance is "preconciliar." To Ratzinger's mind, this distinction, if not divorce, is deeply unhelpful. Under the pretext of subjective responsibility, people yield to dictatorial "social conformism." Someone subscribing to this putative "postconciliar" view must indeed expect to meet members of the inhumane Nazi SS troop in heaven, as they had perpetrated unimaginably heinous crimes in the name of a clean conscience.[89]

In contradiction, a psychologist, Albert Görres (1918–1996), discovered that pangs of conscience belong to every healthy psyche. Lacking guilt is the mark of a brute, such as Hitler, Himmler, Stalin, or a Mafia *padrone*. It is unrealistic to conflate the self-awareness of the ego with "subjective moral certitude."[90] Such confusion leads many to follow ineluctably and uncritically popular opinion and into a deprivation of truth.

Ratzinger then discusses how Newman had fought such a view in his day. Here he delves into Newman's understanding of conscience. He mentions Newman's "Lead Kindly Light": "I was not ever thus, nor pray'd that Thou shouldst lead me on."[91] Much like the sovereign statesmen Cicero and St. Thomas More, Newman emphasized the need not to seek consensus but truth. In this light, Ratzinger discusses Socrates and the Sophists.

Ratzinger's truly original contribution to the question of conscience is his distinguishing two medieval planes of conscience: *synt(d)eresis* and *conscientia*. The significant distinction has been much neglected, he argues. The actual meaning of *synteresis* was never firmly defined,[92] and sometimes,

---

88 Ratzinger, *God Is near Us*, 105–6.

89 Ratzinger, *Vom Wiederauffinden der Mitte*, 270. See also Ratzinger, *On Conscience*, 13–17.

90 Ratzinger, *Vom Wiederauffinden der Mitte*, 273.

91 Ratzinger, *Vom Wiederauffinden der Mitte*, 276.

92 See Levering, *Abuse of Conscience*, 188–90, for a lucid exposition.

this ambiguity invites a teleological reduction. Ratzinger suggests replacing it with the Platonic concept of *anamnesis,* as memory of the good in its winsome quality. It exists as an echo of a primordial moral order partially lost sight of after the fall—and Ratzinger equates it with *Urerinnerung* (primordial memory) in German. Levering elaborates, "This basic moral knowledge is found in the Decalogue, whose precepts find an echo in other cultures, even if without the same clarity."[93] It is in the sacramental life of the Church that this *Urerinnerung* is recovered in its integrity. "Otherwise, Christians would be threatened by moral enslavement to their own subjectivity in conformity with the wider culture(s) in which they live," Levering concludes.[94]

Ratzinger holds that such recollective meaning finds expression, *inter alia*, in the monastic rule of St. Basil: "Loving God rests not on a discipline imposed upon us from outside, rather it is a constitutive element of an [interior] ability and necessity rooted in us as rational beings."[95] There is a spark of divine love in every human being, as the medievals will often repeat. This is the primordial memory of the good and true present in the one created in the image and likeness of God. "The anamnesis of the Creator is identical with the ground of our being,"[96] Ratzinger states. Living in "fear of God" (Acts 10:34), a person permits *anamnesis* to work in him. Echoing Newman's *Letter to the Duke of Norfolk*, Ratzinger notes that papal authority cannot contradict such *anamnesis* but only promote its flowering. The now deceased pope is an advocate of such a recollective memory: "Loving God rests not on an exterior discipline imposed upon us from outside, rather it is constitutive as ability and necessity rooted in us as rational beings." Newman did not explain sufficiently the relationship between conscience and the ecclesial charism, and Ratzinger also admits that *Gaudium et Spes* 16 does not go beyond providing a "general outline of a Christian doctrine of conscience."[97] Ultimately, the ecclesial knowledge of God guarantees the unity of the human race and enables

---

93 Levering, *Abuse of Conscience*, 189.

94 Levering, *Abuse of Conscience*, 189.

95 Ratzinger, *Vom Wiederauffinden der Mitte*, 280.

96 Ratzinger, *Vom Wiederauffinden der Mitte*, 281.

97 Ratzinger, commentary on *Gaudium et Spes* in *Commentary on the Documents of Vatican II*, vol. 5, ed. Herbert Vorgrimler (New York: Herder, 1969), 134–36.

the individual to encounter God again and again as "the common good and binding character of one and the same good."[98]

By interpreting *synteresis* as *anamnesis*, Ratzinger sees better articulated "the original memory of the good and true that has been implanted in us."[99] It is a record innate to everyone. Guilt lies then not so much in following an aberrant conscience as in neglecting to cultivate one's being in such a way that the *anamnesis* comes better to the fore. Far from moralizing, this view shows how gladdening it is to live in a relationship with the divine: "The *actual novelty of Christianity is the Logos,* the Truth in Person who *is also* the *atonement, the transformative forgiveness* beyond our own capacity and incapacity."[100]

With the clarity and simplicity of a church father, Ratzinger writes:

> Psalm 19:12 contains words that deserve constant meditation: 'But who can discern his errors? Clear my hidden faults.' The wisdom of the Old Testament takes a very different line from my professorial colleagues: the loss of the ability to see one's guilt, the falling silent of conscience in so many areas, is a more dangerous illness of the soul than guilt that is recognized as guilt. One who no longer pays heed to the fact that killing is a sin has fallen more deeply than one who still recognizes the abhorrent quality of his actions, since the former person is further away from truth and from repentance. It is not by chance that the self-righteous person is revealed in the encounter with Jesus to be the one who is really lost: when the tax collector with all his undisputed sins is more righteous in the eyes of God than the Pharisee with all his genuinely good deeds (Lk 18:9–14), this is not because the sins of the tax collector were not sins or the good deeds of the Pharisee not good deeds. Jesus does not intend to say that man's virtuous deeds are not good in God's sight or that his evil deeds are not evil (or, at any rate, not particularly serious).
>
> The reason for this paradoxical verdict by God is directly connected to the question we are examining here. The Pharisee is no longer aware that he too is guilty. He is perfectly at ease with his own conscience. But this silence of his conscience makes it impossible for God and men to penetrate his carapace—whereas the cry of conscience

---

98 Ratzinger, *Truth and Tolerance*, 207.

99 Amadasu, "Conscience and Holiness," 102.

100 Ratzinger, *Vom Wiederauffinden der Mitte*, 286. Emphases in the original German.

that torments the tax collector opens him to receive truth and love. Jesus can work effectively among sinners because they have not become inaccessible behind the screen of an erring conscience, which would put them out of reach of the changes that God awaits from them—and from us. Jesus cannot work effectively among the righteous because they sense no need for forgiveness and repentance; their conscience no longer accuses them but only justifies them.[101]

CONCLUSION:
CONSONANCES, NOT DISSONANCES

From the onset of his theological studies, Ratzinger was much influenced by Newman.[102] Both Newman and Ratzinger are confronted with the supposed alternative between a morality grounded in a supposedly autonomous (namely self-legislating) conscience à la Kant and one grounded in heteronomous authority. For Newman and Ratzinger, such putative opposition is postlapsarian fiction. Both thinkers contend that conscience is divinely instituted: more precisely, that the Christian establishment of a personal, living relationship with the one and only God, who is the most intense form of personal life as the Blessed Trinity, is redemptive. Fully *d'accord* with the ancients and scripture, Newman and Ratzinger posit an inherent transparency of the moral agent to the divine that constitutes man's dignity. Assuming a congeniality between creation and Creator, and hence a "moral" analogy of being, there exists on the part of every human being an ontic tendency toward God both in his absolute goodness and as *the* origin of morality.

Newman and Ratzinger accept the fact of an erroneous conscience and suggest that sin often lies in a poorly formed conscience, or in a lack of forming one's conscience altogether. It is ultimately a lack of love: "the good must be loved and made reality."[103] While Newman does not systematically harmonize the individual conscience and the ecclesial charism as an expression of the full

---

101 Ratzinger, *Values in a Time of Upheaval*, 81–82.

102 Joseph Ratzinger, "Presentation: The Theology of Cardinal Newman," https://www.ewtn.com/catholicism/library/1990-presentation-the-theology-of-cardinal-newman-10157.

103 Josef Pieper, *The Four Cardinal Virtues* (Notre Dame, IN: University of Notre Dame Press, 1965), 11.

truth of God and man,[104] Ratzinger attempts a synthesis: between the church and the individual Catholic, between bishops and theologians, and even between the church and the political realm.[105] Both agree that conscience is "man's openness to the ground of his being."[106] When in his essay "Conscience and Truth" Ratzinger pithily states that "the power of conscience consists in suffering, in the power of the Crucified,"[107] Newman and every martyr would underscore this statement.

Both thinkers are very much Platonic, as both believe conscience to be a memory of the good, and yet, Newman sees it from a more biographical perspective, while Ratzinger approaches it more from an ontological one. In sacramental life, it becomes the communal *sensus fidei*, formed deep within the objective reality of the church as the primordial sacrament (*Ursakrament*), whence the seven induvial sacraments issue forth. Thus, both the papal and ecclesial magisterium are not extrinsic to but rather the logical organic manifestation and rightful locus for the full flourishing of conscience.

Little wonder, then, that both thinkers almost seamlessly see in conscience something personal, enriched by and coming fully into its own in a person's ecclesial existence. Both consider its subjectivist reinterpretation as doing violence to the creaturely nature of conscience. While Newman regards this threat as originating in "doctrinal liberalism," Ratzinger apprehends the same danger coming from the almost all-pervasive Critical Theory and its numerous popular variations.

By introducing the term *anamnesis*, Ratzinger spells out further what Newman means by conscience: the "echo of the voice of God." By developing the crucial role of God addressing us personally in the conscience, both Newman and Ratzinger react also to neoscholasticism and its emphasis on a timeless, objectivistic, impersonal theology. Ratzinger had experienced such theology while in seminary in Freising and Newman while briefly studying in Rome.[108] When Newman, writing about his conversion in 1816, refers to "the thought

---

104 As regards Newman and ecclesiological, see the syntheses of Rino La Delfa, *A Personal Church? The Foundation of Newman's Ecclesiological Thought* (Palermo: ILA Palma, 1997); Edward Jeremy Miller, *John Henry Newman: On the Idea of the Church* (Shepherdstown, WV: Patmos, 1987).

105 For a good summary, see Twomey, *Pope Benedict XVI, the Conscience of Our Age.*

106 Joseph Ratzinger, "Conscience and Truth," in *Crisis of Conscience*, ed. John M. Haas (New York: Crossroad, 1996), 4.

107 Ratzinger, "Conscience in Time," 22.

108 Ratzinger, *Milestones*, 41–46; Ker, *John Henry Newman*, 321–32.

of two and two only absolute and luminously self-evident beings, myself and my Creator,"[109] Ratzinger sees Newman giving pride of place to a personal and moral dimension of religious experience, perhaps never thematized as eloquently since Augustine. It is logical for Newman to conclude: "Many a man will live and die upon a dogma: no man will be a martyr for a conclusion."[110]

Ratzinger does not address postmodernity *per se*, but he does see contemporary society becoming "free-floating and impersonal."[111] Such deconstruction of the ethical subject leads ineluctably to "the dictatorship of relativism."[112] The denial of the objectivity of truth and the divine origin of a person's conscience lead[113] to an alienation from God and from the individual self and to a fragmented society incapable of real dialogue.

Whoever ignores this remarkable consistency in thought on conscience spanning at least 2,500 years must assume that divine revelation is not possible and that there is neither a collective human memory nor an overarching intelligence.

The above survey evidences Newman's and Ratzinger's thoughts on conscience not as idiosyncratic musings of peripheral thinkers but as standing in the very center of Christian existence and in direct and organic continuity with the biblical testimony and the thoughts of classical philosophy. Similar basic notions are held by all cultures and religions, and they assume an inescapable relationality between the divine and humankind. While for ancient philosophy it is the at-times impersonal numinous, and for the Old Testament the God of Abraham, Isaac, and Jacob, for the New Testament and for Newman and Ratzinger, it is Jesus Christ speaking to human beings through their consciences. Putting to shame all earthly criteria for a happy life, for all four—ancient philosophy, scripture, Newman, and Ratzinger—serene obedience to the call of conscience defines a fulfilled life.

109 Newman, *Apologia Pro Vita Sua*, 4.

110 John Henry Newman, *Newman Reader*, http://www.newmanreader.org/works/arguments/tamworth/section6.html.

111 Frederic Jameson, "Postmodernism, or The Cultural Logic of Late Capitalism," in *Postmodernism: A Reader*, ed. Thomas Docherty (New York: Columbia University Press, 1992), 72.

112 Joseph Ratzinger, "Mass 'Pro Eligendo Romano Pontifice,' Homily of His Eminence Cardinal Joseph Ratzinger, Dean of the College of Cardinals," April 18, 2005, http://www.vatican.va/gpII/documents/homily-pro-eligendo-pontifice_20050418_en.html.

113 See Newman, *Grammar of Assent*, 74–75. See also Karl Rahner, *Foundations of Christian Faith: An Introduction to the Idea of Christianity* (New York: Crossroad, 1986), 83.

The beauty of human life does not lie in being perfect in the sense of being morally irreproachable but rather in the toil for truth. Such travail is redemptive as it is the privileged place of *"cor ad cor loquitur."*[114]

---

[114] Charles Stephen Dessain et al., eds., *The Letters and Diaries of John Henry Newman* (Oxford: Oxford University Press, 1976), 29:108.

7

THE "SIGNS OF THE TIMES" IN NEWMAN AND TWENTIETH-CENTURY CATHOLIC THEOLOGY

Andrew Meszaros

Many believe that Newman's theological concerns were vindicated at the Second Vatican Council.[1] There are, it is true, many reasons why Newman merits titles such as "father of Vatican II," but his understanding of the expression "signs of the times" is not one of them. I will argue that Newman's approach to the signs of the times is more akin to a biblical understanding of the term that is fundamentally different than, but not incompatible with, the council's understanding as expressed in *Gaudium et Spes*. In fact, Newman's

---

[1] Pope Paul VI called the period of Second Vatican Council and beyond "Newman's hour." See Paul VI, "Una luce sul cammino dell'anno Santo il pensiero del Cardinale Newman," in *Insegnamenti di Paolo VI*, 13 (Vatican City: Tipografia Poliglotta Vaticana, 1976), 277. For an extended reflection on the similarities between Newman's theological priorities and those of the Second Vatican Council, albeit with a particular viewpoint and methodology, see Ian Ker, *Newman and Vatican II* (Oxford: Oxford University Press, 2014). A study that systematically examines the influence that Newman's writings had on the redaction of the conciliar documents has, to my knowledge, yet to be undertaken. Work on Newman's influence on particular conciliar *periti*, however, has begun. See, for example, Andrew Meszaros, *The Prophetic Church: History and Doctrinal Development in John Henry Newman and Yves Congar* (Oxford: Oxford University Press, 2016).

understanding, along with Joseph Ratzinger's, is the prerequisite for enacting what the council exhorts with respect to the signs of the times.

The argument proceeds in three steps. I first show that the biblical expression ushered into the twentieth-century Catholic theological idiom by John XXIII was, by the time it got to *Gaudium et Spes*, uprooted from its scriptural foundation; I then show how subsequent receptions of *Gaudium et Spes* either continued this trajectory or criticized it. Second, I provide a brief exegesis of the expression as it appears in the synoptic gospels. Third, I show how Newman's usage of the expression manifests the biblical understanding of it; I also examine Newman's eschatological view of the world. Finally, appealing to Newman and Ratzinger, I propose how it is that the biblical and conciliar understanding of the category are not only compatible or complementary but indissoluble.

THE "SIGNS OF THE TIMES" UP TO AND IN VATICAN II

THE PAPAL DOCUMENTS

The first time we find the expression "signs of the times" in John XXIII's pontificate is probably in his convocation of the council, *Humanae salutis* (December 25, 1961). In it, John XXIII points to Jesus' promise of his presence within the church in his great commission (Mt 28), teaching that Christ's presence is most noticeable in times of crisis. Pope John then proceeds to observe some destructive contemporary trends, which include a weakened aspiration toward things spiritual, an exclusive pursuit of earthly pleasures, and the existence of a militant atheism. It is only at this point that Pope John refers to the signs of the times, appealing to Matthew 16:4:

> These painful considerations remind us of the duty to be vigilant and keep our sense of responsibility awake. While distrustful souls see nothing but darkness falling upon the face of the earth, we prefer to restate our confidence in our Savior, who has not left the world he redeemed. Indeed, making our own Jesus' recommendation that we learn to discern "the signs of the times" (Mt 16:4), it seems to us that we can make out, in the midst of so much darkness, more than a few

THE "SIGNS OF THE TIMES"

indications that enable us to have hope for the fate of the Church and of humanity.[2]

John XXIII then attempts to highlight some of the silver-lining in the midst of this darkness. The world wars and materialistic ideologies have lessons to offer. Scientific progress raises key questions about human limitations and vulnerability, questions that stimulate a conscientiousness and a desire for peace and collaboration. In other words, when John XXIII invokes the signs of the times, he is in fact discerning opportunities and tendencies that elicit hope for the power of the Gospel amid desolation. John observes that the darkness and threats of the modern world have actually made people more open and ready for the Gospel.[3]

More influential than this first appearance, however, was John XXIII's 1963 encyclical, *Pacem in Terris*, which was novel in its scope and popular reception. Published not two months before his death during the council, the encyclical served as a kind of celebratory last testament of his pontificate for the council and for the world at large. *Signa temporum*, however, never featured in the official Latin version of the *AAS*.[4] The phrase, however, was included in the Italian [*segni dei tempi*] version in the form of four section headings and later made its way into subsequent translations [e.g., *signes des temps*; *Zeichen der Zeit*]. From the context, one can see that, generally, the positive social developments in the world—the workers' movement, the entry of women into public life, increased political sovereignty, the creation of the UN, etc.[5]—are what, according to the encyclical, count as signs of the times.

---

2 John XXIII, *Humanae Salutis*, 1861, no. 4, trans. Joseph Komonchak, https://jakomonchak.files. wordpress.com/2011/12/humanae-salutis.pdf. The official Latin text is in *Acta Apostolica Sedis* 54 (1962): 5–13, hereafter cited as *AAS*.

3 John XXIII, *Humanae Salutis*, no. 4: "The successive bloody wars of our times . . . have not been without useful lessons. Scientific progress itself, which has given man the ability to create catastrophic implements for his own destruction, has raised anxious questions; it has forced human beings to become thoughtful, more aware of their own limitations, desirous of peace, alert to the importance of spiritual values."

4 John XXIII, *Pacem in Terris* in *AAS* 55 (1963): 257–304. An English translation can be found on the Vatican website: https://www.vatican.va/content/john-xxiii/en/encyclicals/documents/ hf_j-xxiii_enc_11041963_pacem.html, accessed June 13, 2024.

5 The one exception to this apparently positive trend are the paragraphs on war and nuclear weapons (nos. 126–29). In the English numeration, the relevant paragraphs on contemporary "signs" include *Pacem in Terris*, §40–45; §75–79; §126–29; §142–45. Where other vernacular versions use the equivalent of "signs of the times" for the headings, the first two English headings are

No reference, however, is made in the encyclical to Mt 16 or any other relevant text. The upshot is candidly summarized by Russell Hittinger:

> Thus, *signa temporum* was detached from its original context in Mt. 16.3. Rather than the richly ambiguous and the pointedly admonitory meanings of both the scripture and Pope John's use of it in 1961, the phrase seemed to be an empty placeholder for organizing pronouncements about current affairs.[6]

The significance of this lies in the fact that when it came to its controversial use in *Gaudium et Spes*, Mark McGrath[7] defended the expression when presenting a draft by explicitly stating that the expression was used not in its scriptural sense but in the sense used by John XXIII's encyclical.[8]

Relative to the scripturally rooted ambiguity of *Humanae salutis*, we can recognize a transition to a more positive approach to discerning the signs of the times in Paul VI's encyclical of 1964 on the church, *Ecclesiam suam.* Admittedly, the expression Paul uses is not *signa temporum* but rather *indicia temporum*, which might explain why there is no reference to Mt 16. But all the major translations use the same vernacular that had previously rendered—and would later render in translations of *Gaudium et Spes—signa temporum: signs of the times, segni dei tempi, signes des temps, Zeichen der Zeit.* The stage was further solidified for *Gaudium et Spes* and for postconciliar theology to use a scriptural expression without its scriptural anchor. What is more, the notion of *aggiornamento* is appealed to as a stimulant for considering the signs of the times.

"Characteristics of the Present Day" (which appears twice), the third, "Signs of the Times," and the fourth, "Modern Developments."

6 Russell Hittinger, "*Quinquagesimo Ante:* Reflections on *Pacem in Terris* Fifty Years Later," *Pontifical Academy of Social Sciences* 18 (2013): 54n32.

7 Marcos Gregorio McGrath, CSC (1924–2000), was active in drafting, elaborating, and promoting the document as archbishop of Panama. For a fuller picture, see Robert S. Pelton, "CELAM and the Emerging Reception of the 'Bridge Theology' of Pope Francis: From Marcos Gregorio McGrath to the Latin American Church Today," *Horizonte* 16 (2018): 454–81.

8 Charles Moeller, "Preface and Introductory Statement," in *Commentary on the Documents of Vatican II*, ed. Herbert Vorgrimler (New York: Herder & Herder, 1969), 5:94: "The words 'signs of the times' are used on this single occasion not in a technical but in a general sense, as they are found in several documents of Popes John XXIII and Paul VI." These words are from McGrath's *relatio* to the council fathers. See also 97–98, 93–94, and Moeller's first essay in the same volume, "History of the Constitution," 35, 64.

THE "SIGNS OF THE TIMES"

> It [aggiornamento] should prove a stimulus to the Church to increase its ever growing vitality and its ability to take stock of itself and give careful consideration to the signs of the times, always and everywhere "proving all things and holding fast that which is good" (Cf. 1 Thes 5. 21.) with the enthusiasm of youth.[9]

The expression, then, is bound up with the project of aggiornamento. Furthering the positivity behind the use here is the appeal to Paul's admonition to the Thessalonians to test and maintain all that is good. While the original context of the passage refers to prophetic charisms, with the encyclical's use, the indicia temporum—not prophecies—are to be tested, retaining and cultivating the good ones. In this sense, the indicia temporum can be interpreted as taking on a prophetic character: God is not working solely through the church but also in and through the world's initiatives which, in turn, the church ought to heed.

VATICAN II AND *GAUDIUM ET SPES*

Vatican II as a whole saw the signs in a positive light. In *Dignitatis Humanae*, for example, the fathers recognize two sociological data: the increasing constitutional guarantee of religious freedom on the one hand, and some governments' dereliction of their duty to recognize that freedom on the other. While the council "deplores" the latter, it "greets with joy the first of these two facts as among the signs of the times."[10] In *Apostolicam actuositatem*, the council fathers recognize also the increasing sense of solidarity among nations as a sign of the times. This sense, the fathers exhort, ought to be transformed into a "sincere and genuine form of brotherhood."[11]

One of the last documents to be promulgated, swimming in the wake of *Pacem in Terris* (1963) and *Ecclesiam Suam* (1964), *Gaudium et Spes* (1965)

---

9 Paul VI, *Ecclesiam Suam*, 1964, no. 50. (Unless otherwise noted, all magisterial documents are taken from the Vatican website, https://www.vatican.va/content/vatican/en.html.)
John O'Malley observes that at the council, "Updating as such was not a problem to either party. It became a problem only in terms of its limits (how far could it legitimately go?). . . . *During the council bishops and theologians sometimes invoked 'development' to cover almost any kind of change.*" See John O'Malley, *What Happened at Vatican II?* (Cambridge, MA: Belknap Press of Harvard University Press, 2008), 300 (emphasis added).

10 Vatican II, *Dignitatis Humanae*, 1965, no. 15.

11 Vatican II, *Apostolicam Actuasitatem*, 1965, no. 10.

contains the council's most celebrated passage on the signs of the times, found immediately after the preface:

> To carry out such a task, the Church has always had the duty of scrutinizing the signs of the times and of interpreting them in the light of the Gospel. Thus, in language intelligible to each generation, she can respond to the perennial questions which men ask about this present life and the life to come, and about the relationship of the one to the other. We must therefore recognize and understand the world in which we live, its explanations, its longings, and its often dramatic characteristics. Some of the main features of the modern world can be sketched as follows.[12]

The following paragraphs proceed to present the then-contemporary existential situation. The more neutral interpretation of the signs is given by the *peritus* Moehler, for whom "the expression 'signa temporum' . . . bears John XXIII's sense of the main facts which characterize an age."[13] The expression, according to Moehler, "at once attracted attention because it was so well chosen to express the new phenomena which had arisen in the world, and which the Church must 'read' in order to discern the opportunity they offer for it to deepen its own teaching."[14] Although the description of these new phenomena or characteristics of the age include a recognition of the causes of anxiety, the general tendency of the document is to view the developments not only as progress but to associate them with divine work. Attention is drawn, for example, to the Latin subtitle given to §11 (a subtitle, which is not rendered in the English translation): *Impulsionibus Spiritus respondendum.*[15]

Similarly, that Catholic theology today opts to take "signs of the times" as an affirmative sign of God's presence is evident in how readers of the document associate—by showing the similarities and indeed parallels between—§4, §11, and §44. The church has the task of scrutinizing [*perscrutandi* in §4) or discerning (*discernere* in §11) or hearing, deciphering, interpreting, and judging (*auscultare, discernere, interpretari,* and *diiudicare* in §44) the signs

---

12 Vatican II, *Gaudium et Spes*, 1965, no. 4.

13 Moehler, "Preface and Introductory Statement," 99.

14 Moehler, "Preface and Introductory Statement," 93.

15 See, for example, Ellen Van Stichel and Yves De Maeseneer, "*Gaudium et Spes*: Impulses of the Spirit for an Age of Globalisation," *Louvain Studies* 39 (2015–2016): 63–73, esp. 63.

of the times (§4), authentic signs of God's presence and purpose [*vera signa praesentiae vel consilii Dei* in §11), and the voices of our age (*loquelas nostri temporis* in §44) in the light of the Gospel (§4), under the light of faith (§11),[16] or in light of the divine word (§44).

Crucially, the Gospel, the divine word, and the light of faith are the measures of contemporary discernment of signs in the world, but this naturally lies in tension with the document's stated purpose for the church to follow Christ, who came "to rescue and not to sit in judgment" (§3). With the church's posture still perceived as antiworld, the desired change in tone had the council fathers present a relationship to the world that was more collaborative and dialogical than rivalrous and condemnatory.

The church, then, simultaneously exhorts the faithful to discern, scrutinize, assess, and judge the movements of the world while not to "sit in judgment" of the world. The resolution of this apparent tension is achieved in two ways: first, whatever judging is taking place by Christians is done at the service of helping bring humanity to its true end and fulfilment, and second and more concretely, to avoid the semblance of condemnation, "the words that the text uses to express that relationship [between Church and world] are words of mutuality, friendship, partnership, cooperation—and dialogue."[17]

One of the great novelties of the council, as far as John O'Malley is concerned, is the admission that, far from having ready-made answers to all the world's problems, the church not only teaches the world but must also learn from it:[18]

> In its general orientation, as articulated especially in its most characteristic vocabulary, the council devised a profile of the ideal Christian. That ideal, drawn in greatest length in *Gaudium et Spes*, is more incarnational than eschatological, closer to Thomas Aquinas than to Karl Barth, more reminiscent of the Fathers of the Eastern Church than of Augustine—more inclined to reconciliation with human culture than to alienation from it, more inclined to see goodness than sin, more inclined to speaking words of friendship and encouragement than of indictment.

---

16 Vatican II, *Gaudium et Spes*, no. 11, in "*sub hoc lumen*"; the hoc refers to the faith that illuminates all things.

17 O'Malley, *What Happened at Vatican II?* 267.

18 O'Malley, *What Happened at Vatican II?* 268.

Significantly, "the style choice," concludes O'Malley, "fostered a theological choice."[19]

THE RECEPTIONS OF *GAUDIUM ET SPES*

The "theological choice" registered by O'Malley was, in fairness, more of a tendency, albeit the dominant one. Moehler observes that the final version of the document

> put to the vote by the fathers before its promulgation represented the consensus of the two main tendencies which had stood confronted since the beginning of work on Schema 13: one a concrete outlook marked by a certain fundamental optimism, the other a dialectical, paradoxical attitude insisting on the polyvalency of the world in which the church lives.[20]

That the theology of history at the time had two tendencies—let us call them the enthusiastic/incarnational and the cautious/eschatological—is indisputable. One cannot qualify or temper the two tendencies without either affirming them (implicitly) or otherwise diminishing what many consider to be the achievement of *Gaudium et Spes*. As Benedict Viviano colorfully sums up the issue, the phrase *signs of the times* "by no means implies an idiotic naive uncritical optimism, but it did lead the Fathers to want to accent the positive in the spirit of Pope John 23 [*sic*]."[21] The cautious eschatologists warn against the "naïve uncritical optimism"; the enthusiastic incarnationalists "accent the positive."

These two tendencies persist to the present day, in large part because both the theologically enthusiastic and the cautious can appeal to *Gaudium et Spes*. There is something in it for both.[22] Contrary to what some conservative critics might allege, such an appeal for both tendencies is a strike against

---

19 O'Malley, *What Happened at Vatican II?* 310–11.

20 Moehler, "History of the Constitution," 60.

21 Benedict Viviano, "The Reception of the Second Vatican Council in Light of Its Prehistory and the Discernment of the Signs of the Times," *Verba theologica* 2 (2013): 6.

22 For a balanced reading of *Gaudium et Spes* that affirms its doctrinal principles but frankly points out the limitations of its relevance due to the radical cultural changes after the council, see Thomas Joseph White, "*Gaudium et Spes*," in *The Reception of Vatican II*, ed. Matthew L. Lamb and Matthew Levering (Oxford: Oxford University Press, 2017), 113–43.

THE "SIGNS OF THE TIMES"

any portrayal of the document as being a lop-sided and naïve capitulation to modernity; *Gaudium et Spes*, for example, does not ignore the reality of sin but teaches the fallenness of man.[23] Conversely, however, the existence of subsequent (very) optimistic readings of the text vindicates critics of the document—past and present—whose misgivings might still be met with skepticism by the enthusiasts on the grounds that the critics (e.g., de Lubac) objected more to potential consequences of the document rather than actual shortcomings in the document itself.[24]

With Richard Schenk, we note that these "two main tendencies," although present from the get-go, did not always enjoy the same popularity. The first, more optimistic wave of postconciliar reception was followed by a second, more critical one, one wherein historical events and movements were not seen as the ultimate, inevitable unfolding of God's plan but as realities that demanded sober analysis and differentiated responses. The rise of liberation theology was just one indicator of a growing dissatisfaction not only with the optimism but a kind of evolutionary understanding of history, marching toward freedom in the spirit, inherent in the Rahnerian system.[25] This shift was manifested in the 1990s by a "changed spirit . . . one more likely to appreciate the objections that Lukas Vischer had raised twenty-five years earlier about answering the key anthropological question, 'What should I do?' by simply pointing to the signs of assumed progress visible in the culture of the day."[26]

Despite the accuracy of Schenk's observations, there are some today who are still surfing on that *first* wave of reception. Let us consider these tendencies more closely.

---

23 For example, *Gaudium et Spes*, nos. 13, 15, 16, 37, 40.

24 Joachim Sander, for example, suggests that the criticisms of *Gaudium et Spes*'s one-sidedness are unfounded, based as they are primarily on previous drafts, and that the Constitution's text itself puts paid to any kind of historical progressivism. See Hans-Joachim Sander, "Theologischer Kommentar zur Pastoralkonstitution über die Kirche in der Welt von heute," in *Herders theologischer Kommentar zum Zweiten Vatikanischen Konzil*, ed. Bernd Jochen Hilberath and Peter Hünermann (Freiburg-i.-Br.: Herder, 2005), 4:716. In a similar vein, see the subtle critique of de Lubac's misgivings in Joseph Komonchak's review of Loïc Figoureux, *Henri de Lubac et le Concile Vatican II (1960–1965)*, in *Cristianesimo nella storia* 40 (2019): 739–50.

25 Richard Schenk, "Officium Signa Temporum Perscrutandi: New Encounters of Gospel and Culture in the Context of the New Evangelization," in *Scrutinizing the Signs of the Times in the Light of the Gospel*, ed. Johan Verstraeten, Bibliotheca Ephemeridum Theologicarum Lovaniensium 208 (Leuven: Peeters, 2007), 167–203, esp. 182–95. The irony here is Rahner's own dissatisfaction with the text, one reason being its—in his eyes—excessive optimism. See the summary of the issue in Sander, "Theologischer Kommentar," 630–31.

26 Schenk, "Officium Signa Temporum Perscrutandi," 195.

THE OPTIMISTIC RECEPTION AND DEVELOPMENT

Between *Gaudium et Spes* and *Ecclesiam Suam*, the message seemed clear: in order to bring the church "up to date"—and thereby render more effective her efforts at evangelization in a modern context—we need to scrutinize the signs of the times. Such scrutiny, then, is at the service of updating the church with a pastoral program that actively engages with the contemporary context. This was the program, for example, of Marie-Dominique Chenu.

SIGNS OF THE TIMES ACCORDING TO CHENU

Chenu's influence on *Gaudium et Spes*, even if at times indirect and behind-the-scenes, was indisputable. His stamp is all over the text, especially with regard to the signs of the times.[27]

Already in the 1930s, Chenu was laying out a theological program that sought to reflect not only on the scriptures and monuments of tradition but also on the life and experiences of Christians who were present to their time. The incarnational logic for Chenu meant viewing Christ's presence in the world as working itself out *now* on a societal level (e.g., in lay apostolates, political and worker movements, the Jocists, etc.). All these movements—what Chenu would later dub signs of the times—were already considered theological *loci*.[28]

Like others, Chenu registers the expression's biblical roots, but instead of contenting himself with saying that its contemporary meaning—catalyzed by John XXIII's use of it—is simply different from its original biblical meaning, he insists that its primordial biblical and gospel roots are of primary value and that all other uses of the expression must refer to this biblical meaning. For Chenu, the biblical meaning lays hold of the historical economy of Christianity "whose development in history includes in its essential framework 'signs.'"[29]

---

27 Ratzinger, apparently, perceived it this way, too. See Sander, "Theologischer Kommentar," 658–62n201). For a summary of Chenu's stance vis-à-vis the Pastoral Constitution, see Joseph Komonchak, "The Redaction and Reception of *Gaudium et Spes: Tensions within the Majority at Vatican II*," 4–7, https://jakomonchak.files.wordpress.com/2013/04/jak-views-of-gaudium-et-spes.pdf. This is an English translation of "Le valutazioni sulla *Gaudium et spes*: Chenu, Dossetti, Ratzinger," in *Volti di fine Concilio: Studi di storia e teologia sulla conclusione del Vaticano II*, ed. Joseph Doré and Alberto Melloni (Bologna: Il Mulino, 2000), 115–53.

28 Joseph Komonchak, "Returning from Exile: Catholic Theology in the 1930s," in *The Twentieth Century: A Theological Overview*, ed. Gregory Baum (Maryknoll, NY: Orbis Books, 1999), 39–45.

29 Chenu, "Les signes des temps," *Nouvelle revue théologique* 87, no. 1 (1965): 30.

THE "SIGNS OF THE TIMES"

Ultimately, however, Chenu will not make much ado about the exegetical questions surrounding the signs. In order to maintain some connection with the biblical-eschatological meaning of the term, it is enough for him—so Chenu thinks—to insist that Christianity (and Judaism along with it), is essentially historical; that God's plan unfolds in time; that grace presupposes and works in and through nature; and that great events have meaning in God's plan. In other words, the sociological signs of our times for Chenu qualify as eschatological because we live in messianic times.[30]

From this, Chenu with ease proceeds to identify certain signs of the time, following John XXIII's *Pacem in Terris*: socialization, promotion of the working classes, the emergence of women in public life, the emancipation of colonized peoples, technological progress, a sense of the universal connectedness of human kind, international collaboration, etc.

On a sociological level, these historical developments, for Chenu, only become signs by virtue of their status as an event that strikes the human consciousness as something new and propels society to a new stage. For a historical development to qualify as a sign, it must awaken humanity and capture its energies and hopes.[31]

The theological significance of such a sign, once one is detected by the church, amounts to an opportunity to evangelize. The sign refers to some social, cultural, or technological reality, development, or aspiration that is ripe for the Gospel. That reality has an "aptitude," "capacity," or a possible "opening" to embody a Gospel value.[32] Perhaps the most suggestive image Chenu provides is that of *pierres d'attente*, or toothing stones, the bricks or stones that are purposely laid so as to protrude beyond the edge of the wall so that, at some future point, another construction can be added to it.[33] Literally, the French translates to "stones of expectation." In a similar but more theologically technical vein, Chenu at one point uses the expression *obediential potency* and extends its application to communal or social realities (rather than just to individual natures). Appealing to Romans 8, the signs show creation in "eager longing" to be set free from its "bondage to decay."[34] The signs of the

30 Komonchak, "Redaction and Reception of *Gaudium et Spes*," 5, esp. n. 14.
31 Chenu, "Les signes des temps," 32–33.
32 Chenu, "Les signes des temps," 34.
33 Chenu, "Les signes des temps," 37.
34 Chenu, "Les signes des temps," 37.

times reveal the aspirations and even the expectation of the Messiah; they reveal "the coherence of the Gospel with the hope of humankind."[35] Just as the Fathers of the Church saw the Roman Empire's values of order, justice, and law, and its literary and cultural riches as various *preparationes evangelica*, so, too, is it the case with the contemporary situation. It, too, contains "possible resources in preparation for the Gospel, good material for the construction of the Kingdom of God."[36]

Chenu's optimism does not conflate Christianity—supernatural and gratuitous—with human progress,[37] nor is his optimism oblivious to the risks involved in this project. He simply does not invest much time in assessing them. There are risks, certainly, but there is, for Chenu, echoing the Pastoral Constitution, great opportunity "for the Christian who will have to discern [the signs] and measure them in light of her faith and under the instinct of her charity."[38]

The signs of the times ultimately function, then, for Chenu, as something that can enrich the church's mission to evangelize. Subordinate to this—but with just as much, if not more ink dedicated to it—is the call for the church to acknowledge its historicity or temporal nature, to be open to new developments within the church, to heed the questions of contemporary society, to affirm the positive values that the world has both begun to embody and to which it beckons the church to respond.

SIGNS OF THE TIMES FOR SUBSEQUENT TWENTIETH-CENTURY CATHOLIC THEOLOGIANS

Similar to Chenu's line is someone like the Third Order Dominican and Schillebeeckx scholar Erik Borgman, for whom "recognizing the signs of the times means finding the places where one can see that the reign of God is in the

---

35 Chenu, "Les signes des temps," 35. Another significant word is *disponibilité* (36), which denotes an openness, readiness, or even willingness.

36 Chenu, "Les signes des temps," 38.

37 Chenu offers one crucial paragraph that reins in what otherwise might be considered "correlationism-gone-wild": "D'aucune manière la construction du monde et la promotion de l'homme ne débouchent de soi sur l'avènement du Royaume; ni la nature ni l'histoire n'ont capacité de révéler le mystère de Dieu: sa Parole vient 'd'en haut,' par l'initiative d'un amour gratuit, s'engageant dans une communion amoureuse. La grâce est grâce, et l'histoire profane n'est pas source de salut. L'Evangélisation est d'un autre ordre que la civilisation" (Chenu, "Les signes des temps," 36).

38 Chenu, "Les signes des temps," 38.

process of breaking through, seeing where that breakthrough is at stake and where the struggle to bring it about is being carried on."[39] Borgman's take is like Chenu's: the *signs of the times* are closely akin to *semen evangelii*, Gospel values in inchoate form, sometimes flourishing, sometimes struggling, and always in need of divine aid.

Contemporary Catholic theology, however, includes a more radical interpretation of the signs that makes of them not so much markers of a context in need of a pastoral response that brings to it the grace of Christ but rather privileged indicators for steering and shaping the church's doctrine and practice. In other words, the signs begin to dictate the terms of *aggiornamento*.[40] For example, Massimo Faggioli appeals to the signs of the times in order to recognize a culture of "communicative dissent" in both society and within the church. With the "the present time" as a *locus theologicus*,[41] the learning church can look into the world and see "where the gospel already exists even without the church, and where the church can recognize it and be inspired by it."[42]

Whether or not such a schema is in keeping with *Gaudium et Spes*, however, is disputable. Does not an assertion such as : "*Gaudium et Spes* faced new issues and addressed old issues . . . in light of the 'signs of the times,'"[43]

---

39 Erik Borgman, *Want de plaats waarop je staat is heilige grond: God als onderzoeksprogramma* (Amsterdam: Uitgeverij Boom, 2008), 68, translated by and quoted in Van Stichel and De Maeseneer, "*Gaudium et spes*," 67–68.

40 An excellent summary and analysis of this trend with numerous examples, especially from the German-speaking theological context, can be found in Thomas Marschler, "Signs of the Times as a New Locus Theologicus?" *Church Life Journal*, August 18, 2022, https://churchlifejournal.nd.edu/articles/signs-of-the-times-as-a-new-locus-theologicus/#_ftnref53. In the North American context, see, for example, Massimo Faggioli, "Reading the Signs of the Times through a Hermeneutics of Recognition: *Gaudium et Spes* and Its Meaning for a Learning Church," *Horizons* 43 (2016): 339.

41 Faggioli, "Reading the Signs of the Times," 345. Cf. Chenu's position, as summarized by Sander, in "Theologischer Kommentar," 660.

42 Faggioli, "Reading the Signs of the Times," 345. Judith Gruber, appealing to a roundtable contribution by Richard Gaillardetz, goes so far as to assert that the contestations around social justifice are "signs of the times" and that they "are of highest theological authority for ecclesial theology." See Judith Gruber, "Conclusion: Dissent in the Roman Catholic Church; A Response," *Horizons* 45, no. 1 (2018): 157. In a similar vein, theologians place scripture and tradition, on the one hand, and the signs of the times, on the other, on the same level as dual authorities. See, for example, the theologian's contributions in this popular theological interview conducted by Inés San Martín, "Experts Debate Meaning of 'Synodality' for Global Church," *Crux*, June 13. 2022, https://cruxnow.com/church-in-the-americas/2022/06/experts-debate-meaning-of-synodality-for-global-church.

43 Massimo Faggioli, "The Battle over *Gaudium et Spes* Then and Now: Dialogue with the Modern World after Vatican II," *Origins* 42, no. 34 (2013): 546.

completely reverse the dynamic of the Constitution according to which the "new issues" we face are indicated by the signs of the times, and these signs, in turn, are to be addressed, not as Faggioli states, "in light of the 'signs of the times,'" but rather *in light of the Gospel*? Characteristic of this trend is a confusion about what is illuminating what.

In much of contemporary theology, the signs of the times are used to exhort the theologian to rethink certain interpretations of the Gospel in light of the contemporary context. According to this interpretation, the signs challenge the church to examine critically itself and its tradition, and the way in which it is attempting to transmit the Gospel.[44] According to such interpretations, scrutinizing the signs is not simply at the service of a more effective evangelization or a more pastorally sensitive response to contemporary straits. Instead, the *signs* take on a quasi-normative character because they help us find God here and now. The present helps explain to us the meaning of the present.[45] The signs take on a certain dogmatic weight [*dogmatische Größe*] because they are a constitutive part of the framework in which the faith is presented.[46]

At the bottom of this way of viewing the relationship between the church's teaching and the world is a radically contextual or historicist understanding of doctrine that relativizes any enduring content it purports to have. While these reflections cannot address this more foundational issue, it highlights the consequences of these two very different paths down the line, as it were.

---

44 See, for example, Tina Beattie, who writes, "If the custodians of Catholic tradition are to regain their moral authority as trustworthy interpreters of natural law, then they must recognize that it is and always has been a dynamic, culturally conditioned way of understanding how the human flourishes. . . . *This means reading the signs of the times*, and recognizing that what seems right and natural to one generation is likely to be viewed as anachronistic or reactionary by another." See Tina Beattie, "*Humanae Vitae*—Nature, Sex, and Reason in Conflict," *Pastoral Review* 4, no. 4 (2008): 60 (emphasis added).

45 Sander expresses this with more rhetorical flare: "in ihnen wird die schiere Gegenwart auf eine Praesenz hin überschritten, welche die Bedeutung dieser Gegenwart aufschließt" (Sander, "Theologischer Kommentar," 717).

46 Sander, "Theologischer Kommentar," 638–39. See also 624, 699, 725–27. Compare the slightly more restrained interpretation expressed by Yves Congar in "Église et monde," *Esprit* 335 (1965): 347: "L'idée demande à être précisée mais elle est, par elle-même, porteuse de signification. L'Église apprend du temps. Elle y discerne des moments et des faits qui intéressent l'histoire du salut. Les mutations qui affectent l'homme d'aujourd'hui ont leur impact sur l'Église et la théologie."

THE DIALECTICAL RECEPTION AND CRITIQUE

The controversy over Schema 13 (or what would become GS) during the council itself is well documented. At the time, critical voices with what Moehler called a more dialectical vision of the economy of salvation were effective in reigning in some of the passages that were incautious (to say the least). An earlier draft in Text 3 contained the words: In voce ergo temporis vocem Dei audire oportet ... [In the voice of time we must hear the voice of God]."[47]

It was ultimately on biblical grounds that German periti and the Protestant observer Lukas Vischer objected to an optimistic reading of the signs of the times as *vox temporis, vox Dei*.[48] Joseph Ratzinger points out that the jump from Matthew 16:3 to *vox temporis, vox Dei* was both exegetically and theologically problematic.[49] Christ, Ratzinger observed, was *the sign* of the time, not the secular *chronos* of the Roman proverb.[50]

The *vox temporis, vox Dei* line was thrown out of the earlier draft, and what was substituted in its place was the more theologically sober exhortation to scrutinize the signs of the times in light of the Gospel. Even so, the creativity in the deployment of the expression amounted to deanchoring the expression from scripture, thereby driving a wedge between scripture and pastoral teaching.[51]

Perhaps the most prevalent critique, persisting even after the council, is the document's persistent—but not exclusive—focus on the world's positive or humanizing tendencies, which uncritically seems to usher the church toward this dialogical stance.[52] As Ratzinger later pointed out, the tension—and even contradiction—between the Gospel and the world is understated. A theology

---

[47] Moehler, "Preface and Introductory Statement," 93.

[48] Moehler, "History of the Constitution," 36.

[49] See Ratzinger, "The Dignity of the Human Person," in Vorgrimler, *Commentary on the Documents of Vatican II*, 5:115. Ratzinger had already published some criticisms *during* the council as "Angesichts der Welt von heute: Überlegungen zur Konfrontation mit der Kirche im Schema XIII," in *Wort und Wahrheit* 20 (1965): 493–504.

[50] Ratzinger, "Dignity of the Human Person," 115. Gerald O'Collins echoes this view in *Fundamental Theology* (Eugene, OR: Wipf & Stock, 2001), 106.

[51] Mathias Nebel describes John XXIII's usage of the expression as "slightly different" and an "innovation" relative to both scripture and spirituality. See P. Bisson, "Breaking Open the Mysteries," in Verstraeten, *Scrutinizing the Signs of the Times*, 121–22.

[52] For a concise but informative summary, see Brandon Peterson, "Critical Voices: The Reactions of Rahner and Ratzinger to 'Schema XIII' (*Gaudium et Spes*)," *Modern Theology* 31, no. 1 (2015): 1–26.

of the cross yields too easily to that of glory; the recalcitrance of the world to its openness to the Gospel, sin to conversion, a broken nature to grace. The paragraphs on human sin (e.g., *GS* §10, 13) stand in an uneasy tension with what Ratzinger described as the downright Pelagian terminology in *GS* §17: "Man achieves ... emancipating himself ... he pursues his goal ... and procures for himself."[53] For its critics, a certain asymmetry in the document's tone-setting preface (*GS* §1–11) manifests itself in the weight given to the enumeration of the positive or neutral signs relative to their worrying counterparts in the modern world. Contemporary atheism (or infidelity, generally) is not counted as a sign of the time in *Gaudium et Spes*.[54] Little if any mention is made of materialism, historicism, moral relativism, and the "invocation of rights for bad ends," to name just a few.[55]

For his part, Joseph Ratzinger contends that *Gaudium et Spes*, ironically, presents a ghettoized understanding of the church because, by all indications, the world is defined in contrast to the church or as its counterpart.[56] If the "world" is the "totality of those human behaviors in which man is related to the shaping of his earthly forms of existence," then the world is inseparable from the human person. And if this is the case, then the world "cannot be neatly separated from and set in opposition to the Church ... thus the dialogue with the world is always to some extent dialogue of Christians with themselves."[57] What is at issue in this Church-world relationship is the precise way in which one's earthly existence is coordinated with one's eternal destiny.

---

53 Ratzinger, "Dignity of the Human Person," 138. This concern is shared by those who, for example, argue that the overly optimistic anthropology might be at least partially responsible for the drop off in the sacrament of reconciliation. See Luigi M. Rulla, Franco Imoda, and Sr. Joyce Ridick, "Anthropology of the Christian Vocation: Conciliar and Postconciliar Aspects," in *Vatican II: Assessment and Perspectives; Twenty-Five Years After (1962–1987)*, ed. René Latourelle, 3 vols. (New York: Paulist Press, 1989), 2:417–18.

54 *Gaudium et Spes*, no. 19. See Sander, "Theologischer Kommentar," 736.

55 J. Brian Benestad, "Doctrinal Perspectives on the Church in the Modern World," in *Vatican II: Renewal within Tradition*, ed. Matthew L. Lamb and Matthew Levering (Oxford: Oxford University Press, 2008), 147–48. A passing reference to materialism is contained in the more lamenting *Gaudium et* Spes, no. 10.

56 Ratzinger, *Principles of Catholic Theology* (San Francisco: Ignatius Press, 1987), 379. The parallel is the case with *Gaudium et Spes*'s apparent church-humanity dualism. See Ratzinger, "Dignity of the Human Person," 119. See also Tracey Rowland, "The World in the Theology of Joseph Ratzinger/Benedict XVI," *Journal of Moral Theology* 2, no. 2 (2013): 116.

57 Ratzinger, "Christian and the Modern World," in *Dogma and Preaching: Applying Christian Doctrine to Daily Life* (San Francisco: Ignatius Press, 2005), 168.

THE "SIGNS OF THE TIMES"

The biblical view of the world, by contrast, is described by Ratzinger as the "totality of behaviors contrary to the faith," or man's ambitions that are exclusively for this world and against God.[58] To the extent that the Christian separates oneself from God, the world is "in the Christian," as it were. Calling this "anti-God tendency" *world* indicates its universal character, in which everyone, including the Christian, finds herself.[59]

According to Ratzinger, *Gaudium et Spes*'s understanding of the world is not the biblical one. It is coterminous not only with *humanitas* but, more specifically, with *homines bonae voluntatis*.[60] Besides the vagueness of the dialogue partner, the text, according to Ratzinger, struggles to admit that the church "cannot stand outside the human race."[61] As Augustine claims, the church is not something separate from the world but *is* the world *as reconciled to God*.[62] In order to foster a dialogue with the world in contradistinction to the Church, however, this world had to consist of "the reasonable and perfectly free human being described in the first articles" of the Constitution.[63] Such a critique indicates that Ratzinger's unease with *Gaudium et Spes* is primarily attributable neither to its ceding too much ground to a theology of glory to the exclusion of the cross (although this is not irrelevant) nor to an alleged but false antihumanism on his part.[64] Rather, it is due to the document's insufficient account of the historical-existential situation of man, his sin, and the power and necessity of grace.

Despite Ratzinger's defense of the council as a whole, and of the merits of *Gaudium et Spes* in particular—namely, its presentation of a Christological anthropology that is all too easily bypassed—his enduring unease with the

58 Ratzinger, "Christian and the Modern World," 169–70.

59 Ratzinger, "Christian and the Modern World," 170.

60 Ratzinger, "Dignity of the Human Person," 117.

61 Ratzinger, "Dignity of the Human Person," 119.

62 Rowland, "World in the Theology of Joseph Ratzinger," 114. See also Congar's reference to Augustine's understanding of the church as *mundus reconciliatus* (*Sermo. 96*, 8) in Congar, "Église et monde," 348.

63 Ratzinger, "Dignity of the Human Person," 120.

64 Tracey Rowland defends Ratzinger's critique of *Gaudium et Spes* against those who caricature his position as "antiworld" or pessimistic. See Rowland, "World in the Theology of Joseph Ratzinger," 109–32. Cf. Ratzinger, "Dignity of the Human Person," 119–20.

general tenor of *Gaudium et Spes* can be traced, in part, to his work on St. Augustine, especially the latter's doctrine of the two cities.[65]

For Augustine, the City of God and the City of Man are "different from and inimical to one another." One of them lives according to the "flesh" and "man"; the other according to the spirit and God.[66] The City of God and the City of Man, then, are not only different but opposed. The latter is a constant source of temptation, a distraction from, and even an obstacle in the path to, the City of God.[67]

Ratzinger observes that each city is its own community of love [*Liebesgemeinschaft*] and worship [*Kultgemeinschaft*] but with inverted objects: the love and worship of the highest good and the idolatry of lower goods; an openness to the other, and self-closing.[68]

Elsewhere, Ratzinger further explains that for Augustine, this community and cult, dedicated to God for the sake of heavenly beatitude, is chiefly a cult of the heart [*Herzenskult*]: "Cum ad illum sursum est, eius est altare cor nostrum."[69] The signs by which it is chiefly recognized are not achievements that witness to this world but instead its sacramental participation in Christ's

---

65 One of the more focused treatments of Augustine's two-cities doctrine is in Ratzinger's doctoral dissertation, *Volk und Haus Gottes in Augustins Lehre von der Kirche*, in *Joseph Ratzinger Gesammelte Schriften*, vol. 1 (Freiburg-i.-Br.: Herder, 2011). For his treatment of the two cities, see 367–80.
For a defense of the thesis that these theological options—Thomist or Augustinian—help account for the very different perceptions of *Gaudium et Spes*, see Komonchak, "The Redaction and Reception of *Gaudium et Spes*." For Komonchak's criticism of Rowland's particular deployment of the same categories and of her criticisms of the Council text, see Komonchak's "'A Postmodern Augustinian Thomism?'" in *Augustine and Postmodern Thought: A New Alliance against Modernity?* ed. L. Boeve, M. Lamberigts, and M. Wisse, Bibliotheca Ephemeridum Theologicarum Lovaniensium 219 (Leuven: Peeters, 2009), 123–46.
For a well-argued and necessary corrective to using "neo-augustinian" and "neo-thomist" as tropes to describe a rigid pessimism and open optimism toward the world, respectively, see Frederick Christian Bauerschmidt, "Augustine and Aquinas," in *T&T Clark Companion to Augustine and Modern Theology*, ed. C. C. Pecknold and Tarmo Toom (London: Bloomsbury, 2013), 113–30, esp. 121–29.

66 Augustine, *The City of God*, ed. and trans. R. W. Dyson (Cambridge: Cambridge University Press, 2015), 15.27. See also 14.4.

67 For example, Augustine, *The City of God*, 15.18. See also Aidan Nichols, *The Thought of Pope Benedict XVI: An Introduction to the Theology of Joseph Ratzinger* (London: Burns & Oates, 2007), 32. For the influence of Augustine on Ratzinger, see also Joseph Lam Cong Quy, "Der Einfluss des Augustinus auf die Theologie des Papstes Benedikt XVI," *Augustiniana* 56, no. 3/4 (2006): 411–32.

68 Ratzinger, *Volk und Haus Gottes*, 376.

69 Joseph Ratzinger, "Herkunft und Sinn der Civitas-Lehre Augustins," in *Augustinus Magister, Congrès International Augustinien, Paris, 21–24 Septembre 1954*, 3 vols. (Paris: Études Augustiniennes, 1954), 2:977, citing *City of God* 10.

THE "SIGNS OF THE TIMES"

body. For Augustine, there is no fundamental collaboration between the City of God and the City of Man because such a collaboration would presuppose shared ends. But one either loves God before all things or does not. The City of Man is not neutral. It is not, for example, a good but incomplete end. Instead, it is hostile to the City of God.

In a preconciliar lecture on "The Unity of the Nations," Ratzinger offers a sustained reflection on Augustine's political theology.[70] Essential to Augustine's argument against Christianity's detractors after the fall of Rome is the Gospel teaching that temporal greatness is subordinate to eternal greatness and that, consequently, the absolute is always beyond the political.[71] Expressed in a Tillichian idiom, one might say that only eternity with God is of ultimate concern.[72] The upshot for Augustine is that the imperial success of Rome becomes a moral example. Ratzinger explains:

> the immense effort that people had committed to the transitory goal of an earthly state and earthly greatness should provide a powerful impetus for the believer to spend all his energies on the eternal goal that had become visible and accessible for him in the person of Christ Jesus.[73]

Ratzinger observes that, for Augustine, Christians ought to imitate the world's earnestness, but not the end toward which that earnestness is directed.

SUMMARY

For the optimistic or enthusiastic interpreters, the "signs of the times" is an expression that connotes a situation in which the church learns as much as it teaches. It assumes that the church, sent to be *in* the world, is inherently relational; that it takes the world seriously; and that it does not have a ready-made answer to all the world's problems.[74] Along with the document's critics, there is a consensus that the Constitution's most effective and lasting characteristic is

---

70 Joseph Ratzinger, "Die Einheit der Nationen: Eine Vision der Kirchenväter," in *Gesammelte Schriften*, 1:553–607; English translation by Boniface Ramsey in *The Unity of the Nations: A Vision of the Church Fathers* (Washington, DC: The Catholic University of America Press, 2015).

71 Ratzinger, *Unity of the Nations*, 77–83.

72 Ratzinger, *Unity of the Nations*, 88–101.

73 Ratzinger, *Unity of the Nations*, 92.

74 Chenu, "Les signes des temps," 39.

not its content—which is acknowledged to be a context-dependent prudential judgment about particulars—but the change it sought in conceptualizing the church's relationship to the world. It was a counter-syllabus to the ninth and tenth Pian popes. Ratzinger and O'Malley, for example, could not agree more on what the document sought and in fact achieved. It seems they simply disagree on how the document is to be evaluated.[75] Joseph Komonchak, when summarizing Ratzinger's attitude toward *Gaudium et Spes,* and referring to Chenu's image of the toothing stones, declares that, for Ratzinger, "there are no cultural or social *pierres d'attente.* Instead, dichotomies abound, contrasts between the Christian notions of truth, freedom, nature, and those current in Western culture."[76]

To fill out this comparison, we now to turn to a consideration of the signs as they appear in Scripture and how Newman understands them.

SIGNS OF THE TIMES IN SCRIPTURE

THE SIGNS IN THE SYNOPTIC
ESCHATOLOGICAL DISCOURSES

Before we look to Matthew 16 (to which John XXIII's *Humanae Salutis* refers), we would do well to consider briefly the theology of the signs more generally among the eschatological discourses in the synoptics.[77] Matthew 24, Mark 13, and Luke 21 are not identical but parallel discourses on signs. Of particular note is that the apocalyptic discourses in all three synoptics are situated right between the end of Jesus' ministry and the beginning of his passion. His preaching of the kingdom is punctuated by a final discourse on the hostility and provocation caused by the advent of this kingdom. And this same hostility between his disciples and the world sets the stage for his crucifixion.[78]

While Matthew and Luke contain unique material relative to Mark, all three share (1) the foretelling of the Temple's destruction and the question posed about the "signs" that will accompany this event; (2) persecution and

---

[75] For example, Ratzinger, *Principles of Catholic Theology,* 379.

[76] Joseph A. Komonchak, "The Church in Crisis: Pope Benedict's Theological Vision," *Commonweal,* June 3, 2005, 13.

[77] Here, the synoptic "signs" are different to the Johannine "signs," which are tantamount to divine epiphanies.

[78] Cf. Eric Franklin, "Luke," in *The Oxford Bible Commentary*, ed. John Barton and John Muddiman (Oxford: Oxford University Press, 2001), 953.

THE "SIGNS OF THE TIMES"

false prophets; (3) the "signs" in the sky and the coming of the Son of Man; and (4) the parable of the fig tree.

The first two are concerned about the course of history and its ambiguity (i.e., the destruction of Jerusalem and the false signs and prophets). Jesus' teaching about the End includes clear warnings against false signs and messiahs, constituting a certain "dampening down" of an enthusiasm for the End, which is ultimately unpredictable.[79] Luke's Gospel especially tries to explain the delay of the Parousia (v. 9: "for this must first take place, but the end will not be at once"). But once one gets to (3), the text turns to the end of history.[80] While the discourses' more immediate concern as a whole may have to do with Jerusalem's destruction, they do not preclude a more ultimate eschatological meaning: the end of Jerusalem is the foreshadowing of the end of the world.[81]

In the Lucan version of number 3, Jesus teaches:

> there will be signs in sun and moon and stars, and upon the earth distress of nations in perplexity at the roaring of the sea and the waves, men fainting with fear and foreboding of what is coming on the world (Lk 21: 25–26).

In Matthew's version, the "sun will be darkened and the moon will not give its light" (v. 29), which darkness relates the predicted end with an allusion to the beginning in Genesis 1:2.[82] These signs are cosmic and open for all to see, constituting a "break-up of the present cosmic order,"[83] and they can be likened to a standard raised up in battle for the soldiers to follow, if, indeed, it is the case that sign here means nēs, or ensign.[84]

---

79 C. M. Tuckett, "Mark," in Barton and Muddiman, *Oxford Bible Commentary*, 913.

80 Tuckett, "Mark," 914, commenting on Mark 13:24ff: "With the next verse, the scene changes dramatically and quite clearly to the future. Now we have a description of the End itself."

81 I am following the fourth interpretative option set out by Dale C. Allison, "Matthew," in Barton and Muddiman, *Oxford Bible Commentary*, 876: "A fourth approach also thinks of both 70 CE *and* the end. Unlike the third, however, it finds not a chronological sequence—the destruction of the temple, then (soon) the end—but a single prophecy with two fulfilments." For a more theological approach to the same, see *The Navarre Bible: New Testament* (Dublin: Four Courts, 2008), 338.

82 Allison, "Matthew," 877.

83 Tuckett, "Mark," 914.

84 Allison, "Matthew," 877: "The Son of Man will signal the eschatological battle by raising an eschatological sign. . . . The old tradition that the cross will accompany Jesus at his Parousia has a straightforward explanation if 'sign' means nēs, for the nēs had a crossbar and would naturally have encouraged Christians to think of a cross." (Cf. Isa 11:10; 13:2–4.)

Jesus later exhorts his disciples to be alert and watchful, to pay attention to these signs, for they indicate the coming of the Son of Man in Matthew and Mark (or of the kingdom in Luke). Nevertheless, the true signs will be there for all to see, that is, if one pays attention. The signs are like the leaves of the fig tree: when the leaves shoot forth, one knows summer is near. The parable is meant to communicate that no esoteric "insider" information is needed; the coming of the end should be obvious, provided one pays attention.

In Luke's discourse, Jesus is particularly insistent on the sobriety and focus that must accompany this watchfulness, lest someone be caught off guard due to pursuits of pleasure and the "cares of this life" (Lk 21:34). In a similar vein, Matthew's Gospel alludes to the carousing of Noah's generation caught off guard by the flood (Mt 24:37–39). Boring and Craddock rightly observe that Jesus is encouraging not speculation about an unpredictable future but obedience and fidelity. This is why Jesus teaches to turn toward the Lord and rely on his mercy: "But watch at all times, praying that you may have strength to escape all these things that will take place, and to stand before the Son of man" (Lk 21:36). In this respect, Dale C. Allison observes that "Eschatology does not simply console: it also demands discernment and adherence to Jesus' commands. The eschatological imagination does not displace practical moral concern."[85] The eschatological discourse is not so much about predicting the future as it is an exhortation to repentance and service in preparation for Jesus' second coming.[86]

MATTHEW 16 AND THE SIGNS OF THE TIMES

The context of this passage is important, as the entire test with the Pharisees and Sadducees is against the backdrop of the Matthean dualistic tension between two kingdoms.[87] It is also not the first time members of the Jewish leadership are asking for a sign (the other is in Mt 12, while the parallel is in Mk 8). The exchange precedes both (i) Peter's confession, (ii) Peter's rebuke, and (iii) Jesus' teaching on discipleship. First, Jesus repeats to his enemies

---

85 Allison, "Matthew," 876.

86 M. Eugene Boring and Fred B. Craddock, *The People's New Testament Commentary* (Louisville: Westminster John Knox, 2009), 264–66. On the parallel passage in Mark on
158: "Mark warns against eschatological speculation. . . . The responsibility of his slaves is to carry out their responsibilities during the master's absence."

87 Boring and Craddock, *People's New Testament Commentary*, 68.

THE "SIGNS OF THE TIMES"

that he will only give them the sign of Jonah because they have no faith; next, Peter confesses his faith in Christ; then Jesus admonishes Peter for dodging the cross. Finally, the chapter ends with Jesus' instruction on discipleship.

Such considerations become more important if one offers a narrative reading of the entire Gospel. The background to the signs of the times, then, is a tension between the way the world thinks and the way God thinks. Peter embodies this tension in his oscillation between thinking the way God thinks ("flesh and blood has not revealed this to you, but my Father who is in heaven") and thinking the way man thinks ("for you are not on the side of God, but of men" [RSV]. The NIV renders it as: "You do not have in mind the concerns of God, but merely human concerns.") The same proud, skeptical, and self-absorbed dynamic is at play in Matthew 16:1–4. Jesus has just multiplied loaves to feed four thousand (Mt 15:32–39), but then Jesus is confronted with this:

> And the Pharisees and Sadducees came, and to test him they asked
> him to show them a sign from heaven.

The Greek here is *semeion*, not *dynamis*, the common word for miracle. The Pharisees and Sadducees are looking not for some wonder but for some divine testimony. Jesus will refuse them, for they are spiritually blind; nothing he has done or can do will be enough for them.

> He answered them, "When it is evening, you say, 'It will be fair weather;
> for the sky is red.' And in the morning, 'It will be stormy today, for the
> sky is red and threatening.' You know how to interpret the appearance
> of the sky, but you cannot interpret the signs of the times. An evil and
> adulterous generation seeks for a sign, but no sign shall be given to it
> except the sign of Jonah." So he left them and departed.

Against the backdrop of the two rival kingdoms in Matthew, the Pharisees and Sadducees embody the way of seeing things, not as God does but as man does. That is why Jesus can tell the Pharisees and Sadducees that they are well able to discern the weather, but due to their lack of faith, they cannot discern spiritual things, including the very obvious eschatological sign of Jesus himself, who is the ultimate "sign from heaven" that Jesus' interlocutors sought.[88] It is one thing to read the signs of the world but quite another to read

---

88 Allison, "Matthew," 864.

the signs from the kingdom of Heaven. Without faith, one is preoccupied with the concerns of this world and cannot read the signs. The only sign Jesus will offer is the sign of Jonah, or Jesus' exit after three days, not from the belly of the whale but from the depths of the tomb.

This is significant. Jesus' offering of his own resurrection as a sign is a choice one for a Sadducee who denies its possibility *a priori*.[89] But any other allusion that might be evoked is confirmed earlier in Matthew 12, where this very sign of Jonah is spelled out:

> The men of Nin'eveh will arise at the judgment with this generation and condemn it; for they repented at the preaching of Jonah, and behold, something greater than Jonah is here. (Mt 12:41)

The sign of Jonah is not simply his being spit out of the whale but his preaching,[90] which the Ninevites took to be a sign, in reaction to which they repented and thereby received new life. The dynamic is the same with Jesus, but in reverse order. Jonah exits the whale and then preaches repentance; Jesus preaches repentance, and then rises from the dead. There is, then, with this allusion to the Ninevites, coupled with Jesus' naming his adversaries "an evil and adulterous generation," an exhortation to repentance.[91]

The second reference in the first test of Matthew 12 is to the Queen of the South, or the Queen of Sheba. In 1 Kings 10, the Queen of Sheba travels to Solomon to inquire whether all that she has heard about his wisdom is true; her face-to-face visit with Solomon confirms and surpasses the reports she had received. Jesus reminds the Pharisees and Sadducees of this story:

> the queen of the South will arise at the judgment with this genera-tion and condemn it; for she came from the ends of the earth to hear the wisdom of Solomon, and behold, something greater than Solomon is here.

Now it is true that the queen, having heard the reports only, was skeptical and did not believe them. But she goes to the trouble of traveling very far—from the ends of the earth—to seek and find. She had embarked on a quest, not for a

---

89 Allison, "Matthew," 864.

90 Benedict T. Viviano, "The Gospel according to Matthew," in *The New Jerome Biblical Commentary* (Englewood Cliffs, NJ: Prentice Hall, 1968), no. 81, 655.

91 Viviano, "Gospel according to Matthew," no. 81, 654.

sign but for wisdom.[92] She is an active seeker, and because of her disposition, the signs of confirmation she beholds—the wisdom of Solomon, his house and household, etc.—are enough to convince her of both the authenticity of the reports and, as a consequence, Solomon's wisdom. Jesus' interlocutors, on the other hand, are also face-to-face with Jesus, but they have not travelled far, nor are they convinced that he is the sign of God. Jesus' healings relayed in chapters 8 and 9 are not good enough for them.[93] They are testing Jesus, not seeking him.

In sum, the characteristics of the biblical understanding of the signs include, first, being on the lookout, or seeking the truth, and second, the necessity of conversion: in short, vigilance and repentance.

To the extent that the exegesis above is a sound one, it seems we have at least three understandings, then, of the signs of the times. First, we have the eschatological–biblical understanding of the signs; then (2) John XXIII's and the conciliar text's understanding of the signs; and, finally, (3) what we might call the "spirit of the council's" understanding of the signs. Matthew's Gospel contrasts the ability to read the signs of the world versus the signs from heaven. By intentionally using the expression in a nonbiblical way, *Gaudium et Spes* avoids teaching that societal developments (or signs of the world) are signs from heaven. The more enthusiastic interpreters of *Gaudium et Spes* risk conflating the two.

We can now turn to Newman's own approach to the signs of the times, which is ultimately a reading of spiritual—not sociological—realities. Newman's understanding, as we shall see, is more in tune with scripture and the critics of *Gaudium et Spes* than with John XXIII's and its further development.

NEWMAN AND THE SIGNS OF THE TIMES

Many theologians, such as Gerald O'Collins, state that scrutinizing the signs of the times is not simply about "taking account" of a sociological datum and reacting to it as a Christian but also identifying divine intentions behind it, positive or negative.[94] Like twentieth-century theologians, Newman views the signs as ways in which one can discern God's activity in history:

---

92 Viviano, "Gospel according to Matthew," no. 81, 654.

93 Anthony J. Saldarini, "Matthew," in *Eerdmans Commentary on the Bible*, ed. James D. G. Dunn (Grand Rapids, MI: Eerdmans, 2003), 1029.

94 O'Collins, *Fundamental Theology*, 105.

He still whispers to us, He still makes signs to us. But His voice is so low, and the world's din is so loud, and His signs are so covert, and the world is so restless, that it is difficult to determine when He addresses us, and what He says.[95]

Newman believes that, as in the Incarnation, God continues to speak through history; unlike for many of these theologians, however, the signs are not inchoate manifestations of the kingdom breaking into history but usually foreboding signs of warning.

The signs are tantamount to what Newman and the scriptural tradition calls "visitations." They are historical events or circumstances that, to the one with open eyes, communicate a divine warning. Vigilance and obedience are, for Newman, the hallmarks of the Christian on the lookout, and what is sought is Christ's second coming.

Persons who are looking out for Christ are not only, in that they look out, acting in obedience to Him, but are looking out,—in their very way of looking out, through the very signs through which they look out,—in obedience to Him. Always since the first, Christians have been looking out for Christ in the signs of the natural and moral world. . . . wars, revolutions, and the like,—have been additional circumstances which served to impress them, and kept their hearts awake for Christ. . . . "There shall be signs," He says, "in the sun, and in the moon, and in the stars." One day the lights of heaven will be signs; one day the affairs of nations also will be signs. . . . We may be wrong in the particulars we rest upon, and may show our ignorance in doing so. . . . [but] It is better to be wrong in our watching, than not to watch at all.[96]

For Newman, following the Gospel of Luke, the signs are primarily negative and indicative of the end or, at the very least, draw our attention to the end that is sure to come because it was promised by Christ. The horizon of the signs, for Newman, is eschatological. He likens the signs of the times to those things which constitute the bleakness and "tumult" of this world and these, in turn, elicit in us—believers and unbelievers alike—an expectation of the

---

95 Newman, "Waiting for Christ," *Parochial and Plain Sermons* i–viii (London: Longmans, Green, and Co., 1907–1909), vi, 248, hereafter cited as *PS*.

96 Newman, "Waiting for Christ," *PS* vi, 245–46.

end. But whereas the unbeliever believes the church and religion will come to an end, the Christian believes that the world will come to an end.[97]

Akin to Augustine's two loves that determine the posture of two cities, the fault line between the church and the world (taken, again, in the biblical sense) is the object of their love and hence the object of their expectation: "Such is the difference between Scripture and the world; judging by Scripture, you would ever be expecting Christ; judging by the world, you would never expect Him."[98] There is, then, for Newman, a competitive, indeed combative, relationship between the church and the world, a relationship to which we will return below.

The signs of the times for Newman also challenge the moral conscience. The category is almost always used to describe some sobering reality that amounts to a call to penitence and humility, especially of those whom God has chosen.

In his novel *Callista,* for example, Newman mentions the signs of the times twice. In the first instance, the opposite dynamic is at work from that which is most evident in *Gaudium et Spes*. The dynamic of *Gaudium et Spes* is fundamentally correlative in that the church seeks common cause and cooperation with the world's desires that are noble and humanizing. In *Callista*, Newman casts the signs in negative terms that are the result of a fifty-year peace in which the hiatus in Christian persecutions accounts for their simultaneous proliferation and social ascendance. The third-century Christians in the city of Sicca, at least from appearances, seem to be thriving, or at least are enjoying a peace that allows them to immerse themselves in, and be accepted by, the local culture. But underneath this temporary peace is something foreboding. The Christians' increased immersion into Roman society renders them less the objects of scorn and more the causes of fear. Heathen philosophers are working out intellectual grounds for paganism, while Christianity's inroads into the lower-classes are seen as a threat. The tension between Christians and heathens is brewing underneath relations which, by all worldly appearances, seem steady and amicable.

> But, while the signs of the times led to the anticipation that a struggle
> was impending between the heads of the state religion and of the

---

97 Newman, "Waiting for Christ," *PS* vi, 238–39.
98 Newman, "Waiting for Christ," *PS* vi, 237.

new worship which was taking its place, the great body of Christians, laymen and ecclesiastics, were on better and better terms, individually, with the members of society, or what is now called the public; and without losing their faith or those embers of charity which favourable circumstances would promptly rekindle, were, it must be confessed, in a state of considerable relaxation.[99]

Newman's third-century portrait of Sicca is obviously a commentary on his own times. Amicable relations between Christians and heathens hide a darker reality which only the conscientious Christian on the lookout can discern. Those in the midst of these amicable relations, by contrast, are subject to a certain religious complacency. The tokens of the "state of considerable relaxation" that Newman mentions include sinful indulgences, poor catechesis, and mixed marriages. The amicable relations and religious complacency hid from view the true signs of the times, which was a pagan vulnerability anticipating an impending confrontation between the heads of the state religion and Christianity.[100] A facile treaty with the world, for Newman, leaves Christians unprepared for the confrontation that inevitably boils over between Christians and the world. To prepare, religious complacency must be met with a call to repentance.

This rivalry is found in Newman's other writings. In his *Idea of a University*, for instance, Newman uses the signs of the times within the context of a battle against unbelief in the nineteenth century: far from indicating the movements of a morally neutral world, the signs are in fact indicative of the "enemy's" movements. Like a soldier on the battlefield, Newman takes his cue from the signs in order to determine the next course of action.[101] Even when the signs are hopeful, Newman immediately warns that they should be "accompanied with Godly fear" on the part of those who are fortunate enough to witness them.[102]

To return to another example from *Callista*, however, Newman intends for a plague of locusts descending on Sicca to be a sign from heaven and a call

---

99 John Henry Newman, *Callista: A Tale of the Third Century* (London: Longmans, Green, and Co., 1901), 17, hereafter cited as *Call*.

100 Newman, *Call*, 16–18.

101 Newman, *The Idea of a University* (London: Longmans, Green, and Co., 1907), 385–86, hereafter cited as *Idea*.

102 Newman, *Sermons Bearing on Subjects of the Day* (London: Longmans, Green, and Co., 1902), 116–17, hereafter cited as *SD*.

THE "SIGNS OF THE TIMES"

to repentance. The locusts are described by Newman as a "visitation" and "an instrument of divine power."[103] As if the herd's sole purpose was to sack Sicca, they die soon after they move beyond the city, but, as if things could not get worse, "a poisonous element, issuing from their remains, mingled with the atmosphere, and corrupted it," and a pandemic breaks out in Sicca:[104]

> "O wretched minds of men! O blind hearts!" truly cries out a great heathen poet, but on grounds far other than the true ones. The true ground of such a lamentation is, that men do not interpret the signs of the times and of the world as He intends who has placed these signs in the heavens; that when Mane, Thecel, Phares, is written upon the ethereal wall, they have no inward faculty to read them withal; and that when they go elsewhere for one learned in tongues, instead of taking Daniel, who is used to converse with Angels, they rely on Magi or Chaldeans, who know only the languages of earth.[105]

First of note is that the sign Newman uses is not a positive sociological development but a terrible plague. Elsewhere, Newman deploys signs or visitations similarly. In his "The Rise and Progress of Universities," "the time of visitation" for Newman is associated with the "judgments of God," and this divine judgment takes the form of a "great pestilence."[106] Newman spares no risk in violating modern senses of decency: in *Callista*, the plague was sent by God. Newman's allusion to the book of Daniel is an obvious clue that the sign is meant as an unambiguous condemnation of the status praesens of Sicca,[107] and those who have a chance at reading the signs are those who are, like Daniel, not only spiritually gifted but also committed to the God of Abraham and Jesus Christ. Like Jesus' refusal to give another sign to the Sadducees and Pharisees for whom Jesus' previous works were not obvious enough, so, too, the meaning of this pestilence ought to be obvious for the people—including the Christians—of Sicca:

---

103 Newman, *Call*, 170.

104 Newman, *Call*, 176–77.

105 Newman, *Call*, 178.

106 John Henry Newman, *Historical Sketches*, i–iii (London: Longmans, Green, and Co., 1906–1909), iii, 117–20, hereafter cited as *HS*.

107 Daniel 5:24–28.

> So it was with the miserable population of Sicca now; half famished, seized with a pestilence . . . they never fancied that the real cause of the visitation which we have been describing was their own iniquity in their Maker's sight, that His arm inflicted it, and that its natural and direct interpretation was, "Do penance, and be converted." On the contrary, they looked only at their own vain idols, and at the vain rites which these idols demanded, and they thought there was no surer escape from their misery than by upholding a lie, and putting down all who revolted from it; and thus the visitation which was sent to do them good turned through their wilful blindness to their greater condemnation.[108]

Newman is explicit that the message of this visitation, like Jonah's sign to the Ninevites, is to repent, but only those who have the spiritual eyes to see it get it. Between these two examples in Newman's *Callista*, we can infer that the signs of the times for Newman are calls to repentance that need to be interpreted by those spiritually in tune.

Let us consider another example, this time not a fictional one from one of his novels but from his gloss on the scriptures and its relaying of divine visitations. In this sermon, "The Secrecy and Suddenness of Divine Visitations," Newman points out that the divine visitation of God in the form of a small baby brought to the temple for a routine purification of his mother was recognized by Simeon and Anna who had been "*looking* for redemption in Jerusalem."[109] There were clues and prophecies, but only those who were "on the lookout," as it were, could read the signs and prepare. The same is true of the flood in Genesis, the destruction of Sodom and Gomorrah, etc. Those who were busy with worldly pursuits—"they were eating and drinking, marrying and given in marriage" (Mt 24:38)—were not ready. And so will it be with the final visitation at the end of time.

> In spite of warnings ever so clear, considering how the world goes on in every age. Men, who are plunged in the pursuits of active life, are no judges of its course and tendency on the whole. They confuse great events with little. . . . "The sun was risen upon the earth," bright as usual, on that very day of wrath in which Sodom was destroyed.

---

108 Newman, *Call*, 178–79.

109 Newman, "Secrecy and Suddenness of Divine Visitations," *PS*, ii, 108.

THE "SIGNS OF THE TIMES"

Ultimately, Newman identifies a lack of religious zeal as that which inhibits a proper reading of the signs. He writes:

> Men cannot believe their own time is an especially wicked time; for, with Scripture unstudied and hearts untrained in holiness, they have no standard to compare it with. When the power of Assyria became great (we might suppose), the Jews had a plain call to repentance. Far from it; they were led to set power against power. . . . Probably they reasoned themselves into what they considered a temperate, enlightened, cheerful view of national affairs. . . . Certain it is, we find them connecting themselves first with one kingdom, and then with the other, as men who could read (as they thought) "the signs of the times," and made some pretences to political wisdom.[110]

In this passage, Newman sees the rise of Assyria as a visitation or sign from God calling the Jews to repent. They, however, think themselves wise (by the standards of the world) and engage in a sort of pragmatic *Realpolitik*, thinking they are reading the signs of the times in doing so. The above example goes to show how easily even religious or the "chosen" can be deceived, and how important it is to cultivate humility and a fear of God whilst reading the signs.

In another sermon, Newman commends a "religious waiting" for signs of Christ's coming. Such a waiter is willing, even at the world's ridicule, to maintain open eyes in obedience to the Lord's command. The final inference from such watching is something deeply personal for Newman and cannot be insisted on, urged upon, and argued for. Signs raise in awe the religious mind. Such seekers are those who are "thoughtful and conscientious"; they do their duty as they can.[111]

Just as striking but no less audacious are Newman's comments concerning Arius's "stroke of death that suddenly overtook him" as he was entering the city of Alexandria. For Newman, Arius's sudden death is Providence's way of stimulating the conscience.

> Though we may not infer the sin from the circumstance of the temporal infliction, yet, the commission of the sin being ascertained, we may well account, that its guilt is providentially impressed on the minds

---

110 Newman, "Secrecy and Suddenness of Divine Visitations," *PS*, ii, 112–13.
111 Newman, "Waiting for Christ," *PS* vi, 250.

and enlarged in the estimation of the multitude, by the visible penalty by which it is followed.[112]

The surprising death that visits Arius is for Newman a divine visitation that, for the spiritually attuned person on the lookout, is intelligible: repent and do not dabble in heresy, Arian or otherwise.

Before anyone is tempted to dismiss this excerpt of Newman's as theologically crass, the importance of Newman's careful wording must be noted: the sinfulness of the act (Arius's heresy) is not recognized as such by virtue of the extraordinary event (in this case, his death); rather, the extraordinary act is interpreted to be a judgment of that which has *already been established* as being out of the divine favor. Hence, Newman cannot be accused of some pedestrian fundamentalism according to which tragedy (or fortune) becomes a criterion for the evaluation of something. Rather, the purpose of the event qua 'visitation' is to harness our attention, not to reveal a divine smile or frown on something about which, before any such sign, we had no way of assessing. Signs direct our attention to some already-intelligible aspect about something, in this case, the perverseness of Arius's heretical teaching. The point here is that, according to Newman (at least in this passage), this perverseness could have been ascertained regardless of Arius's unpredictable death, in the same way that conscience's call to follow the moral law is there for all to hear, regardless of whether something extraordinary draws one's attention to it. The condemnation of Arianism is as obvious to the orthodox Christian as the call to repentance is to the practicing Christian. The signs of the times, in this respect, are not revealing something new for Newman: they are calls or reminders to return to Gospel principles.

From this, one can infer that, for the most part, Newman associates the signs of the times as occasions for divine judgment and human conversion or focus on God and his plan. And even when the signs are hopeful or neutral, what is crucial for Newman is the religious and fearful disposition of the one reading them.[113] Only the general outlines of God's plan have been revealed to us, whereas the significance of the particulars of daily life escape us except in

---

112 Newman, *The Arians of the Fourth Century* (London: Longmans, Green, and Co., 1908), 269, hereafter cited as *Ari*.

113 For example, Newman, "The Nature of Faith in Relation to Reason," in *Fifteen Sermons Preached before the University of Oxford: Between A.D. 1826 and 1843*, ed. James David Earnest and Gerard Tracey (Oxford: Clarendon, 2006), 209–10.

the measure that revelation can shed light on it, and this revelation is closed; hence, the interpretation of post-apostolic events is not guaranteed but requires a prophetic gift whose foundation is baptism, and whose perspicacity requires conscientiousness, a fervent spiritual life, and firm adherence to the Gospel.[114]

Latent in Newman's deployment of the 'signs of the times' is his more general understanding of the world and how the Gospel (or the church) relates to it. Let us turn to consider Newman's understanding of the world.

THE WORLD ACCORDING TO NEWMAN

For Newman, the world understood in its biblical sense has multiple meanings. At his most combative, Newman uses "the world," "unbelievers," and "enemies of Christ" synonymously.[115] In its most neutral sense, the world is the visible order or system of things which occupy humans, and this is necessarily so; God, in fact, ordained it. Things and pursuits in the world are good in themselves, but—and here is Newman's pastoral realism at work—they are not good in the hands of sinners.[116] "This well-ordered and divinely-governed world, with all its blessings of sense and knowledge," writes Newman, "may lead us to neglect those interests which will endure when" the world "has passed away."[117] Human aspirations—for example, the sciences of "good government, of acquiring wealth, of preventing and relieving want"—might be good in themselves, but they are dangerous and ought to be considered "enemies" to the extent that (i) they cannot deliver what they promise ("they are short-lived"),[118] and (ii) their visible and therefore more immediate presence in the world distracts us from the invisible world to which we truly belong. In a word, "they go far to persuade us that they have no other end" or, worse, they might convince us that religion is the problem and not the solution to the world's problems.[119]

---

114 Some might understandably ask whether Newman ventures too far on occasion. An example of this might be his speculation about the significance of the thunderstorm in Rome in the aftermath of the definition of papal infallibility. See Charles Stephen Dessain et al. (eds.), *The Letters and Diaries of John Henry Newman,* i–xxxii (Oxford and London: Clarendon Press, 1978–2008), xxv, 262, hereafter cited as *LD*; W. J. Sparrow Simpson, *Roman Catholic Opposition to Papal Infallibility* (London: John Murray, 1909), 273–74.

115 For example, Newman, "Waiting for Christ," *PS* vi, 238, 248.

116 Newman, "World Our Enemy," *PS* vii, 29.

117 Newman, "World Our Enemy," *PS* vii, 30.

118 Newman, "World Our Enemy," *PS* vii, 30.

119 Newman, "World Our Enemy," *PS* vii, 30, 34.

Hence, Newman exhorts a certain detachment from, and caution in, worldly engagement. For him, worldly goods are precisely that: goods. The fault lies not with things but with the human heart that fails to see in these goods gifts from God, and therefore, fails to see them as part of a larger creation that includes not only visible but also invisible things.[120] In this way, Newman shows his Augustinian detachment from temporal pursuits. For Augustine, those who live by faith "make use of earthly and temporal things like pilgrims: they are not captivated by them, nor are they deflected by them from their progress towards God."[121]

In addition to the temptations that are inherent in an intrinsically good world inhabited by fallen man, however, the Christian also has to confront the world in the diabolical sense of that which has been taken over by the powers of darkness through the sin of Adam that permeates the entire system. "The world lieth in wickedness" (1 Jn 5:19).[122] Good things, divinely appointed things, become perverted. Good and natural things, such as statehood and government, are sometimes achieved by breaking God's law, through bloodshed, for the sake of a debased, worldly honor.[123]

Not only, then, does the good world promise more than it can deliver, and seduce us and distract us, but it has also been corrupted such that, in pursuing worldly goods, it is an incredibly difficult task to enjoy those goods without partaking also of the evil concomitant with them.

In sum, then, Newman's approach combines a robust affirmation of the goodness of creation and human endeavor with a realistic appreciation of the temptations and distractions these pose, along with a sober view of the fallen human condition. More industrialization, socialization, literacy, etc., though not without merit, are no balm for the human condition.[124] "You must go to a higher source for renovation of the heart and of the will,"[125] he says.

Newman's appeal to a true and authentic peace cannot but remind one of St. Augustine, for whom the state of the heart or *caritas* is the maker of

---

120 Newman, "World Our Enemy," *PS* vii, 31.

121 Augustine, *City of God* 19.17.

122 RSV: "The whole world is in the power of the evil one."

123 Newman, "World Our Enemy," *PS* vii, 33.

124 For example, Newman, *Discussions and Arguments on Various Subjects* (London: Longmans, Green, and Co., 1907), 268, hereafter cited as *DA*.

125 Newman, *DA*, 273.

true progress.[126] Also characteristic of Augustine is the subordination of the visible and created to the invisible and uncreated, a recurrent theme in the *City of God*. Like St. Paul, Augustine reminds us that this world is passing away (cf. 1 Cor 7:31). Only in vain does one seek happiness in the "miserable pilgrimage"[127] that is the "transitory vapour of this mortal life."[128] In this temporal life, the "greatest of human attainment and exaltation is but smoke."[129] Believing in the Gospel is tantamount to God "by degrees withdrawing His servants from a world decaying and collapsing under these evils, in order to build with them an eternal and most glorious City."[130] The achievements of humanity are impressive, but transitory and disproportionate to our ultimate end.[131]

Practical knowledge, for example, not only fails to save us from our sins but does not even lead to moral improvement. The world's newest trends, technologies, recreations, and even knowledge are not only useless with respect to salvation but are not entirely neutral, either. While Newman's enlightened age sees these diversions as a help and a welcome distraction from life's darker sides, Newman sees in them distractions and diversions from the requisite confrontation with ourselves, our sin, and the grace offered to us.[132]

Everything from foot pain to the death of a loved one is not something to escape but a call to confront reality, our place in it, and its ultimate meaning. In other words, these events, pains, and sufferings are the opportunities God provides us to work out our salvation.[133]

In Chenu's schema, the world's aspirations and desires—however noble they might appear to be at first glance—are like the toothing stones onto which Christianity can latch itself and bring the edifice to completion. For Newman, the dynamics are the opposite. While speaking specifically about education, Newman's words, I think, can be expanded to apply to all the various aspects of human endeavor:

---

126 This is similar to Ratzinger's take on technological progress in Ratzinger, *Theological Highlights of Vatican II* (New York: Paulist Press, 1966), 159–60.

127 Augustine, *City of God* 17.13.

128 Augustine, *City of God* 7. preface.

129 Augustine, *City of God* 5.26.

130 Augustine, *City of God* 2.18.

131 Ratzinger, *Unity of the Nations*, 77–79.

132 Newman, *DA*, 261–68.

133 Newman, *DA*, 266.

> Christianity, and nothing short of it, must be made the element and principle of all education. Where it has been laid as the first stone, and acknowledged as the governing spirit, it will take up into itself, assimilate, and give a character to literature and science. Where revealed truth has given the aim and direction to knowledge, knowledge of all kinds will minister to revealed truth. . .But if in education we begin with nature before grace . . . we shall be doing much the same as if we were to indulge the appetites and passions and turn a deaf ear to the reason.[134]

Christianity is not added on to an already-sufficient edifice that lacks nothing except the elevation and transformation that comes from grace.[135] The world and human nature are not simply incomplete and in need of completion, imperfect and in need of perfection. Rather, they are broken and in need of conversion, reorientation, or—to use Newman's word—"recasting."[136]

It would seem that much of the difference between the view of Chenu and the conciliar commentators who follow his line, on the one hand, and the view of Newman, on the other, has to do with what contextual data—that is, the recognizable social movements and priorities of a given culture—are qualified as human aspirations. Because Chenu attends to generally positive developments, the "transformation" required of these developments amounts to ushering an already positive dynamic toward its Christian fulfilment. With Newman it is different. It is not the case that Newman simply focuses on negative aspirations. Knowledge, even functional knowledge, and technological advances are not inherently contrary to the Gospel, but if they are detached from God, these aspirations do not enjoy any dynamism toward the Gospel. They do not particularly reach out for it, as it were. Science, for example,—and, presumably other human endeavors such as progress in economics or international relations—does not "lead to religion."[137] In fact, human endeavours in themselves "tend to infidelity."[138] Without religion, science leads the mind "to acquiesce" to atheism.[139]

---

134 Newman, *DA*, 274–75.

135 Cf. Ratzinger, "Dignity of the Human Person," 119–20.

136 Newman, *DA*, 277.

137 Newman, *DA*, 298.

138 Newman, *DA*, 299.

139 Newman, *DA*, 300.

THE "SIGNS OF THE TIMES"

In this sense, the world's aspirations—insofar as they belong to a world that does not know God—are not toothing-stones; it is the church that is the foundation stone that can support, direct, and—with apologies for mixing metaphors—purify, the hopes and aspirations of the world. This is not to deny Newman's correlationism; for Newman, Christianity does indeed answer to the human person's deepest longings and aspirations,[140] but the locus of these aspirations is the conscience,[141] not the *polis*, and Christianity's answering of them involves a simultaneous transformation of them. The hopes and aspirations that come from a view limited to the "immanent frame" are by that very fact defective and misleading.[142]

In his own day, Newman was arguing, among other points, "that apprehension of the unseen[143] is the only known principle capable of subduing moral evil, educating the multitude, and organizing society."[144] With due reticence for speaking on behalf of someone else, I think it is fair to say that were Newman confronted with someone like Chenu today, he would not dispute the worthiness of attempts to subdue evil, educate the multitude, and organize society. He would simply point out that such attempts do not aim at, or lead toward, the Gospel, even though they are in dire need of it (for without it, they tend toward idolatry or Babel). Any evangelization, as a consequence, ought to appeal, not to earthly aspirations of a *humanitas* on its way but to moral conscience.

CONCLUSION

At this point, we are now in a position to compare Newman's understanding of the *signs of the times* with that of *Gaudium et Spes*. There are obvious differences. *Gaudium et Spes*, following John XXIII, deployed the phrase to characterize developments in history (or the world)—positive or negative, but with an emphasis on the former—which could be starting points for

---

140 Newman, *DA*, 277.

141 Newman, *DA*, 302–5. See also the commentary on these pages by David P. Delio, *"An Aristocracy of Exalted Spirits": The Idea of the Church in Newman's Tamworth Reading Room* (Leominster: Gracewing, 2016), 168–76.

142 The phrase is taken by Charles Taylor in *A Secular Age*. Cf. Newman's reference to "the frame of things" (*DA*, 298). See also how Newman characterizes a secular view of contrary intellectual positions in *DA*, 284–85.

143 The phrase "apprehension of the unseen" was substituted in 1872 for "faith" in the original.

144 Newman, *DA*, 304.

dialogue, mutual collaboration, and evangelization. It was a fundamentally correlational use of the term. Newman, by contrast, deploys the term usually to characterize moments—usually catastrophes—which seize us and shake us into repentance. According to *Gaudium et Spes* and both the theology inspired by it and inspiring it, the signs are "opportunities" and preparations for the Gospel, though with acknowledgement of the risks involved in pursuing these developments without the Gospel.

In a similar vein, the world in the conciliar schema is not an enemy but an ally whose potential is unfulfilled, similar to a broken, beleaguered friend who needs help. The world is not, to be sure, the helpless one on the roadside helped by the Good Samaritan, who really has nothing to offer, but a real mover and shaker, a player, a change agent who, the church recognizes, is susceptible to error and needs help.

As a consequence, then, because the signs are positive opportunities for the evangelization of a collaborative partner, the focus is exclusively on intersections, analogies, continuities, or correlations between the church and the world. The main concern according to this understanding of the signs is not repentance or the coming of the end. While repentance and the expectation of Christ's coming are not incompatible with *Gaudium et Spes*'s theology, the conciliar use of the expression is intelligible and theologically deployable without such concerns.[145]

Newman's usage, by contrast, is thoroughly biblical. *Gaudium et Spes*'s use of the expression was presented explicitly as not being so. A more traditional understanding of signs of the times includes this conciliar-correlational dynamic, but it also includes—and, indeed, emphasizes—the possibility that there are signs of God's presence in a mode of judgment, not of affirmation. But does that mean that there is ultimately no exegetical connection between the theology behind *Gaudium et Spes*'s usage and scripture's? Can we really declare (with McGrath) that John XIII's usage is simply different from scripture's and that, therefore, the former is in no way rooted in the latter?

I think the key here is the Christocentric focus on the signs highlighted by both Newman and Ratzinger, or to reintegrate into our understanding of the *signa* that forgotten phrase in *Gaudium et Spes* 4: *sub Evangelii luce*

---

145 For example, Sander's treatment of no. 4 in his "Theologischer Kommentar," 715–19, is representative.

THE "SIGNS OF THE TIMES"

interpretandi. Scrutinizing the signs of the times *in light of the Gospel* is tantamount to investigating what the light of Christ illuminates for us in the world.

In a way more helpful than many commentators, O'Collins provides a link between the synoptic (Matthew and Luke) understanding of the signs and John XXIII's more recent use of it:

> We find Jesus reproaching his audience for failing to read the signs of their times—namely, those indications in his person and work which pointed to the messianic climax of divine revelation and salvation (Mt 16:2–4). But in that case the signs of the times concerned the foundational history of revelation and salvation. Pope John, the council, the bishops and contemporary theologians, however, have attended rather to those signs which in their particular ways indicate God's intentions to reveal and save now: in short, the signs of the dependent revelation and salvation. The central question is: Where in the world and its history today does God appear to be especially present and active?[146]

As can be gleaned from this text, the link between John XXIII's usage and its biblical precedent is based on O'Collins's distinction between foundational revelation and dependent revelation.[147] As Lord of history, God is especially present and active (i.e., reveals himself) in certain events and movements in history, but the meaning of God's presence and activity in dependent history is determined by (or dependent on) the foundational events of salvation history. The "light of the Gospel," then, is what ultimately determines the meaning of contemporary signs of divine promptings (and *not* vice versa).[148]

---

146 O'Collins, *Fundamental* Theology, 102–3.

147 This distinction is substantially the same, though conceptually distinct, from the earlier scholastic terminology, *traditio constitutiva* and a *traditio continuativa*. Congar explains it like this: "They [the time of the apostles and the time of the Church] are different not only in that the time of the apostles is constitutive of the *objects*, whereas that of the Church is not; they are different even in the matter of the *traditio activa,* for the apostles were *inspired,* receiving the grace of revelation, whereas the Church is only *assisted* in transmitting and announcing it.... The difference between [the Holy Spirit's] action at the level of the apostolic foundation of the Church and the level of the ministry based upon it has been well put by Fr Deneffe himself, in the categories of *traditio constitutiva* and *traditio continuative,* which could also be termed *explicativa.*" See Congar, *Tradition and Traditions: An Historical and a Theological Essay* (London: Burns & Oates, 1966), 208–9. Congar's language is indicative of O'Collins's distinction: *traditio constitutiva* is an "apostolic foundation" (i.e., foundational revelation), whereas the *traditio continuativa* is "based upon it" (i.e., dependent).

148 A similar solution to the biblical and conciliar usage of "signs of the times" is proposed by Brian Pedraza, who, appealing to *Dei Verbum,* no. 8—which reads, "God . . . uninterruptedly

With this in mind, we can see that, while Newman's usage is simply more biblical, his theology of discerning the movements in the world in light of the Gospel in fact echoes the intention of Vatican II. In fact, his own sermon on the subject provides a theological commentary on *Gaudium et Spes* §4. Key to Newman's commentary is his Christocentric seeking rooted in the Gospel:

> When, then, a man, thus formed and fortified within, with these living principles in his heart, with this firm hold and sight of things invisible, with likings, opinions, views, aims, moulded upon God's revealed law, looks abroad into the world, he does not come to the world for a revelation,—he has one already. He does not take his religion from the world, nor does he set an over-value upon the tokens and presages which he sees there. But far different is the case when a man is not thus enlightened and informed by revealed truth. Then he is but a prey, he becomes the slave, of the occurrences and events, the sights and sounds, the omens and prodigies, which meet him in the world, natural and moral.[149]

This is a key observation by Newman: Christ and his Gospel are the measure of the signs of God in the world. While Newman's understanding of the phrase signs of the times is very different from the council's, his Christocentric attentiveness to the world is consonant with *Gaudium et Spes* §4.

To use the more contemporary idiom of O'Collins, the scrutinizing of the signs of the times—for Newman, Ratzinger, Chenu, and *Gaudium et Spes*—is squarely within the realm of dependent revelation; the signs' intelligibility is wholly reliant on what is communicated to us through the foundational revelation that comes to its peak in the Incarnation.

One reason for the struggles surrounding *Gaudium et Spes*, both during and after the council, was undoubtedly the drafters' desire to speak to "modern

---

converses with the bride . . . and the Holy Spirit, through whom the living voice of the Gospel resounds in the Church, and through her, in the world"—argues that "any revelation 'outside' the Church (in the signs of the times) is then ordered to union with God in the Church." This is because scripture and church teaching are "objective manifestations of the revelation already received by the people of God in the past, and, since the Church by nature is united to this experience, it must continue to be informed by it." See Brian Pedraza, "Signs of the Times: Origin and Meaning," *Church Life Journal*, November 8, 2022, https://churchlifejournal.nd.edu/articles/signs-of-the-times-origin-and-meaning/#_ftnref19.

149 Newman, "Waiting for Christ," *PS* vi, 251–52. See also 253: "He does not seek a Lord and Saviour. He has "found the Messias" long since. . . . His Lord Himself has bid him look for Him in the signs of the world, and therefore he looks out."

THE "SIGNS OF THE TIMES"

man," which, according to some who were working on the document, was impossible if one began with ultimate theological considerations. But as Ratzinger observed, it would be no better to begin inoffensively with points of consensus only to later concede that, from the Christian perspective, the world is lost without Christ.[150]

For Ratzinger, the most desirable path between brash pronouncement and a dialogue without teeth is proclamation. This might help explain why Ratzinger, with John Paul II,[151] honed in on the most kerygmatic dimension of *Gaudium et Spes*: their Christocentric reading of it finds its clearest expression in *Gaudium et Spes* §22, that famous and extensive paragraph on Christocentric anthropology that begins: "only in the mystery of the incarnate Word does the mystery of man take on light."

Ratzinger's incarnationalism is not a bald affirmation of the world. With Chenu, Ratzinger believes the Incarnation manifests the object of God's love: the world, *this* world. But in a way uncharacteristic of Chenu, Ratzinger prioritizes the cross—along with its contradiction and scandal—and the transformation it brings about as the end for which the Son assumes flesh:

> Contrary to the express assurances of those who based their optimistic way of thinking on the idea of the Incarnation, the idea of the Cross takes a clear precedence in the New Testament over the idea of the Incarnation.[152]

With this Christocentric reading of the document, the signs of the times are not cultural or societal thrusts of which the church is to take account in order to accommodate itself to them,[153] but rather concrete (i.e., historical contextualized) witnesses or manifestations of human aspirations that can be healed, purified, transformed, or fulfilled, but only by Christ's cross. The

---

150 Ratzinger, *Theological Highlights*, 153–54.

151 See, for example, John Paul II's *Discorso di Giovanni Paolo II nel XXX Anniversario della proclamazione della Costituzione pastorale 'Gaudium et Spes,"* November 8, 1995, https://www.vatican.va/content/john-paul-ii/it/speeches/1995/november/documents/hf_jp-ii_spe_19951108_anniv-gaudium.html. A partial English translation can be found at https://www.vatican.va/jubilee_2000/magazine/documents/ju_mag_01051997_p-28_en.html.

152 Joseph Ratzinger, "Catholicism after the Council," *The Furrow* 18, no. 1 (1967): 16.

153 This does not exclude the perennially important and delicate task of adjusting the Gospel content's terms of expression or style of delivery in order to render it intelligible in shifting historical contexts on the part of those involved in the transmission of the faith—for example, the theologian, evangelist, catechist, apologist, and, indeed, parent.

Gospel is not only "in harmony" with these aspirations; it not only enriches them: it is ultimately the only answer to them: "Apart from this message nothing will avail to fill up the heart of man: 'Thou hast made us for Thyself', O Lord, 'and our hearts are restless till they rest in Thee'" (*GS* §21). Further: "Through Christ and in Christ, the riddles of sorrow and death grow meaningful. Apart from His Gospel, they overwhelm us."

On a speculative theological level, if our exegesis, following Ratzinger's and others,' is correct and Jesus himself is God's sign of the times,[154] then the church, the sacrament of salvation, ought to be considered the sign of our times.[155] It is like a standard raised above for all nations to see (cf. Is 49:42; 59:19; 62:10). That is why, according to Ratzinger's gloss on Augustine's *City of God*'s ecclesiology, the sign and instrument of human unity is the church, whose unifying capacity is manifested at Pentecost.[156]

And yet such a view sits with us uneasily; wrongly understood, its latent triumphalism chafes. This is where, however, Ratzinger's contribution is so important. It is because his understanding of the words Church and world militates precisely against the "us vs. them" mentality, a mentality which caricatures of his thought seek to substantiate. The church and *humanitas* are not two communities at loggerheads. The church, for Ratzinger is the world, but the world *as converted*. The church is the world repentant, the Body of Christ penitent. And to the extent, then, that the church is not repenting, it is not signaling that salvation is at hand.[157]

---

154 Ratzinger [Benedict XVI], *Jesus of Nazareth: From the Baptism in the Jordan to the Transfiguration* (New York: Doubleday, 2007), 217: "One thing is clear: God's sign for men is the Son of Man; it is Jesus himself. . . . He himself is the 'the sign of Jonah.'"

155 The crucial point here is that the church as "sacrament of salvation" is, in fact, the sacrament of Christ. See Vatican II, *Lumen Gentium*, 1964, nos. 1, 9, 48; Cf. Vatican II, *Gaudium et Spes*, nos. 42 and 45; Vatican II, *Sacrosanctum concilium*, 1963, nos. 5, 26, 7; Vatican II, *Ad Gentes*, nos. 1, 5; Vatican II, *Presbyterorum ordinis*, no. 22.

156 Ratzinger, *Unity of the Nations*, 107–9. For the church as sign, see also 113–16; Ratzinger, "The Christian and the Modern World," in *Dogma and Preaching: Applying Christian Doctrine to Daily Life* (San Francisco: Ignatius Press, 2011), 179.

157 Lieven Boeve is no doubt correct in his hypothesis that Benedict XVI was distressed at "the immense lack within the church of what he perceived to be the most fundamental structure of the Christian faith: *metanoia*." See Lieven Boeve, "Conversion and Cognitive Dissonance: Evaluating the Theological-Ecclesial Program of Joseph Ratzinger/Pope Benedict XVI," *Horizons* 40, no. 2 (2013): 252. I believe, however, that Boeve in his assessment of Benedict's papacy does not do justice to the intrinsic relationship between *metanoia* and church, or the church as the world reconciled. Naturally, the question of the proper subject of the church and her holiness arises. It is a fundamental ecclesiological issue. For those who would disagree with Boeve's assessment, the reality of the church is more than the sum-total of her members; and those members reflect God's

THE "SIGNS OF THE TIMES"

Newman has a similar conception of the church–world relationship. The church is in the world and only "*in a process* of separation from it." "All Christians," writes Newman, "are in the world, *and of the world*, so far as sin still has dominion over them."[158] The outward conduct of Christians and unbelievers might not be radically different. The lack of visible holiness in the church is explained by Newman by the fact that first, there is actually not a lot of it, but also second, that part of this holiness, which is only in utero, has its beginning in repentance and contrition, which we do not see.[159] "Instead of attempting to judge of mankind on a large scale, and to settle deep questions," Newman exhorts us to "take what is close at hand and concerns ourselves," and to "work practically," for the "improvement of our hearts and conduct."[160]

Newman's program is a humble one to be sure, but its return to spiritual basics is not a rejection of, or aloofness, over the world but instead one at its service. *Gaudium et Spes*'s primary concern, on this reading, is to scrutinize and discern the signs of the times in order to offer a credible, intelligent, and intelligible presentation of the Gospel in response to the hopes and anxieties of humankind. Such scrutiny and discernment, not only of the sociological data but of the proper deployment of the Gospel remedy, require a series of virtues, intellectual and moral, that are cultivated through Christian discipleship. As Ratzinger argues, daily self-abandonment or Christian asceticism is the precondition for a "whole-hearted service" to the modern world, a relationship characterized by a loving responsibility.[161]

This life of grace, however, is impossible without daily conversion to, and watchfulness for, Christ. In other words, Newman's biblical understanding of the signs of the times is the prerequisite for scrutinizing the signs according to the light of the Gospel. Together, *Gaudium et Spes* and Newman teach us that, before the signs of the times manifest an in-breaking of the Gospel into our world, they are first a call to conversion. Or as Ratzinger echoes Newman:

---

grace to the extent that they participate in the church's life. On this question, see, for example, Jacques Maritain, *On the Church of Christ*, trans. Joseph W. Evans (Notre Dame, IN: University of Notre Dame Press, 1973).

158 Newman, "World Our Enemy," *PS* vii, 36 (emphasis added). Newman continues: "Though then, in our idea of the two, and in their principles, and in their future prospects, the Church is one thing, and the world is another, yet in present matter of fact, the Church is of the world, not separate from it."

159 Newman, "The World Our Enemy," *PS* vii, 37–38.

160 Newman, "The World Our Enemy," *PS* vii, 39.

161 Ratzinger, "The Christian and the Modern World," 177–78.

187

The decisive thing is the attempt to arouse the conscience and to summon it to responsibility before God, who has shown himself in Jesus Christ as Word and Love, which on the Cross became both the crisis and the hope of the world.[162]

Newman's and Ratzinger's view of the *signs*, though different from that of *Gaudium et Spes*, is indissoluble from it.

162 Ratzinger, "The Christian and the Modern World," 180.

8

APPROACHING RATZINGER'S INTERCULTURALITY THROUGH NEWMAN'S POWER OF ASSIMILATION

Jacob Phillips

Joseph Ratzinger was famously caricatured as a *Panzerkardinal* while prefect of the Congregation for the Doctrine of the Faith (CDF), implying he was eurocentric, reactionary, and unaccommodating to non-Catholic ideas.[1] This caricature was, of course, jarring for those familiar with his theology, many of whom consider it measured, attentive to contemporary thought, and undertaken in faithful humility to the church.[2] Few theologians regard the *Panzerkardinal* caricature as accurate, but there are still characterizations of the theology as eurocentric, retrograde, and intolerant. The most obvious examples come from Hans Küng, but more subtle examples crop-up in scholars attentive to

---

1 The term reappeared in an article by Joachim Frank in 2018: "Die Rückkehr des 'Panzerkardinals,'" *Katholisch*, March 21, 2018.

2 Cf. Tracey Rowland, in *Ratzinger's Faith: The Theology of Pope Benedict XVI* (Oxford: Oxford University Press, 2008), 9: "Ratzinger's Augustinian dispositions should not be construed as having anything to do with wanting the Church to retreat from the world, or wanting her scholars to close down conversations with the rest of non-Catholic humanity." See also Emery de Gaál, *The Theology of Benedict XVI: the Christocentric Shift* (London: Palgrave Macmillan, 2010), x–xi.

Ratzinger's work, such as Lieven Boeve,[3] who draws attention to Benedict XVI's "explicitly European programme" as having a pre-modern "neo-Platonic Augustinian vision of the world." [4] He acknowledges Ratzinger's contention that "truth is located in the great religious and cultural traditions of humanity" but highlights that Ratzinger's "first concern remains the relation between Christianity and the Enlightenment," which is, of course, an essentially European concern.[5] Moreover, Ratzinger's pattern for understanding that relation is the encounter of the classical world with Christianity. Boeve writes that the "providential marriage between Jewish-Christian faith and Greek (Platonic) rationality," rooted in Augustine, "conveys a profoundly dual understanding of reality," with "a hierarchical and asymmetrical view" of the relationship between "Church and world," which "tends to underline a clear distinction between both."[6]

Boeve concludes that Ratzinger's classical scheme results in a dualist theology that is ill-equipped to respond adequately to "multiculturality," meaning the contemporary situation of abundant "images of humanity and the world" rooted in a "plurality of religions and convictions."[7] This provides an impression of Ratzinger's theology as inimical to particularity, to the multiplicity of variations in ways of apprehending and expressing truth. The same criticism can also be applied to Ratzinger's "intraecclesial" positions, perhaps most famously around liturgy and worship, but with bearing on Catholic life more broadly.[8] This is the criticism that regards Ratzinger's perpetual recourse to the classical paradigm again to render the particularity of, and difference between, various expressions of Catholic life as merely superficial and never significant. As Boeve suggests, because everything is schematized in terms

---

3 For Küng, cf. his interview with *Le Monde* from February 24, 2009, "Pour le théologien Hans Küng, l'Eglise 'risque de devenir une secte.'"

4 Lieven Boeve, "Thinking Sacramental Presence in a Postmodern Context," in *Sacramental Presence in a Postmodern Context: Contemporary Sacramental Contours of a God Incarnate; The Presence of Transcendence*, ed. Lieven Boeve and Lambert Leijssen (Leuven: Leuven University Press, 2001), 3–37; Boeve, "Europe in Crisis: A Question of Belief or Unbelief?," *Modern Theology* 23 (2007): 205–27.

5 Boeve, "Europe in Crisis," 215.

6 Boeve, "Europe in Crisis," 219.

7 Boeve, "Europe in Crisis," 222.

8 Cf. Jacob Phillips, "After Etsi Veluti Si Deus Daretur: Joseph Ratzinger and Cardinal Robert Sarah," in *Joseph Ratzinger and the Promise of African Theology*, ed. Matthew Levering and Maurice Ashley Agbaw-Ebai (Eugene, OR: Pickwick, 2021), 98–121, 102.

of the classical context, particular developments in thought or practice are always superseded by the universality of Christianity as the Augustinian *vera philosophia.*

Approached intraecclesially, the issues at stake here pertain to theologies of culture. Multiple academic disciplines have in recent decades affirmed a deep, even incommensurable particularity between different cultures, which threatens to make Boeve's criticisms seem yet more acute. Sustained attention should perhaps therefore be given to Ratzinger's own approach to culture, although this area of his thought receives little attention in the secondary literature. Ratzinger outlines an alternative to the dominant Catholic theology of culture, inculturation, with what he terms "interculturality."[9] Interculturality seems at first glance to evince the same features that have occasionally made Ratzinger's reception contentious. It certainly makes more space for friction between Catholicism and non-Catholic contexts than inculturation, and indeed presents the encounter between Christianity and Greco-Roman thought as paradigmatic for all intercultural encounters henceforth. He also critiques the "transcultural," globalized provenance of consumer technology in a way some might consider hostile to contemporary life. At the same time, however, the "inter-" of interculturality points to Ratzinger's overarching contention that encounters between Catholicism and non-Catholic cultures can and should involve significant mutual interaction between each, resulting eventually in the universality of Catholic truth becoming profoundly intertwined with a particular culture. Interculturality suggests there are particular outworkings and articulations of the faith that can answer some of his critics and result in local and particular variations of the faith that are more than merely superficially different.

Ultimately, interculturality presents dynamics for understanding how the particular is elevated to having universal purchase or provenance; how one cultural setting can inform and enlighten other settings that share in the universal *catholicum.* In order to investigate how effective interculturality is in achieving this end, it needs to be brought into conversation with a

---

9 Interculturality is discussed at length directly in only two of Ratzinger's published talks: "Christ, Faith and the Challenge of Cultures: Meeting with the Doctrinal Commissions in Asia," March 3, 1993, https://www.vatican.va/roman_curia//congregations/cfaith/incontri/rc_con_ cfaith_19930303_hong-kong-ratzinger_en.html, and "Culture and Truth: Reflections on *Fides et Ratio*," originally given at St. Patrick's Seminary, New York, February 13, 1999, https://www. ratzinger.us/Some-Reflections-on-the-Encyclical-Letter-Fides-et-Ratio/.

context other than the encounter between Christianity and the classical world. This is because criticisms like those of Boeve imply that all Ratzinger's openness to difference really applies only to the classical context, and other differences ae approached dualistically and asymmetrically. For this reason, I want to explore how Ratzinger's dynamics apply to the encounter between Catholicism and the Protestant culture of Victorian England, which of course has its nexus in the life of St. John Henry Newman. This is fitting because it involves genuine conflict, resulting in what Newman calls "loss," meaning a loss of long-cherished elements of English self-understanding. But it also results eventually in an intertwining of Catholicism and received notions of Englishness that Newman calls "gain"; in which "our own habits of mind, our own manner of reason, our own tastes, and our own virtues" find "a place and thereby a sanctification, in the Catholic Church."[10] In short, the mature Newman sought to find space for Catholic universality to correct and sanctify English particularity, with absolutely no compromise to the truth of the former as the *vera philosophia*.

I have three tasks in this chapter: the first is to situate Ratzinger's interculturality in relation to other well-known theologies of culture of the twentieth century, to bring out the distinctiveness of his contribution to those discussions. The second is to highlight the marked similarities between interculturality and what Newman calls in *An Essay on the Development of Christian Doctrine* a "power of assimilation" that authentic Christian doctrine exhibits in encounter with the world at large. The third task is for me to demonstrate how Newman's power of assimilation can be applied to his own context, to the power of contemporary Catholicism to assimilate his own cultural setting. This will enable me to conclude by arguing that insofar as interculturality applies to Newman's life, Ratzinger's thinking can and does bear applications to contexts other than the classical world.

INTERCULTURALITY AMONG THEOLOGIES OF CULTURE

In two talks given during the 1990s, Ratzinger presented his approach to theology of culture as an alternative to inculturation.[11] These talks were

---

10 John Henry Newman, *Apologia Pro Vita Sua* (London: J. M. Dent, 1993), 296.

11 Cf. n. 9, and for a fuller discussion, see Jacob Phillips, *Mary Star of Evangelization* (Mahwah, NJ: Paulist Press, 2018); Jacob Phillips, "John Henry Newman and the English Sensibility," *Logos* 24, no. 3 (Summer 2021): 108–29.

given in ecclesial and pastoral contexts, so they contain little reference to the complex developments in theologies of culture of the preceding decades. It is nevertheless necessary to mention those developments in order to bring the distinctiveness of Ratzinger's contribution fully into view. Beginning in the period immediately after the First World War, theologians had been grappling with the emergence of "culture" as an apparently autonomous (nonreligious) domain of activity. The complexity of this task was then further intensified by the development of a more "global consciousness," with anthropologists intensely extenuating the depth of cultural particularity. Theologies of culture thus grapple with two closely related tensions. There is first the task for theologians to navigate ways of understanding non-Christian settings in ways that are evaluative or nonevaluative, which means deciding whether to present the faith as intrinsically superior to other worldviews or trying somehow to meet those worldviews on an equal footing. This immediately leads to a second tension, for a strongly evaluative theology of culture will obviously tend toward a confident universality, while nonevaluative theologies of culture are highly sympathetic to local particularity. The challenge of this second tension is to discern how to be sympathetic and attentive to local contexts without downplaying the intrinsically universal claims of Christian faith, or whether to forfeit one for the other.

The challenges at stake were first made explicit for academic theology by Paul Tillich, whose *Theology of Culture* remains an authoritative work in the field. Although the book was published in 1959, the positions he outlines there were first presented in a lecture from 1919.[12] As is well-known, Tillich considers religion to be "an aspect of the human spirit," meaning it is not "a special function of man's spiritual life" but rather "the dimension of depth in all of its functions."[13] This means there is no discrete or delineated realm of human experience to which religion belongs more than any other: religion is not a particular element among others and has no special domain within culture.[14] Tillich's term "depth" enables him to express that religion can pervade all elements of human life, insofar as those elements plumb the depths of the human condition, pointing "to that which is ultimate, infinite, [and]

---

12 Paul Tillich, *Über die Idee einer Theologie der Kultur* (Berlin: Reuther & Reichard, 1919).

13 Paul Tillich, *Theology of Culture* (Oxford: Oxford University Press, 1959), 5.

14 Tillich, *Theology of Culture*, 6–7.

unconditional."[15] The sphere of culture is always transfigured by the human longing for the ultimate, and this ultimate is the object of religion. Tillich writes that the "word 'God' is filled with concrete symbols in which mankind has expressed its ultimate concern,"[16] that is, God is the ultimate, God is that which is "beyond" or transcendent, not conditioned by material existence, by time and space, the limits of a perceptive standpoint, or, indeed, by culture.

Tillich's approach is evaluative, insofar as he provides a framework for distinguishing between meaningful culture (evincing depth) and meaningless culture (evincing the shallowness of merely "penultimate" concerns). This theology of culture certainly purports to have universality, but it does so at the expense of particularity. Cultural specificity is superficial and transient, pertaining to "concrete symbols" that can be disambiguated from their depth, or import, which is their ultimate and abiding concerns.[17] Indeed, Tillich's theology of culture is not only ambivalent to local specificity but at times even hostile to it. Perhaps understandably, given his experience of the Third Reich, Tillich goes so far as to problematize *locality* as itself tending toward division and hatred. For Tillich, positive developments in culture are victories of time over space. He connects conditioned time, or time bound to space, with cyclical repetition. Decisive events like the calling of Abraham break out of the cycle, leaving space behind with the emergence of an hitherto unforeseen future, the promised land.[18] An example of staying in the conditioned, penultimate sphere, by contrast, is shown in nationalism, which Tillich believes tends toward an atavistic re-emergence of paganism: "the elevation of a special space to ultimate value and dignity."[19] As he writes, "there are many soils and many sections of the earth and each of them has creative force for some group of people' and is 'consequently given divine honor'" by that group.[20] Tillich's theological evaluation of culture requires that specificity is removed,

---

15 Tillich, *Theology of Culture*, 6–7.

16 Tillich, *Theology of Culture*, 3.

17 The word *Gehalt* has been translated as "depth," "import," and "substance"; see William Schweiker, "Theology of Culture and its Future," in *Cambridge Companion to Paul Tillich*, ed. Russell Manning (Cambridge: Cambridge University Press, 2009), 142.

18 Tillich, *Theology of Culture*, 31.

19 Tillich, *Theology of Culture*, 31.

20 Tillich, *Theology of Culture*, 31.

or at least drastically minimized, for otherwise a "god of space" will destroy the universalism of ultimate concern.[21]

There are various problems with Tillich's approach that would require a lengthy discussion to be done justice here, but suffice to say that he provides a stark example of how an evaluative approach to culture can work against particularity. The main challenge for our present purposes is to ask how local, particular contexts might be approached more positively, with a less strident means of evaluation. H. Richard Niebuhr provides an early example of a non-evaluative approach, as his *Christ and Culture* (1951) is more accommodating to particular circumstances. Niebuhr gathers together different models for Christian encounters with culture and sorts them into "types," with differing degrees and styles of interpenetration between Christ and culture pertaining to each. On one end of the spectrum is "Christ against culture," for which Tertullian serves as the archetype, and on the other is "Christ as transformer of culture," for which St. Thomas Aquinas is the archetype.[22] Interestingly, when *Christ and Culture* was first published, there was some confusion about which, if any, of the types were deemed optimal by Niebuhr himself.[23] This is instructive, I suggest, insofar as what Niebuhr is attempting is to meet the challenge of universality by sidestepping evaluation by forfeiting the notion that particular cultural variants of Christianity are more proximate to Christ than others. The universality of Christ is represented by the range of options available, and by their mutual equidistance from Christ himself, who always stands above and beyond any particular culture. As Niebuhr writes, "every description falls short of completeness" when it comes to Jesus Christ, and so a particular perspective "must fail to satisfy others who have encountered him."[24]

Christ and Culture deals only with cultures that have come into some contact with Christianity, which perhaps enables a nonevaluative approach, insofar as one might assume that non-Christian cultures must surely be deemed as deficient (albeit with "invincible ignorance") from a Christian standpoint. It is precisely here that Catholic theology joins the discussion with the theology of culture that Ratzinger would later critique: inculturation. This approach is first outlined at length in the writings of Pedro Arrupe SJ, who applied two

---

21 Tillich, *Theology of Culture*, 37.

22 H. Richard Niebuhr, *Christ and Culture* (London: Harper Collins, 2002).

23 Niebuhr, *Christ and Culture*, introduction.

24 Niebuhr, *Christ and Culture*, 14.

elements from magisterial documents to the newly urgent question of relating culture and Christian faith after Vatican II. The first element is §53 of *Gaudium et spes*, in which culture is defined as: "everything whereby man develops and perfects his many bodily and spiritual qualities."[25] This means culture is edification (as in the cultivation) of human nature, the ordering of human life toward fulfilment and flourishing. The second element is §20 of *Evangelii Nuntiandi*, which states that the Gospel is "independent in regard to all cultures" yet "capable of permeating" every culture "without becoming subject to any one of them."[26] These statements provide Arrupe's basic coordinates for a scheme whereby culture itself is evaluated as always intrinsically good, as the tending toward perfection of human nature. If culture is intrinsically good, then the Catholic faith can take shape within (or permeate) the terms of any cultural setting. It means that cultures can by definition be ordered to Christ, for Christ is human perfection. As Arrupe defines it, "inculturation is the incarnation of Christian life and of the Christian message in a particular cultural context, in such a way that this experience . . . becomes a principle that animates, directs and unifies the culture . . . so as to bring about a new creation."[27] Inculturation is thus evaluative, but in such a way that all culture is more-or-less positively evaluated. It is also universal, albeit in a way rather like Niebuhr's, for all cultural settings are equidistant from Christ himself, who inhabits cultural settings from outside or beyond culture.

Before moving on to Ratzinger's criticisms of inculturation, it is necessary to touch briefly on two more recent contributions to the field. These contributions are specifically postmodern and challenge Arrupe's presupposition that Christ can inhabit cultural settings by coming from some domain beyond culture. The first is Kathryn Tanner's *Theories of Culture: A New Agenda for Theology* (1997). Tanner is a helpful interlocuter for this discussion insofar as she pursues the implications of a nonevaluative definition of culture more thoroughly than most.[28] She draws on postmodern anthropologies to untangle what are deemed Eurocentric definitions of culture as presupposing

---

25 *Gaudium et Spes*, 1965, no. 53.

26 Paul VI, *Evangelii Nuntiandi*, 1975, no. 20, https://www.vatican.va/content/paul-vi/en/apost_exhortations/documents/hf_p-vi_exh_19751208_evangelii-nuntiandi.html.

27 Pedro Arrupe, SJ, *Jesuit Apostolates Today: An Anthology of Letters and Addresses III*, ed. Jerome Aixala, SJ (Anand: Sahitya Prakash, 1981), 171.

28 Kathryn Tanner, *Theories of Culture: A New Agenda for Theology* (Minneapolis: Augsburg Fortress, 1997), 61.

"general processes of refinement" that destroy differences with an overarching framework, illustrating a typically postmodern unease about what Lyotard called "metanarrative."[29] *Gaudium et Spes* cannot survive this postmodern critique, of course, nor can any claim to universality, as such. Importantly, Tanner's utilization of postmodern anthropology means she defines culture as constitutive of human nature: it "makes human life from the first."[30] This works from the view that all definitions of being human are not only cultural products themselves but also that the parameters of being human cannot be disambiguated from the cultures that delineate them. This also means that theology itself is culturally constituted: theology *is* culture, it is always "historically and socially conditioned."[31] Arrupe's view of Christ as coming from outside culture is thus unsustainable for Tanner, as is Paul VI's comment that the "Gospel is independent of culture." Tanner thereby offers a theology of culture that is not only nonevaluative but accepts that radical particularity should supplant universality. For Tanner, any grasping at universality is always only the product of a particular culture and thus has imperial or colonial pretensions.[32]

The decisive postmodern development of culture's constitutive status does not challenge only Arrupe. It also challenges Tillich and Niebuhr, for prior to postmodern thought, theologians nearly always tended to think in terms of Christian faith and culture as two relatively discrete and autonomous spheres that can be differentiated from each other, even if only abstractly. This postmodern insight proves important for the final theology of culture to be mentioned here: John Milbank's *Word made Strange: Theology, Language, and Culture*. Milbank criticizes "approaches to theology which seek for it foundations supposedly prior to linguistic mediation,"[33] and, assuming language to be cultural, thus celebrates "the inescapability of culture."[34] He even goes so far as to claim that God himself is cultural, that there is "a cultured God."[35] This

---

29 Tanner, *Theories of Culture*, 5.

30 Tanner, *Theories of Culture*, 53.

31 Tanner, *Theories of Culture*, 63.

32 Modern universalist anthropologies are described as "vitiated by associations with nationalism, colonialism, and the power plays of intellectual elites" (Tanner, *Theories of Culture*, 38).

33 John Milbank, *Word Made Strange: Theology, Language, and Culture* (London: Blackwell, 1997), 2.

34 Milbank, *Word Made Strange*, 2.

35 Milbank, *Word Made Strange*, 80.

is not intended to surrender the notion of revelation but to approach culture "as an integral element of Christian being" and not "a 'problem' external to faith."[36] Unlike Tanner, moreover, Milbank's theology of culture is evaluative, albeit in a complexly nuanced way. He draws on Johann Georg Hamann's contention that language becomes "determinate and thereby fully conceptual through the *repeated* use of the sign in different contexts."[37] This implies that the repeated use of language by a specific community through time will develop into fruitful or effective or accurate approximations to that which is signified *by* language, which is itself never accessible apart from language. On this basis, Milbank freely uses supremely evaluative terms like orthodox and heterodox, presumably as terms built into a developed evaluative framework like that just described, namely the tradition of creedal Christianity.

However, a difficult question remains surrounding the universality of Milbank's approach. If there is no access to any purely extracultural reality, and our proximity to that reality is accrued by degrees in the highly particular realms of developing linguistic traditions, in what concrete sense can Christianity be universal? Milbank's answer to this arises in a discussion with Umberto Eco. He presents Eco's view that there are two options for theories of culture after postmodernity: "the only real cultural choice is between a clearly 'coded' and generally understood set of conventions on the one hand, and the control of interpretation by arbitrary authority on the other."[38] Eco defends "modern, liberal society" as offering the former of these, while Milbank presents thinkers like Derrida and Deleuze as having submitted to the latter.[39] Milbank, however, argues that theology is a "metasemiotics" transcending this aporia, because that which is signified by theology can never be collapsed into either a clearly coded set of conventions or the wielding of language with arbitrary authority. God's transcendence means that theology is, as it were, relatively immune (at least in principle) from being subsumed by particularity, that God's difference from language is always remaking and disrupting language itself, and that theology therefore has an ultimate breadth over time and space that all other semiotic systems do not.

36 Milbank, *Word Made Strange*, 79.
37 Milbank, *Word Made Strange*, 76.
38 Milbank, *Word Made Strange*, 112; see n. 92.
39 Milbank, *Word Made Strange*, 111.

Nonetheless, it is hard to discern how Milbank's scheme might indeed be as safe from collapsing into particularity as he wishes. For Milbank, we have no access to God *in se* apart from linguistic applications, which are always determined by use within communities. God's universality (or difference from particular semiotic expressions) can therefore never be articulated, as such: semiotic systems are all distant from God himself, albeit with degrees of proximity (or varying degrees of orthodoxy). This presents a situation whereby there is a concept of God as the ultimately universal meaning of Christian language, without any conceptual tools to articulate it *as* universal. We are left with a conceived dimension of universality obliquely residing within structures of determined meaning. Strangely, theologies of culture seem to have travelled full-circle. Tillich considers theology to articulate the "dimension of depth" to human culture, which expresses "ultimate meaning."[40] Tanner considers theology to articulate "the meaning dimension of Christian practices."[41] For Milbank, God is a metasemiotic fount of universal meaning that is never apprehensible apart from culturally determined meaning in particularity. Yet the original challenge remains: discerning how to arrive at a theology of culture that is evaluative without subsuming particularity to universality, or vice versa.

INTERCULTURALITY AND THE POWER OF ASSIMILATION

In this section, I will first show how Ratzinger's interculturality responds to the challenges presented by the trajectory of theologies of culture described in section 1 and then point to marked similarities between interculturality and Newman's power of assimilation. It is my contention that while interculturality is approached by Ratzinger as an alternative to inculturation, it bears certain characteristics that enable it to respond to theologies of culture more broadly, especially for the primary challenge of harmonizing evaluation with both universality and particularity. The first point to make in working toward this end is that Ratzinger critiques inculturation on grounds which apply to those who differentiate postmodern from modern theologians of culture. That is, he goes to great lengths to argue that Christian faith and culture are not discrete and autonomous realms. Rather, human culture is always already religious.

40 Tillich, *Theology of Culture*, 8.
41 Tanner, *Theories of Culture*, 63; cf. 70.

As he writes, "in all known historical cultures, religion is the essential element and its determining core."[42] Moreover, the same is true of Christian faith, especially Catholicism. There is no faith apart from its culture, as such. He always speaks of "faith *and* its culture" or of faith's "cultural physiognomy" and argues that a supposedly "pre-cultural or decultured Christianity" results in just "an empty collection of ideas."[43] Theology of culture is therefore intercultural, insofar as it explores the encounter between cultural subjects, not a decultured Christ and a cultural subject.

At first glance, this might seem nonevaluative, but Ratzinger does not take that route. On the contrary, interculturality is intensely evaluative. In the context of postmodern thinking—of suppositions about culture as constitutive of reality—this of course threatens to provoke allegations of imperialism, something Ratzinger acknowledges. But he points out that "mission" was not originally "perceived as expansion for the wielding of power, but as the obligatory transmission of what was intended for everyone and which everyone needed."[44] Theologies of culture, as we have seen, tend to adopt "meaning" as their primary category, no doubt because meaning serves as a primary category for the "human" or "cultural" sciences, the humanities,[45] but a preference for meaning tends toward relativism, insofar as it proves extremely difficult to posit one framework of meaning as somehow better than any other. Ratzinger avoids this problem by presenting a different primary category for this discussion, namely *truth*.[46] That is, while he accepts that Christianity is always cultured, and that non-Christian culture is always religious, he maintains that the most effective means of distinguishing and relating the two is to recall that Christianity is true. Here, he parts with postmodern thought. It is not

---

42 Ratzinger, "Christ, Faith and the Challenge of Cultures."

43 Ratzinger, "Christ, Faith and the Challenge of Cultures" (emphasis added).

44 Ratzinger, "Christ, Faith and the Challenge of Cultures."

45 On "meaning" as the primary categories for the humanities, see Wilhelm Dilthey, *Selected Works IV: Hermeneutics and the Study of History*, ed., with an introduction by Rudolf A. Makkreel and Frithjof Rodi (Princeton, NJ: Princeton University Press, 1996), also discussed in Jacob Phillips, *Human Subjectivity in Christ in Dietrich Bonhoeffer's Theology: Simplicity and Wisdom* (London: Bloomsbury, 2019), 120—23.

46 On truth as arguably the most pervasive theme in Ratzinger's writings, see his discussion of the scholastic "verum est ens" (Being is truth) in Joseph Ratzinger, *Introduction to Christianity* (London: Burns & Oates, 1969), 34, and his discussion of his episcopal motto "co-worker in truth" in his final autobiographical work, Benedict XVI and Peter Seewald, *Last Testament*, trans. Jacob Phillips (London: Bloomsbury, 2016), 241.

so much that truth is beyond culture, as that truth cannot contradict itself. This means that even if culture constitutes reality, two differently constituted apprehensions of reality can share common ground insofar as reality is being truthfully apprehended in each.

Put in terms of *Evangelii Nuntiandi*, then, Ratzinger would disagree that "the Gospel is independent of culture" if we take this to mean that the transmission of the Gospel is not itself always configured by the cultural history of the Gospel texts themselves and the cultural identity of those apprehending or communicating them. Yet he would agree strongly with the statement insofar as the Gospel uniquely corresponds to ultimate reality. Meaning does not confer independence, just a diffraction of competing possibilities. Ultimately, we read, people find they cannot "keep referring" the "word of God" to "one interpretation after another." Human beings, he writes, are "not trapped in a hall of mirrors of interpretations; one can and must seek a breakthough to what is really true."[47] For Ratzinger, God's Word is just this: "simply true."[48] Putting truth to work in service in distinguishing one culture from another is evaluative. It is to ask how far the values and worldviews and ways of life of different peoples correspond with reality, and with the ultimate correspondence to the reality that is Jesus Christ.

Being so unabashedly evaluative, Ratzinger is vulnerable to some of the most damning characterizations of Christian mission as the imperial imposition of one set of beliefs on others. This is not a fair representation of his approach, however. Yes, of course Ratzinger wants to deny relativism, and challenge popular misgivings about "the universality of Christian faith,"[49] but truth is for him not just a means of distinguishing one culture from another. It is also a means of establishing commonality between them because truth can be a constructive point of communication between all cultures. While Christ is truth as person, Christ can and will take shape in differing cultural forms insofar as those forms are ordered to the truth. In this, he shares a certain element with Arrupe, the view that Christ can permeate different cultures. Yet he differs from Arrupe on two fronts. First, he does not maintain that all cultures are equally ordered to the truth. He can be said to hold firm to *Gaudium et Spes* §53, but only if we accept that culture *should* cultivate human nature, that a

---

47 Ratzinger, "Culture and Truth."

48 Ratzinger, "Culture and Truth" (quoting *Fides et Ratio*, no. 84).

49 Ratzinger, "Christ, Faith and the Challenge of Cultures."

culture ordered to truth will be edifying, and that unedifying or degrading elements of cultures are reflective of error or falsehood. Second, the church is itself a cultural subject precisely because those cultures ordered to truth that she has encountered now participate in it. Christ is not beyond culture, as such, but brings with him those cultures that he has transformed through history. Because truth is a constructive point of interaction, Christianity itself bears the elements of truth of the cultures that contributed to it, just as those cultures themselves bear witness to the influence of Christianity. The main reference for this comes from *Fides et ratio*, in which St. John Paul II writes that "the Church cannot abandon what she has gained from her inculturation in the world of Greco Latin thought." In and of itself, this is relatively uncontestable. It is extremely difficult to envisage an interpretation of Christianity entirely shorn of the influence of Greco-Roman culture, especially if we assume that culture includes philosophy.[50] At the same time, however, it does suggest that Christian mission will involve a measure of acculturation, of adjusting non-Christian contexts to the cultured norms of the church.

Maintaining that truth is the primary category for his discussion means Ratzinger gives a certain priority to philosophy and an interpretation of philosophy in relation to truth as "correspondence" (and not just "coherence," and therefore "meaning"). This approach maintains that certain linguistic constellations are particularly appropriate for articulating Christian faith and able in particular to bear crosscultural transposition without diminution. Metaphysics is one such constellation. As put by Thomas Joseph White, "theological knowledge of the mysteries of faith" *is* close "to the form of natural knowledge that is properly metaphysical, or ontological."[51] A further remark should be made about Ratzinger's own admission that *Fides et ratio* threatens "the canonization of a eurocentrism." His response is that it is not that Greco-Roman thought was simply closer to God than the thinking of other cultures *per se*, in any straightforward sense. Rather, it was that Greco-Roman thought had itself encroached upon universality, "it had begun to open itself to universal truth" and so was particularly amenable to the universality personified in Christ.[52] This is why the culture of the classical world came to be so profoundly

---

[50] The most well-known attempt at this is probably Adolf von Harnack's *Essence of Christianity*.

[51] Thomas Joseph White, *The Incarnate Lord* (Washington, DC: The Catholic University of America Press, 2015), 55.

[52] Ratzinger, "Culture and Truth."

intertwined with the Christian faith, and—importantly—how it is that other cultures might bear the promise of an analogous intercultural fusing. Arrupe's inculturation presupposes "a faith stripped of culture is transplanted into a religiously indifferent culture," but Ratzinger's interculturality maintains that "cultures are potentially universal and open to each other."[53]

Now I can bring Newman into the discussion, with the aim of pointing to the similarities he shares with Ratzinger. These similarities are particularly striking considering that Ratzinger is engaging in a lively dialogue with postmodern thought, and Newman lived in the nineteenth century. In the *Essay on the Development of Christian Doctrine*, Newman outlines seven notes of authentic doctrinal developments, the fourth of which he calls "the power of assimilation." He writes that the "idea of Christianity" develops by way of "incorporation" of elements from its contexts.[54] The "more readily" Christianity "coalesces" the "raw material" of its context, indicates the degree to which there is "an antecedent affinity" between them.[55] Christianity also corrects its contexts. He writes that Christianity succeeds by "purifying" and "transmuting" but also "assimilating" and "taking into itself the many-colored beliefs, forms of worship, codes of duty, [and] schools of thought, through which it was ever moving."[56]

For Ratzinger, antecedent affinities mean an openness to universal truth inherent to a particular cultural setting. For Newman, universality is certainly assumed, but the key point of contact he shares with Ratzinger surrounds the importance he places on truth. For Newman, Christianity has this capacity to assimilate elements only from its multitude of contexts *because* it has a strong sense of its own truth. Otherwise, it would not assimilate, as such, because it would not have what he terms a "continuity of principle" that serves as the backbone for the organism, as it were. Without this truth, the development would not be assimilation, but mere "change."[57] As he writes, "Christianity has

---

53 Ratzinger, "Christ, Faith and the Challenge of Cultures."

54 John Henry Cardinal Newman, *An Essay on the Development of Christian Doctrine* (Notre Dame, IN: University of Notre Dame Press, 1989), 186.

55 Newman, *Essay on the Development*, 187.

56 Newman, *Essay on the Development*, 356–57.

57 The commitment to universality and its connection with truth is also show, intraecclesially, by the debate between Ratzinger and Walter Kasper over the priority or complementarity of the universal church and particular/local churches. Indeed, universal singularity is necessary to doctrinal development; see Emery de Gaál, *O Lord, I Seek Your Countenance: Explorations and Discoveries in Pope Benedict XVI's Theology* (Steubenville, OH: Emmaus Academic, 2018), 41; Jacob

from first to last kept fixed principles in view in the course of its developments, and *thereby* has been able to incorporate doctrine which was external to it without losing its own."[58] The note of authentic development that precedes "the power of assimilation" is therefore "continuity of principle." An authentic development of doctrine will thus not disrupt the essential truth of the faith but instead will incorporate elements from its contexts. His first example of continuity of principle in action is what he calls the "dogmatic principle": that truth is "one, unalterable, consistent, imperative, and saving."[59] He says it was this, specifically, that was the "cardinal distinction between Christianity and the religions and philosophies by which it was surrounded" in the centuries after Christ.[60] Because Christianity maintained that "there is a truth" and "there is one truth," it was no match against "the old established paganism." The two opinions encountered each other as each "abstractedly true," but only one maintained that truth is "a matter of life and death."[61]

Ratzinger's interculturality and Newman's power of assimilation thus share important similarities. In the first place, there is an overarching commitment to truth, not as something to suspend in order to understand the encounters of Christianity and culture, but as the very means by which to make sense of those encounters themselves. Hence, both are evaluative, and evaluative in the same way, as based on truth. Secondly, both approaches bespeak the inherent universality of Christianity itself. Because Christianity is true, it is universal, and because it is universal, there must be a framework for understanding its capacity to speak to contexts radically different from its first origins. To revisit the two tensions inherent in theologies of culture mentioned at the outset of this chapter, however, we would seem simply to have reverted back to an evaluative approach that threatens to subsume particularity. The problem is how to evaluate contexts with Christian faith as a benchmark of ultimate truth, without simply supplanting those particular contexts with the universal faith. On this front, a third shared element between Ratzinger and Newman is potentially fruitful. Both approaches involve an understanding of

---

Phillips, "Lumen Gentium: The Church as Mystical Body and the Communion of the Faithful," in *The Oxford Handbook of Joseph Ratzinger*, ed. Tracey Rowland and Francesca Aran Murphy (Oxford: Oxford University Press, forthcoming).

58 Newman, *Essay on the Development*, 352 (emphasis added).

59 Newman, *Essay on the Development*, 352.

60 Newman, *Essay on the Development*, 352.

61 Newman, *Essay on the Development*, 357.

Christianity and culture by which Christianity itself develops *through* encounters with culture and forever bears the marks *of* those developments from then on. For Ratzinger, this is expressed in terms of a paradigmatic inculturation in the Greco-Roman world, for Newman in terms of an assimilation of foreign elements into the bosom of the church.

INTERCULTURALITY APPLIED TO NEWMAN'S THEOLOGY

As it stands, neither interculturality nor the power of assimilation can be said to withstand criticisms about being retrograde and therefore hostile to the world outside the church. This is because when these criticisms are levelled at Ratzinger, they fall back on how he returns again and again to the classical paradigm. The implication is that the openness to culture Ratzinger professes is never actually applied to any context other than the Greco-Roman, and that elsewhere his evaluations are always negative. Bringing interculturality into conversation with the power of assimilation does not answer to these suspicions, for the obvious reason Newman's *Development* essay is itself similarly concerned with Christian antiquity. So here, I want close this chapter by showing how Newman's work on doctrinal development applies to a different setting, being inseparable from his own struggles with his own culture.

Little attention has been given by Newman scholarship to the possibilities for transposing the dynamics of the power of assimilation into Newman's own context. There are good grounds for proceeding in this direction, however, because Newman himself does so in a series of lectures given some five years after the publication of the *Development* essay. In his lectures on the *Difficulties of Anglicans*, he describes the Anglican Church in the exact terms he used for the Catholic Church a few years previously. That is, the power of assimilation is put to work negatively, he tries to show how the Anglican Church could not assimilate the Oxford Movement. Newman argues that the Anglo-Catholic movement was doomed to failure because the principles on which it is founded are not in continuity with the principles of Anglicanism. Because the movement thus fails the third note of authentic development, it fails the fourth, the Power of Assimilation. That is, because there was no continuity of principle between the Oxford Movement and the Anglican Church, the Anglican Church simply could not assimilate Anglo-Catholic teaching. The issue here is, of course, truth. The Anglican *via media* held truth to be a mean between extremes, to reside somewhere in the middle of Protestantism and Romanism.[62] It simply could not assimilate those who held truth as defined by the "dogmatic principle" of Rome, that is, that truth is "one, unalterable, [and] consistent." Here, Newman enters into precisely the analogies he uses for doctrinal development. He says, "as physical life assimilates to itself, or casts off, whatever it encounters, allowing no interference with the supremacy of its own proper principles, so it is with life civil and social." The "Anglo-catholic teaching" could thus not be "supplemental, or complemental, or collateral, or correlative to" Anglicanism. Because it is not "developed from it," it is not "capable of absorption into it." On the contrary, he continues, it is actually "most uncongenial and heterogenous" to it and thus destined to ever float upon it, "like oil upon the water."[63]

We can be confident that Newman applied his reading of the fathers to his own context, therefore, which should be uncontentious considering his transposition of the dynamics of Anglicanism to the Monophysite, Donatist, and Arian controversies relayed in some of the most famous passages of the *Apologia*. In all these examples, however, the transposition is negative; it is focused on criticizing Anglicanism rather than engaging in a constructive dialogue between Catholicism and his context. Looking closely at his corpus, however, it can be argued that Newman's belief in assimilation is central for understanding his work as a Catholic theologian. That is, his mature works like the *Apologia* and the *Essay in Aid of a Grammar of Assent* take widely acknowledged facets of Englishness and recast them in the context of Catholic thought.[64] These facets include, for example, the empiricism connected with the scientific and industrial revolutions, British empiricist philosophy, and the pragmatism of common law and the unwritten English constitution. The *Grammar* evinces a thoroughly empirical means of inquiry, foreshadowing much later philosophical developments with his descriptive phenomenology of empirical consciousness: "the facts of human nature, as they are found in

---

62 John Henry Newman, *The Via Media of the Anglican Church*, vol. 1, *On the Prophetical Office of the Church* (London: Basil Montagu Pickering, 1877), 7–10.

63 John Henry Newman, *Certain Difficulties Felt by Anglicans in Catholic Teaching* (London: Longmans, Green, and Co., 1901), 19, 35.

64 For a full treatment of Newman and Englishness, see Jacob Phillips, *John Henry Newman and the English Sensibility: Distant Scene* (London: Bloomsbury, 2023).

the concrete action of life."[65] Assent is described in this book by way of the "illative sense," which is a sort of common sense, is deeply pragmatic, and in which the premises of decisionmaking are largely unthematized and implicit as spontaneously "coalescing probabilities" on the basis of which we draw a sense of how to proceed that is described as an "unwritten summing up" of the matter at hand.[66]

There is correction at play between Newman and Englishness, too, I suggest, which can be seen in another facet of a received notion of Englishness in Victorian society, with traditions around reserve or discretion. As a Tractarian, this theme was paramount in his *Arians of the Fourth Century*, particularly with regard to his use of the idea of a *disciplina arcani* pertaining to the Alexandrian Church. Following his conversion, however, he came out strongly against the idea that decorum in speaking of sacred things was an indicator of sanctity, arguing that the "supernatural virtue of faith" meant those baptized Catholic could speak freely, albeit profanely, about the most supremely spiritual matters. He thus describes "Catholic populations," meaning French, Italians, and Spanish, in ways typical of the nineteenth century English: as "rude where they should be reverent, jocose where they should be grave, and loquacious where they should be silent."[9] Contrary to appearances, however, this is not a bad thing. Newman is teasing his audience with their popular stereotypes of Catholics in order to highlight the great spiritual benefit of their Catholic faith. The supernatural virtue of faith, defined specifically as knowledge rather than the more amorphous Protestant sense of faith as an existential state, meant for Newman that they could speak freely about divine things because those things were genuinely given to their hearts and minds. Just as the Englishman "*knows* about railroads and electric telegraphs" regardless of his "moral state," in a Catholic country, "the ideas of heaven and hell, Christ and the evil spirit, saints, angels" and so on are straightforwardly known as self-evident facts of life: "facts attested by each to all, and by all to each."[67] There is thus no need to speak with great discretion and reserve, because the lofty mysteries of the faith can be immanent and accessible.

---

65 John Henry Newman, *An Essay in Aid of a Grammar of Assent* (London: Burns, Oates, and Co., 1870), 168.

66 Newman, *Grammar of Assent*, 284–85.

67 Newman, *Difficulties Felt by Anglicans*, 275–76; for a particularly vivid illustration of this tension between decorum and devotion is given by Newman's discussions of Marian devotion in an English context, see Phillips, *John Henry Newman and the English Sensibility*, 78.

The two examples just outlined, empiricism and reserve, combine to indicate that Newman treats his own cultural identity as something subject to both loss and gain through his conversion, and ultimately that the Second Spring of English Catholicism will involve elements of Englishness being assimilated to Catholic truth, while shorn of those overbearing, self-confident, and deluded features of the national identity he ferociously critiques. Hence it is that he can arrive at the position where he thanks Pope Pius IX for having "prepared the way for our own habits of mind, our own manner of reason, our own tastes and our own virtues, finding a place and thereby a sanctification, in the Catholic Church."[68]

Put in terms of interculturality, the truth of Catholicism serves for Newman as a corrective to English excesses. At the same time however, what Newman calls "antecedent affinities" are also present, and these might perhaps constitute what Ratzinger considers a tending toward universality. That is, there might be something important for the worldwide Church, for example, in Newman's empiricism, something that was neglected by the formalism of the dominant neoscholasticism he encountered in the Rome of the 1840s. On this front, I suggest, Newman's own nineteenth-century experience offers a way to apply to Ratzinger's interculturality beyond the classical context and shows it can have a much broader provenance than critics of Ratzinger might assume. Indeed, for Newman, the interaction between cultures and Rome is beneficial to both parties. He says "the multitude of the nations which are within the fold of the Church will be found to have acted for its protection, against any narrowness," and "national influences have a providential effect in moderating the bias which the local influences of Italy may exert on the See of St Peter."[69] It is clear from this that Newman's approach considers local tendencies and variations of emphasis to have enduring warrant within Catholic universality, and there is a profound attentiveness to the local and the particular. But for both Ratzinger and Newman, this comes without conceding the evaluation of truth and therefore universality itself. This is aimed at the dictatorship of relativism in Ratzinger's case, and to an overly confident Protestantism in Newman's. If the power of assimilation is as similar to interculturality as I suggest, we have an example of Ratzinger's theology showing an openness to

---

68 Newman, *Apologia Pro Vita Sua*, 296.

69 Newman, *Apologia Pro Vita Sua*, 296.

local developments that is not retrograde and that is attentive to contemporary settings.

Moreover, it is fitting that Newman serves as an illustration of Ratzinger's thought following the former's canonization, which is, after all, the raising of local veneration to universal provenance.[70] As Benedict XVI said on his visit to England in 2010: Newman's "insights . . . were not only of profound importance for Victorian England, but continue today to inspire and enlighten many all over the world."[71]

---

70 This is also, I suggest, closely related to the document from Benedict XVI's papacy *Anglicanorum Coetibus*, as a offering a fulfilment of ecumenical dialogue as conversion to Catholic norms while maintaining a distinctive cultural patrimony.

71 Quoted by Mary Katherine Tillman, *John Henry Newman: Man of Letters* (Milwaukee: Marquette University Press, 2015), 16n4.

9

CONCEPTIONS OF THE ECCLESIA

MYSTICAL BODY IMAGERY IN JOHN HENRY NEWMAN AND JOSEPH RATZINGER

Elizabeth A. Huddleston

For as in one body, we have many members,
and all the members do not have the same function,
so we, though many, are one body in Christ,
and individually members one of another. (Rom 12:4)

The image of the church as Christ's "body" is found in both the genuine and disputed letters of Saint Paul.[1] The scriptural image of the church as the body of Christ would later develop into a robust theology of the "Mystical Body" of Christ, though the term "mystical" as a reference to the body of Christ is not mentioned in the Pauline corpus.[2] This image of the church—"body of

[1] The primary places St. Paul refers to the church as a "body" are 1 Corinthians 12:12–31, Romans 12:4–5, Ephesians 4:16, and Colossians 1:18: It is understood here the distinction between the disputed and genuine letters of Paul. When I speak of "St. Paul," in a letter that is disputed, I am including the author writing under the name of St. Paul as well.

[2] For an in-depth study of the development of the doctrine of the Mystical Body of Christ prior to the doctrine's boon in the 1940s, see Émile Mersch, *The Whole Christ: The Historical Development of the Doctrine of the Mystical Body in Scripture and Tradition*, trans. John R. Kelly (Milwaukee: Bruce Publishing, 1938); the original was published under the title *Le corps mystique du Christ: Études de théologie historique* and was composed of vol. 1, *Ecriture, tradition grecque*, and vol.

Christ"—has been foundational for Christian understanding of both what the church is and how it functions for two millennia. This is true of both Saint John Henry Newman (1801–1890) and Joseph Ratzinger/Pope Benedict XVI (1927–2022). Newman, especially as a high church Anglican pastor and during the years on his "Anglican deathbed," in which he composed his famous *Essay on Development*, tended to employ the image of the church as the Mystical Body of Christ in his sermons and in his more ecclesio-political writings. Ratzinger focused on the church as the people of God in writings prior to the Second Vatican Council, though he would later refer to the church as the Mystical Body of Christ in his writings after the council, particularly in his work with the *Communio* movement.

Newman's years leading the Oxford Movement produced a robust theology of the church as the Mystical Body of Christ as he was working to instill an Anglo-Catholic ecclesiology within the national church.[3] One emphasis of the Oxford Movement was to demonstrate how the church is both an imperfect visible reality and perfect invisible reality.[4] For his part, Ratzinger, along with his *Ressourcement* confrères, founded the academic journal *Communio* as a way to lead the church into a movement of *aggiornamento*, which necessarily demanded a *ressourcement* of the early Christian sources.[5] Both the Oxford Movement and the *Communio* movement were interested in an ecclesiological

---

2, *Tradition occidentale* (Brussels: L'Edition Universelle, S.A., 1936). Pope Pius XII's encyclical *Mystici Corporis Christi* (1943) helped to resuscitate the doctrine of the Mystical Body of Christ in the modern Roman Catholic world.

3 The project of the Oxford Movement was to interpret the Anglican Church in terms of a more "Catholic," though not Roman Catholic, theological and ecclesiological schema. See Stewart J. Brown, Peter Nockles, and James Pereiro, eds., *The Oxford Handbook of the Oxford Movement* (Oxford: Oxford University Press, 2017), 7–27; Peter B. Nockles, "The Oxford Movement," in *The Oxford Handbook of John Henry Newman*, ed. Frederick D. Aquino and Benjamin J. King (Oxford: Clarendon, 2018), 7–27; Peter B. Nockles, *The Oxford Movement in Context: Anglican High Church-manship, 1760–1857* (Cambridge: Cambridge University Press, 1994); and Marvin R. O'Connell, *The Oxford Conspirators: A History of the Oxford Movement, 1833–1845* (New York: University Press of America, 1991). For an exposition into Newman's shift from evangelicalism to high church Anglicanism, see Geertjan Zuijdwegt, *An Evangelical Adrift: The Making of John Henry Newman's Theology* (Washington, DC: The Catholic University of America Press, 2023).

4 Newman's sermon "The Invisible World" is a good example of this idea. See Newman, "The Invisible World," in *Parochial and Plain Sermons*, vol. IV (London: Longmans, Green, and Co., 1909), 200–213, hereafter cited as *PS*. See also James Pereiro, *"Ethos" and the Oxford Movement: At the Heart of Tractarianism* (Oxford: Oxford University Press, 2008), 125–29; Donald Graham, *From Eastertide to Ecclesia: John Henry Newman, the Holy Spirit, and the Church* (Milwaukee: Marquette University Press, 2011).

5 The founders of *Communio* along with Ratzinger were Hans Urs von Balthasar and Henri de Lubac. Other prominent theologians involved were Louis Bouyer, H. Medina, and Marie-Joseph Le Guillou.

reformation, and at the heart of both was the notion that the church is constituted as a physical and spiritual body, harkening back in their own ways to the Pauline notion of the church as the body of Christ. Indeed, at the heart of both the Oxford Movement[6] and the *Ressourcement* movement, was the issue of how precisely the church is—and functions as—the Mystical Body of Christ.

JOHN HENRY NEWMAN

It has become commonplace to say that Newman's vision of the church includes language of an "organism."[7] While it is true that many philosophers, politicians, scientists, and theologians began to use language associated with biology to describe the church, it is a mischaracterization of Newman's work to claim that he viewed the church itself as an organism.[8] Though Newman uses the analogy of a butterfly, which is obviously an organism, to describe how different

---

6 While Newman's ecclesiology undoubtedly shifted during the interim years between exit from the Oxford Movement and his conversion to the Roman Church in 1845, the typology of the church as the Mystical Body of Christ is found in writings from both before and after his conversion. Similarly, Newman never wavered on his explanation of the church as both an invisible and visible reality.

7 There is a common pithy saying spreading through the more popular places on the internet (Pinterest, memes, social media, etc.) like wildfire that misattributes the saying "The church is not an organization, it is an organism," to John Henry Newman. See, for example, the prayer card by Bishop Barron's *Word on Fire*: https://www.prayergraphics.com/project/the-church-is-not-an-organization-it-is-an-organism-bl-john-henry-newman/. Erich Przywara parses the idea of the church as an "organism" as it appeared in two differing Augustinianisms in his essay "Newman: Saint and Modern Doctor of the Church?" trans. Christopher M. Wojtulewicz, *Church Life Journal*, October 11, 2019, https://churchlifejournal.nd.edu/articles/newman-possible-saint-and-modern-doctor-of-the-church/. For more discussion on how Newman does or does not deem the church an "organism," see Daniel Lattier, "John Henry Newman and Georges Florovsky: An Orthodox-Catholic Dialogue on the Development of Doctrine" (PhD diss., Duquesne University, 2012).

8 Tübingen theologian Johann Adam Möhler, for example, spoke of the church as an organism in his *Unity of the Church*, published in 1825, which can be considered in a sense ahead of his time. For a good translation of this text, see Johann Adam Möhler, *Unity in the Church, or the Principle of Catholicism Presented in the Spirit of the Church Fathers of the First Three Centuries*, trans. Peter C. Erb (Washington, DC: The Catholic University of America Press, 2015). The language of "organism" can also be seen in Vincent of Lérins's *Commmonitorium*. See Thomas G. Guarino, "Tradition and Doctrinal Development: Can Vincent of Lérins Still Teach the Church?" *Theological Studies* 67 (2006): 34–72; Thomas G. Guarino, *Vincent of Lérins and the Development of Christian Doctrine* (Grand Rapids, MI: Baker Academic, 2013). While Charles Darwin's *Origin of Species* would not be published until a few decades after Newman's *Essay on the Development of Christian Doctrine* (1845), Darwin's thought would influence some of the reception history of Newman's theory of doctrinal development, particularly during the Modernist Crisis. See, for example, Valentine G. Moran, "Loisy's Theological Development," *Theological Studies* 40, no. 3 (September 1989): 421.

the church's doctrine may look after an authentic development,[9] he never actually refers to the church as an organism. What he does say in his *Essay on Development*—the ideas of which were conceived during his participation in the Oxford Movement and published in the months after his conversion to Catholicism—is that there are rules required to distinguish authentic developments in the church's teachings from corruptions.[10] To illustrate this, Newman observes that "the adult animal has the same make as it had on its birth; young birds do not grow into fishes; nor does the child degenerate into the brute."[11] Incorporating similar biological language, Newman also explains that some doctrinal developments appear quite different from their original form. Newman states that "the fledged bird differs from its rudimental form in the egg," and "the butterfly is the development, but not in any sense the image, of the grub."[12] This demonstrates how sometimes developments within the church's doctrine may appear to be completely different, though if they are authentic developments, these doctrines still pertain to the same divine revelation rather than being a corruption of the divine revelation. This description of how the church's doctrines develop is quite different from saying that the church itself is a living, breathing organism.[13] If Newman is not conceptualizing the church as an organism, how then did he understand the nature of the church in the years leading up to his *Essay on Development*?

---

9 False "developments" for Newman are considered "corruptions." For an excellent exposition of how Newman understands doctrinal corruption, see Matthew Levering, *Newman on Doctrinal Corruption* (Skokie, IL: Word on Fire Academic, 2022).

10 See John Henry Newman, *Essay on the Development of Christian Doctrine*, hereafter cited as *Dev.*, (London: James Toovey, 1845), section 3, "On the Corruption of an Idea."

11 Newman, *Dev.*, 58.

12 Newman, *Dev.*, 58.

13 It is important to note that nowhere—at least that I have been able to uncover—does Newman refer to the church directly as an "organism." In his *Grammar of Assent* (New York: Catholic Publication Society, 1870, hereafter cited as *GA*, which was penned much later than his *Essay on the Development*, Newman mentions an *organon*, which he describes as a process by which we come to know truth in our minds, though a full discussion falls outside the purview of this essay. The *organon* for Newman is more of a way in which we receive knowledge in our imaginations, rather than a thing: "Here then again, as in the other instances, it seems clear, that methodical processes of inference, useful as they are, as far as they go, are only instruments of the mind, and need, in order to their due exercise, that real ratiocination and present imagination which gives them a sense beyond their letter, and which, while acting through them, reaches to conclusions beyond and above them. Such a living *organon* is a personal gift, and not a mere method or calculus" (Newman, *GA*, 303–4).

"ETHOS" OF THE OXFORD MOVEMENT

Central to Newman's ecclesiology during his Tractarian years was an emphasis on the mystical, or invisible, nature of the church, evidenced particularly in his sermons, which were often preached at the University Church of St. Mary the Virgin in Oxford.[14] Newman and his Tractarian companions often spoke of their movement in terms of an "ethos." This ethos appeared in the way in which they carried out their tutorial duties. John Keble, for example, said to John Taylor Coleridge that he accepted his position on the grounds that he considered the tutorial office "as a species of pastoral care."[15]

A major emphasis in the Tractarian ethos is an ecclesiology in which the mind of Jesus Christ is understood as "the secret inspiration of His Holy Spirit communicated to His whole Mystical Body, informing, guiding, moving it, as He will."[16] The ethos of the Oxford Movement did not shy away from mystery. On the contrary, it focused on mystical interpretation of scripture, various patristic mystical language (including that of mystical scriptural interpretation), and poetic and moral sensibilities.[17] As Pereiro states: "He [Keble] considered religion and poetry closely related, for God has used poetical language to communicate himself to man, employing symbolical associations—whether poetical, moral, or mystical—to reveal a world beyond sense perception."[18] Influenced by the Romantic imagination common in the Victorian era, the

---

14 See his *Parochial and Plain Sermons*, *Tracts for the Times*, and *Lyra Apostolica*, for examples. The University Church was, and still is, one of the main parishes of Oxford, which is intimately connected to Oriel College, where Newman was a Fellow. While Newman's Tractarian theology does not necessarily contradict his ecclesiology in later writings, his theology of the Mystical Body was much more prevalent in Newman's Anglican years, particularly his Tractarian years, than it would be in his ecclesiology as a Catholic. Newman never ceased to adhere to his ecclesiology built on the threefold office of the church, though he would emphasize the notion of an *ecclesia discens*, *ecclesia docens*, or a church learning, church teaching, model of the church at times as a Catholic. See, for example, Newman, "On Consulting the Faithful in Matters of Doctrine," *The Rambler* (July 1859): 198–230. It was commonplace for Newman to lightly edit and republish his Anglican writings as a Catholic. His *Parochial and Plain Sermons*, for example, was originally published in 1843 and reissued in 1868, well after Newman's conversion to Catholicism. See Eamon Duffy, "The Anglican Parish Sermons," in Aquino and King, *Oxford Handbook of John Henry Newman*, 221.

15 John Keble to John Taylor Coleridge, January 29, 1818, quoted in John Taylor Coleridge, *A Memoir of the Rev. John Keble* (Oxford and London: James Parker and Co. 1869), 73, cited in Pereiro, *"Ethos" and the Oxford Movement*, 85.

16 John Henry Newman, "Remains of the late Reverend Richard Froude, M.A.," *British Critic* 27, no. 54 (April 1840): 401.

17 See Pereiro, *"Ethos" and the Oxford Movement*, 96–97.

18 Pereiro, *"Ethos" and the Oxford Movement*, 98.

Tractarians were interested in how the sacramental imagination could be employed as a way to reveal this divine world beyond our sense perception.[19]

In his Tractarian years, Newman understood the Anglican Church as 1) Apostolic, 2) a *via media* between "the so-called Reformers and the Romanists," and 3) one of three branches that makes up the One, Holy, Catholic, and Apostolic Church.[20] As Coulson writes, "as an Anglican Newman makes a . . . simple two-fold distinction between what gives the Church life—the prophetical tradition—and what gives the Church form—the episcopal tradition."[21] In his sermon "The Communion of Saints," Newman preached that "The Ministry and Sacraments, the bodily presence of Bishop and people, are given us as keys and spells, by which we bring ourselves into the presence of the great company of the saints."[22] Newman adds that though the church appears imperfect, it is perfect in the invisible realm of the saints. In his view, it is "through the English, or the Greek, or the Roman porch into the one invisible company of elect souls, which is independent of time and place, and untinctured with the imperfections or errors of that visible porch by which entrance is made."[23] "The efficacy" of baptism, Newman preached, "lies in the inflowing upon the soul of the grace of God lodged in that unseen body into which it opens, not, in any respect, in the personal character of those who administer or assist in it."[24]

BAPTISM AS THE FORMATION OF THE MYSTICAL BODY OF CHRIST

The Anglican Newman often preached about the importance of baptism for the Christian life.[25] The way in which Newman speaks of baptism as a "grafting

---

[19] For a deeper exposition of the relationship between English Romanticism and the Oxford Movement, see David Nichols and Fergus Kerr, eds., *John Henry Newman: Reason, Rhetoric and Romanticism* (Carbondale: Southern Illinois University Press, 1991); Mirko Starčević, "John Henry Newman and the Oxford Movement: A Poet of the Church," *English Language Overseas Perspectives and Enquiries* 12, no. 2 (November 2015): 129–45; and David Goslee, *Romanticism and the Anglican Newman* (Athens: Ohio University Press, 1996).

[20] Newman, *Tracts for the Times*, xxxviii, hereafter cited as *TT*. See Geoffrey Rowell, "The Ecclesiology of the Oxford Movement," in Brown, Nockles, and Pereiro, *Oxford Handbook of the Oxford Movement*, 216–30.

[21] John Coulson and A. M. Allchin, eds., *The Rediscovery of Newman: An Oxford Symposium* (London: Sheed & Ward, 1967), 127, quoted in Rowell, "Ecclesiology of the Oxford Movement."

[22] Newman, *PS* iv, "The Communion of Saints."

[23] Newman, *PS* iv, "The Communion of Saints."

[24] Newman, *PS* iv, "The Communion of Saints."

[25] As a priest at the University Church parish of St. Mary the Virgin, Newman was responsible for the people of Littlemore as part of his appointment. From the very start of his tenure, he advocated

into" a mystical community is quite striking. For example, in Tract 88, along patristic lines, Newman translates from Bishop Andrewes: "Thou hast hallowed me in regeneration, destroy not Thy holy work;—that Thou has grafted me into the good olive tree, the member of Thy mystical body; the member of thy mystical body cut not off."[26] Newman expresses a similar understanding of baptism in his sermon "The Unity of Church," in which he makes clear to his parishioners that the sacrament of baptism is a "visible rite" by which "individuals are incorporated into an already existing body."[27] It is at baptism, Newman preaches, that we are ontologically changed as we participate in the common baptism of the church. At our baptism, "God visits us, penetrates through our whole soul and body" and "leaves no part of us uncleansed, unsanctified."[28] In this same sermon, we see Newman explain that we are not only changed as individuals as we are washed clean at baptism: we also enter into a physical and mystical communion with others who have been baptized in the waters sanctified by Christ's baptism. Newman explains that the baptismal stamp of the image of Christ is the "revealed design of Christ to connect all his followers in one by a visible ordinance of incorporation."[29]

Similarly, Newman writes that when we are incorporated into the "invisible Body of Christ mystical," we are "so knit together in Him [Christ] by Divine Grace, that all have what He [Christ] has, and each has what all has."[30] The individual stamp of Christ's image procured at baptism incorporates the new Christian into the Mystical Body of Christ. It is the collective stamp of the image shared by all the baptized that allows for Christians to be considered Christ's body.[31] Newman comments that at baptism, "they are considered

---

for Littlemore to be its own parish because of how different the needs were from those of the parishioners of University Church. He built the chapel of St. Mary and St. Nicholas in 1835–1836 and dedicated it to his mother, Jemima Newman.

26 Newman, *TT* 88, *The Greek Devotions of Bishop Andrewes, Translated and Arranged* (London: J. G. & F. Rivington, 1840), 66. Bishop Lancelot Andrewes (1555–1626) was a bishop during the reign of Elizabeth I and fought against the reduction of the power of the Anglican Church during one of the most turbulent eras of Anglican history. For more on the context and history leading up to Bishop Andrewes, see Eamon Duffy, *The Stripping of the Altars: Traditional Religion in England, 1400–1580* (New Haven, CT: Yale University Press, 1992).

27 Newman, *PS* vii, Sermon 17, "The Unity of the Church."

28 Newman, *PS* vii, Sermon 17, "The Unity of the Church."

29 Newman, *PS* vii, Sermon 17, "The Unity of the Church."

30 Newman, *PS* vii, Sermon 17, "The Unity of the Church."

31 While this language is similar to that of the doctrine of our being created in the image of God (*imago Dei*), the idea that Newman is expounding on is similar to the early church language of baptism and chrismation as providing an indelible mark on the human soul in the participation in the sacraments of initiation. This was a common theological motif in the early church baptismal

one; so that henceforth the whole multitude" are "no longer viewed as mere individuals."[32] The body of Christ, for Newman, is simultaneously a physical reality and a mystical reality.

THE MYSTICAL/INVISIBLE CHURCH
AND THE VISIBLE CHURCH

Newman's Anglican literature is teeming with examples of his adherence to the Platonic notion of an invisible world that is more real than our visible material world. Newman writes in his homily entitled "The Invisible World," for example, that God "exists more really and absolutely than any of those fellow-men whose existence is conveyed to us through the senses."[33] We also see in many of Newman's *Tracts for the Times* that while he often preaches about the beauty of the invisible world and the mystical church, he also emphasizes the necessity of the visible church to be a beacon of light to the world and to reveal the reality of the perfected invisible world and church. We see this most profoundly when Newman remarks in Tract 20:

> In order then to supply this need of our minds, to satisfy the imagination, and so to help our faith, for this among other reasons Christ set up a visible Society, His Church, to be as a light upon a hill, to all the ends of the earth, while time endures. It is a witness of the unseen world; a pledge of it; and a prefiguration of what hereafter will take place. It prefigures the ultimate separation of good and bad, holds up

---

theologies. The language is also common of the early Anglican theologians, such as Lancelot Andrews, who Newman translates in his *Tract 88* and the *Book of Common Prayer*.

32 Newman, *PS* vii, Sermon 17, "The Unity of the Church."

33 Newman, *PS* iv, "The Invisible World." For a more complete picture of Newman's theology of the invisible world, see Frédéric Libaud, *Voir l'invisible: Le monde surnaturel chez John Henry Newman* (Paris: Saint-Léger Éditions, 2016). See also Louis Bouyer, *L'Église de Dieu* (Paris: Cerf, 1970); Bouyer, *Newman's Vision of Faith: A Theology for Times of General Apostasy* (San Francisco: Ignatius Press, 1986); Keith Beaumont, *Dieu Intérieur: La théologie spirituelle de John Henry Newman*, Études Newmaniennes (Paris: Éditions Ad Solem, 2014); Elizabeth Huddleston, "To Witness the Unseen: A Portrait of Sanctity according to John Henry Newman and Wilfrid Ward," in *"Heart Speaks to Heart": Saint John Henry Newman and the Call to Holiness*, ed. Kevin J. O'Reilly (Leominster: Gracewing, 2021), chap. 6; and Robert A. O'Donnell, "The Two Worlds of John Henry Newman," *New Oxford Review* 78, no. 7 (September 2011): 36–38. For a good analysis of the practical historical import of Newman's visible and invisible ecclesiology in his Tractarian years, see Kenneth J. Stewart, "The Tractarian Critique of the Evangelical Invisible: Tracts 2, 11, 20 and 47 in Historical Context," *Churchman* 121, no. 4 (Winter 2007): 349–62; Brian Horne, "Church and Nation: Newman and the Tractarians," *International Journal for the Study of the Christian Church* 5, no. 1 (2005): 25–40.

the great laws of God's Moral Governance, and preaches the blessed truths of the Gospel. It pledges to us the promises of the next world, for it is something (so to say) in hand; CHRIST has done one work as the earnest of another. And it witnesses the truth to the whole world; awing sinners, while it enspirits the fainting believer. And in all these ways it helps forward the world to come; and further, as the keeper of the Sacraments, it is an essential means of the realizing it at present in our fallen race.[34]

The visible church and the invisible church should not be understood as two distinct entities, according to Newman. They are in essence one, though the visible church is bound by the flesh and holds a more obscure vision of the divine truth than that of the invisible church. The veil of our sensory world does not cloud the church's entire vision, and so the visible church in her sacraments stands as a beacon of light, even amid the sins of its people.

Thus, for Newman and his Tractarian friends, the church exists at the intersection of the invisible and material. The Mystical Body, which Christians enter into at their baptism, is what the church is at its very core. At the same time, the church exists in our sensory world, in which we participate by our particular way of life—laity, clergy, magisterium, etc. We are grafted into Christ's Mystical Body, which enables us to participate in the visible church. Again, Newman does not separate the mystical and physical churches. He understands them as the full reality of what the church is, though he does make the point that the mystical church, because it does not pass away as our material world does, is more "real" or perfected.

As noted above, we should not interpret Newman as understanding the church as an organism, which can be pitted against the notion of an "institutional" church.[35] While Newman did explore organic language to describe how we might understand the nature of authentic developments—as opposed to corruptions—his ecclesiology is not such that the church is in any real sense understood as an organism. This is important because many in the generations after Newman—particularly during the Modernist Crisis—would

---

34 Newman, *TT* 20, "The Visible Church" (December 24, 1833). See also *TT* 11.

35 The notion of an "institutional" church was popularized by Avery Dulles in his *Models of the Church*—chapter 2, to be precise. Given Newman's ecclesiology of a threefold office described here, and even his notion of an *ecclesia discens* and *ecclesia docens*, it seems unlikely that Newman would have categorized the church, or any part of it, as strictly an institution.

explicate Newman's theory of development in a way that pushed much further than Newman's ecclesiology and theory of development allows.[36]

THE YEARS BETWEEN NEWMAN AND RATZINGER: *MYSTICI CORPORIS*

The historical interlude and geographical and ecclesiological space between Newman and Ratzinger are important for understanding the ethos of Ratzinger's ecclesiology. The years between Newman's writings on the church as the Mystical Body of Christ and Joseph Ratzinger's ecclesiological writings included the Roman Catholic Modernist Crisis and two world wars.[37] Likewise, if one places the early Newman's body of Christ theology, written during his Anglican years, in conjunction with Ratzinger's writings after the Second Vatican Council, then two Vatican Councils can also be included in the list of major transitions between the eras of these two great theologians.[38] Both the church and the world inhabited by Ratzinger had changed significantly since the time of Victorian England and the English Romanticism in which Newman thrived. Ecclesiologically, the promulgation of the encyclical *Mystici Corporis Christi* is one of the most significant events in the time between Newman and the height of Ratzinger's writing career.

In June 1943, while World War II raged, Pope Pius XII published the encyclical *Mystici Corporis Christi*, which only grew in popularity after the Second World War.[39] *Mystici Corporis* sought to establish that the Catholic

---

36 George Tyrrell, for example, interiorized much the language of development and would eventually argue that the church has developed past that of the deposit of faith. See, for example, George Tyrrell, "Lex Orandi, Lex Credendi," in *Through Scylla and Charybdis, or The Old Theology and the New* (London: Longmans, Green, and Co., 1907), 85–86. See also Elizabeth A. Clark, "'Historical Development' and Early Christianity: George Tyrrell's Modernist Adaptation and Critique," in *Christians Shaping Identity from the Roman Empire to Byzantium* (Leiden: Brill, 2015), 454–77.

37 The Modernist Crisis is typically dated from the promulgation of Leo XIII's encyclical *Providentissimus Deus* in 1893 and two events in 1914, the beginning of the First World War and the death of Pope Pius X. World War I is dated from 1914 to 1918, and World War II is dated from 1939 to 1945.

38 Vatican I began on June 29, 1868, and was adjourned on October 20, 1870, a month after the Capture of Rome (September 20, 1870). Pope John XXIII convened the Second Vatican Council on October 11, 1962, and the council officially ended on December 8, 1965.

39 *Mystici Corporis* is generally recognized as penned by Sebastian Tromp and Réginald Garrigou-Lagrange. See Sebastian Tromp, "Annotations ad enc. *Mystici Corporis*," *Periodica de re morali, canonica, liturgica* 32 (1943): 377–401; Alexandra von Teuffenbach, *Pius XII: Neue Erkenntnisse über sein Leben und Wirken* (Aachen: MM Verlag, 2010); David Berger, "Kommentar zur Enzyklika *Mystici Corporis*," *Einsicht: Römisch-Katholische Zeitschrift* 34, no. 2 (February 2004): 40; and Jose

Church is both a mystical/invisible body and a visible/sociological reality. Paragraph 64 states:

> It is clear . . . how grievously they err who arbitrarily claim that the Church is something hidden and invisible, as they also do who look upon her as a mere human institution possessing a certain disciplinary code and external ritual, but lacking power to communicate supernatural life. On the contrary, Christ, Head and Exemplar of the Church "is not complete, if only His visible human nature is considered, or if only His divine, invisible nature, but He is one through the union of both and one in both . . . so is it with His Mystical Body" since the Word of God took unto himself a human nature liable to sufferings, so that He might consecrate in His blood the visible Society founded by Him and "lead man back to things invisible under a visible rule."[40]

With this pronouncement, *Mystici Corporis* rejected two extremes that had become popular in the decades before the war. The first was a rationalistic notion of the church that overemphasized the visible reality of the church to the detriment of a healthy Mystical Body theology. Against the notion that the church is solely formed of human structures and activities, Pius XII writes that the Holy Spirit acts as the church's guide:

> Although the juridical principles, on which the Church rests and is established, derive from the divine constitution given to it by Christ and contribute to the attaining of its supernatural end, nevertheless that which lifts the Society of Christians far above the whole natural order is the Spirit of our Redeemer who penetrates and fills every part of the Church's being and is active within it until the end of time as the source of every grace and every gift and every miraculous power. Just as our composite mortal body, although it is a marvelous work of the Creator, falls far short of the eminent dignity of our soul, so the social structure of the Christian community, though it proclaims the wisdom of its divine Architect, still remains something inferior when

---

Isidro Belleza, "Joseph Ratzinger, Student of Thomas," *Berkeley Journal of Religion and Theology* 5, no. 1 (2019): 107.

40 Pius XII, *Mystici Corporis Christi*, June 29, 1943, https://www.vatican.va/content/pius-xii/en/encyclicals/documents/hf_p-xii_enc_29061943_mystici-corporis-christi.html.

compared to the spiritual gifts which give it beauty and life, and to the divine source whence they flow.[41]

The other extreme involved exaggerated tendencies that had crept into some Mystical Body theologies that tended to equate the works of the members of the body of Christ with the works of Christ himself.[42] To dispel this notion, Pius XII noted that the *una mystica persona* does not refer to an individual but rather to a social, physical, and mystical church:

> For there are some who neglect the fact that the Apostle Paul has used metaphorical language in speaking of this doctrine, and failing to distinguish as they should the precise and proper meaning of the terms the physical body, the social body, and the Mystical Body, arrive at a distorted idea of unity. They make the Divine Redeemer and the members of the Church coalesce in one physical person, and while they bestow divine attributes on man, they make Christ our Lord subject to error and to human inclination to evil. But Catholic faith and the writings of the holy Fathers reject such false teaching as impious and sacrilegious; and to the mind of the Apostle of the Gentiles it is equally abhorrent, for although he brings Christ and His Mystical Body into a

---

41 Pius XII, *Mystici Corporis*, no. 63.

42 Five months prior to the publication of *Mystici Coporis*, Archbishop Conrad Gröber of Fribourg wrote to his German colleagues: "I am concerned by the sublime supernaturalism and the new mystical attitude that is spreading in our theology. It can degenerate into a mysticism in which the borders of creation vanish." Quoted in Timothy R. Gabrielli, *One in Christ: Virgil Michel, Louis-Marie Chauvet, and Mystical Body Theology* (Collegeville, MN: Liturgical Press Academic, 2019), 11. The letter is found in Theodor Maas-Ewerd, *Die Krise der liturgischen Bewegung in Deutschland und Österreich: Zu den Auseinandersetzungen um die "liturgische Frage" in den Jahren 1939 bis 1944* (Regensburg: Pustet, 1981), 540–69. See Gabrielli, *One in Christ*, 11–15. Mersch had also warned of a false mysticism: "The error lies in mistaking the image [mystical body of Christ] for a definition and in thinking that just because they are able to conceive some huge ethereal and invisible organism or a kind of living atmosphere in which men's souls are somehow fused one into the other, they therefore possess a perfect knowledge of the mystery of the mystery of the Head and members" (Mersch, *Whole Christ*, 7). Thomas Merton also warns of a false mysticism in the decade after *Mystici Corporis*, which he sees as intimately related to Nazi ideology: "We are living in a time when false mysticism is a much greater danger than rationalism. It has now become much easier to play on men's emotions with a political terminology that sounds religious than with one that sounds scientific. This is all the more true in an age in which the religious instincts of millions of men have never received their proper fulfillment. A nation that is starved with the need to worship something will turn to the first false god that is presented to it. Hitler showed the world what could be done with an ersatz mysticism of 'Race' and 'Blood.'" See Thomas Merton, *The Ascent to Truth: A Study of St. John of the Cross* (New York: Harcourt and Brace, 1951), 44–54, quoted in Gabrielli, *One in Christ*, 13n42.

wonderfully intimate union, he nevertheless distinguishes one from the other as Bridegroom from Bride.[43]

Ratzinger would later praise *Mystici Corporis* as one of the gems of Pius XII's encyclicals, writing that "*Mystici Corporis* stands out, in which the Pope deals with the theme of the true and intimate nature of the Church."[44] Ratzinger continues, "On the scale of research he [Pius XII] sheds light on our profound ontological union with Christ and in him, through him and with him all the other faithful moved by his Spirit, who are nourished by his Body and, transformed in Him, are able to continue to extend his salvific work in the world."[45] Ratzinger links *Mystici Corporis* with two other encyclicals, *Divino Afflante Spiritu* (1943) and *Mediator Dei* (1947). It is within the ecclesiological landscape of these encyclicals of the 1940s and Vatican II and their respective reception histories that we witness a transition in Ratzinger's ecclesiology from conceptualizing the church as the people of God to also employing Mystical Body language.

JOSEPH RATZINGER

While Ratzinger focused on the church as the people of God in his earliest writings, he began to also focus on the church as the Mystical Body of Christ due to the shifting interpretation in the reception of Vatican II's ecclesiological statements.[46] While the documents of Vatican II point to the church as both the Mystical Body of Christ and the people of God, the reception of the meaning

---

43 Pius XII, *Mystici Corporis*, no. 86.

44 Benedict XVI, "Address of His Holiness Benedict XVI to Participants at a Congress on 'The Heritage of the Magisterium of Pius XII and the Second Vatican Council' Promoted by the Pontifical Lateran University and the Pontifical Gregorian University," November 8, 2008, https://www.vatican.va/content/benedict-xvi/en/speeches/2008/november/documents/hf_ben-xvi_spe_20081108_con-gresso-pioxii.html.

45 Benedict XVI, "Address to 'The Heritage of the Magisterium of Pius XII and the Second Vatican Council,'" Rome, November 8, 2008.

46 Ratzinger's earliest publications tend to focus on the church as the people of God. His dissertation, for example, was entitled *Volk und Haus Gottes in Augustins Lehre von der Kirche* (*The People of God in Augustine's Doctrine of the Church*) and focused on the theological terms "people of God" and "house of God" in Augustine's writings, in particular his *De Civitate Dei*. Avery Dulles (1918–2008) outlines the shift in Ratzinger/Pope Benedict XVI's employment of the images of people of God and Mystical Body of Christ. See Avery Cardinal Dulles, "On Ecclesiology," *Nova et Vetera* 15, no. 3 (2017): 779–93; Joseph Ratzinger, "Volk und Haus Gottes in Augustins Lehre von der Kirche" (PhD diss., University of Munich, 1951).

of these images in the years following the council led to some division among theologians concerning how the church ought to be conceptualized. This led to at least two strands of ecclesiological thinking that were at times opposed to one another. As Tracey Rowland notes:

> The event of the Second Vatican Council had the effect of doing away with the idea that Catholic theology was a monolithic intellectual system. The luminaries among the Conciliar *Periti* all agreed on this but as the decade of the 1960s wore on it became apparent that the leading theologians of the Church could agree only on their opposition to the pre-Conciliar 'monolithic system,' not on alternative ways forward.[47]

As tensions arose, two publication outlets—*Concilium* and *Communio*—became the exemplary signposts of the two poles to which theologians tended to gravitate.[48]

COMMUNIO VS. CONCILIUM

Concilium is more associated with "spirit of Vatican II," which includes a general openness to many kinds of new ecclesiological ideas. Ratzinger labeled the *Concilium* perspective a "hermeneutic of rupture"—"an interpretation of the Council as a radical irruption in Church history for which, according to Karl Rahner, the only precedent was the Council of Jerusalem in 49 AD."[49] Ratzinger described the *Communio* perspective as conforming to "the hermeneutic of reform" rather than rupture or revolution.[50] The hermeneutic of reform, according to Rowland, adheres to

---

47 Tracey Rowland, *Catholic Theology* (London: Bloomsbury T&T Clark, 2017), 91. For further background into what helped shape Ratzinger's theology, see Tracey Rowland, *The Culture of the Incarnation: Essays in Catholic Theology* (Steubenville, OH: Emmaus Academic, 2017); Tracey Rowland, *Ratzinger's Faith: The Theology of Pope Benedict XVI* (Oxford: Oxford University Press, 2008); Emery de Gaál, *O Lord, I Seek Your Countenance: Explorations and Discoveries in Pope Benedict XVI's Theology* (Steubenville, OH: Emmaus Academic, 2018); and Emery de Gaál, *The Theology of Pope Benedict XVI: The Christocentric Shift* (London: Palgrave Macmillan, 2010).

48 Philip Trower, *Turmoil and Truth: The Historical Roots of the Modern Crisis in the Catholic Church* (San Francisco: Ignatius Press, 2003), 32. See also Rowland, *Catholic Theology*, 93.

49 Rowland, *Catholic Theology*, 93.

50 Rowland, *Catholic Theology*, 93. Rowland notes that sometimes Ratzinger used the phrase "hermeneutic of continuity" interchangeably with "hermeneutic of reform," which was true until he became Pope Benedict XVI, when he clarified that what he intended was a "hermeneutic of reform," which encompassed continuity and discontinuity on varying levels. See chap. 1 in Shaun

an interpretation of the Conciliar documents that views them as merely reforming certain aspects of the intellectual presentation of the faith to overcome a lopsided emphasis on one or other teaching, or to overcome a dualistic mode of thinking, or to place Church teachings on stronger scriptural and Christological foundations but in no sense overturning centuries of settled dogmatic teachings.[51]

Communio theology "tended to reflect upon theological questions with reference to the whole intellectual history of a doctrine or practice from patristic times to present, and to approach such studies with a disposition of respect for the received teaching."[52]

One hallmark difference between the *Concilium* and *Communio* theological outlooks, according to Rowland, has to do with how they interpreted Christ's call to read the "signs of the times." The typical *Concilium* scholar, according to Rowland, "wants to read the Second Vatican Council as an event that exhorted Catholics to be aware of the signs of the times and to enter into dialogue with the world on the world's terms."[53] By contrast, the typical *Communio* scholar "wants to read the Second Vatican Council as an event that emphasized the importance of Christocentrism and therefore the renewal of theological anthropology and Trinitarian theology."[54] The *Communio/Concilium* theological divide contributes to the context of how Ratzinger's ecclesiology is formulated after the council, especially with respect to his conception of the church as the Mystical Body of Christ.

COMMUNIO ECCLESIOLOGY

Ratzinger begins his 1986 essay, "The Ecclesiology of the Second Vatican Council," with a reflection on the church as something much more than an organization. Unlike Newman, he claims that the church is in fact an organism. He interprets Romano Guardini's statement, "The Church is awakening in

---

Blanchard, *The Synod of Pistoia and Vatican II: Jansenism and the Struggle for Catholic Reform* (Oxford: Oxford University Press, 2020).

51 Rowland, *Catholic Theology*, 93.

52 Rowland, *Catholic Theology*, 93.

53 Rowland, *Catholic Theology*, 94.

54 Rowland, *Catholic Theology*, 94.

people's souls,"[55] to mean that the church should "be known and experienced as something inward, as something that does not stand in opposition to us like some mechanical device, but is alive in us."[56] Ratzinger pushes back against the notion that the human-run exterior organization is the most important aspect of the church. Speaking in relation to Guardini, he writes:

> If the Church had been seen until then as all structure and organization, the insight now arose that we ourselves are the Church. It is more than an organization, it is an organism of the Holy Spirit, something alive encompassing us all from within. This new consciousness of the Church found its linguistic form in the term "the mystical body of Christ." A new and liberating experience of the Church expressed itself in this formula. At the end of his life, in the year in which the Second Vatican Council's Constitution on the Church was adopted, Guardini once again formulated the new view: the Church "is not an institution that was thought out and constructed . . . but a living being. . . . It lives again through time; becoming, just as everything alive becomes; changing . . . and nevertheless always the same in essence, for its innermost core is Christ. . . . As long as we see the Church as only an organization . . .' as an authority . . . ; as a coalition . . . , we do not yet have a correct understanding of it. It is a living being, and our relation to it must itself be life.[57]

The primary characteristic of Ratzinger's Mystical Body theology is that the church is living and is distinctly Christological. It is the body that Christ has built for himself, and we must find a way to humbly fit into it.[58]

One must ask, if the church is a fully alive *corpus mysticum*, how Ratzinger explains our participation in this living body. He argues that "*communio*-ecclesiology became the core of the teaching of the Second Vatican Council on

---

55 See Romano Guardini, *The Church and the Catholic*, trans. Ada Lane (New York: Sheed & Ward, 1935).

56 Joseph Ratzinger, "Die Ekklesiologie des Zweiten Vatikanums," *Internationale katholische Zeitschrift: Communio* 15, no. 1 (January 1986): 41–52. The English publication appeared as "The Ecclesiology of the Second Vatican Council," *Communio: International Catholic Review* 13, no. 3 (Fall 1986): 239–52. The translated essay used here is from Benedict XVI, *Ratzinger in "Communio,"* vol. 1, *The Unity of the Church* (Grand Rapids, MI: Eerdmans, 2010), 63.

57 Ratzinger, *Unity of the Church*, 63. See also Romano Guardini, *The Church of the Lord: On the Nature and Mission of the Church*, trans. Stella Lange (Washington, DC: Henry Regnery, 1966).

58 Ratzinger, *Unity of the Church*, 64.

the Church, and at the same time the central element the Council wished to convey."[59] It is through the liturgical life of the church, with the Eucharist at the height, that Christians participate in the Mystical Body.[60] Eucharistic participation is by nature communal, as Ratzinger says. The Eucharistic local church represents "the inner, sacramental reason for the doctrine of collegiality."[61] Ratzinger clarifies this statement against Lutheran/Protestant and Russian Orthodox understandings of how the local community is related to the whole Mystical Body by looking closely at the text of *Lumen Gentium*. He states, "The Church is really present in all legitimately organized local groups of the faithful, which, insofar as they are united to their pastors are also quite appropriately called Churches."[62] At the same time, he says, "The Church exists wholly in every community celebrating the Eucharist."[63]

Ratzinger emphasizes that no community can make itself into the church; "a group cannot simply get together, read the New Testament, and say 'We are now the Church because the Lord is there wherever two or three are gathered in his name.'"[64] We cannot "make" the church; rather, the church is something given to us, which we receive as a gift: "One cannot make the Church but only receive it, that is receive it from where it already is and where is really is: from the sacramental community of Christ's body passing through history."[65]

Francesca Aran Murphy identifies three aspects of Ratzinger's *Communio* ecclesiology that help deepen our understanding of the church as Christ's

---

59 Ratzinger, *Unity of the Church*, 66.

60 See Kimberly Hope Belcher, "The Feast of Peace: The Eucharist as a Sacrifice and a Meal in Benedict XVI's Theology," in *Explorations in the Theology of Benedict XVI*, ed. John C. Cavadini (Notre Dame, IN: University of Notre Dame Press, 2012), 254–75.

61 Ratzinger, *Unity of the Church*, 67.

62 Vatican II, *Lumen Gentium* (Dogmatic Constitution on the Church) (November 21, 1964), 26, hereafter cited as *LG*, quoted in Ratzinger, *Unity of the Church*, 68. *LG*, 8, states: "This Church constituted and organized in the world as a society, subsists in the Catholic Church, which is governed by the successor of Peter and by the Bishops in communion with him, although many elements of sanctification and of truth are found outside of its visible structure," https://www. vatican.va/archive/hist_councils/ii_vatican_council/documents/vat-ii_const_19641121_lumen-gentium_en.html. This is a different formulation than is found in *Mystici Corporis* (1943) and *Humane Generis* (1950), both of which totally identify the church as the Catholic Church.

63 Ratzinger, *Unity of the Church*, 68.

64 Ratzinger, *Unity of the Church*, 68.

65 Ratzinger, *Unity of the Church*, 69.

body.[66] The first, "the Church as 'Subject,'" expresses the notion that the church "is the *subject* of revelation," which "means God speaks about himself *to* her."[67] Similarly, the church as subject allows the church to see Christ in his divinity through the revelation passed down by the Apostles, which Ratzinger notes is the foundation of the church.[68] The church as the subject of God's initiative is a *communio* "because the Triune God is communion, an 'ecstatic' and entire 'going out from himself.' The divine dialogue partner shapes his Thou as Communio."[69]

The second aspect of Ratzinger's *Communio* ecclesiology is "the Church as 'Communion,'" which "flows from the dialogue between God and humanity as not just verbal but sacramental."[70] This aspect sees a new relationship formed between persons in the church and transforms our participation in God's eternal love. Murphy argues that "the ecclesiology of communion is a development of 'mystical body theology,' which imagines the Church as a human 'participation' in 'that communion between man and God which is the Incarnation.'"[71] This is because through the Incarnation, "'she [the church] is God's communing with men and hence the communion of men with each other.'"[72]

Murphy's third aspect of *Communio* ecclesiology, "the Church as 'Eucharistic,'" serves to "mediate between external conceptions of the Church, such as ultra-papalism, and internalist or charismatic ecclesiologies."[73] Ratzinger

---

66 See Francesca Aran Murphy, "Papal Ecclesiology," in *Explorations in the Theology of Benedict XVI*, 222–24. See also Francesca Aran Murphy, "De Lubac, Ratzinger and von Balthasar: A Communal Adventure in Ecclesiology," in *Ecumenism Today: The Universal Church in the 21st Century* (London: Routledge, 2016), 45–80.

67 Murphy, "Papal Ecclesiology," 222. See also Lawrence Paul Hemming, *Benedict XVI: Fellow Worker for the Truth; An Introduction to His Life and Thought* (London: Continuum, 2005). Hemming notes that "Divine Revelation is God's approach *toward* man. God's divine self-disclosure—. . . his *disclosing* of himself . . . is *God's*, not *our* initiative. Such an initiative . . . is always *for*, and so *given to*, someone" (Hemming, *Benedict XVI*, 145, quoted in Murphy, "Papal Ecclesiology," 222).

68 Murphy, "Papal Ecclesiology," 222.

69 Murphy, "Papal Ecclesiology," 223. See also Joseph Ratzinger, *Principles of Catholic Theology: Building Stones for a Fundamental Theology*, trans. Mary Frances McCarthy, SND (San Francisco: Ignatius Press, 1982), 23–25, 132.

70 Murphy, "Papal Ecclesiology," 223.

71 Murphy, "Papal Ecclesiology," 223; Ratzinger, *Principles of Catholic Theology*, 53.

72 Murphy, "Papal Ecclesiology," 223; Ratzinger, *Principles of Catholic Theology*, 53.

73 Murphy, "Papal Ecclesiology," 224. Ratzinger notes that "there arose a eucharistic ecclesiology which people also likes to term an ecclesiology of union." See Joseph Ratzinger, *Church, Communion,*

describes the church as Eucharistic in his essay, "Communion: Eucharist—Fellowship—Mission," where he states:

> The Eucharist effects our participation in the Paschal Mystery and thus constitutes the Church, the body of Christ. Hence the necessity of the Eucharist for salvation. The Eucharist is necessary in exactly the sense that the Church is necessary, and vice versa. It is in this sense that the saying of the Lord is to be understood: "Unless you eat the flesh of the Son of man and drink his blood, you have no life in you" (Jn 6:53). Yet, thereby appears the necessity of a visible Church and of visible concrete (one might say, "institutional") unity. The inmost mystery of communion between God and man is accessible in the sacrament of the Body of the Risen One; and the mystery, on the other hand, thereby demands our body and draws it in and makes itself a reality in one *Body*. The Church, which is built up on basis of the Sacrament of the Body of Christ, must for her part likewise be one body and, in fact, be a single body so as to correspond to the uniqueness of Jesus Christ, and the way she corresponds to the uniqueness of Jesus Christ, and the way she corresponds to this is seen, again, in her unity and in remaining in the teaching of the apostles.[74]

In a similar vein, Murphy brings together the three aspects of Ratzinger's *Communio* ecclesiology in her statement:

> The Church as subject, as communio, and as Eucharist is created by receiving the Word of the Lord: to "say that the last supper is the origin of the Church . . . means . . . that the eucharist links men and women . . . with Christ and . . . in this way . . . turns people into the Church." Hence the Church both as institution and as charismatic "lives in eucharistic communities."[75]

---

and Politics: New Essays in Ecclesiology, trans. Robert Nowell and Fridesiwide Sandeman, OSB (New York: Crossroad, 1988), 7.

74 Joseph Ratzinger, "Communion: Eucharist—Fellowship—Mission," in *Pilgrim Fellowship of Faith: The Church as Communion*, trans. Henry Taylor (San Francisco: Ignatius Press, 2002), 82–83, quoted in David Vincent Meconi, SJ, "The Mystical Body in the *Nouvelle Théologie*," in *Ressourcement after Vatican II: Essays in Honor of Joseph Fessio, S.J.*, ed. Nicholas J. Healy Jr. and Matthew Levering (San Francisco: Ignatius Press, 2019), 51.

75 Murphy, "Papal Ecclesiology," 224; Joseph Ratzinger, *Church, Ecumenism, and Politics: New Endeavors in Ecclesiology* (San Francisco: Ignatius Press, 2008), 8. For an explanation as to why there are some conflicts with the reception of this type of theology, see Michael Dauphinais,

We see in Ratzinger's *Communio* ecclesiology the reality that our participation in the church is a mystical, intimate communion with the Trinitarian God and with one another. Like Newman, Ratzinger is also reflecting on the nature of the church within the challenges he was experiencing at the time of his writing, including the chasm between *Concilium* and *Communio* theology/ecclesiology and the entrance of postmodernity into the theological and cultural landscape.

CONCLUSION

The scriptural image of the body of Christ has endured through the millennia, though our understanding of the meaning and significance of the image has varied. In Newman's context of the Oxford Movement, we see an emphasis on the sacramental imagination. He explains that at baptism, Christians are grafted into the Mystical Body of Christ and are made a part of a church that exists both in our sensory world and in a divine world beyond our senses. In Ratzinger's context in the wake of Vatican II, we see an ecclesiology based on a deep Eucharistic theology. Even though elements of the contexts of the Oxford Movement and, even more so, the *Communio* movement still influence our ecclesial outlook today, our own context has its own challenges.

Our context, which is ever more secularized by the day, is marked by a drastic exodus from the church, though many of those leaving still claim an affinity for some amorphous spirituality without the "chains" of an organized religion.[76] This growing secularism is often met with a heavy-handed reaction in the form of a traditionalism that seems to long for an imagined golden age of Christendom with a heavy focus on fighting culture wars.[77] In our

---

"The Ratzinger Option: Introducing Christianity in a Postmodern Age," in *Ressourcement after Vatican II*, 112–38.

76 On the exodus of from the Catholic Church, see Stephen Bullivant, *Mass Exodus: Catholic Disaffiliation in Britain and America since Vatican II*, 2nd ed. (Oxford: Oxford University Press, 2019). See also James Emery White, *Rise of the Nones: Understanding and Reaching the Religiously Unaffiliated* (Grand Rapids, MI: Baker Books, 2014); Amy Hollywood, "Spiritual but Not Religious: The Vital Interplay between Submission and Freedom," *Harvard Divinity Bulletin*, Winter/Spring 2010, https://bulletin.hds.harvard.edu/spiritual-but-not-religious/; and Robert C. Fuller, *Spiritual, but Not Religious: Understanding Unchurched America* (Oxford: Oxford University Press, 2021).

77 See Massimo Faggioli, "Traditionalism, American-Style: A New Kind of Opposition to Rome," *Commonweal*, November 23, 2021, https://www.commonwealmagazine.org/traditionalism-american-style; Shaun Blanchard, "*Traditionis Custodes* Was Never Merely about the Liturgy," *Church Life Journal*, August 2, 2021, https://churchlifejournal.nd.edu/articles/traditionis-custodes-was-never-merely-about-the-liturgy/. For an example of the very new rift between traditionalist Catholics

contemporary stratified ecclesial context, it becomes easy to occupy an echo chamber in which those with opposing views are either disregarded as of no consequence or even seen as an enemy, even if they are members of the same communion.[78] We also see in our contemporary context a rise in a new form of Donatism in which one's political views or social stances are what determines a person's participation in the church rather than sacramental standing.[79]

Pope Francis addresses our contemporary climate by calling for the church to act as a "field hospital" responsible for healing wounds:

> I see clearly that the thing the church needs most today is the ability to heal wounds and to warm the hearts of the faithful; it needs nearness, proximity. I see the church as a *field hospital* after battle. It is useless to ask a seriously injured person if he has high cholesterol and about the level of his blood sugars! You have to heal his wounds. Then we can talk about everything else. Heal the wounds, heal the wounds.... And you have to start from the ground up.[80]

While the wounds are often deep, one possible way for the church to act as a field hospital is to reintroduce the church as a great mystery whose identity in Christ overshadows the infighting and ecclesio-political bickering. This is not to say that we should stop fighting injustices or trying to better our church and world; rather, it is to say that the recognition of the church for the divine reality that it is, can and should lead to a sense of humility and charity that allows differing political views and even ecclesial views within the same communion to come together. As members of the Mystical Body of Christ, we worship at the same altar because we are baptized into the same body of Christ and share the same body and blood of Christ in the Eucharist.

---

and Rome, see Peter Kwasniewski, ed., *From Benedict's Peace to Francis's War: Catholics Respond to the* Motu Proprio Traditionis Custodes *on the Latin Mass* (New York: Angelico, 2021).

78 Some of the discourse from both sides surrounding Pope Francis's *Traditionis Custodes* has reached this level of vitriol.

79 This goes hand in hand with cancel culture from both sides of the metaphorical aisle. For example, see John E. Thiel, "The New Donatism: An Old Controversy Illuminates the Bishops' Biden Gambit," *Commonweal*, July 5, 2021, https://www.commonwealmagazine.org/new-donatism.

80 Antonio Spadaro, SJ, "A Big Heart Open to God: An Interview with Pope Francis," *America Magazine*, September 30, 2013, https://www.americamagazine.org/faith/2013/09/30/big-heart-open-god-interview-pope-francis.

10

NEWMAN AND RATZINGER ON ECCLESIAL AUTHORITY

Ryan Marr

St. John Henry Newman and Joseph Cardinal Ratzinger are indisputably two of the most influential Catholic theologians of the modern era. While their theological writings span a range of topics, the area in which they have had the most significant impact is in the realm of ecclesiology. Newman, of course, did groundbreaking work on the sense of the faithful and also pushed Catholic thought to move beyond an excessively juridical understanding of the Church.[1] Ratzinger, as well, wrote extensively on the nature of the church, its relationship to the world, and the mutuality that ought to exist between different parts of the body of Christ. In the case of Ratzinger, we were able to witness his fascinating ecclesiology in practice, in that he served in highly influential positions of ecclesiastical authority—first as Archbishop of Munich and Freising, later as Prefect of the Congregation for the Doctrine of the Faith, and finally as Supreme Pontiff of the Universal Church. Newman, by contrast, never possessed comparable ecclesiastical power. His influence on the hierarchy was from a distance—in the vein of prophetic challenge, primarily through the medium of his writing.

---

1 Avery Dulles, "The Threefold Office in Newman's Ecclesiology," in *Newman after a Hundred Years*, ed. Ian Ker and Alan G. Hill (Oxford: Clarendon, 1990), 378.

Considering this difference between the two, it's noteworthy that Ratzinger—like Newman—ended up publishing a great deal on the limits of ecclesial authority. One might assume that a cleric such as Ratzinger, who held some of the most powerful positions within the church hierarchy, would be tempted to adopt an inflated understanding of episcopal authority. While it may be possible to critique how Ratzinger wielded authority, his theology of the church could hardly be described as ultramontane or excessively monarchical. In this area, at least, we see a remarkable convergence between Ratzinger's ecclesiology and Newman's. Both theologians articulate a communion ecclesiology, both affirm development of doctrine as an important dynamic in the life of the church, and both seek to place reasonable boundaries around the exercise of papal authority. Newman is remembered today, in part, for resisting his neoultramontane counterparts in the church. He was willing to raise a toast to the pope, but said that if he did so, he would drink "to Conscience first, and to the Pope afterwards."[2] "The Apostles were inspired," Newman insisted; "the Pope is not."[3] The pope, in other words, is a custodian of tradition, not a generator of it. Ratzinger similarly noted that "the pope is not an absolute monarch whose will is law."[4] The pope's "rule," Ratzinger maintained, "is not that of arbitrary power, but that of obedience in faith."[5] It's telling that Ratzinger felt compelled to assert these points in the early twenty-first century. In spite of a renewed emphasis on collegiality and communion ecclesiology after Vatican II, some elements of ultramontanism, in the negative sense of the term, survived the reforming efforts initiated by the council and remain in the church today. As I hope to show, the views of Newman and Ratzinger on ecclesial authority offer a corrective to this lingering problem. Viewed together, their ecclesiologies present a personalist vision of the church, one that emphasizes the mutuality that should exist between different parts of

---

2 John Henry Newman, *Certain Difficulties Felt by Anglicans in Catholic Teaching*, vol. 2 (1875; reprint, London: Longmans, Green, and Co., 1900), 261, hereafter cited as *Diff.*

3 Newman to Arthur Arnold, September 22, 1872, in *The Letters and Diaries of John Henry Newman*. ed. C. S. Dessain et al., 32 vols. (London: Thomas Nelson, 1961–72; Oxford: Clarendon, 1978–2008), xxvi, 173, hereafter cited as *LD*.

4 Joseph Ratzinger, preface to *The Organic Development of the Liturgy: The Principles of Liturgical Reform and Their Relation to the Twentieth-Century Liturgical Movement Prior to the Second Vatican Council*, by Dom Alcuin Reid (San Francisco: Ignatius Press, 2005), 10.

5 Ratzinger, preface to *The Organic Development of the Liturgy*, 11.

the body of Christ as a safeguard against authoritarianism, in one direction, and against anarchy, in the other.

FOUNDATIONAL PRINCIPLES IN NEWMAN AND RATZINGER'S ECCLESIOLOGIES

Noticeably, both Newman and Ratzinger are nonscholastic in their theologizing. While neither manifests a strong aversion to scholasticism, they both write in more of a patristic key, heavily reliant upon biblical categories and less systematic than one would find in, say, neoscholastic treatments of the church. For Newman, this characteristic was rooted in the reality of his spiritual journey. Since the bulk of his theological formation took place within the Church of England, he was not well-versed in the manualist tradition, as most nineteenth-century Catholic theologians would have been.[6] Newman, rather, was steeped in the writings of the early church fathers. During his formative years, he dove headlong into the rich heritage of the patristic tradition, and his way of thinking about God, faith, and the church was indelibly marked by these studies. Even after becoming Roman Catholic, his default theological outlook remained more patristic than scholastic in its style and general orientation.

Ratzinger, too, displays a strong devotion to the great works of the first four centuries of Christian history.[7] As Fergus Kerr notes, in Ratzinger's landmark *Introduction to Christianity*, Ratzinger "avoids any sign of neoscholasticism."[8] Per his own testimony, Ratzinger admits being underwhelmed by the "rigid

---

6 In fact, it was partly for this reason that after becoming Catholic, Newman did not consider himself a theologian. For Newman, the vocation of the theologian meant being able to quickly recall the key sources of tradition, such as conciliar teachings and papal bulls—a skill that he said he lacked. See Newman's remarks to Miss Maria Giberne, dated February 10, 1869, in *LD* xxiv, 212–13: "Really and truly I am *not* a theologian. A theologian is one who has mastered theology—who can say how many opinions there are on every point, what authors have taken which, and which is the best—who can discriminate exactly between proposition and proposition, argument and argument, who can pronounce which are safe, which allowable, which dangerous—who can trace the history of doctrines in successive centuries, and apply the principles of former times to the conditions of the present."

7 For a helpful overview of the influence of the fathers on Ratzinger's theology, see Christopher Collins, *The Word Made Love: The Dialogical Theology of Joseph Ratzinger/Benedict XVI* (Collegeville, MN: Liturgical Press, 2013), 9–13. Regarding specifically St. Augustine's influence on Ratzinger's eucharistic ecclesiology, see Theodore Dieter, "Joseph Ratzinger," in *The Oxford Handbook of Ecclesiology*, ed. Paul Avis (Oxford: Oxford University Press, 2022), 449–52.

8 Fergus Kerr, *Twentieth-Century Catholic Theologians: From Neoscholasticism to Nuptial Mysticism* (Malden, MA: Blackwell, 2007), 190.

neothomism" that characterized his early seminary formation, the experience of which motivated him to root his thought in the earliest sources of the Catholic tradition.[9] A key turning point in Ratzinger's theological trajectory occurred during his studies in Munich, when his mentor Alfred Läpple gifted him with a copy of Henri de Lubac's *Catholicism*. Ratzinger was mesmerized with de Lubac's masterful re-sourcing of the fathers, which he says provided him "a new way of looking at theology and faith as such."[10] According to Tracey Rowland's research, it was also around this time that Ratzinger developed a deep appreciation for Newman's theology, which further solidified Ratzinger's commitment to a patristic mode of theological reflection.[11]

Because of their indebtedness to patristic thought, Newman and Ratzinger in their writings on the church eschew a heavily juridical approach in favor of more personalistic and dynamic descriptions of the body of Christ. It was common in Newman's time for works of ecclesiology to make their starting point the notion of the church as a *societas perfecta*, a "perfect society" endowed by God with all of the resources necessary for leading the faithful to salvation.[12] While Newman does not reject this idea, his guiding image for the church is the New Testament concept of the body of Christ, a living organism analogous to a person and animated by the indwelling of the Holy Spirit.[13] This theme was prominent in Newman's preaching from the very beginning of his ministry. In an entry from volume 3 of the *Parochial Sermons*, for instance, he writes that, "The word Church applied to the body of Christians in the world, means but one thing in Scripture, a visible body invested with invisible privileges."[14] At

---

9 Quoted in Kerr, *Twentieth-Century Catholic Theologians*, 187.

10 Quoted in Tracey Rowland, *Ratzinger's Faith: The Theology of Pope Benedict XVI* (Oxford: Oxford University Press, 2008), 3.

11 Rowland, *Ratzinger's Faith*, 3. Rowland references an interview with Läpple by Gianni Valente and Pierluca Azzardo, *30 Days*, I (2006), 60.

12 Susan Wood treats the post-Reformation background to this concept in "Continuity and Development in Roman Catholic Ecclesiology," *Ecclesiology* 7, no. 2 (May 2011): 149–50. As she notes, theologians such as Robert Bellarmine used this term to emphasize that "the church contains all the necessary elements to accomplish the end for which it was intended, namely the salvation of all humanity."

13 Among studies of Newman's ecclesiology, Edward Jeremy Miller's has stood the test of time—*John Henry Newman on the Idea of Church* (Shepherdstown, WV: Patmos, 1987). Miller specifically treats Newman's understanding of the church as a visible body on pages 136–38. See also Andrew Meszaros, *The Prophetic Church: History and Doctrinal Development in John Henry Newman and Yves Congar* (Oxford: Oxford University Press, 2016), especially 232–39.

14 Newman, "The Church Visible and Invisible," in *Parochial and Plain Sermons*, 8 vols., ed. W. J. Copeland (London: Rivingtons, 1868; reprint, Westminster, MD: Christian Classics, 1968), iii, 224.

the time of his conversion to Catholicism, this idea had practical implications for his explanation of how doctrine develops. In the Newman-Perrone paper—written in Latin and intended to test the orthodoxy of his theory of development—Newman employs personalist imagery to describe how the church's grasp of the apostolic tradition deepens over time.[15] While the deposit of faith is objective and immutable, the church, according to Newman, grows in its understanding of the faith through prayerful reflection on the mysteries handed on by Jesus to the apostles.[16] In other words, Newman was attuned to the human element of the church, which during the earliest centuries of its existence did not grasp the fullness of the mystery of faith but grew in understanding through ongoing reflection on the teachings handed down by the apostles.[17] "Even though possessing the whole deposit of faith from the very beginning, [the Church]," Newman argues, "can be said to have more theological knowledge now than it did in former ages."[18] In this sense, the body of Christ is like a person whose knowledge increases through experience of the world around her and through critical reflection upon that experience.

Ratzinger viewed the church from a similar perspective. As early as 1956, in an article entitled "The Church as the Mystery of Faith," Ratzinger identified the New Testament concept of the church and the perspective of the church fathers as his two primary sources for understanding the body of Christ. Within this article, Ratzinger contrasts his view with the image of a *societas perfecta*. According to Maximilian Heim, Ratzinger's goal in this essay was "to overcome the narrowly juridical view of the Church and the reduction of her to her visible structure."[19] This motif is a thread running throughout several of Ratzinger's works. Pointing to the mid-twentieth-century reemphasis on the

---

15 T. Lynch, ed., "The Newman-Perrone Paper on Development," *Gregorianum* 16 (1935): 402–47; English translation: John Henry Newman, *Roman Catholic Writings on Doctrinal Development*, ed. and trans. James Gaffney (Kansas City, MO: Sheed & Ward, 1997).

16 Lynch, "Newman-Perrone Paper," 406–7; English translation, 11–12.

17 The bishops gathered at the Second Vatican Council officially affirmed this process of development and indicated that it would continue for the church "until the words of God reach their complete fulfillment in her." See Vatican II, *Dei Verbum*, no. 8, 1965, https://www.vatican.va/archive/hist_councils/ii_vatican_council/documents/vat-ii_const_19651118_dei-verbum_en.html. All quotations from Vatican II are taken from the Vatican's website.

18 Lynch, "Newman-Perrone Paper," 415; English translation, 20.

19 Maximilian Heinrich Heim, *Joseph Ratzinger—Life in the Church and Living Theology: Fundamentals of Ecclesiology with Reference to Lumen Gentium*, trans. Michael J. Miller (San Francisco: Ignatius Press, 2007), 231.

church as the body of Christ, Ratzinger frames his own ecclesiological project as participating in a movement meant to overcome a legalistic and institutional vison of the church that was prone to the danger of "hierarchology."[20]

At the start of *Church, Ecumenism, and Politics*—one of Ratzinger's most important studies on these topics—he quotes the great twentieth-century theologian Romano Guardini as an exemplification of the "new and liberating experience of the Church" as the Mystical Body of Christ, an idea that Ratzinger sees as central to the ecclesiology articulated in *Lumen Gentium*. The quote from Guardini reads as follows:

> [The Church] is not an invented and constructed institution . . . but a living being . . . She lives on through time, in the process of becoming, like every living thing. She changes . . . and yet essentially she is always the same, and her inmost core is Christ . . . . So long as we regard the Church as merely an organization . . . as a governing body . . . as a federation [that is, an association] . . . we do not have the right relation to her. She is a living being, and our relation to her must itself be a vital one.[21]

One hears in this remark important themes that we have already identified in the thought of Newman: the church is a living organism, one that experiences growth like any living being yet remains essentially the same in her core identity. Not surprisingly, then, in this same section of his book, Ratzinger draws directly upon Newman's theology in order to illustrate "the historical dynamism of the Church" as a body whose understanding of the faith deepens. Ratzinger writes:

> A body maintains its identity by the fact that it constantly becomes new in the process of living. For Cardinal Newman, the idea of development was the real bridge to his conversion to the Catholic faith. I believe that this idea is indeed one of the critical basic concepts of Catholicism on which there still has not been sufficient reflection, although here, too,

---

20 Ratzinger, *Volk und Haus Gottes in Augustins Lehre von der Kirche* (1954; unamended reprint, St. Ottilien: EOS-Verlag, 1992), xi, quoted in Heim, *Joseph Ratzinger*, 232. On Ratzinger's eucharistic ecclesiology as a counterbalance to excessive hierarchology, see Aidan Nichols, *The Thought of Pope Benedict XVI: An Introduction to the Theology of Joseph Ratzinger*, new ed. (London: Burns & Oates, 2007), 96–99.

21 Quoted in Joseph Ratzinger, *Church, Ecumenism, and Politics: New Endeavors in Ecclesiology* (San Francisco: Ignatius Press, 2008), 14.

the Second Vatican Council is to be credited with having formulated the idea for the first time in a solemn magisterial document. Anyone who wants to cling exclusively to the wording of Scripture or to the formulas and structures of the patristic Church banishes Christ to yesterday. The result is, then, either a completely sterile faith that has nothing to say to today or else an arbitrariness that skips over two thousand years of history, tosses it onto the scrap heap of failed enterprise, and now decides to figure out what Christianity should really look like according to the Scriptures or according to Jesus. But that can only amount to an artificial product of our own making that has no inherent stability. There is real identity with the origin only when there is at the same time a living continuity that unfolds it and thereby preserves it.[22]

This lengthy quotation is pretty much a reformulation of Newman's famous description of the development of doctrine, according to which the church's sense of the faith becomes purer and stronger over time, as the deposit of faith's vital element disengages with what is foreign to it and as old principles reappear under new forms.[23] When Ratzinger mentions that real identity with the origin occurs only through an unfolding process of growth that preserves what is essential, the reader's mind automatically thinks of Newman's claim that doctrine "changes . . . in order to remain the same."[24] When it comes to their understanding of the church's vocation of passing on doctrine across time, the

---

22 Ratzinger, *Church, Ecumenism, and Politics*, 16–17. Ratzinger's mention of the Second Vatican Council is a gesture to *Dei Verbum* (no. 8), a document that he helped compose. One of Ratzinger's collaborators in this effort was Yves Congar, who was equally indebted to Newman's work. On Congar's contribution to *Dei Verbum*, see Éric Mahieu, introduction to Yves Congar, *My Journal of the Council* (Collegeville, MN: Liturgical Press, 2012), xvii. Cf. Meszaros, *Prophetic Church*, 183–84.

23 See Newman, *An Essay on the Development of Christian Doctrine*, 6th ed. (1878; reprint, Notre Dame, IN: University of Notre Dame Press, 1989), 40, hereafter cited as *Dev.* In a 2020 monograph, Reinhard Hütter provides a constructive engagement with Newman's theory of development. Particularly helpful is Hütter's discussion of the seven notes of development and how these can be used to distinguish between authentic developments and corruptions. See Hütter, *John Henry Newman on Truth & Its Counterfeits: A Guide for Our Times* (Washington, DC: The Catholic University of America Press, 2020), 138–43. For a critical evaluation of Newman's theory, cf. the recent study of David Bentley Hart, who admits that the *Essay on the Development* was "nothing less than epochal in its importance" but concludes that in the end it was "a self-defeating exercise." See Hart, *Tradition and Apocalypse: An Essay on the Future of Christian Belief* (Grand Rapids, MI: Baker Academic, 2022), 3. Matthew Levering convincingly rebuts some of Hart's charges in *Newman on Doctrinal Corruption* (Park Ridge, IL: Word on Fire Academic), 261–70.

24 Newman, *Dev.*, 40.

basic parameters sketched out by Newman and Ratzinger are fundamentally the same.

AN EXCURSUS ON THE HISTORICAL BACKGROUND TO NEWMAN AND RATZINGER'S ECCLESIOLOGY

Regarding the historical background to their theologies, it's striking that Newman and Ratzinger both played significant roles in the reception of an ecumenical council. Ratzinger, of course, was a peritus at Vatican II and, with Karl Rahner, helped to compose the final form of *Dei Verbum*. After the council ended, Ratzinger made a significant contribution to the interpretation of its documents through his involvement in the five-volume *Commentary on the Documents of Vatican II*, edited by Herbert Vorgrimler, and more accessibly through the publication of his concise monograph *Theological Highlights of Vatican II*.[25] Once he was elected pope, his judgments on the legacy of the council took on heightened importance. As with his predecessor, Benedict XVI made the reception of Vatican II a central facet of his pontificate. Particularly significant in this regard was his 2005 Christmas address to the Roman Curia, in which Benedict sought to defend, in his words, "the correct interpretation of the council."[26]

In that address, Benedict argued that the difficulties of the postconciliar period were caused not by the documents themselves but by erroneous interpretations of the documents. For the council to bear abundant fruit, he said, its interpreters must adhere to a proper hermeneutic, which he described as a "'hermeneutic of reform,' of renewal in the continuity of the one subject-Church which the Lord has given to us."[27] His emphasis on reform is significant. Since Benedict condemned in this address a hermeneutic of discontinuity, commentators will sometimes use the phrase "hermeneutic of continuity" as a

---

25 Herbert Vorgrimler, ed., *Commentary on the Documents of Vatican II* (New York: Herder and Herder, 1969); Joseph Ratzinger, *Theological Highlights of Vatican II* (New York: Paulist Press, 2009), vii.

26 Benedict XVI, "Christmas Greetings to the Members of the Roman Curia and Prelature," December 22, 2005, https://www.vatican.va/content/benedict-xvi/en/speeches/2005/december/documents/hf_ben_xvi_spe_ 20051222_roman-curia.html.

27 Benedict XVI, "Christmas Greetings to the Members of the Roman Curia," no. 36.

counterpoint to the mentality of rupture,[28] but Benedict here speaks specifically of the hermeneutic of *reform*. In other words, he readily acknowledges that something significant happened at Vatican II. It would be foolish to pretend otherwise. This renewal, however, must be understood in continuity with the tradition. The problem with a "hermeneutic of discontinuity and rupture" is that it posits a sharp break between the pre- and postconciliar church and, in turn, equates progress with newness. From Benedict's vantage point, the way forward for unleashing the forces of renewal intended by the council fathers is to root interpretation of Vatican II's documents in the venerable tradition that preceded the council and to reject any reading that posits a rupture with the so-called preconciliar church.[29]

Considering his close study of church history, Newman almost certainly would not have been surprised by the turbulence that has followed the Second Vatican Council. "Councils have ever been times of great *trial*," he observed in a letter from July 1870.[30] Now, Newman offered this remark specifically in response to the political machinations that took place at Vatican I, but he was also well acquainted with the complexities of interpreting the teachings of an ecumenical council. From his Anglican days, Newman had held a theory that dogmatic formulae should be hammered out only in cases of necessity, when a heretical idea threatened to undermine some part of the deposit of faith. As he put it in his *Arians of the Fourth Century*, "freedom from symbols and articles is abstractedly the highest state of Christian communion, and the peculiar privilege of the primitive Church," adding that "technicality and formalism

---

28 Cf. Ian Ker, "Newman Can Lead Us out of Our Post-Vatican II Turmoil," *Catholic Herald*, July 10, 2009: "If there has been one keynote of Benedict XVI's pontificate, it has been 'the hermeneutic,' or interpretation, 'of continuity.' By that the Pope means that the post-Vatican II Church needs to be understood in continuity, rather than disruption, with the Church of the past. It is not that the Pope denies the significance of the achievements of the Second Vatican Council but that he insists that that Council did not somehow cancel out all the other Councils or constitute so radical a disruption as to be equivalent to a revolution." Ker's article was originally published online at http://www.catholicherald.co.uk/ but has since been taken down. An excerpt is still available at https://www.newliturgicalmovement.org/2009/07/newman-and-vatican-ii-according-to-fr.html#.YeMgTHrMLb1.

29 Edward Mushi offers an appreciative, though critical, engagement with Benedict XVI's proposal in "Benedict XVI's Hermeneutics of Reform and Its Implication for the Renewal of the Church," *Pacifica: Australasian Theological Studies*, no. 26 (2013): 279–94. Cf. John W. O'Malley, "'The Hermeneutic of Reform': A Historical Analysis," *Theological Studies* 73, no. 3 (September 2012): 517–46.

30 Newman to Mrs. F. R. Ward, July 9, 1870, *LD* xxv, 158.

are, in their degree, inevitable results of public confessions of faith."[31] These judgments shaped Newman's view on the actions of the majority bishops at the First Vatican Council. While the council was underway, he was troubled by the push to force through a definition of papal infallibility when, in his mind, the vast majority of Catholics already believed the doctrine. From his vantage point, the definition of a dogma should only ever come about as a stern painful necessity, not as a luxury of devotion.[32] Furthermore, Newman believed the church had not dedicated sufficient time toward working through the historical and theological questions raised by such a definition. "We are not ripe yet for the Pope's Infallibility," he remarked to a Jesuit friend.[33] In contrast to the careful consultation and deliberation that went into defining the dogma of the Immaculate Conception, this decision was being rushed, and to outsiders, it seemed "as if a grave dogmatic question was being treated merely as a move in ecclesiastical politics."[34] What was needed, Newman said, was "a careful consideration of the acts of Councils, the deeds of Popes, the Bullarium."[35] Theologians would have to try the doctrine's "future working by the past"—an undertaking that would require years, not months.[36]

Once he learned of the council's outcome—that it had promulgated a definition of papal infallibiliy—Newman shifted his energies toward providing an interpretation of the teaching that was historically tenable and restrained in its claims. He employed a minimizing hermeneutic and argued that the *schola theologorum* would be responsible for testing the doctrine and applying it to concrete cases.[37] When Newman first saw the final form of the definition, he remarked to a friend that he was "pleased at its moderation," noting that

---

31 John Henry Newman, *The Arians of the Fourth Century* (London: E. Lumley, 1871; reprint, Notre Dame, IN: University of Notre Dame Press, 2001), 36–37.

32 Newman to Bishop Ullathorne, January 28, 1870, *LD* xxv, 18–19.

33 Newman to Robert Whitty, April 12, 1870, *LD* xxv, 93.

34 Newman to Robert Whitty, 94.

35 Newman to Robert Whitty, 94.

36 Newman to Robert Whitty, 94.

37 The most in-depth study of Newman's use of the concept of the *schola theologorum* is Michael Pahls's 2015 dissertation, "School of the Prophets: John Henry Newman's Anglican *Schola* and the Ecclesial Vocation of Theology" (Saint Louis University). For a condensed study of the same topic, see Pahls, "Development in the Service of Rectification: John Henry Newman's Understanding of the *Schola Theologorum*," in *Authority, Dogma, and History: The Role of the Oxford Movement Converts in the Papal Infallibility Debates*, ed. Kenneth L. Parker and Michael J. G. Pahls (Bethesda, MD: Academica Press, 2009), 195–211.

"the terms used are vague and comprehensive."[38] The definition, Newman noted, "says that the Pope is infallible, when he speaks ex cathedrâ, but what ex cathedrâ is has never been defined."[39] It would be the responsibility of the *schola theologorum* to determine what constitutes an *ex cathedra* statement, and they would settle this matter, in part, by looking to the past.[40] So, for instance, theologians would have to take into account the infamous case of Pope Honorius (rd. 625–638) in determining what kind of papal statements fall under the umbrella of an *ex cathedra* pronouncement. In the midst of a controversy over whether or not there were two sources of action in Christ, Honorius in a letter to the patriarch Sergius of Constantinople had endorsed the notion that Christ had only one will.[41] This position, commonly known as *monothelitism*, was later condemned as heretical at the Third Council of Constantinople (680), and that anathema was subsequently ratified by Pope Leo II. As Newman put it, "Historical facts, which are objections to [the] definition, must ever be elements in its interpretation. Though a Pope does all that Honorius did, he would not determine ex cathedrâ."[42]

This overview of Newman's response to Vatican I merely touches the surface of what he wrote on the matter, but already some similarities between his reception of that council and Ratzinger's reception of Vatican II are evident. Both figures affirm, as a working principle, that doctrinal development can take place at an ecumenical council. In his famous essay on development, in fact, Newman set forth a series of examples from ecumenical councils as instances of legitimate development.[43] His issue with the ultramontane faction at Vatican I did not have to do with their openness to development but with them pushing for a dogmatic definition that went beyond what could be demonstrated from

---

38 Newman to Ambrose Phillipps de Lisle, July 24, 1870, *LD* xxv, 164.

39 Newman to Alfred Plummer, March 12, 1871, *LD* xxv, 301.

40 See, for example, Newman to Mrs. William Froude, November 21, 1869, *LD* xxiv, 378: "Councils are formal things—and there is no need of drawing the line between their acts, or not much need, but a Pope is a living man, ever living, and it will be a great work to through this questioning well. You have to treat it doctrinally—and then again historically, reconciling what you teach with the verdict of history."

41 Pope Honorius I, *Epistle 4*, PL 80:473–75. Jaroslav Pelikan provides an informative historical overview of the monothelite controversy in *The Christian Tradition: A History of the Development of Doctrine*, vol. 2, *The Spirit of Eastern Christendom (600–1700)* (Chicago: University of Chicago Press, 1974), 63–75.

42 Newman to E. B. Pusey, August 28, 1870, *LD* xxv,198.

43 See the section in *Dev.* on "Instances in Illustration," beginning at p. 130.

the historical record. Their ultramontane conclusions foundered not against the theory of development but against the witness of history.[44]

The idea of doctrinal development figures prominently in Ratzinger's approach to conciliar theology, as well. In contrast to Newman's reception of Vatican I, Ratzinger during and shortly after Vatican II was enthusiastic about the council fathers' theological achievements. He helped to draft the final version of the Constitution on Divine Revelation and later defended its understanding of revelation as a necessary corrective to "the superficial approach of scholastic theology" that had been employed at Vatican I.[45] Meanwhile, Ratzinger described *Gaudium et Spes*, the Pastoral Constitution on the Church in the Modern World, as constituting a "revision of [Pius IX's] Syllabus" of Errors, that is as "a kind of counter-syllabus."[46] From Ratzinger's vantage point, the council kickstarted a process of renewal in the church's understanding of its relation to the modern state by moving beyond the defensive posture that had been the de facto stance of the church since the promulgation of Pius IX's 1864 encyclical *Quanta cura*. Later in his life, even as Ratzinger became increasingly concerned about misguided interpretations

---

44 One of the finest recent studies of Newman's theory of development is C. Michael Shea, "Development," in *The Oxford Handbook of John Henry Newman*, ed. Frederick Aquino and Benjamin King (Oxford: Oxford University Press, 2018), 284–303. Although the standard narrative has been that Newman's theory came under early suspicion by Roman authorities, Shea's 2017 monograph convincingly demonstrates that Newman's idea had a profound influence on the dogmatic definition of the Immaculate Conception. See Shea, *Newman's Early Roman Catholic Legacy, 1845–1854* (Oxford: Oxford University Press, 2017).

45 Joseph Ratzinger, "Dogmatic Constitution on Divine Revelation," trans. William Glen-Doepel, in *Commentary on the Documents of Vatican II*, vol. 3, ed. Herbert Vorgrimler (London: Burns & Oates, 1968), 191. On Ratzinger's contribution to the composition of *Dei Verbum*, see Jared Wicks, "Vatican II on Revelation—From behind the Scenes," *Theological Studies* 71, no. 3 (September 2010): 641–47. In his role as *peritus*, Ratzinger's affinity for biblical and patristic modes of theologizing played into his understanding of how the council should communicate: "As a matter of principle, Ratzinger stated that the conciliar texts 'should not be treatises in a scholastic style, as if they were taken over from textbooks of theologians, but should instead speak the language of Holy Scripture and the holy Fathers of the Church'" (Wicks, "Vatican II on Revelation," 643).

46 Joseph Ratzinger, *Principles of Catholic Theology: Building Stones for a Fundamental Theology* (San Francisco: Ignatius Press, 1987; original German edition, 1982), 381. According to Wicks, the designation "counter-syllabus," as adopted by Ratzinger, "does not refer to a revocation of the condemnations issued by Popes Pius IX and Pius X." Rather, it has to do with the way that Vatican II's documents, especially *Gaudium et Spes*, stand "in sharp contrast to earlier papal ways of addressing the world." Wicks concludes: "In Vatican II, the Catholic church turned a quite different 'face' to the world as it declined to issue censures but chose instead to speak to an about the world in respectful, hopeful, and encouraging ways." See Wicks, *Investigating Vatican II: Its Theologians, Ecumenical Turn, and Biblical Commitment* (Washington, DC: The Catholic University of America Press, 2018), 231.

of the council, he did not retreat to an outlook that denied the reality of development but simply insisted that a sound reception of Vatican II calls for "innovation in continuity," along the lines of what Pope John XXIII proposed at the start of the council when he challenged the bishops to express ancient truths in a new way through creatively harnessing the methods of research and literary forms of modern thought.[47] Ratzinger understood the application of the conciliar documents precisely in those terms and committed his pontificate to the project of the new evangelization that had been energetically launched by his predecessor as an extension of what John XXIII had hoped for when he convened the Second Vatican Council.

Ratzinger's aversion to a hermeneutic of discontinuity brings into relief another similarity between his outlook and Newman's: they both settled on a fundamentally conservative approach to conciliar teaching, insisting that a correct interpretation demands repect for the actual wording that was approved at a council. Ratzinger, as is well known, was critical of appeals to the spirit of the council, which advocate "courageously [going] beyond the texts" in order to "make room for the newness in which the Council's deepest intention [c] ould be expressed, even if it were still vague."[48] Ratzinger claimed that this methodology misunderstands the nature of a council by wrongly assuming that the bishops gathered had a mandate to create a new constitution for the church, as it were, when in fact the essential constitution of the church comes from the Lord himself and cannot be replaced.[49] Newman similarly adopted a conservative stance when it came to the definition of papal infallibility promulgated at Vatican I. Following the council, he counseled theologians

---

47 John XXIII, *Gaudet Mater Ecclesia*, October 11, 1962, in *Acta Apostolicae Sedis* 54 (1962): 786–96; English translation: *The Documents of Vatican II*, ed. Walter M. Abbott (New York: Crossroad, 1989), 1:715.

48 Benedict XVI, "Christmas Greetings to the Members of the Roman Curia" (2005), no. 38.

49 Benedict XVI, "Christmas Greetings to the Members of the Roman Curia," no. 39. Though it cannot be determined with certainty, one wonders if Ratzinger's comments in this section of the address were a response to Peter Hünermann's proposal that Vatican II represents "a constitutional text of faith." The substance of Hünermann's thesis can be found in "Der Text: Werden—Gestalt— Bedeutung; Eine hermeneutische Reflexion," in *Herders theologischer Kommentar zum Zweiten Vatikanischen Konzil*, vol. 5, ed. Peter Hünermann and Bernd Jochen Hilberath (Freiburg: Herder, 2006), 7ff. This volume was published in 2006, but Hünermann had written on the topic before that time, for example, in "Zu den Kategorien 'Konzil' und 'Konzilsentscheidung': Vorüberlegungen zur Interpretation des II. Vatikanums," in *Das II. Vatikanum: Christlicher Glaube im Horizont globaler Modernisierung*, ed. Peter Hünermann (Paderborn: Ferdinand Schöningh, 1998), 67–82. Grant Kaplan brings Hünermann's thesis into conversation with Ratzinger's hermeneutic of reform in "Vatican II as a Constitutional Text of Faith," *Horizons* 41, no. 1 (2014): 1–21.

to apply a minimizing hermeneutic to that teaching.[50] And like Ratzinger, he was insistent that what was binding on Catholics was the actual wording of the document, not the more exaggerated interpretations of its advocates. When making this point, Newman actually argued that *Pastor Aeternus* did not significantly develop what Catholic doctrine already affirmed regarding the papal office. As he put it, historically theologians had long asserted

> that what the Pope said ex cathedra, was true, *when* the Bishops had received it—what has been passed, is to the effect that what he determines ex cathedra is true independently of the reception by the Bishops—but nothing has been passed as to what is meant by "ex cathedrâ"—and this falls back to the Bishops and the Church to determine quite as much as before. Really therefore nothing has been passed of consequence.[51]

Now, Christians from other traditions—particularly the Eastern Orthodox—might balk at the idea that nothing of consequence was passed at Vatican I, but however we assess Newman's claim here, the quote nevertheless highlights the fundamentally conservative nature of his interpretive strategy. In sum, he and Ratzinger both advocate for a hermeneutic of reform in continuity that emphasizes interpreting recent conciliar decisions in light of previously articulated teachings.

NEWMAN AND RATZINGER ON THE NATURE AND LIMITS OF ECCLESIAL AUTHORITY

These commonalities naturally segue into the final section of this chapter, which analyzes the respective approaches of Newman and Ratzinger to ecclesial authority. Since the mid-nineteenth century, the Catholic Church has been wrestling with the changes in society brought about by the waning of Christendom and the ascendancy of secularization. It was only natural, under the circumstances, for a pope like Pius IX (rd. 1846–1878) to feel under attack and therefore to resort to a bunker mentality in relation to the broader society. At that stage in church history, a monarchical framework for ecclesiology looked

---

50 For more on Newman's minimizing hermeneutic, see my remarks in Marr, "Infallibility," in *Oxford Handbook of John Henry Newman*, 346–49.

51 Newman to Lady Simeon, November 1, 1870, *LD* xxv, 224.

appealing to many theologians, with its clear line of authority and as a kind of buffer to the democratizing currents driving the secular order. Newman prophetically recognized the limits of such a framework. Certainly, kingship is a prominent theme in different parts of scripture, but the biblical witness, in its totality—along with the patristic inheritance of this witness—highlights other equally significant characteristics of the church, ones that can be obscured if the regal element is overemphasized. Thus, even though Newman's early Catholic perspective could be described as moderately ultramontane,[52] over time he mitigated this dynamic by highlighting such factors as the responsibility of the hierarchy to consult the faithful and the role of the *schola theologorum* in the reception and application of dogmatic decrees.

In his most mature treatment of ecclesiology—the 1877 preface to the Via Media—Newman provided a seminal analysis of the church's threefold office, in which he described how the church, as a body, exhibits the three offices that belonged in a perfect way to Christ. According to this schema, each office—prophetical, priestly, and kingly—has its proper sphere of influence and, in turn, boundaries or limits to its operation. In this sense, the regal office, while important, does not have grounds to govern the church in a despotic manner. Within the context of his argument, Newman observes that each office is prone to a particular temptation or exaggeration. Since the regal office has as its vocation governance of the church, it must sometimes act with a view to expediency, but it oversteps its bounds when this characteristic mode of operating devolves into tyranny.[53] In this light, the regal office must be counterbalanced by healthily functioning priestly and prophetical offices. As Avery Dulles comments, "All three of [the offices] enter into the idea of the Church, standing in a dialectical relationship of mutual tension and support."[54]

---

52 Owen Chadwick arguably overstates the case when he contends that Newman was "at times an extreme Ultramontane in certain directions." See Owen Chadwick, *From Bossuet to Newman*, 2nd ed. (London: Cambridge University Press, 1987), 194. In *To Be Perfect Is to Have Changed Often*, I make the case that it is more accurate to describe Newman's early Roman Catholic ecclesiology as moderately ultramontane. See Marr, *To Be Perfect Is to Have Changed Often: The Development of John Henry Newman's Ecclesiological Outlook, 1845–1877* (Lanham, MD: Fortress Academic, 2018), 4–6.

53 John Henry Newman, preface, *The Via Media of the Anglican Church; In Two Volumes with a Preface and Notes*, 3rd ed., vol. 1 (London: Basil Montagu Pickering, 1877), xli, hereafter cited as *VM*. On this facet of Newman's argument, see the insightful commentary of Miller in *John Henry Newman on the Idea of Church*, 121–27.

54 Dulles, "Threefold Office in Newman's Ecclesiology," 13.

Corruption tends to emerge whenever one office encroaches upon the territory of another, disrupting the balance that is meant to exist among them.

Although Newman never applied this terminology directly to contemporary ecclesiastical affairs, as he watched Pio Nono's pontificate in action, he made comments that signaled his concern about the overreach of the regal office. Near the end of 1870, for instance, in a letter to Lady Simeon he remarked:

> We have come to a climax of tyranny. It is not good for a Pope to live 20 years. It is anomaly and bears no good fruit; he becomes a god, has no one to contradict him, does not know facts, and does cruel things without meaning it. For years past my only consolation personally has been in our Lord's Presence in the Tabernacle. I turn from the sternness of external authority to Him who can immeasurably compensate trials which after all are not real.[55]

Around that same time, he lamented that "the present Pope . . . has lived too long" but reiterated his trust that, no matter how long Pius ended up living, he would not be permitted in his acts to "go beyond the limit which God has assigned him."[56] Following the acceptance of *Pastor Aeternus*, Newman anticipated the day when a future pope or council would "trim the boat" by supplying what was lacking in Vatican I's theology of the papacy. As he reassured one friend, "the Latin race will not always have a monopoly [on] the magisterium of Catholicism. We must be patient in our time . . . God will take care of His Church—and, when the hour strikes, the reform will begin."[57]

From Ratzinger's perspective, the ecclesiological vision articulated at Vatican II could be seen as part of the reform that Newman anticipated. In his *Theological Highlights of Vatican II,* Ratzinger lauds the dogma of 1870 as progress, in that the spiritual essence of the papacy was reemphasized "after centuries of papal primacy in the political realm."[58] Nevertheless, "the outcome [of Vatican I] was still dubious in many ways," Ratzinger claims, for "theology seemed to lose its freedom in the face of an all too smoothly functioning central teaching office which prejudged every question almost before it had come up

---

55 Newman, *LD* xxv, 231.
56 Newman, *LD* xxv, 224.
57 Newman, *LD* xxv, 327.
58 Ratzinger, *Theological Highlights*, 136.

for discussion."[59] To transplant Newman's language, Ratzinger's basic assertion here is that the regal office was unduly hampering the prophetical office by preemptively shutting down theological discussions before they had time to bear real fruit. Vatican II, then, represented a genuine advancement in the church's self-understanding in that it formulated "a genuinely spiritual view of the episcopate as a complement to papal primacy."[60] With its doctrine of collegiality, the council offered a corrective to the papal centralism that had taken hold in the wake of Vatican I. Building on this theology, Ratzinger notes that "the Church is neither a parliamentary nor monarchical super-State, but rather a fabric of worshipping congregations."[61] Relatedly, the function of the papal office is "not monarchical rule, but rather coordination of the plurality which belongs to the Church's essence."[62]

Later on in this same work, Ratzinger develops a robust theology of collegiality, describing the college of bishops as "the form in which the apostolic community continues through the time of the Church."[63] While this college exercises its power in a solemn way when convened in council, "the collegiality of the bishops, as a medium for achieving unity" in diversity, he says, "supplies the normal pattern of orderly life in the Church."[64] Without denigrating in any way the papal office, Ratzinger affirms the rightful authority of the bishops in college as deriving from the sacramentality of episcopal ordination. Properly speaking, "collegiality is not based on a papally conferred jurisdiction" but instead "reaches into the very essence of the sacrament."[65] For all of these

---

59 Ratzinger, *Theological Highlights*, 136. Ratzinger commends Pope St. Pius X for having intervened when a "radically evolutionist" conception of doctrine threatened to overwhelm the study of historical theology. Nevertheless, he laments the fact that Pius's campaign against modernism ended up precipitating an antihistorical and overly defensive posture toward theological scholarship. See Ratzinger, *Storia e dogma* (Milan: Jaca Book, 1971), 16.

60 Ratzinger, *Theological Highlights*, 137.

61 Ratzinger, *Theological Highlights*, 137.

62 Ratzinger, *Theological Highlights*, 138.

63 Ratzinger, *Theological Highlights*, 167. Though some scholars accuse Ratzinger of abandoning the commitment to collegiality that he espoused around the time of the council, Christopher Collins challenges this notion. For an example of the former argument, see Massimo Faggioli, "Which Ratzinger?" *Commonweal*, February 2020, 9–10. The online version of the article is entitled, "Theological Drift: Benedict's Estrangement from Ratzinger." Collins, in contrast, recognizes an underlying continuity in Ratzinger's ecclesiology, which he describes as essentially "dialogical," or collegial; see Collins, *Word Made Love*, 93–99.

64 Ratzinger, *Theological Highlights*, 190.

65 Ratzinger, *Theological Highlights*, 187.

reasons, Ratzinger identifies papal centralism as the "most important problem" that was confronting the council fathers at the third session of Vatican II.[66] As Newman did, Ratzinger harbors concern about the prospect of a pope who would refuse to recognize the proper limits of his office and, in so doing, could threaten to choke the life out of the other offices that make up the church.

In the decades following the publication of his commentary on Vatican II, Ratzinger continued to warn against the possibility of papal overreach. For instance, in his 2005 introduction to Dom Alcuin Reid's *The Organic Development of the Liturgy*, Ratzinger stresses that, "The pope is not an absolute monarch whose will is law; rather, he is the guardian of the authentic Tradition and, thereby, the premier guarantor of obedience."[67] The pope, in other words, "cannot do as he likes. . . . His will is not that of arbitrary power, but that of obedience in faith." It is precisely the pope's accountability to tradition that enables him to oppose those who are tempted "to do whatever comes into their head."[68] With respect to the liturgy, therefore, the pope, in Ratzinger's words, "has the task of a gardener, not that of a technician who builds new machines and throws the old ones on the junk-pile."[69] The liturgy, as it has organically developed over the centuries, is a tradition unto itself and demands a humble reverence from those who are called to oversee it. To borrow a principle from *Sacrosanctum Concilium*, there should be "no innovations [to the liturgy] unless the good of the Church genuinely and certainly requires them; and care must be taken that any new forms adopted should in some way grow organically from forms already existing."[70] In line with these ideas, Ratzinger refers to the Roman rite as "a condensed form of living tradition."[71] It reflects the faith of generations and is the means by which we participate in the fellowship of those who came before us and those who will follow after us. Again, the pope's vocation in handling this living tradition is to tend to it as a gardener. He has no right to discard or radically alter what has been handed down to the church.

---

66 Ratzinger, *Theological Highlights*, 151.

67 Ratzinger, preface to *Organic Development of the Liturgy*, 10.

68 Ratzinger, preface to *Organic Development of the Liturgy*, 11.

69 Ratzinger, preface to *Organic Development of the Liturgy*, 11.

70 Vatican II, *Sacrosanctum concilium*, 1963, no. 23, https://www.vatican.va/archive/hist_councils/ii_vatican_council/documents/vat-ii_const_19631204_ sacrosanctum-concilium _en.html.

71 Ratzinger, preface to *Organic Development of the Liturgy*, 11. Christopher Collins argues that Ratzinger's liturgical theology is the effective expression of his eucharistic ecclesiology, grounded in a robust conception of *communio*; see Collins, *Word Made Love*, 109–13.

Dramatic alterations to the liturgy comprise just one area where someone might conclude that papal authority has become unduly inflated. The ultramontane element in the church manifests itself in other, sometimes surprising ways. One can see it, for instance, in the cult of personality that has surrounded recent pontiffs, perhaps most especially in the case of John Paul II. This intense devotion to the person of the Holy Father has also fed the phenomenon of creeping infallibility, or the tendency among Catholics to treat personal statements of the pope—say, from an interview or in a published work—as if they bear the weight of dogmatic authority. In turn, secular journalists rarely possess the acumen to perceive the difference between authoritative statements of the pope and his personal judgments, such that any word uttered by the present occupant of the Holy See is presented as the church's definitive take on a given issue. The magnitude of authority projected onto the Petrine office leaves Catholics who pay close attention to ecclesiastical affairs in breathless anticipation at the election of a new pope, hoping that whoever is chosen will side with their own values and concerns.

As Newman and Ratzinger both tried to show, this is an unsustainable state of affairs. The essential purpose of the bishop of Rome is to serve as the "perpetual and visible principle of unity" in the church.[72] When a holder of the office wields power in a heavy-handed or arbitrary manner, he acts contrary to his vocation. Serving in this capacity is undoubtably a difficult job, particularly considering that the pope pastors a global church in which news travels instantaneously and where the concerns among Catholics in one part of the world may be completely different from those in another. The challenge for the church today is that of remaining faithful to the received tradition while mediating the content of that tradition in such a way that it proves life-giving to Catholics inhabiting diverse and rapidly changing societies. Newman's theology prophetically anticipated some of these complexities. In contrast to some of his contemporaries, he recognized that the church in the modern world would not be able to evangelize persuasively without thinking critically about the history of doctrine. A simplistic, ahistorical construal of the faith would not suffice. The reality of development is, today, taken for granted, and it's the proverbial oxygen of our ecclesial ecosystem. What is far less settled is the question of how far development can proceed. To borrow a phrase from

---

72 John Paul II, *Ut Unum Sint*, 1995, no. 88, https://www.vatican.va/content/john-paul-ii/en/encyclicals/documents/hf_jp-ii_enc_25051995_ut-unum-sint.html.

John T. Noonan, we inhabit "a Church that can and cannot change," and some of the most contentious theological debates in recent decades have been waged over which parts of the tradition are open to development and which are not.[73]

Newman established the basic framework for this conversation. It's impossible today to talk about development without addressing the core features of his argument. It is my contention that Joseph Ratzinger represents a natural heir to Newman's legacy, in that he carried forward key components of Newman's ecclesiology by applying them in creative ways to a changed context. For all of his openness to development, Ratzinger, like Newman, never abandoned a fundamental commitment to continuity.[74] Doctrine develops, to be sure, but it is able to retain its liberative power, Ratzinger contended, only if it remains in essential continuity with the apostolic faith. It's noteworthy, therefore, that in his famous Christmas address in which he made a case on behalf of the hermeneutic continuity, Benedict/Ratzinger set forth as a guide for this hermeneutic Pope John XXIII, who noted at the opening of Vatican II, "The substance of the ancient doctrine of the deposit of faith is one thing, and the way in which it is presented is another."[75] The challenge that John XXIII set forth on that occasion remains, in many ways, the central task for theologians today. We have moved essentially from the first part of Newman's famous essay—the case for development—to the conclusion of his essay, which sketches a plan for applying the notes of authentic development.

As to the role of ecclesial authority in this process, Newman and Ratzinger have left us rich images of what a life-giving regal office can look like. Admittedly, there is a certain appeal to the idea of a papacy that resolves doctrinal disagreements immediately and by fiat.[76] But as we know from scripture, that is not the way Christ has constituted his church. St. Peter was the Prince

---

[73] See John T. Noonan, *A Church That Can and Cannot Change: The Development of Catholic Moral Teaching* (Notre Dame, IN: University of Notre Dame Press, 2006). In his 2014 work on the doctrine of revelation, Matthew Levering exposes some of the weakness in Noonan's approach. See Levering, *Engaging the Doctrine of Revelation: The Mediation of the Gospel through Church and Scripture* (Grand Rapids, MI: Baker Academic, 2014), 185–97.

[74] See, for example, Ratzinger's comments on the objective nature of revelation—"a message that has been given to us"—and how "we have no right to change it as we wish," in *Co-Workers of the Truth* (San Francisco: Ignatius Press, 1992), 265.

[75] John XXIII, *Gaudet Mater Ecclesia*, in *The Documents of Vatican II*, 715.

[76] The biblical basis of Ratzinger's ecclesiology is evident in his 2005 work *Pilgrim Fellowship of Faith: The Church as Communion* (San Francisco: Ignatius Press, 2005). Particularly important to him is Acts 2:42, which he says sets forth four essential characteristics of the church catholic: that it would devote itself to the apostles' teaching, to the breaking of bread, to life in communion,

of the Apostles, but he did not act alone. When the first major controversy erupted in the church, the Apostles convened a council in Jerusalem (Acts 15), and on one occasion, St. Paul opposed Peter to his face (Gal 2:11–14). These dynamics persisted in the life of the church in the centuries following the apostolic age, and the relation between pope and other members of the body of Christ has remained a live issue into modern times. Newman, for his part, fought strenuously against expansions to papal powers that could occlude the sense of the faithful. As he noted in his famous *Rambler* article of 1859, the hierarchy with the pope as its head has something to benefit from consulting the faithful on matters of doctrine, for "there is something in the *pastorum et fidelium conspiratio*, which is not in the pastors alone."[77] In other words, the shepherds (*pastorum*) of the church can lead more effectively when they "breathe together" (*conspiratio*) with the lay faithful (*fidelium*). This notion is foundational to Newman's vision of the threefold office of the church—prophetical, sacerdotal, and regal—existing in a dialectical relationship of mutual tension and support. The regal office must be careful not to govern in such a way that it stifles the full flourishing of theologians and lay faithful. Ratzinger makes a similar point when he contends that the pope is not an absolute monarch whose will holds the force of law but rather the guardian of authentic tradition.[78] The bishop of Rome fulfills his calling as minister of unity precisely through obedience in faith. Ratzinger's comments about the binding nature of the doctrinal tradition echoes Newman's conviction that the prophetical office, whose sphere is theology, regulates the regal and sacerdotal offices, since revelation is, in his words, "the original and essential idea of Christianity."[79]

Of course, the onus in these matters does not fall only on the shoulders of ecclesial authority. The faithful—in a particular way, theologians—are also called to protect and transmit the tradition in line with our station in life. In recent decades, a fair number of academic theologians have come to view ecclesial authority only as a burden—something not to be respected but

---

and to regular worship. In *Pilgrim Fellowship of Faith*, 61, Ratzinger describes the book of Acts as a "first [or, primordial] ecclesiology."

77 John Henry Newman, *On Consulting the Faithful in Matters of Doctrine*, ed. John Coulson (London: Geoffrey Chapman, 1961), 104.

78 Ratzinger, preface to *Organic Development of the Liturgy*, 10.

79 Newman, *VM* i, xlvii.

overcome. In light of this temptation, it's worth recalling (in closing) a warning given by Ratzinger in his 2001 work *Called to Communion*. This quote succinctly captures the heart of his ecclesiology:

> Because Christ is never alone but came in order to unite the world in his Body, love for the Church becomes an additional component: we do not seek a Christ whom we have invented, for only in the real communion of the Church do we encounter the real Christ. And once again the depth and seriousness of one's relation to the Lord himself is revealed in the ready willingness to love the Church, to live together with her and to serve Christ in her.[80]

The real Christ, we might add, was a healer and comforter but also a lawgiver. The real Christ built his church upon St. Peter and has sustained that body across time through the means of apostolic succession. Communion in this body, therefore, means fostering due respect for and practicing obedience to the authorities that providence has chosen to lead this body. Communion, authority, and adherence to tradition are, ultimately, all intertwined. As Newman warned, each office in the church is prone to a particular temptation: if authority can sometimes adopt tyrannical modes of governing, theologians must recognize that their own vocation runs the risk of falling into rationalism. For while theology can offer prophetical correctives to the misuse of power, if cut off from the real communion of the church, it cannot bear fruit.

---

[80] Joseph Cardinal Ratzinger, *Called to Communion: Understanding the Church Today*, trans. Adrian Walker (San Francisco: Ignatius Press, 1991), 130.

11

"A LARGER IDEA OF DIVINE SKILL"

NEWMAN, RATZINGER, AND THE THEORY OF EVOLUTION

Matthew J. Ramage

In an age when many believe that Christianity and evolutionary theory are mutually incompatible, St. John Henry Newman and Joseph Ratzinger stand out as two towering ecclesiastical figures who belie this common misconception. These theological giants made remarkably complementary contributions toward an engagement of evolution in the light of faith. Yet, as far as I have been able to tell, no attempt has been made to put the two into direct conversation with one another on this topic.

I seek to do just this, focusing on two fundamental areas of convergence in their thought. First, I will survey the thinkers' overall assessment of evolutionary theory and their shared conviction regarding the possibility of a mutual enrichment between evolutionary science and theology. Second—and this is what interests me most—I will reflect on each thinker's respective epistemology in relation to a reception of evolutionary theory. Specifically, each boasts a conceptual framework that when applied to this scientific matter enable us to recognize it as a discovery that while not infallible or complete is nevertheless sufficiently certain to require that we revisit certain traditional assumptions in its light. I believe that the way each of these scholars arrives at this conclusion is crucial, for my experience has been that believers who fail to acknowledge the evidence that supports life's evolutionary history often end up—to borrow an expression from Aquinas—making the faith look ridiculous to would-be believers and placing obstacles to their belief.[1]

In the end, my hope is that this chapter's engagement with Ratzinger and Newman will bolster the proclamation of the gospel in today's world by removing the common obstacle to belief that occurs when believers reject well-grounded scientific conclusions on the basis that they are not absolutely certain. In this sense, this endeavor serves as a sort of *apologia* for human reason that serves to make space for intellectually compelling Christian apologetics.

OVERALL APPROACH TO ENGAGING EVOLUTIONARY THEORY IN THE LIGHT OF FAITH

JOHN HENRY NEWMAN

Mutual Enrichment of Faith and Science Generally
As a contemporary of Charles Darwin, Newman's writings give us a privileged lens into a faithful Catholic reception of the modern theory of evolution by natural selection at its origin. A fitting entry point into Newman's thought in this domain can be found in an 1855 lecture on faith and science that would eventually be included in his *Idea of a University*. In this text, which predates Darwin's *On the Origin of Species* by four years, Newman speaks of science and theology as "two worlds" and "two great circles of knowledge" that are "mismatched" and "cannot on the whole contradict each other."[2] Describing

---

1 Aquinas, *Summa theologiae*, trans. Fathers of the English Dominican Province (Westminster, MD: Christian Classics, 1981), I, q. 68, a. 1, hereafter cited as *ST*; Augustine, *The Literal Meaning of Genesis*, trans. J. H. Taylor, Ancient Christian Writers 41 (New York: Newman Press, 1982), 42–43. For a similar text in which Augustine warns believers ignorant of the physical universe against making misguided claims in the name of defending the faith, see his *Confessions* (Oxford: Oxford University Press, 2008), 5.3.9, 76–77. Galileo referenced this last text in the debate over heliocentrism that raged in his own day. See Galileo Galilei, "Letter to the Grand Duchess Christina," in *The Galileo Affair: A Documentary History*, ed. Maurice Finocchiaro (Berkeley: University of California Press, 1989), 103, 112: "For how can [outsiders] believe our books in regard to the resurrection of the dead, the hope of eternal life, and the kingdom of heaven when they catch a Christian committing an error about something they know very well . . . things they have been able to observe or to establish by unquestionable argument?"

2 John Henry Newman, "Christianity and Physical Science," in *The Idea of a University Defined and Illustrated in Nine Discourses Delivered to the Catholics of Dublin in Occasional Lectures and Essays Addressed to the Members of the Catholic University*, ed. Martin J. Svaglic (Notre Dame,

theology as "just what such science is not," the rector of the new Catholic University in Dublin explained that the scientist "contemplates the facts before him" and treats of efficient causes and laws, whereas the theologian "gives the reasons of these facts," unveiling their divine origin and final cause.[3] While recognizing that theology is "the highest indeed, and widest" science, Newman nevertheless insists that it "does not interfere with the real freedom of any secular science in its own particular department."[4] As these quotes illustrate, for Newman as for the Catholic tradition at large, faith and science are compatible and indeed mutually enriching, provided each respects the limits of its particular expertise.[5]

Divine Design and the Presence of Chance and Instrumental Causality in Evolution

Newman's positive appreciation of "the Darwin theory," as he called it, was evident in his first written remarks on the subject in 1863.[6] Unlike many at the time, Newman found the science to be consistent with the teachings of the church. In 1874, for example, he wrote, "I see nothing in the theory of evolution inconsistent with an Almighty Creator and Protector."[7]

The role of chance and an apparent absence of design in evolution did not pose deep problems for Newman, and this for a very simple reason: "I believe in design because I believe in God; not in God because I see design,"

IN: University of Notre Dame Press, 1982), 323, 337. For helpful surveys of Newman's thought on faith and science in general and the theory of evolution in particular, see Ryan Vilbig, "John Henry Newman's View of the 'Darwin Theory,'" *Newman Studies Journal* 8, no. 2 (2011): 52–61; Mark Kalthoff, "A Different Voice from the Eve of *The Origin*: Reconsidering John Henry Newman on Christianity, Science, and Intelligent Design," *Perspectives in Science and Christian Belief* 53 (2001): 14–23; Berta Moritz, "A Patron Saint of Evolution?" *Church Life Journal*, October 16, 2019); and Stanley Jaki, *Newman's Challenge* (Grand Rapids, MI: Eerdmans, 2000), 265–90.

3 Newman, "Christianity and Physical Science," 326. Newman adds, "The physicist tells us of laws; the Theologian of the Author, Maintainer, and Controller of them; of their scope, of their suspension, if so be; of their beginning and their end" (326).

4 John Henry Newman, *Discourses on the Scope and Nature of University Education Addressed to the Catholics of Dublin* (Dublin: James Duffy, 1852), 152–53.

5 For a treatment of this point, see Jonathan Chappell, "A Grammar of Descent: John Henry Newman and the Compatibility of Evolution with Christian Doctrine," *Science & Christian Belief* 27, no. 2 (2015): 183–86.

6 For this term, see John Henry Newman to William Monsell, 22, June 1863, in *The Letters and Diaries of John Henry Newman*, vol. 20 (London: Nelson, 1970), 479–80.

7 John Henry Newman to David Brown, 1874, in *The Letters and Diaries of John Henry Newman*, vol. 25 (Oxford: Clarendon, 1973), 137.

he said.[8] Newman therefore parts ways with those who look at what they consider to be "the accidental evolution of organic beings" and the "blind instrumentality" of nature's laws and assume that the element of chance in evolution is inconsistent with divine design. In reality, the saint responds that it is "an instance of incomprehensibly and infinitely marvelous Wisdom and Design to have given certain laws to matter millions of ages ago, which have surely and precisely worked out, in the long course of those ages, those effects which He from the first proposed." Accordingly, he observes that "Mr. Darwin's theory need not, then, be atheistical, be it true or not," and that the role of contingency in creation "is accidental to *us*, not to *God*." Indeed, Newman suggests that the role of secondary creaturely agents in evolution (including chance causes) "may simply be suggesting a larger idea of Divine Prescience and Skill" than would shine forth if God had created all of our planet's myriad species independently of one another by divine fiat.[9]

Compatibility of Evolutionary Theory and the Testimony of Scripture

Newman's thought on the Bible in relation to modern science coheres with his broader outlook that I have just sketched. In an unpublished revised introduction to his essay on biblical inspiration, the saint described nature and revelation as "nothing but two separate communications from the same infinite Truth," adding, "Scripture is not inspired to convey mere secular knowledge, whether about the heaven or the earth, or the race of man. As a consequence of this, Newman held, "I need not fear for Revelation whatever truths may be brought to light by means of observation and experience out of the world of phenomena which environ us."[10] Or as he wrote to E. B. Pusey,

---

8 John Henry Newman to William Brownlow, April 13, 1870, in *The Letters and Diaries of John Henry Newman*, vol. 25, ed. C. S. Dessain and T. Gornall (Oxford: Clarendon, 1978), 97, 137–38; John Henry Newman, *An Essay in Aid of a Grammar of Assent* (Notre Dame, IN: University of Notre Dame Press, 1979), 109–11. All references to the *Grammar* will be to this version, except in the instance further below when Gilson's introduction to another edition is mentioned.

9 John Henry Newman to J. Walker of Scarborough on Darwin's theory of evolution, May 22, 1868, in *The Letters and Diaries of John Henry Newman*, vol. 24, 77–78 (emphasis in original).

10 John Henry Newman, *The Theological Papers of John Henry Newman on Biblical Inspiration and on Infallibility*, ed. J. Derek Holmes (Oxford: Clarendon, 1979), 29, 31. Concerning the common fear that engaging new scientific discoveries will damage the faith, Newman emphasizes that *not* tackling these issues presents the greater danger: "Do not let us make real difficulties for the cause of truth by running away from fancied ones. . . . I must say distinctly that I have no sympathy at all in that policy, which will not look difficulties or apparent difficulties in the face, and puts off the evil day of considering them as long as it can" (32–33).

THEORY OF EVOLUTION

"little is determined about the inspiration of Scripture, except in matters of faith and morals." Noting that other traditional assumptions about life on our planet may eventually turn out to be just as inaccurate as geocentrism was shown to be beginning with Galileo, Newman expresses the wish "that divine and human science might each be suffered in peace to take its own line, the one not interfering with the other," seeing as "their circles scarcely intersect each other."[11] Yet in violating this dynamic by restricting inquirers in their free exercise of reason, Newman noted that the "injurious" suspicion of science entertained by some religious men ironically impedes discoveries that would eventually turn out to favor the Christian cause.[12]

If a particular scientific discovery appears to contradict a passage of scripture, Newman therefore urges believers not to hastily reject it. On the contrary, as he wrote in another 1855 essay, the faithful should be open to three different eventualities when an empirical datum appears to contradict a revealed dogma:

> If anything seems to be proved by astronomer, or geologist, or chronologist, or antiquarian, or ethnologist, in contradiction to the dogmas of faith, that point will eventually turn out, first, *not* to be proved, or, secondly, not *contradictory*, or thirdly, not contradictory to anything *really revealed*, but to something which has been confused with revelation.[13]

While this last text was composed before Darwin published his theory, it is easy to see that the third of the above categories aptly characterizes the situation of evolution vis-à-vis the text of scripture. If we interpret scripture in a wooden and literalistic manner, then, yes, the discoveries of evolutionary science do in fact contradict it. However, if properly understood according to its truly literal—or, perhaps better, literary—sense, the revealed message of Genesis is in no way contradicted by evolutionary science, and the only tension lies between evolution and what has been *confused* with its revealed teaching. Indeed, so convinced is Newman of this that in his view even the evolution of human beings poses no intrinsic obstacle for faith, provided that

---

11 John Henry Newman to Edward B. Pusey, April 13,1858, in *The Letters and Diaries of John Henry Newman*, vol. 18 (Oxford: Clarendon, 1973), 322.

12 Newman, *Theological Papers of John Henry Newman*, 31.

13 Newman, "Christianity and Scientific Investigation," in *The Idea of a University*, 351 (emphasis in original).

we take care to uphold the Catholic doctrine of man as the *imago Dei* and the immortality of his soul."[14]

JOSEPH RATZINGER

Mutual Enrichment of Faith and Science Generally

In line with Newman, Ratzinger is consistently respectful of the modern sciences as independent disciplines of inquiry that have much to contribute to our understanding of the truth of things. Indeed, to compellingly repropose the faith in today's world, Ratzinger insists on the importance of an intelligent faith that is conversant with the discoveries of modern science. As this endeavor requires considerable virtue, Benedict said in his Regensburg address that today's disciple must have the willingness to "enter into the debates of our time," armed with "the courage to engage the whole breadth of reason."[15] Yet even as this task may seem overwhelming, he adds, "Today's man must be able to recognize again that the Church is neither afraid of nor need be afraid of science, because she is sheltered in the truth of God."[16]

---

14 John Henry Newman to E. B. Pusey, 5, June 1870, in *The Letters and Diaries of John Henry Newman*, vol. 25 (Oxford: Clarendon, 1978), 138. Asking whether it is possible that the first man was *not* immediately taken from the dust of the earth, Newman replies that, while all of us are dust (Ecc 3:20), it is also the case that "we never were dust—we are from fathers." To this, he humbly proceeds to ask, "Why may not the same be the case with Adam? I don't say that it is so—but if the sun does not go round the earth and the earth stand still, as Scripture seems to say, I don't know why Adam needs be immediately out of dust."
For an informative essay that explores Newman on the above point, see Vilbig, "John Henry Newman's View of the 'Darwin Theory,'" 55–56. Summarizing Newman's approach to this topic, Vilbig writes, "The human mind is itself a distinct act of Creation, ensouling a body that was constructed in an evolutionary way— thereby making the human body the crowning product of evolution." On Newman, evolution, and the soul, see also Jonathan Chappell, "A Grammar of Descent," 180–206. As Chappell notes, for Newman "a judicious and scientifically informed reading of the Genesis narrative concerning the origins of humankind shows that there is scope within the text itself for accepting the findings of palaeontology that *Homo sapiens* has descended from a non-human progenitor" (206). For Newman's texts on the subject of the human soul being immortal and not subject to evolutionary change while allowing for a mediate generation of man's body from parent species, see 192–93n38. Drawing a helpful analogy and connecting Newman's thought to the biblical text, Chappell writes: "Just as in a post-Copernican age it is no longer possible to subscribe to a (supposedly) biblically sanctioned geocentric cosmology, so a careful exegesis of Genesis reveals that the text itself appears to have the resources to allow for a mediate generation of Adam's body out of 'dust and mud' via the intermediary of a parent species" (205).

15 Benedict XVI, "Faith, Reason and the University: Memories and Reflections," September 12, 2006.

16 Josef Frings, "Das Konzil und die moderne Gedankenwelt," *Herder Korrespondenz* 16 (1961–62): 174. For an enlightening discussion of this speech, see Emery de Gaál, *O Lord, I Seek Your Countenance: Explorations and Discoveries in Pope Benedict XVI's Theology* (Steubenville, OH: Emmaus

In empirical matters that touch on issues like the role of chance in creation, Benedict—like his predecessor, John Paul II—advocates a "principle of autonomy" that allows sciences to operate according to their respective methods, without theology seeking to fix their conclusions in advance.[17] Ratzinger believes that this is the right approach to evolution given that the theory itself neither invalidates not corroborates the faith but rather represents an opportunity to probe the faith more profoundly.[18] As the then-cardinal once memorably said in a homily, "We cannot say: creation or evolution . . . we are faced here with two complementary—rather than mutually exclusive—realities."[19] As pope, Benedict would later remark that the opposition between creation and evolution that one often encounters is "absurd."[20] According to the pontiff, the question of whether the Christian ought to privilege either the authority of science or of the faith is a red herring. Put simply, his view is that we should judge science by science, and theology by theology, for the claims of faith and evolutionary theory can never contradict one another provided we remain clear on what lies within the purview of each.

Academic, 2018), 149. For the English translation of an abridged version of the speech, see Jared Wicks, SJ, "Six Texts by Prof. Joseph Ratzinger as *Peritus* before and during Vatican Council II," *Gregorianum* 89 (2008): 258–59. On this topic, see also Aquinas, *Summa theologiae*, I-II, q. 109, a. 1, ad 1; Aquinas, *De veritate* q. 1, a. 8.

17 For the "principle of autonomy," see John Paul II, *Fides et Ratio*, nos. 13, 77. See also Second Vatican Council, *Gaudium et Spes*, no. 36, wherein we read that the council "cannot but deplore certain habits of mind, which are sometimes found too among Christians, which do not sufficiently attend to the rightful independence of science and which, from the arguments and controversies they spark, lead many minds to conclude that faith and science are mutually opposed." Citing the First Vatican Council's constitution *Dei Filius*, chap.. 4, §5, it adds, "Therefore if methodical investigation within every branch of learning is carried out in a genuinely scientific manner and in accord with moral norms, it never truly conflicts with faith, for earthly matters and the concerns of faith derive from the same God." These more recent formulations are consonant with the Angelic Doctor's classic statement, "It is impossible that the truth of faith should be opposed to those principles that the human reason knows naturally." See Aquinas, *Summa Contra Gentiles*, trans. Anton C. Pegis (Garden City, NY: Hanover House, 1955), 7, §1.

18 Ratzinger, "Belief in Creation and the Theory of Evolution," in *Dogma and Preaching* (San Francisco: Ignatius Press, 2011), 142; Ratzinger, preface to *Evolutionismus und Christentum*, ed. Robert Spaemann, R. Löw, and P. Koslowski (Weinheim: Acta Humaniora, 1986), viii.

19 Ratzinger, *In the Beginning: A Catholic Understanding of the Story of Creation and the Fall* (Grand Rapids, MI: Eerdmans, 1995), 50 (emphasis added).

20 Benedict XVI, "Meeting with Clergy of the Dioceses of Belluno-Feltre and Treviso," July 24, 2007.

Divine Design and the Presence of Chance
and Instrumental Causality in Evolution

Provided that empirical science does not profess to account for the entirety of existence by means of its methods alone, Benedict, like Newman, has no hesitancy in acknowledging the role played by chance in evolution.[21] This outlook, which emerges in his private writings, is articulated especially clearly in a document that the International Theological Commission (ITC) penned under the leadership of its then-president Cardinal Ratzinger: "Even the outcome of a truly contingent natural process can nonetheless fall within God's providential plan for creation. . . . Divine causality can be active in a process that is both contingent and guided. Any evolutionary mechanism that is contingent can only be contingent because God made it so."[22] In contrast with those who would seek design in the complexity of discrete structures in our universe, the word "design" in this text envisions God's hand operative at a more fundamental order: the providential design of creation *as a whole*.[23]

Beyond the phenomenon of chance operative at the minutest of levels in our genetic code, Ratzinger is equally attentive to the more fundamental fact that new creatures arise through the agency of secondary creaturely causes without the need for any direct divine intervention as is sometimes assumed.

---

[21] Ratzinger, preface to *Evolutionismus und Christentum*, vi–viii; Ratzinger, *Truth and Tolerance: Christian Belief and World Religions* (San Francisco: Ignatius Press, 2003), 178–83; and John Paul II, *Fides et Ratio*, no. 88. As Benedict observes, some who are enamored by the explanatory power of science unfortunately can be led to embrace what Benedict and his predecessor called scient*ism*—an ideology that refuses to admit the validity of any other form of knowledge than that which comes from the empirical sciences, thus relegating religious, theological, ethical and aesthetic knowledge to the realm of the subjective.
In this vein, Ratzinger insists that the Christian faith stand its ground against totalizing "mythical philosophies" which allege that evolutionary theory can explain everything while failing to acknowledge that many details of the theory (e.g., when and how life first originated, when and how our hominin ancestors finally became truly human, etc.) remain at the level of hypothesis and will continue to be refined as research progresses. See Ratzinger, *Salt of the Earth* (San Francisco: Ignatius Press, 1997), 31. Here we find a parallel with Ratzinger's famous call for a "criticism of the criticism" within the field of biblical studies. On this subject, see Ratzinger, "Biblical Interpretation in Crisis: On the Question of the Foundations and Approaches of Exegesis Today," in *Biblical Interpretation in Crisis: The Ratzinger Conference on Bible and Church* (Grand Rapids, MI: Eerdmans, 1989), 6.

[22] International Theological Commission, *Communion and Stewardship*, no. 69. See also Aquinas, *ST* I, q. 22, a. 2. What the ITC is suggesting here aligns well with what Aquinas has to say about the place of contingent events of chance in relation to God's providence. For a helpful discussion of this topic, see Mariusz Tabaczek, OP, "What Do God and Creatures Really Do in an Evolutionary Change? Divine Concurrence and Transformism from the Thomistic Perspective," *American Catholic Philosophical Quarterly* 00 (2019): 445–82.

[23] International Theological Commission, *Communion and Stewardship*, no. 68.

For Ratzinger, this is no obstacle to an affirmation of God's essential role in the evolutionary dynamic: on the contrary, it is an occasion for wonder at the reality that creatures, including man, arise "not next to [nicht neben] but rather precisely in" [gerade in] the processes of a living being, i.e. the biological process by which a sperm and egg come together to form an embryo."[24] At the same time, Ratzinger echoes Newman in steadfastly insisting that the origin of humans is not reducible to a biological explanation—that man's soul is "not the mere product of development, even though it comes to light by way of development."[25]

Compatibility of Evolutionary Theory and the Testimony of Scripture

Like Newman, the emeritus pontiff understands man's origin in a way that eschews not only biological reductionism on the one extreme but also biblical literalism on the other. This can be seen in many of his writings, such as when he writes that the biblical depiction of Adam's creation "is valid for each human being in the same way." In other words, he continues, "Each human is Adam [Jeder Mensch ist Adam], a new beginning; Adam is each human being [Adam ist jeder Mensch]. The physiological event is more than a physiological event."[26]

As Ratzinger understands well, the biblical portrait of man's creation from the "dust" and his reception of the divine "breath" were never meant to provide a physical account of the first man's origin along the lines of what we would capture with a video camera. Rather, the meaning of these statements is more fundamental. Adam ("human being") is all of us, and what we all are is "dust" (i.e., intimately connected to the earth and the rest of creation) and "breath" (i.e., more than the rest of creation, as our species alone enjoys the capacity for relationship with God). Accordingly, for Ratzinger, Genesis's narrative and the Catholic doctrine that mankind has an immediate or direct origin distinct from that of other creatures "is not meant to suggest any miraculous tinkering by God."[27] This account, penned by a German cleric a

---

24 Ratzinger, "Man between Reproduction and Creation," in *Dogma and Preaching*, 79 ["Der Mensch zwischen Reproduktion and Schöpfung," *Internationale Katholische Zeitschrift* 1 (1989), 68].

25 Ratzinger, "Belief in Creation and the Theory of Evolution," 141.

26 Ratzinger, "Man between Reproduction and Creation," 79 ["Der Mensch zwischen Reproduktion und Schöpfung," 68].

27 Ratzinger, *Schöpfungslehre* (1964), 178, cited in Santiago Sanz, "Joseph Ratzinger y la doctrina de la creación: Los apuntes de Münster de 1964 (y III)," *Revista Española de Teología* 74 (2014): 475n58.

century after our Englishman's account, is profoundly consistent with the latter's conviction that God's governance of the universe through the natures of his creatures—allowing life to evolve by means of nature's own internal laws—constitutes an even greater manifestation of divine wisdom than would shine forth in a scenario in which God were to override creaturely causality and "tinkering" with creation.

AN EPISTEMOLOGY FOR ENGAGING EVOLUTIONARY THEORY IN THE LIGHT OF FAITH

Beyond the affinities between their overarching approaches to faith and evolutionary theory, I would now like to explore another remarkable point of contact between the thought of Newman and Ratzinger: each thinker's epistemological approach to evolution, the manner in which each comes to recognize it as a scientific certainty. As I mentioned above, I find that this approach—as opposed to rejecting evolution on the one hand or deeming everything about it to be an infallible certitude on the other—can be of great assistance in the church's ongoing proclamation of the gospel in our scientific age. Specifically, I hope to show that thinkers do not believe that we need to have absolute certitude in order to draw sound scientific conclusions concerning evolutionary theory, thereby removing the common obstacle to belief that occurs when believers reject well-grounded scientific insights on the grounds that they are not sufficiently certain.

At the time of the Galileo controversy, Cardinal Robert Bellarmine wrote that if science were to demonstrate something that contradicts the way we have heretofore interpreted the Bible (which it in fact ending up doing), "then one would have to proceed with great care in explaining the Scriptures that appear contrary; and say rather that we do not understand them than that what is demonstrated is false." To this, however, Bellarmine also immediately added an important requirement: "I will not believe that there is such a demonstration, until it is shown me."[28]

That geocentrism debate has long come and gone, but a parallel question presses upon us today: namely, has the truth of evolution indeed been shown convincingly enough that a traditional reading of Genesis's account of man's

---

28 Robert Bellarmine to Foscarini, April 12, 1516, in Maurice Finocchiaro, *The Galileo Affair: A Documentary History* (Berkeley: University of California Press, 1989), 68.

direct creation by God is now untenable? And what would it take to arrive at the point where it becomes necessary to reinterpret this narrative along symbolic lines or else risk doing great harm to the faithful? To be sure, it is imprudent to jump on the bandwagon of every latest alleged scientific discovery or subordinate the faith to fleeting trends. Moreover, it must be acknowledged that evolutionary theory will always remain an incomplete science, and we are only in the nascent stage of grappling with its theological implications. Yet if we set our epistemological bar unreasonably high and ask evolutionary theory to fill in every one of its lacunae before giving it the serious attention that it deserves, then we will never be able to make needed developments and will thereby damage the credibility of the faith as well as hinder its ability to illumine new discoveries. Let us see what insight Newman and Ratzinger might shed on this subject.

JOSEPH RATZINGER

Ratzinger's stance with respect to Darwin's theory is that the science is well-founded and in of itself noncontroversial, provided it is not wedded to materialist assumptions. His thought concerning the epistemic status of evolutionary theory can be glimpsed in *Introduction to Christianity*, where in 1968 the then-professor already described the theory evolution as a discovery that "for practical purposes already lies behind us as self-evident."[29] As Benedict XVI, he would further remark that "there are so many scientific proofs in favor of evolution which appears as a reality that we can see and enriches our knowledge of life and being as such."[30]

This stance was also taken by the ITC after studying the topic from the years 2000 to 2002 at a time when the commission was helmed by Cardinal Ratzinger. Noting that the general scientific consensus places the first organism on this planet between 3.5 to 4 billion years ago, the ITC significantly states that "*it has been demonstrated* that all living organisms on earth are genetically related," to which the commission adds that "it is *virtually certain* that all living organisms have descended from this first organism."[31] What grounds such

---

29 Joseph Ratzinger, *Introduction to Christianity* (San Francisco: Ignatius Press, 2004), 66.

30 Benedict XVI, "Meeting with Clergy of the Dioceses of Belluno-Feltre and Treviso," July 24, 2007. As will be discussed further below, these "proofs" are not strict demonstrations of evolution but are better understood as strong pieces of *evidence*, as the Italian word *prova* can indeed be translated.

31 International Theological Commission, *Communion and Stewardship*, no. 63 (emphasis added).

certitude? Echoing the thought of then-pontiff John Paul II, the ITC explains, "Converging evidence from many studies in the physical and biological sciences furnishes mounting support for some theory of evolution to account for the development and diversification of life on earth, while controversy continues over the pace and mechanisms of evolution."[32] Wrapping up its summary of man's evolutionary history, the document finally notes that while the precise narrative "is complex and subject to revision, physical anthropology and molecular biology combine to make a convincing case for the origin of the human species in Africa about 150,000 years ago in a humanoid population of common genetic lineage."[33] As we will become evident below with the help of Newman, the ITC is able to draw this conclusion because it is operating on the basis of inductive inferences drawn from independent converging bodies of evidence, which is the epistemology suited to the study of biology in general and evolution in particular.

JOHN HENRY NEWMAN

As discussed earlier,, Newman perceived that nothing in evolutionary science itself is incompatible with God, and indeed he suggested that God's governance of the universe through evolution may even suggest "a larger idea of Divine Prescience and Skill." Having briefly examined evolutionary theory's epistemic status according to Ratzinger and other recent high-level Catholic writings, I now wish to explore Newman's approach in some depth. For while Ratzinger's corpus addresses evolution much more extensively as a whole, Newman's thought is especially rich when it comes to discussion of the theory's epistemic status, a point that brings with it important implications for effectively proclaiming the gospel today. In particular, I find Newman helpful in addressing the claim that despite the overwhelming evidence that points to a long history of evolution on this planet, this does not amount to a definitive *proof* of evolutionary theory. Such an outlook, which tends to characterize evolution as "just a theory," implies that the science behind it need not be

---

32 International Theological Commission, *Communion and Stewardship*, no. 63 (emphasis added). John Paul II famously called evolution "more than a hypothesis," adding, "The convergence in the results of these independent studies—which was neither planned nor sought—constitutes in itself a significant argument in favor of the theory." See John Paul II, Message to the Pontifical Academy of Sciences on Evolution, October 22, 1996, no. 4.

33 International Theological Commission, *Communion and Stewardship*, no. 63 (emphasis added).

taken seriously—a response that unfortunately damages the credibility of the faith in the eyes of would-be and struggling believers.

Unfortunately, to make such claims is to fundamentally misunderstand the nature of the theory at hand. For in science, theory is not a mere conjecture but rather refers to *a well- substantiated explanation of a multitude of facts observed in the natural world that makes predictions whose accuracy has been repeatedly confirmed through testing.*[34] In the case of evolutionary theory, for those who are competent in this scientific field, the debate is not over *whether* evolution occurred—that is, whether every living organism on our planet descended from a common ancestor or a pool of common ancestors through incremental change across the ages—but rather in the details of *how precisely it happened.* Like the theories of general relativity, plate tectonics, the Big Bang, heliocentrism, and many other theories, evolutionary theory is—precisely because it is a *scientific* theory (as opposed to an individual person's unfalsifiable pet "theory" in the sense of a conjecture)—always fundamentally open to refinement and even rejection from any new evidence that emerges.

The "Want of Simplicity" in Creationism's Account of Life's Origins

One way that some Christians deal with the lack of correspondence between all the evidence that favors evolution and an attempt to read the Bible scientifically is to raise the possibility that God made it *look like* things evolved in order to test our faith.

While the effort to counter evolutionary theory has taken many forms over the years, it is remarkable that Newman—just a year after the publication of Darwin's *On the Origin of Species*—wrote to a friend who held precisely the view just mentioned, which one sometimes still encounters a century and a half later. Having been told that God placed the fossils in the rocks so as to give species the *appearance* of having evolved, Newman shrugged and drew this notion to

---

34 For helpful discussions on the meaning of theory in the scientific sense, see Tia Ghose, "'Just a Theory': 7 Misused Science Words," *Scientific American*, April 2, 2013; Alina Bradford, "What Is a Scientific Theory?" *Live Science*, July 29, 2017; and Kenneth Angielczyk, "What Do We Mean by 'Theory' in Science?" Chicago Field Museum, March 10, 2017.
Concerning the epistemic status of evolutionary theory, Dominican biologist Nicanor Austriaco writes, "I am often asked if evolution is a fact. If gravity is a fact, then evolution is a fact as well. The evidence [i.e., facts, in Gould's language] is so overwhelming in favor of evolution that there really is no rival explanatory theory of repute for the origin and diversity of life on our planet, in the same way that there is no rival explanatory theory to the theory of gravity for the attraction of bodies." See Nicanor Austriaco, OP, et al., *Thomistic Evolution: A Catholic Approach to Understanding Evolution in the Light of Faith*, 2nd ed. (Tacoma, WA: Cluny Media, 2019), 138–39.

its logical conclusion, noting that "there is as much want of simplicity" in the suggestion that God created each species directly as there is in the notion that a given tree we encounter was created fully grown and that rocks were crafted with fossils already in them. Further, Newman continues, the supposition that "monkeys should be so like men, with no historical connection between them" is just as "strange" as the notion that fossils got into rocks apart from a significant expanse of history elapsing. Clearly not averse to the notion of human evolution and our species' real family ties with the other great apes, the saint concludes, "I will either go whole hog with Darwin or, dispensing with time and history altogether, hold, not only the theory of distinct species but that also of the creation of the fossil-bearing rocks."[35]

This passage is remarkable, for it reveals that at a time when Darwin's theory was brand new, Newman already recognized that some form of evolutionary explanation was clearly needed to account for phenomena like the presence of fossils in fossils in rocks and physical similarities between humans and other species. As we will see, such a comment fits well with Newman's overall thought concerning the role of reasoning from converging or accumulated evidences and the way inductive reasoning works in science and in our everyday experiences. While the various pieces of evidence it brings into play do not infallibly guarantee the soundness of its conclusions, a good argument that reasons from particulars to the more general aligns with our broader knowledge of the world, is open to being challenged by a potentially superior explanation of the evidence or by the discovery of new evidence, and is simpler than its alternatives.

This last characteristic of a good inductive argument alluded to by Newman relates to the principle commonly known as Ockham's Razor but which has long been deployed by the likes of Aristotle and Aquinas to help evaluate the quality of arguments.[36] Sometimes also referred to as the principle of parsimony or principle of economy, its basic premise is that the simplest proposed explanation of a given set of phenomena is more likely to be true than its more complex alternatives. As Aristotle said, "We may assume the

---

35 John Henry Newman, letter of December 9, 1863, in *Sundries*, 83, cited in Dwight Culler, *The Imperial Intellect* (New Haven, CT: Yale University Press, 1955), 267.

36 While the fundamentals of this principle may be found in the writings in William of Ockham, the precise words "Entities must not be multiplied beyond necessity" are not found in his extant corpus but are traceable to a seventeenth-century commentary on the works of Duns Scotus by another Franciscan, John Punch.

superiority *ceteris paribus* of the demonstration which derives from fewer postulates or hypotheses."[37] Aquinas for his part recalls this axiom in an objection to God's existence according to which "it is superfluous to suppose that what can be accounted for by a few principles has been produced by many,"[38] and in another case noting, "When a thing can be done adequately by one agent, it is superfluous for it to be done by many; in fact, we see that nature does not do with two instruments what it can do with one."[39]

Assenting Not to What Is Conceivable but to What Is Plausible

Note that in the above text Newman does not claim to have *disproven* his friend's assertion. Like other good inductive reasoners, Newman is willing to admit that it is, indeed, always *conceivable* that all the scientific evidence of evolution is wrong or that it has been globally misinterpreted. This reveals the need to reflect more deeply on how it is that humans come to know truth more generally—especially when it comes to navigating apparently contradictory truth claims from the domains of faith and science.

Newman's writings contain some striking statements in which he admits, for instance: "No line can be drawn between such real certitudes as have truth for their object, and apparent certitudes. No distinct test can be named, sufficient to discriminate between what may be called the false prophet and the true." To this assertijon from the *Grammar of Assent*, Newman adds, that "what looks like certitude always is exposed to the chance of turning out to be a mistake."[40] The saint proceeds to explain that it is common to confuse infallibility (a gift belonging to the institution of the Catholic Church) with certitude (pertaining to specific truths all of us can come to know even apart from a special gift of the Holy Spirit). For instance, he notes that I may remember for certain what I did yesterday, yet my memory remains fallible. And, while I have confidence in a particular mathematical calculation, I have made mistakes

---

37 Aristotle, *Posterior Analytics* 1.25. For this translation and commentary, see Aquinas, *Commentary on the Posterior Analytics* (Notre Dame, IN: Dumb Ox Books, 2008), l. 39.

38 Aquinas, *ST* I, q. 1, a. 3.

39 Aquinas, *Summa Contra Gentiles*, bk. 3, *Providence, Part 1*, trans. Vernon Bourke (Notre Dame, Ind: University of Notre Dame Press, 1975), LXX, obj. 2.

40 Newman, *Grammar of Assent*, 182. Worth consideration here is the entirety of chap. 7, §2 on the indefectibility of certitude from which this material is drawn.

before. Further, I have no doubt that my best friend is a true friend, but it is always possible that my trust will tragically turn out to have been misplaced.[41]

Hearing this, one might get the impression that Newman's fallibilism amounts to a denial that man enjoys any certitudes whatsoever in life. However, I now wish to show that this is far from his view. *Could* all the evidence that points toward all life's common evolutionary history someday turn out to entail an entirely different conclusion? In other words, is it possible that the entire scientific community is wrong in its convictions concerning evolution and that biblical literalism is correct? According to Newman's epistemology, the answer to this question has to be "yes."

This, however, is not the truly important issue. Rather, it is: do we have any good reason to suppose that the broad evolutionary narrative is indeed wrong? And do we foresee any good reason this conviction should change at some point in the future? To drive home this point, Newman raises the possibility that his honest father is in actuality a murderer, to which he responds: "I have not absolute demonstration that my father was not a murderer, or my intimate friend a sharper, but it would not only be heartless, but irrational, not to disbelieve these hypotheses or possibilities *utterly*."[42] While it is certainly logically possible that my late father (God rest his soul) was a serial killer, for most of us, it would be irrational to entertain such a proposition seriously.

Applying this to the relationship of faith and evolution, we might ask: Is an antievolutionist explanation that is merely possible any more credible than the claim that one's father is a murderer when all the evidence in both cases points to the contrary? Newman's principles reveal that when weighing the evidence for these rival accounts, our main concern should not be whether a given explanation is *technically possible* but rather whether it is *plausible*. In other words, if the harmony of faith and reason is to be made manifest to would-be believers, we must be in the business of seeking not just any possible narrative of the way things are but the most *compelling* account of the relationship of revealed doctrine and evolutionary history.

---

41 Newman, *Grammar of Assent*, 183.

42 John Henry Newman to William Robert Brownlow, in *The Letters and Diaries of John Henry Newman*, vol. 25, ed. C. S. Dessain and T. Gornall (Oxford: Clarendon, 1978), 324. Similarly, G. K. Chesterton quipped that the possibility that cows might start fasting on Fridays or bending their knees in prayer is no good reason to suppose it will ever be the case. G. K. Chesterton, *The Everlasting Man*, in *The Collected Works of G. K. Chesterton* (San Francisco: Ignatius Press, 1986), 2:181.

The Role of Deductive and Inductive Reasoning

If evolution is such a compelling scientific theory, it is only fitting to ask: How is it that evolutionary theory has come to take on the epistemic status that nearly universally enjoys within the scientific community? How do we arrive at confidence in its findings in the first place, and why should we take the evidence so seriously as to be ready to revisit longstanding theological traditions in their wake? What makes it plausible in a way that creationism is not? Aside from the comments already noted, Newman does not apply his epistemological principles to the subject of evolution, likely because he considers its truth or lack thereof incidental to the substance of faith. Yet in an age where many have lost sight of this last point, it is instructive to recall his approach and apply it to the subject at hand.

Particularly helpful is Newman's understanding of the ability of inductive reasoning to yield real knowledge in matters of science. Observing that theology and the physical sciences each have their own respective method "which is best for its own science," Newman describes theology as "advancing syllogistically from premises to conclusion" (i.e., *deductive*), whereas he notes that physical science is, "just the reverse" (i.e., *inductive*).[43] Insistent upon the compatibility of these respective methods of argumentation, Newman issues a salutary reminder of a historic danger that we would do well to avoid today: "Each has at different times thought to impose it upon the other science, to

---

43 Newman, "Christianity and Physical Science," 332. For another helpful treatment of the type of certitude that is obtainable through the various empirical sciences (e.g., physics, biology, psychology) as distinct from one another and philosophy, see Jacques Maritain, *The Degrees of Knowledge* (Long: Geoffrey Bles, 1937), especially 181, 235–36. In these pages, Maritain affirms that biological science yields real knowledge, yet one (which he calls "empirico-schematic") that is distinct from that of physics (which he terms "'empirico-mathematical"). As for Newman, in Maritain's understanding, biological science is descriptive and inductive in nature and "not thought out or rationalised according to the laws of mathematical conceptualisation, but in accord with the schemas which have themselves been experimentally discovered by the reason in phenomena" (181n1).

In considering the type of knowledge that comes from the empirical sciences, it may also be helpful to recall that, for medievals like Aquinas, science and understanding had technical meanings that differ from the way we use the terms today. *Scientia*, or science, is knowledge of things attained by proofs which are necessarily true and cannot change (think the Pythagorean Theorem). Meanwhile, *intellectus*, or understanding, is knowledge that is self-evidently true or too obvious to need proven. That knowledge that we have obtained of evolution by means of multiple converging scientific disciplines clearly does not fit neatly into either of these categories, and yet neither is evolution a mere "opinion," which in Thomas's nomenclature refers to a state of accepting a proposition yet with fear that the opposite might be true.

the disparagement or rejection of that opposite method which legitimately belongs to it."[44]

Having acknowledged that the inductive nature of empirical science yields bona fide knowledge, we are now in a position to investigate whether Newman's principles might shed some light on the epistemic status of evolutionary theory and its importance in relation to theology. To begin, it should be stated plainly that the conclusion that all life on our planet descends from a common ancestor will never be mathematically proven along the lines of the Pythagorean Theorem. Yet, this is not to say that the theory is somehow unreliable or that those competent in the field lack confidence in its repeated, time-tested discoveries. It is due, rather, to the nature of the scientific method itself, which requires that its findings always remain subject to refinement and revision by further discoveries. Accordingly, we can have confidence in such theories as general relativity, plate tectonics, the Big Bang, heliocentrism, evolution, and the like while granting that they could in principle be falsified at some point in the future. Indeed, as Alasdair MacIntyre says of healthy traditions and disciplines, the only rational way for them to remain such is for their adherents to approach rivals allowing for the possibility that an alien tradition may eventually be proven superior in some respect.[45]

Evolution and Converging Evidences

As an empirical and therefore inductive science, the conclusions of evolutionary biology are arrived at "from below," reasoning inductively from particular pieces of evidence to more general conclusions that do not follow from them by strict logical necessity. Keen insight into this dynamic can be found in Newman's method of inductive reasoning, which he refers to as reasoning from "converging probabilities," or, perhaps better in today's English, "converging evidences."[46] Specifically, in the *Apologia*, the saint contends that firm

---

44 Newman, "Christianity and Physical Science," 331.

45 Alasdair MacIntyre, *Whose Justice? Which Rationality?* (Notre Dame, IN: University of Notre Dame Press, 1988), 388. MacIntyre then proceeds to add, "Only those whose tradition allows for the possibility of its hegemony being put into question can have rational warrant for asserting such hegemony."

46 Thomas Dubay suggests the word "evidences" as a replacement for "probabilities," for Newman is using the word in a technical sense not intended in contrast with certitude as in common parlance but rather to capture the reality that a conclusion can be well-founded yet not immune to objection from one who does not see the whole. See Dubay, *Faith and Certitude: Can We Be Sure of the Things That Matter Most to Us?* (San Francisco: Ignatius Press, 1998), 108–9.

certitudes may be attained on the basis of "an assemblage of concurring and converging probabilities." While not reaching the level of logical certainty, he indicates that these convergences can suffice for a mental certitude that "might equal in measure and strength the certitude which was created by the strictest scientific demonstration."[47] Just as the power of converging lines of attestation may compel one to give his assent to the Christian faith while not being able to exhaustively prove every single doctrine in isolation, so a deep acquaintance with the many bodies of evidence that support evolutionary theory also may compel a person to accept its major findings.

While not discussing evolution in particular at this juncture, Newman lays the groundwork for this claim on the subject of "informal inference" in the *Grammar*:

> It is plain that formal logical sequence is not in fact the method by which we are enabled to become certain of what is concrete; and it is equally plain, from what has been already suggested, what the real and necessary method is. It is the cumulation of probabilities, independent of each other, arising out of the nature and circumstances of the particular case which is under review; probabilities too fine to avail separately, too subtle and circuitous to be convertible into syllogisms, too numerous and various for such conversion, even were they convertible.[48]

In another passage from this same monograph, our saint further explains:

> It is by the strength, variety, or multiplicity of premises, which are only probable, not by invincible syllogisms—by objections overcome, by adverse theories neutralized, by difficulties gradually clearing up, by exceptions proving the rule, by un-looked-for correlations found with received truths, by suspense and delay in the process issuing in triumphant reactions—by all these ways, and many others, it is that the practised and experienced mind is able to make a sure divination

---

47 John Henry Newman, *Apologia Pro Vita Sua* (New York: Longmans, Green, and Co., 1908), 20. Later in this text, Newman proceeds to describe certitude as "the consequence . . . of the accumulative force of certain given reasons which, taken one by one, were only probabilities" (199). In the section on inference and assent in his *Grammar*, he likewise notes that, with regard to revealed religion that from "an accumulation of various probabilities we may construct legitimate proof, sufficient for certitude" (320).

48 Newman, *Grammar of Assent*, 230.

that a conclusion is inevitable, of which his lines of reasoning do not actually put him in possession.[49]

As in the case of evidence that supports the truth of the Christian faith, none of the individual pieces of evidence that support evolutionary theory admits of absolute certitude, yet, to adopt Newman's language, each "carries with it a number of independent probable arguments, sufficient, when united, for a reasonable conclusion about itself."[50] In a letter to Charles Appleton, the saint adds that certitude achieved by way of accumulated probabilities "bestows on us a certitude which rises higher than the logical force of our conclusions."[51]

All this is eminently relevant to the matter of evolution, whose truth is arrived at by means of myriad "concrete" bodies of evidence in the created world, like the *fossil record* with its evidence of "transitional" species, *biogeography* (distribution of species across space and time), *comparative anatomy* with its observations of astonishingly similar structures across species as well as odd vestigial structures and atavisms that are entirely out of place unless within an evolutionary narrative, *embryology* (temporary vestigial structures like gill slits in humans and hind limbs in whales), *comparative genomics* (which studies affinities between our DNA and that of other species), and *direct observation* of evolutionary change in organisms with short life spans (e.g., bacteria, viruses, fruit flies, mosquitos).[52]

According to Wilfred Ward, Newman's first biographer, the saint once compared a conclusion drawn by reasoning from such bodies of evidence to:

> a cable, which is made up of a number of separate threads, each feeble, yet together as sufficient as an iron rod. An iron rod represents mathematical or strict demonstration; a cable represents moral demonstration,

---

49 Newman, *Grammar of Assent*, 254.

50 Newman, *Grammar of Assent*, 232.

51 John Henry Newman to Charles Appleton, January 12, 1874, in *The Letters and Diaries of John Henry Newman*, ed. vol. 27, C. S. Dessain and T. Gornall (Oxford: Clarendon, 1975), 9–10.

52 Among the many sources available that document the evidence for evolution in great detail, see Douglas Futuyma, *Evolution* (Sunderland, MA: Sinauer, 2017); Richard Dawkins, *The Greatest Show on Earth: The Evidence for Evolution* (New York: Free Press, 2009); Jerry Coyne, *Why Evolution Is True* (New York: Penguin Books, 2010). For Christian sources that do the same while contextualizing the evidence from within the perspective of faith, see Christopher Baglow, *Faith, Science, and Reason: Theology on the Cutting Edge* (Downers Grove, IL: Midwest Theological Forum, 2019); Nicanor Austriaco, OP, et al., *Thomistic Evolution: A Catholic Approach to Understanding Evolution in the Light of Faith* (Providence, RI: Cluny Media, 2019); and Scot McKnight and Dennis Venema, *Adam and the Genome: Reading Scripture after Genetic Science* (Grand Rapids, MI: Brazos Press, 2017).

THEORY OF EVOLUTION

which is an assemblage of probabilities, separately insufficient for certainty, but, when put together, irrefragable. A man who said "I cannot trust a cable, must have an iron bar" would in certain given cases, be irrational and unreasonable—so too is a man who says I must have a rigid demonstration, not a moral demonstration, of religious truth.[53]

To explain this dynamic fully, it is illustrative to consider some examples of how we deploy inductive reasoning in every day affairs. In his *Grammar*, Newman discusses the knowledge that he has of his homeland:

> We are all absolutely certain, beyond the possibility of doubt, that Great Britain is an island. We give to that proposition our deliberate and unconditional adhesion. There is no security on which we should be better content to stake our interests, our property, our welfare than on the fact that we are living in an island. We have no fear of any geographical discovery which may reverse our belief.[54]

Having said this, he proceeds to elaborate on the motives for this certainty:

> Our reasons for believing that we are circumnavigable are such as these:—first, we have been so taught in our childhood, and it is so in all the maps; next, we have never heard it contradicted or questioned; on the contrary, every one whom we have heard speak on the subject of Great Britain, every book we have read, invariably took it for granted; our whole national history, the routine transactions and current events of the country, our social and commercial system, our political relations with foreigners, imply it in one way or another. Numberless facts, or what we consider facts, rest on the truth of it; no received fact rests on its being otherwise. If there is anywhere a junction between us and the continent, where is it? . . . There is a manifest *reductio ad absurdum* attached to the notion that we can be deceived on such a point as this.[55]

Just as "numberless facts" rest on the truth of Great Britain being an island and none on its being otherwise, so, too, for evolution. As the now-common adage

---

53 John Henry Newman to Canon Walker, July 6, 1864, in Wilfred Ward, *The Life of John Henry Cardinal Newman: Based on His Private Journals and Correspondence*, vol. 2 (London: Longmans, 1912), 43.

54 Newman, *Grammar of Assent*, 234–35.

55 Newman, *Grammar of Assent*, 235.

goes, nothing in biology makes sense except in light of the theory of evolution.[56] Yet, the truth is that no single piece of evidence in its favor can be considered certain on its own, even if it enjoys a certain strength even in isolation from the others. When considered together, though, these observations mutually reinforce one another in such a way that their cumulative force leads one to the point where, as Étienne Gilson writes in his introduction to the *Grammar*, their "extreme probability is a practical certitude."[57]

The Illative Sense

An innovative dimension of Newman's method of argumentation by converging evidences is that he actually assigns it to a particular faculty of person, for in Newman's own words, "genuine proof in concrete matters we require an *organon* more delicate, versatile, and elastic than verbal argumentation."[58] In the *Grammar*, Newman refers to the inferential capacity connected with drawing conclusions from converging probabilities as man's "illative sense." In the saint's own words, his "illative sense" is "a grand word for a common thing." Analogous to prudence in practical matters, it is that reasoning faculty" that is but a "branch" of judgment that "in all concrete matter is the architectonic faculty."[59]

As Mary Katherine Tillman observes, "According to the *phronesis* tradition, one judges what to do in everyday actions by means of a 'sense' of something more important and ultimate. Very simply, this is Newman's 'illative sense.'"[60] On this analog with prudence, one might say that the illative

---

56 The point that nothing in biology as a whole and in evolution in particular makes sense apart from evolution is explored in Theodosius Dobzhansky's essay "Nothing in Biology Makes Sense Except in the Light of Evolution," *American Biology Teacher* 35, no. 3 (1973): 125–29.

57 Étienne Gilson, introduction to Newman, *An Essay in Aid of a Grammar of Assent* (Garden City, NY: Image Books, 1955).

58 Newman, *Grammar of Assent*, 217. In speaking of the "concrete" things with which the illative sense and prudence are concerned, Newman has in mind what Aristotle refers to as contingent matters. See Newman's notes at 277.

59 John Henry Newman to Charles Meynell, in *The Letters and Diaries of John Henry Newman*, vol. 24 (Oxford: Clarendon, 1973), 375. Brandon Dahm captures this parallel and summarizes Newman's approach well: "Through the convergence of probabilities and a kind of insight analogous to *prudence* in practical matters we attain certainty from probabilities. More formally, if p has Newman certainty for S, then S has rationally attained belief that p through the accumulation of probabilities." See Brandon Dahm, "The Certainty of Faith: A Problem for Christian Fallibilists?" *Journal of Analytic Theology* 3 (2015): 140.

60 Mary Katherine Tillman, "Economies of Reason: Newman and the *Phronesis* Tradition," in *Discourse and Context: An Interdisciplinary Study of John Henry Newman*, ed. Gerard Magill (Carbondale: Southern Illinois University Press, 1993), 47. For another valuable scholarly treatment

THEORY OF EVOLUTION

sense is that instinct that allows one to judge what is worthy of assent when we make informal inferences for whose conclusions incontrovertible proof is not available. Recognizing that it is not possible to attain the existential equivalent of logical certainty in concrete matters, the illative sense enters into these situations to close the gap or "margin" between converging probabilities and what is required for certainty and assent in regard to their conclusion. Comparing this sense to the nonlinear mode of reasoning in concrete matters typical of Aristotle's *phronesis* and noting that our knowledge of God revealed in Christ shares common features with the structure of our knowledge of empirical reality, Newman writes:

> I consider there is no such thing (in the province of facts) as a perfect logical demonstration; there is always a margin of objection. . . .Yet on the other hand it is a paradox to say there is not such a state of mind as certitude. . . . I think it is φρ□νησις which tells us when to discard the logical imperfection and to assent to the conclusion which ought to be drawn in order to demonstration, but is not quite . . . but I am arguing against the principle that φρ□νησις is a higher sort of logic."[61]

---

of the illative sense, see Cyril O'Regan, "John Henry Newman," in *The Oxford Handbook of the Epistemology of Theology*, ed. Frederick D. Aquino and William J. Abraham (Oxford: Oxford University Press, 2017), 511–22. In this essay, O'Regan tackles the potentially "relativistic implications of what appears to be a thoroughly individualistic account of the human being who assents or judges" (520). Given what we know concerning Newman's polemic against private judgment, O'Regan notes that this cannot be the saint's intention. Accordingly, O'Regan suggests that those who find value in Newman's account acknowledge that he likely overplays the personal nature of the illative sense and attend more to those facets of Newman's thought wherein he recognizes that we all operate from within larger communities of consensus.

Similarly, while noting that the illative sense certainly includes a personal element, Frederick Aquino emphasizes that it also has social and progressive dimensions, and "its proper development requires good epistemic practices in which people refine cognitive skills under the tutelage of exemplars of informed judgment." See Frederick Aquino, *Communities of Informed Judgment: Newman and Accounts of Rationality* (Washington, DC: The Catholic University of America Press, 2004), 95.

61 John Henry Newman, "Report to Henry Wilberforce," in *The Letters and Diaries of John Henry Newman*, vol. 24 (Oxford: Clarendon, 1973), 104–5. For Newman's understanding of *phronesis* in Aristotle, see Newman, *Grammar of Assent*, 277–78. See also 68 and 282, where the saint speaks of "the margin . . . intervening between verbal argumentation and conclusions in the concrete." For a lucid summary of Newman's illative sense on this point and within his entire oeuvre, see Nicholas Lash, introduction to Newman, *Grammar of Assent*, 12–19. As Lash remarks, Newman dedicates chapter 9 of the *Grammar* to the illative sense, yet the chapter is comparatively short for it simply brings into explicit focus what had already been under discussion in earlier chapters of the work (i.e., the method of reasoning from accumulated probabilities). With regard to the closing of the "margin" discussed above, Lash emphasizes that this perfective act of the illative sense does not occur through a leap of the will. Rather, Newman's view is that we "grow, rather

To reprise an analogy offered by Newman himself, one way of articulating this point is that the illative sense is what "fills in" the final details needed in order to see a portrait for what it truly is a representation of a *person*:

> As a man's portrait differs from a sketch of him, in having, not merely a continuous outline, but all its details filled in, and shades and colours laid on and harmonized together, such is the multiform and intricate process of ratiocination, necessary for our reaching him as a concrete fact, compared with the rude operation of syllogistic treatment.[62]

The illative sense allows us to perceive the whole and thereby not just to see lines on a page but the *picture* that emerges when the strokes on a canvas are harmonized together. This is the sort of capacity needed to see the truth and coherence of a scientific theory—the ability not merely to consider each piece of evidence in isolation but to reason from these converging lines to a greater whole and to draw conclusions in its regard. As defined by one Newman scholar, illation is "the mind in its perfection, judging and correlating at the highest point of any individual," attending to the entire gamut of our experience in all its complexity—principles, doctrines, facts, memories, experiences, testimonies—"in order to attain insights too delicate and subtle for logical analysis."[63]

Examining the illative sense in light of its etymology, Aidan Nichols defines Newman's illative sense as the "architectonic faculty that in this way gathers up the fragments of experience into a single and unified judgment,"[64] adding:

---

than leap, into conviction," and, while "The discovery that we have come to hold a certain belief, or set of beliefs, may be sudden," further reflection typically allows us "to see something of the process whereby those beliefs were cumulatively, slowly, and often painfully acquired" (17–18). Tillman notes that Newman's illative sense has applications in every subject matter, and that "discussion of the illative sense in his *Essay in Aid of a Grammar of Assent* is disproportionate to its tacit preponderance in all of his writings. . . . Operative in all inferences, the illative sense is 'the moral sense' when Newman shifts into the ethical register, and it becomes 'conscience' when he shifts into the religious dimension of thinking. Again, when he shifts from the individual seat of judgment to that of the ecclesial community, the illative sense becomes the sense of the faithful, and conscience is translated into the principle of tradition in the Church" (Tillman, "Economies of Reason: Newman and the *Phronesis* Tradition," 53).

62 Newman, *Grammar of Assent*, 230.

63 Charles Frederick Harrold, *John Henry Newman: An Expository and Critical Study of His Mind, Thought, and Art* (New York: Longmans, Green, and Co., 1945), 157; Aidan Nichols, *A Grammar of Consent: The Existence of God in Christian Tradition* (Notre Dame, IN: University of Notre Dame Press, 1991), 34.

64 Nichols, *Grammar of Consent*, 32.

A whole host of features of experience conspire to "carry us into" (the original late Latin sense of *illatio*) the more spacious realm of a conclusion that is larger than any of them. The heaping together of tiny indications, none of which by itself is conclusive, produces certitude in ordinary human affairs. At some point, there is a qualitative change in the quantitative amassment of evidence. Spread out the pieces of a jigsaw puzzle on a table, and it may be only probable that they are more than an accidental collocation. Fit them together and there will be no doubt.[65]

A corollary of this is that when viewing an entire complex interlocking puzzle, the absence of a few pieces will often not prevent one from seeing its true form. So it is with evolution: the inability to explain features of the process does not prevent one from attaining an accurate grasp of its overarching form.

Indeed, as in the case of other scientific theories, no architectonic explanation of life's history is perfect, and a certain number of gaps will remain in the theory of evolution. The question is whether one attaches more weight to the ability of this framework to explain a great many things when no other rival comes close to doing so, or whether one remains focused on the presence of issues that the theory has hitherto not fully explained. Darwin himself thus acknowledged:

> Although I am fully convinced of the truth of the views given in this volume under the form of an abstract, I by no means expect to convince experienced naturalists whose minds are stocked with a multitude of facts all viewed, during a long course of years, from a point of view directly opposite to mine. It is so easy to hide our ignorance under such expressions as the "plan of creation," "unity of design," etc. and to think that we give an explanation when we only restate a fact. Anyone whose disposition leads him to attach more weight to unexplained difficulties than to the explanation of a certain number of facts will certainly reject my theory.[66]

Thankfully, the integrity of a person's Christian faith remains regardless of whether he affirms or rejects the science of evolution. As I mentioned in the

---

65 Nichols, *Grammar of Consent*, 33.
66 Darwin, *On the Origin of Species*, 481–82.

introduction of this chapter, the issue is rather about the credibility of the faith: how to better proclaim the truth of Christ in today's world by engaging the full breadth of wisdom, human and divine.

For Josef Pieper, a true lover of wisdom must have a critical attitude, which "does not primarily mean accepting only what is absolutely certain, but being careful not to suppress anything."[67] This point is especially apropos when it comes to addressing evolution. It is tempting for the believer to write off the immense scientific evidence in its favor on the grounds that it is not "absolutely certain." Yet if Pieper is right, this is not the way a lover of wisdom approaches reality, for such an individual is concerned less with keeping out new ideas that would challenge his point of view than with making sure not to miss anything that might require him to refine it.[68]

CONCLUSION

For those believers whose illative sense led them to the conclusion that evolutionary theory's account of life on our planet is superior to that of biblical literalism's, the question then becomes: What next?

Fortunately, here again, Newman and Ratzinger both come to our aid. In fact, Ratzinger explicitly references the English saint's work on doctrinal development as one of his greatest theological influences and a "decisive contribution to the renewal of theology." With his theological reflection, Ratzinger explains, Newman "had placed the key in our hand to build historical thought into theology, or much more, he taught us to think historically in theology and so to recognize the identity of faith in all developments." To this, the then-cardinal added that "Newman's starting point, also in modern theology, has not yet been fully evaluated. Fruitful possibilities awaiting development are still hidden in it."[69]

---

67 Josef Pieper, *In Defense of Philosophy* (San Francisco: Ignatius Press, 1992), 51.

68 Pieper, *In Defense of Philosophy*, 51.

69 Ratzinger, "Presentation on the Occasion of the First Centenary of the Death of Cardinal John Henry Newman," April 28, 1990, http://www.vatican.va/roman_curia/congregations/cfaith/documents/rc_con_cfaith_doc_19900428_ratzinger-newman_en.html. See also Joseph Ratzinger, *Salt of the Earth* (San Francisco: Ignatius Press, 1997), 115–16. For more on Newman's influence on Ratzinger, see Tracey Rowland, *Ratzinger's Faith: The Theology of Pope Benedict XVI* (Oxford: Oxford University Press, 2008), 1–16; Matthew Ramage, *Jesus, Interpreted: Benedict XVI, Bart Ehrman, and the Historical Truth of the Gospels* (Washington, DC: The Catholic University of America Press, 2017), 41–43.

Ratzinger wrote these words in 1990, but they are just as applicable today. And so, once we come to grips with the reality of our planet's evolutionary history, what, indeed, comes next in theology? First, Ratzinger and Newman—along with a chorus of other giants like John XXIII and John Paul II—would say that we must first of all remember that the deposit of faith is not ours to manipulate but rather a gift to safeguard, and that we must always take care to preserve the essential core of the revelation bestowed on the church by her Lord.

Second, ever drawing on the old, we must be eager to learn from what is new, purifying the faith in light of modern discoveries and illumining these same realities in the light of faith. To recall the famous line of Newman that Ratzinger referenced more than once, "to live is to change, and to be perfect is to have changed often."[70] As a professor of theology in the academic arena and a disciple who strives to profess the Catholic faith in daily life, I have too often observed the tragic state of affairs that occurs when a would-be believer feels compelled to choose between faith and science, thereby abandoning the faith, abandoning reason, or leading someone else to do so. Thanks to such towering patrons as Newman and Ratzinger, we are blessed with confidence that the faith is strong enough not only to survive new scientific discoveries but to develop and thrive by engaging the challenges they present. The substance of the Catholic faith will endure until the end of time. Yet, to borrow once again the words of Newman, discoveries in the field of evolutionary theory are a powerful reminder that sometimes "old principles reappear under new forms," and in certain respects, the faith must "change with them in order to remain the same."[71]

---

[70] John Henry Newman, *Essay on the Development of Christian Doctrine* (Notre Dame, IN: University of Notre Dame Press, 1989), 40. Speaking of the "development and change within a fundamental identity" within in his own life and that of the church's doctrine as a whole, the then-cardinal stated, "Here I agree with Cardinal Newman, who says that to live is to change and that the one who was capable of changing has lived much" (Ratzinger, "Presentation on the Occasion of the First Centenary of the Death of Cardinal John Henry Newman").

[71] Newman, *Essay on the Development of Christian Doctrine*, 40.

12

DEIFICATION IN THE WORK OF NEWMAN AND RATZINGER
A COMPARATIVE ANALYSIS

Jeremy Pilch

St. John Henry Newman and the late Pope Emeritus Benedict XVI are figures united in many ways. Both stand out as among the preeminent theological voices of their times; indeed, many today regard both as potential doctors of the church. They were each aware of the secular currents of thought of their age and sought to articulate a theological response to that. Holiness was integral to their witness to the truth of revelation and any authentic evangelization. This chapter will examine the theme of holiness in the work of both Newman and Ratzinger, focusing particularly on their handling of the patristic doctrine of deification. It will proceed in four stages: first, examining the prevalence of this theme in Newman's writings prior to his conversion; second, tracing the emergence of deification as a distinctive feature of Ratzinger's theology in his more mature work; third, examining the different language Newman uses to describe sanctity in his writings as a Catholic; and last, comparing the stature of our Lady and her role in our divinization in the thought of both Newman and Ratzinger.

The significance of deification in Newman's work has been noted by scholars for some time. Indeed, for Stephen Dessain, recognized by Ian Ker as "the founder of Newman studies," Newman was a representative of eastern Christian theology in the West.[1] In his two-part article of 1962, "Cardinal Newman and the Doctrine of Uncreated Grace," he suggests that the doctrine of deification "lay at the foundation of [his] religion life," and certainly Newman's recent canonization would appear to confirm this![2] In terms of the development of Newman's theological mind the Eastern fathers and their writings were undoubtedly formative. This influence took place primarily during that period of change in his religious convictions that eventually led to his reception in to the Catholic Church. "The Fathers made me a Catholic," he would say in his *Letter to Pusey*, chiefly having in mind, we may reasonably assume, St. Athanasius, the Cappadocians, and St. Cyril of Alexandria, for their influence shines through vividly in Newman's historical and doctrinal investigations into the early church, as well as at a more directly spiritual level.[3]

One of the reasons deification is such a valuable teaching is that it served as a marker of orthodoxy. Since it is so rooted in a correct Christology, its absence in a theologian's vision can often indicate that a flawed Christology is present. Indeed, it was in the face of the Arian heresy that St. Athanasius responded with his teaching on deification. The lived experience of the Christian, documented by St. Athanasius in his life of St. Anthony, testified to the deifying power of Christ.[4] If Christ were not truly divine, then the fruits of faith and sacramental life witnessed by Athanasius would not make sense. As Newman explained in the second volume of his *Select Treatises of St. Athanasius*:

> The greatest and special gift is the actual presence as well as the power within us of the Incarnate Son as a principle [arche] of sanctification, or rather of deification. On this point Athan., especially dwells in too many passages to quote or name.[5]

---

1 Ian Ker, *Healing the Wound of Humanity: The Spirituality of John Henry Newman* (London: Darton, Longman and Todd, 1993), 60.

2 C. S. Dessain, "Cardinal Newman and the Doctrine of Uncreated Grace," *Clergy Review* 47 (1962): 207.

3 John Henry Newman, *Certain Difficulties Felt by Anglicans in Catholic Teaching* (London: Longmans, Green, and Co., 1892), 3:24.

4 Athanasius, *The Life of Antony and the Letter to Marcellinus*, trans. by Robert C. Gregg (Mahwah, NJ: Paulist Press, 1980).

5 John Henry Newman, *Selected Treatises of Saint Athanasius in Controversy with the Arians* (London: Longmans, Green, and Co., 1895), 2:130.

It is notable that Newman here implies that sanctification and deification are equivalent terms, a point important to keep in mind when we consider Newman's Catholic homilies and his theology of grace, where the term deification is absent but its reality, the process of sanctification, remains a central principle.

While the fact that the doctrine of deification features most explicitly in Newman's Anglican writings raises the question about the reason for its apparent absence in his Catholic writings, it also points to the truth that the genuine desire of holiness is crucial to any ecumenical endeavor.[6] This is why the contemporary academic interest in the theme is able to foster ecumenical understanding in a more fruitful way than direct focus on doctrinal matters and differences. Newman wasn't alone in his "discovery" of deification, of course; other members of the Oxford Movement, Keble and especially Pusey, were also united by a deep interest in the fathers and a commitment to the truth that God became man so that man might become god. Indeed, for Andrew Louth, Newman already "expresses this central conviction of the Oxford Movement" in his *Lectures on Justification,* namely "the conviction that as we respond to God in Christ, God himself is present to us, in our hearts, drawing us to himself; a conviction which expresses the heart of the patristic doctrine of deification."[7]

Further evidence that Newman's spirituality at this time was especially animated by this teaching is evidenced in his *Letters on Justification,* which was published in 1838. In this work, Newman addressed one of the theological dividing points of the Reformation and was able to move beyond the polemics surrounding faith and works by drawing upon the pneumatology of the Eastern fathers. Newman emphasizes the scriptural and patristic teaching about the indwelling of the Holy Spirit. For Newman, it is this that is the indication of justification, which he writes "is wrought by the power of the Spirit, or rather by its presence within us"; significantly, he adds that "faith and renewal are both present also, but as the fruits of it."[8] Newman develops his exploration very

---

6 For a classic exposition of deification in the Anglican tradition, see A. M. Allchin, *Participation in God: A Forgotten Strand in the Anglican Tradition* (London: Darton, Longman and Todd, 1988). For a more recent engagement with the topic from an Anglican perspective, see Paul M. Collins, *Partaking in Divine Nature: Deification and Communion* (London: T&T Clark, 2010).

7 Andrew Louth, "Manhood into God: The Oxford Movement, the Fathers and the Deification of Man," in *Essays Catholic and Radical,* ed. Kenneth Leech and Rowan Williams (London: Bowerdean Press, 1983), 74–75.

8 Cited in Ian Ker, *Newman on Vatican II* (Oxford: Oxford University Press, 2014), 60.

scripturally and also with an eye to the 39 articles, observing with reference to the 13th article that "justification may fitly be called an 'inspiration of the Spirit of Christ' or a spiritual presence."[9] Further on after consideration of baptism, he writes that "whereas justification is the application of Christ's merits to the individual, it is also an inward gift; . . . the habitation in us of God the Father and the Word Incarnate through the Holy Ghost. . . . This is to be justified, to receive the Divine Presence within us, and be made a Temple of the Holy Ghost."[10]

By the early 1840s, when he was translating Athanasius, Newman could deliver a Christmas Day homily, "Religious Joy," containing as explicit a statement of deification as may be found in the homilies of the Greek fathers, so integral had this doctrine become for him:

> Men we remain, not mere men, but gifted with a measure of all those perfections which Christ has in fullness, partaking each in his own degree of the Divine Nature so fully, that the only reason (so to speak) why His saints are not really like Him, is that it is impossible—that He is the Creator, and they His creatures; yet still so, that they are all but Divine, all that they can be made without violating the incommunicable majesty of the Most High.[11]

Other Christmas homilies from around this period reflect the same emphasis. In "The Mystery of Godliness," Newman reflects on the Incarnation: "He took upon Himself what was ours for the sake of us. . . . He came in that very nature of Adam, in order to communicate to us that nature as it is in His Person, . . . to make us partakers of the Divine Nature."[12] In another Christmas sermon, "Christian Sympathy," reflecting on Christ's submission to temptation, he observes that:

> whereas He was God from everlasting, as the Only-begotten of the Father, He took on Him the thoughts, affections and infirmities of

---

9 John Henry Newman, *Lectures on Justification* (London: J. G. & F. Rivington, 1838), 153.

10 Newman, *Lectures on Justification*, 160.

11 John Henry Newman, *Parochial and Plain Sermons* (San Francisco: Ignatius Press, 1997), 1712. For studies of the theme of deification in the Greek Fathers, see the pioneering work of Jules Gross, *The Divinization of the Christian according to the Greek Fathers*, trans. Paul A. Onica (Anaheim, CA: A & C Press, 2002) and the magisterial study of Norman Russell, *The Doctrine of Deification in the Greek Patristic Tradition* (Oxford: Oxford University Press, 2004).

12 Newman, *Parochial and Plain Sermons*, 1018.

DEIFICATION

man, thereby, through the fulness of His Divine Nature, to raise those thoughts and affections, and destroy those infirmities, that so, by God's becoming man, men, through brotherhood with Him, might in the end become as gods.[13]

Very clearly, then, as Brian Daley has observed, "the theme of Christian salvation as divinization . . . is by the 1840s, at least, an integral aspect of Newman's increasingly Patristic interpretation of the Gospel of Christ."[14]

From the heady heights of Newman preaching explicitly about deification at Christmas 1842, on the threshold of the beginning of the end of his Anglican days, let us now turn to a homily of Joseph Ratzinger from the mid-1960s to begin our exploration of how deification features in his theological outlook. The second of the three sermons that comprise his slim 1965 volume, *What It Means to Be a Christian*, is titled "Faith as Service," comprised of three parts, the second of which at least echoes the patristic axiom of deification in being called "God Becomes Man, Man Becomes Christlike." Ratzinger begins by addressing the question of why the Incarnation took place. He sees this as a second breakthrough moment in history, "from Creator to creature," after an initial "breakthrough from nature to mind," which took place when consciousness arose.[15] This second breakthrough point is, says Ratzinger, "the moment when, in one place, the world and God become one," and he continues with an explicit affirmation of deification:

> The significance of all the history that followed after can only be that of including the entire world within this union and, on that basis, giving it the fulfilled meaning of being at one with its Creator. "God became man, in order that men might become gods," is what Saint Athanasius, Bishop of Alexandria, said. We can say, as a matter of fact, that the actual meaning of history is being announced to us here. In the breakthough from the world to God, everything that went before and everything that followed afterward is given its proper significance as the

---

13 Newman, *Parochial and Plain Sermons*, 1034.

14 Brian E. Daley, "The Church Fathers," in *The Cambridge Companion to John Henry Newman*, ed. Ian Ker and Terrence Merrigan (Cambridge: Cambridge University Press, 2009), 41.

15 Joseph Ratzinger, *What It Means to Be a Christian*, trans. Henry Taylor (San Francisco: Ignatius Press, 2006), 53.

> great movement of the cosmos is drawn into the process of deification,
> into a return to the state from which it originated.[16]

At first sight, despite the portrayal of deification as a simple return to an original state—and this for the cosmos, not simply man—this would seem to be a statement that might resonate with the expansive scope of cosmic deification as expressed by St. Maximus the Confessor.[17] Yet Ratzinger's further reflections move away from the movement of descent and ascent, of kenosis and theosis, that is a characteristic of patristic reflection on the meaning of the mystery of the Incarnation. Instead, Ratzinger identifies the significance of the Incarnation and its deifying potential for humanity as meaning "being ready to engage in a particular service that God requires from us in history" and thus ultimately "moving out of that selfishness which only knows about itself and only refers to itself and passing into the new form of existence of someone who lives for others."[18] Worthy as these sentiments are, the "newness" being considered doesn't reflect on the ontological change effected by Christ assuming and healing human nature. Rather, Ratzinger's stress is horizontal and relational, and while the life of charity and sacrificial love is obviously a central component of any human existence that may be being divinized, what Ratzinger presents here is difficult to distinguish from a purely natural philanthropic humanism.

A couple of years after these homilies, Ratzinger delivered a series of lectures at Tubingen offering modern reflections on the Apostles' Creed, which would form the basis of his significant work, arguably a "twentieth-century classic," that was published in English translation in 1969 as *Introduction to Christianity*. Before considering Ratzinger's handling of Christology in this text, it is worth noting that there is an easily missed footnote to Maximus the Confessor's *Exposition of the Lord's Prayer*, together with comments from von Balthasar's great study of Maximus, *Cosmic Liturgy*.[19] This apparently incidental point highlights the fact that Ratzinger was undoubtedly familiar with the

---

16 Ratzinger, *What It Means to Be a Christian*, 53.

17 For a good selection of the writings of Maximus, along with a helpful introduction, see St. Maximus the Confessor, *On the Cosmic Mystery of Christ*, trans. Paul M. Blowers and Robert Louis Wilken (New York: St. Vladimir's Seminary Press, 2003).

18 St. Maximus the Confessor, *On the Cosmic Mystery of Christ*, 54–55.

19 Joseph Ratzinger, *Introduction to Christianity*, trans. J. R. Foster and Michael J. Miller (San Francisco: Ignatius Press, 2004), 125–26.

DEIFICATION

complete vision of deification expressed by the Christian east, and there is no reason why this could not have entered in to his own theological position in some way. Indeed, Ratzinger's admiration for von Balthasar and for Henri de Lubac, such a key figure in Catholic *ressourcement*, might suggest a certain inevitability of this happening, and perhaps it did much more following the establishment of *Communio*. The Pope Emeritus was, after all, the person through whom these two giants of twentieth-century Catholic theology lived on into our times. And yet, as *Introduction to Christianity* reveals to us, there is surprisingly little of this; the context in which Ratzinger's theology found expression was really quite different to the world of *ressourcement*. As he highlights in the introduction to the 1969 edition, the book "attempts to serve . . . the bonds that unite Catholic and Protestant Christians in the apostolic faith."[20] This is a work very much shaped by the legacy of the Reformation, questions raised by fashionable existentialism, and the experience of post-Auschwitz Germany.

The section of this text of most significance for our purposes is the one focusing on Christology. One may first note Ratzinger's brief critique of "the concept of the divine man or God-man (theos aner)," which he says "occurs nowhere in the New Testament."[21] Whatever the broader merits of Ratzinger's handling of Chalcedon, which is what this critique is linked to (and this merits more attention than there is scope for here), his position on the God-man terminology, does, however, close off for him the post-Chalcedonian Byzantine Christology that adopted language such as "theandric" and "theanthropos."[22] Ironically, this Christology was also concerned with a satisfactory concept of the human person, which is precisely the topic at the heart of Ratzinger's rereading of Chalcedon.

In addition to this, Ratzinger is not satisfied simply with the theology of the Incarnation and is concerned to try to show its necessary connection to the theology of the cross. He will work this out fully and effectively in a brilliant essay on "The Theological Basis for a Spiritual Christology," which dates from the early 1980s. It appears in his little book *Behold the Pierced One*, which we

---

20 Ratzinger, *Introduction to Christianity*, 35.

21 Ratzinger, *Introduction to Christianity*, 215.

22 For an etymological study of this terminology in the later Greek patristic period, see Jeremy Pilch, *"Breathing the Spirit with Both Lungs": Deification in the Work of Vladimir Solov'ev* (Leuven: Peeters, 2018), 67–72.

will consider in due course. For now, however, Ratzinger doesn't draw from that patristic Christology that so nourished Newman, who described the Incarnation as "the central aspect of Christianity" in *An Essay on the Development of Christian Doctrine.*[23] Rather, he goes on to address the significance of Anselm's atonement Christology before his crucial consideration of Christ in terms of St. Paul's "the last man." Christ as this last man, or "exemplary man," "oversteps the bounds of humanity," and he does this because "man is more himself the more he is with 'the other.' He only comes *to* himself by moving away *from* himself. Only through 'the other' and through 'being' with 'the other' does he come to himself."[24] This Buber-esque, I-thou, language seems to be the way Ratzinger wishes to describe what is traditionally seen as the self-emptying or kenosis of Christ. Christ has done in an exemplary way what is seen as the way for all. In this way, Ratzinger offers what could be considered as a reworking of the exchange theory: "Man is finally intended for *the* other, the truly other, for God; he is all the more himself the more he is with the *entirely* Other, with God."[25] Thus, when we step out of ourselves into relationship with Christ, we become fully human, as Christ himself did in an exemplary way. It would seem, therefore, that for Ratzinger, the transformation that Christ brings is one that fulfils us but does not necessarily establish an ontological change; it is fully humanizing and nothing more. Ratzinger expresses this as follows, fleshing out the ideas expressed in his 1965 homily, cited earlier:

> Man's full "hominization" presupposes God becoming man; only by this event is the Rubicon dividing the "animal" from the "logical" finally crossed for ever and the highest possible development accorded to the process that began when a creature of dust and earth looked out beyond itself and its environment and was able to address God as "You." It is openness to the whole, to the infinite, that makes man complete. Man is man by reaching out infinitely beyond himself, and he is consequently more of a man the less enclosed he is in himself, the less "limited" he is. For—let me repeat—that man is most fully man, indeed *the* true man, who is most unlimited, who not only has contact

---

23 John Henry Newman, *An Essay on the Development of Christian Doctrine* (Notre Dame, IN: University of Notre Dame Press, 1989), 36.

24 Ratzinger, *Introduction to Christianity*, 234.

25 Ratzinger, *Introduction to Christianity*, 234.

DEIFICATION

with the infinite—the infinite Being!—but is one with him: Jesus Christ. In him "hominization" has truly reached its goal.[26]

But can hominization be understood in any way pertaining to deification? So far, Ratzinger's exposition hasn't suggested any sense of how this hominization might work at a more than human level. He does, however, develop a second point, that hominization has an intrinsic ecclesial element by virtue of our corporate identity in Christ the New Adam. Thus, Ratzinger explains:

> If Jesus is the exemplary man, in whom the true figure of man, God's intention for him, comes fully to light, then he cannot be destined to be merely an absolute exception, a curiosity, in which God demonstrates to us what sort of things are possible. His existence concerns all mankind. The New Testament makes this perceptible by calling him an "Adam"; in the Bible this word expresses the unity of the whole creature "man," so that one can speak of the biblical idea of a "corporate personality." So if Jesus is called "Adam," this implies that he is intended to gather the whole creature "Adam" in himself. But this means that the reality that Paul calls, in a way that is largely incomprehensible to us today, the "body of Christ" is an intrinsic postulate of this existence, which cannot remain an exception but must "draw to itself" the whole of mankind (cf. Jn 12:32).[27]

It is possible, therefore, to read Ratzinger's emphasis on the hominization of man as an expression of deification on a corporate, ecclesial level, with grace mediated through the Church. Our salvation, our divinization, is not something that happens to us individually apart from others, since we are part of and linked to, the communion of saints. In this sense, it is worth highlighting the way Ratzinger concludes his 1960 work *The Meaning of Christian Brotherhood*:

> When all other ways fail, there will always remain the royal way of vicarious suffering by the side of the Lord. It is in her defeat that the Church constantly achieves her highest victory and stands nearest to Christ. It is when she is called to suffer for others that she achieves her highest mission: the exchange of fate with the wayward brother and thus his secret restoration to full sonship and full brotherhood.

---

26 Ratzinger, *Introduction to Christianity*, 235.

27 Ratzinger, *Introduction to Christianity*, 236.

> Seen in this way, the relationship between the "few" and the "many" reveals the true measure of the Church's catholicity.[28]

This endorsement of vicarious suffering, may we say coredemptive suffering, is striking not least since it is a theme he has explicitly returned to in his rare post-retirement writings. It is also, of course, related to the Marian doctrine of the coredemptrix and is very much the spirituality animating the sense of the church as the Mystical Body of Christ. As Pius XII opened his encyclical *Mystici Corporis Christi* stressing our corporate redemption in Christ, following our corporate fall in Adam, he ends it reminding us that "sufferings are not in vain but will be of immense profit to themselves and to the Church if they bear them patiently for that intention."[29]

For all this, however, there is something unsatisfactory about Ratzinger's emphasis on hominization. The church fathers of the East, as Newman understood clearly, meant far more than simply Christ's nativity in their theology of the Incarnation; what was implied was the whole scope of birth, life, passion, crucifixion, descent into hell, resurrection, and ascension. Ratzinger's Christology in *Introduction to Christianity* appears to neglect the resurrection and ascension. As such, the anthropology he draws from his Christology is somewhat incomplete. In this context, the analysis of Bernard Tissier de Mallerais, in his study of the redemption according to Benedict XVI, is significant. De Mallerais highlights the philosophical influences or context behind Ratzinger's approach, notably the existentialism of Heidegger and the "going out self" of Karl Jaspers, and suggests that Ratzinger has a fatally naturalistic interpretation of redemption in which no account is given of sin. In his efforts to reconcile modern philosophy with the Christian faith, de Mallerais argues that Ratzinger puts "in place of an ascending analogy, a descending reduction of the supernatural mysteries."[30]

Particularly in light of these criticisms, we should mention Ratzinger's important 1966 commentary on articles 12–22 of *Gaudium et Spes* in which he criticizes aspects of the council document for insufficient acknowledgement of sin and inadequate treatment of the question of freedom. Many of the themes we

---

28 Joseph Ratzinger, *The Meaning of Christian Brotherhood* (San Francisco: Ignatius Press, 1993), 84.

29 Pius XII, *Mystici Corporis Christi*, 1943, no. 107, https://www.vatican.va/content/pius-xii/en/encyclicals/documents/hf_p-xii_enc_29061943_mystici-corporis-christi.html.

30 Bernard Tissier de Mallerais, *L'Étrange Théologie de Benoît XVI: Herméneutique de continuité ou rupture?* (Avrillé: Editions du Sel, 2010), 38.

have considered emerge in Ratzinger's analysis, but the highpoint of the text, article 22, introduces features of patristic anthropology that almost compel a humanism more centered on deification. As Ratzinger explains, this "presents Christ as the eschatological Adam to whom the first Adam already pointed; as the true image of God which transforms man once more into likeness to God."[31] Ratzinger acknowledges that "similutudo," is "probably an echo of Irenaeus," whose absence from *Introduction to Christianity* is almost as notable as that of Aquinas. Although he doesn't dwell long on this, Ratzinger highlights two points: first, that Irenaeus anticipated the later distinction between the natural and supernatural image of God with his image and likeness distinction, and second, that the council text actually distorts the classical teaching by suggesting "similitudo" is only mentioned as "deformata," whereas "in the classical doctrine the 'similitude' is lost but the 'imago' is wounded."[32] Perhaps key, however, is that this image and likeness anthropology opened the door to the supernatural in the text and thus ensured an anthropology open to deification, rather than one that would demonstrate that "by Christian faith in God, true humanism, i.e. man's full development as man is attained."[33] One further point is pertinent in Ratzinger's analysis of article 22—Incarnation, cross, and resurrection are considered. He notes that "the idea of the 'assumptio hominis' is first touched upon in its full ontological depth."[34] One can argue that the anthropology posited here challenges Ratzinger to embrace a supernaturalized anthropology.

Indeed, this development in Ratzinger's position can be seen clearly expressed by the end of the 1970s, because following the council, the fruits of the "fully human" anthropology became manifest; indeed, a standard traditionalist critique of the council is that it established the cult of man in place of the cult of God.[35] In other words, in this reading, in its attempts at dialogue and openness, the council achieved precisely what atheistic Marxism does explicitly, and liberalism does eventually, consciously or not. In Henri de

---

31 Joseph Ratzinger, "The Dignity of the Human Person," in *Commentary on the Documents of Vatican II*, vol. 5, *Pastoral Constitution on the Church in the Modern World*, trans. W. J. O'Hara (London: Burns & Oates, 1969), 115–63.

32 Ratzinger, "The Dignity of the Human Person," 159.

33 Ratzinger, "The Dignity of the Human Person," 118.

34 Ratzinger, "The Dignity of the Human Person," 119.

35 Álvaro Calderón, *Prometheus: The Religion of Man; An Essay on the Hermeneutics of the Second Vatican Council*, trans. Inés de Erausquin (St. Marys, KS: Angelus Press, 2021).

Lubac's late work, *A Brief Catechesis on Nature and Grace*, he addresses many elements of this postconciliar phenomenon as they found expression in the church: the views of Abbe Georges de Nantes, the anguish of Paul VI, and the Marxist sympathies of Edward Schillebeeckx are all covered in appendices.[36] In stark contrast to the anthropocentric critique, he offers an illuminating list of texts pertaining to the supernatural from the council, which serves to illustrate how Vatican II can and should be read very much in the light of deification.[37] Particularly striking, from our perspective, is the fact that de Lubac concludes this work with words of Ratzinger from a little-known piece he wrote in *Communio* in 1978: "a Christianity which offers man something less than making him God is too modest. . . . In the struggle for man in which we are engaged, such an answer is insufficient."[38]

What has happened? This is an extraordinary development from "hominization." For Ratzinger now, Christian teaching on deification is suggested as the necessary response to atheism and indifference in the modern world. This change in Ratzinger's position may ascribed in a way to Hans Kung, for the words in question are the conclusion to an article called "*Le christianisme sans peine*," a review of Hans Kung's book *On Being a Christian*.[39] What prompted the observation is Kung's question, "Is there a sensible man today who still wants to become God?" Ratzinger considers Ernst Bloch's adaption and use for his own cause of the serpent's temptation "You will be as gods," as well as the broader passion for emancipation witnessed in the twentieth century—one might say particularly in the previous ten years—and highlights the fact that nothing can satisfy this thirst except the status of divinity. For this reason, what Ratzinger terms the astonishing lack of ambition of modern Christianity is deeply unsatisfactory. Rather, the only response that can satisfy the yearnings of modern man is the traditional Christian doctrine of deification.

In 1982, Ratzinger gave an address at a congress on Christology in Rio de Janiero organized by the Latin American Episcopol Council. The 1,200th anniversary of the Third Council of Chalcedon in 1981 certainly appears to

---

36 Henri de Lubac, *A Brief Catechesis on Nature and Grace*, trans. Richard Arnandez (San Francisco: Ignatius Press, 1984).

37 De Lubac, *Brief Catechesis on Nature and Grace*, 177–90.

38 De Lubac, *Brief Catechesis on Nature and Grace*, 172.

39 Joseph Ratzinger, "Le christianisme sans peine—*Etre chrétien* de Hans Küng," *Communio* (September–October 1978), 84–95.

have stimulated Ratzinger, for he develops his Christology well beyond his 1960's writings. In the fifth of seven theses offered, Ratzinger considers human freedom, and states that "If man is to be free, he must be 'like God.' Wanting to be like God is the inner motive of all mankind's programs of liberation.... Any liberation of man which does not enable him to become divine betrays man, betrays his boundless yearning."[40] In the sixth thesis, Ratzinger reflects on Constantinople III, so-called neo-Chalcedonian Christology and the work of Maximus the Confessor, so centered on what Ratzinger beautifully describes as "the sentence which remains the measure and model of all real prayer: 'Not what I will, but what thou wilt' (Mk 14:36)."[41] Constantinople III, informed so much by Maximus and his exegesis of Gethsemane, shows for Ratzinger how the two wills of Christ become one in a personal manner, while not abrogating the metaphysical "two-ness." In this way, he writes, "we come to grasp the manner of our liberation, our participation in the Son's freedom. As a result of the unity of wills of which we have spoken, the greatest possible change has taken place in man, the only change which meets his desire: he has become divine."[42]

The "ontology of freedom" that Constantinople III expresses is also considered in another essay in *Behold the Pierced One*, which examines the relationship between the Eucharist, Christology, and ecclesiology.[43] Maximus's Christology is also mentioned fulsomely in *The Spirit of the Liturgy*; while not suggesting a direct influence of Maximus's *Mystagogia* on Ratzinger, his statement that "Christian liturgy is liturgy on its way, a liturgy of pilgrimage toward the transfiguration of the world, which will only take place when God is 'all in all,'" echoes the sense of the cosmic reach of the liturgy present in the Byzantine saint's liturgical writing.[44]

Before we return to Newman and consider how the theology of deification is reflected in his Catholic writings and homilies, I would like to briefly consider

---

40 Joseph Ratzinger, *Behold the Pierced One: An Approach to a Spiritual Christology*, trans. Graham Harrison (San Francisco: Ignatius Press, 1986), 33–35.

41 Ratzinger, *Behold the Pierced One*, 41.

42 Ratzinger, *Behold the Pierced One*, 42.

43 "Communion, Community and Mission: On the Connection between Eucharist, (Parish) Community and Mission in the Church," in Ratzinger, *Behold the Pierced One*, 71–100.

44 Joseph Ratzinger, *Collected Works*, vol. 11, *Theology of the Liturgy: The Sacramental Foundation of Christian Existence*, trans. John Saward, Kenneth Baker, Henry Taylor et al. (San Francisco: Ignatius Press, 2014), 30.

whether Ratzinger has implemented his own advice. Since the early 1980s, especially after apparent victory of in the Cold War, aggressive secularism and indifference to the sanctity of human life have been very evident. Technocracy, transhumanism, and a move to a New World Order, identified by Ratzinger in a conference given in September 2001, "Reflections on Europe," as the replacements for the old Marxist ideology of hope, are all in the ascendancy.[45] Ratzinger, as he shows in his 2005 study *Western Culture Today and Tomorrow* and in numerous other works, is one of the most adept commentators on the contemporary situation. Yet having dissected contemporary Western society and values, he very rarely puts forward a positive vision, preferring instead to insist on the need for Christ to be allowed in to our world. There is a peculiar reticence here, which I think in part stems from the difficulty of doing Christian politics once the parameters established by the French Revolution are accepted as normative.[46] If a theology of deification is to be proposed as a practical reality for Christians, and as any sort of corporate ecclesial reality as Ratzinger rightly envisages it, it will necessarily challenge the secular premises of modern political culture. Ultimately, to be able to preach a theology of deification to the modern Christian in a coherent way, one has to be able to complement this with the doctrine of the social reign of Christ the King, and Ratzinger is decidedly reluctant to move in that direction.

Newman's Catholic writings are considerably more combative than Ratzinger's with regard to engagement with the culture. I propose to consider two texts in particular, the *Discourses Addressed to Mixed Congregations* and the *Sermons Preached on Various Occasions*. While explicit expressions of deification in the patristic mode are not noticeable here, unlike in his Anglo-Catholic days, these Catholic homilies are animated by an extraordinary realism about the spiritual life as compared to the natural order, and they contain significant reflections on the relationship between nature and grace, all of which contribute to the supernatural goal to which Newman seeks to lead his flock. While Newman is often invoked as a man of the fathers, a precursor

---

45 Joseph Ratzinger, *Western Culture Today and Tomorrow*, trans. Michael J. Miller (San Francisco: Ignatius Press, 2007), 47–58.

46 On this topic, see "On the Status of Church and Theology Today," Ratzinger's epilogue to his major work of fundamental theology, published in German in 1982: Joseph Ratzinger, *Principles of Catholic Theology: Building Stones for a Fundamental Theology*, trans. Mary Frances McCarthy (San Francisco: Ignatius Press, 1987), 365–93. Here, among other things, he notes that *Gaudium et Spes* "serves as a countersyllabus and, as such, represents, on the part of the Church, an attempt at an official reconciliation with the new era inaugurated in 1789" (382).

to Vatican II, and even an ecumenical figure, these homilies remind us that he was a son of St. Philip Neri, who continued to develop theologically after his conversion, being shaped by the Catholic theological world of his time.

The first of the discourses, "The Salvation of the Hearer, the Motive of the Preacher," sets the tone, as Newman contrasts the views of the world with those of the church. The former "teaches that a man has not much to do to be saved; that either he has committed no great sins, or that he will, as a matter of course, be pardoned for committing them; that he may securely trust in God's mercy for his prospects in eternity; and that he ought to discard all self-reproach, or deprecation, or penance, all mortification and self-discipline, as affronting or derogatory to that mercy."[47] In contrast, the church highlights the fallen state of man, which remains fragile until death; hence, man "requires an extraordinary remedy."[48] Newman is under no illusions about the evil of the world and how it contrasts with the supernatural life of grace, a point he makes powerfully in the fifth of these discourse, "Saintliness the Standard of Christian Principle."

Newman begins this homily with reflections on the idols people revere, which are clearly not attributes of the divine nature, but typically wealth and notoriety, which he nicely describes as "newspaper fame."[49] He contrasts this with an awakening to the life of grace in the soul of believers in a beautiful passage:

> what a change for them when they first begin to see with the eyes of the soul, with the intuition which grace gives, Jesus, the Sun of Justice; and the heaven of Angels and Archangels in which He dwells; and the bright Morning Star, which is His Blessed Mother; and the continual floods of light falling and striking against the earth, and transformed as they fall, into an infinity of hues, which are His Saints.[50]

This, suggests Newman, is something of what the Apostles were introduced to on Mount Tabor, "a new range of ideas . . . a new sphere of contemplation."[51]

---

47 John Henry Newman, *Discourses Addressed to Mixed Congregations* (1849; Leominster: Gracewing, 2002), 7.

48 Newman, *Discourses Addressed to Mixed Congregations*, 8.

49 Newman, *Discourses Addressed to Mixed Congregations*, 91.

50 Newman, *Discourses Addressed to Mixed Congregations*, 92.

51 Newman, *Discourses Addressed to Mixed Congregations*, 93.

Henceforth, a new life begins that recognizes that "the high and precious things" are "saintliness and all its attendants—saintly purity, saintly poverty, heroic fortitude and patience, self-sacrifice for the sake of others, renouncement of the world, the favour of Heaven, the protection of Angels, the smile of the Blessed Virgin, the gifts of grace, the interpositions of miracle, the intercommunion of merits."[52]

In this way, Newman suggests, Catholics "have an idea before them which a Protestant nation has not; they have the idea of a Saint."[53] However weak and fallible they are, "they have a standard for their principles of conduct, and it is the image of Saints which forms it for them."[54] Newman offers a memorable explanation of how the saint is an incomprehensible figure to men of the world who pride themselves on knowing human nature but "know nothing of one great far-spreading phenomenon in man—and that is, his nature under the operation of grace; they know nothing of the second nature, of the supernatural gift, induced by the Almighty Spirit upon our first and fallen nature; they have never met, they have never read of, and they have formed no conception of a Saint."[55] Moreover, this principle of saintliness is something that is not only unknown to the man of the world but, as Newman highlights powerfully in concluding, is also distinct from the national religion, that is, the Anglican Church that he left, which ultimately reinforces worldliness. Newman writes:

> The national religion has many attractions; it leads to decency and order, propriety of conduct, justness of thought, beautiful domestic tastes; but it has not power to lead the multitude upward, or to delineate for them the Heavenly City. It comes of mere nature, and its teaching is of nature. . . . It in no true sense inculcates the Unseen; and by consequence, sights of this world, material tangible objects, become the idols and the ruin of its children, of souls which were made for God and Heaven. It is powerless to resist the world and the world's teaching: it cannot supplant error by truth; it follows where it should lead. There is but one real Antagonist of the world, and that is the faith of Catholics.[56]

---

52 Newman, *Discourses Addressed to Mixed Congregations*, 94.

53 Newman, *Discourses Addressed to Mixed Congregations*, 94.

54 Newman, *Discourses Addressed to Mixed Congregations*, 94–95.

55 Newman, *Discourses Addressed to Mixed Congregations*, 98.

56 Newman, *Discourses Addressed to Mixed Congregations*, 102–3.

This powerful passage is remarkable in its forthrightness and its clear align-
ment with what Pius X would teach with regard to Protestantism giving rise
to naturalism. The church's conflict with the world is taken as a given, and
the gulf between the saint and the ordinary is highlighted. For all the talk
of Newman being a father of Vatican II, this all seems rather too confidently
Catholic and lacking in the spirit of dialogue. It is also interesting to note that
for Newman, the saint, who we can term the deified human being, is one who
is incomprehensible to non-Catholics but intuitively accessible to Catholics.
One might contrast this with Ratzinger's view that the person of the saint
provides one of the most effective ways the Catholic Church can evangelize.[57]

One way in which Newman is aligned with the council fathers is in the
manner in which he handles nature and grace. At first sight, this claim might
seem odd, since as Ratzinger explains in his 1968 piece on *Gaudium et Spes*,
the council sought to avoid the topic of nature and supernature, and the
theology of grace and the supernatural has been somewhat in the background
of postconciliar theology.[58] Indeed, in Ratzinger's work, the topic receives little
explicit treatment, with the exception of a 1962 article written for a *Festschrift*
in honor of Gottlieb Söhngen's 70th birthday.[59] Newman is able to highlight
the distinction between nature and grace and yet resonate with figures like de
Lubac since his theology avoids the extrinsicist positions typically ascribed
to the neoscholastic Roman school.

In this way, Newman's theology of grace is very distinctive. Typical of
all his writing on grace is the clear distinction he makes between nature and
grace, which certainly preserves the gratuity of grace as the so-called two-
tier positions desired. At the same time, however, Newman is able to hold
the two extremes together and integrate them. Here, we can surely see the
translation of the patristic teaching about the indwelling of the Holy Spirit
into more contemporary Catholic language. Thus, in Discourse VIII, "Nature
and Grace," as well as highlighting the fact that "the world does not know of

---

57 See, for example, Joseph Ratzinger with Vittorio Messori, *The Ratzinger Report: An Exclusive
Interview on the State of the Church*, trans. Salvator Attanasio and Graham Harrison (San Francisco:
Ignatius Press, 1985), 129: "The only really effective apologia for Christianity comes down to two
arguments, namely the *saints* the Church has produced and the *art* which has grown in her womb."

58 Ratzinger, "Dignity of the Human Person," 123.

59 Joseph Ratzinger, "*Gratia Praesupponit Naturam*: Grace Presupposes Nature," in *Dogma
and Preaching: Applying Christian Doctrine to Daily Life*, trans. Michael J. Miller and Matthew J.
O'Connell (San Francisco: Ignatius Press, 2011), 143–61.

the existence of grace,"[60] he warns Catholics to be wary of taking for grace what is in fact nature, writing that "the difference is in a great measure an inward, and therefore a secret one. Grace is lodged in the heart; it purifies the thoughts and motives, it raises the soul to God, it sanctifies the body, it corrects and exalts human nature in regard to those sins of which men are ashamed, and do not make a public display."[61] Hence, he continues, "nature may counterfeit grace, nay even to the deception of the man himself in whom the counterfeit occurs."[62]

Newman's teaching on grace merits more detailed analysis than can be given here—other significant discourses in this volume include "Illuminating Grace," "Persevering Grace," and "Mysteries of Nature and Grace." I would like to conclude these reflections on this theme with a look at two of the sermons in the volume *Sermons Preached on Various Occasions*: "Omnipotence in Bonds" and "St. Paul's Characteristic Gift." In the former, Newman offers a reflection on the Incarnation, and it might be thought to be an obvious place for Newman to delineate the patristic teaching about deification, as he had done as an Anglican when preaching on this theme. Instead, what we find here is a consideration of the mystery that instead highlights the majesty of God and the inexhaustible mystery of such majesty taking on human flesh—"He has," Newman writes, "the incomprehensible power of even making himself weak."[63] Hence, his message here is not that we should aspire to become gods by grace but rather that we should simply learn to understand our littleness and "blush at our own pride and self-will" and "call to mind our impatience at God's providence towards us." Newman teaches the way of humility here, and surrender to God, asking, "What was the sin of Lucifer, but the resolve to be his own master? What was the sin of Adam, but impatience of subjection, and a desire to be his own god?"[64] Here, then, we have another instance of the realism of Newman's preaching, his awareness of the reality of sin and our human frailty.

In "St Paul's Characteristic Gift," Newman identifies two types of saints. If we can say that in his Catholic teaching, Newman prefers the language and

---

60 Newman, *Discourses Addressed to Mixed Congregations*, 148.

61 Newman, *Discourses Addressed to Mixed Congregations*, 151.

62 Newman, *Discourses Addressed to Mixed Congregations*, 151.

63 Newman, *Sermons Preached on Various Occasions*, 88.

64 Newman, *Sermons Preached on Various Occasions*, 89.

sanctity and grace over deification, there is a sense that this latter doctrine finds expression no longer in the abstract but in the concrete reality of the saints. In this sermon, Newman suggests that while all saints are alike in that "their excellence is supernatural" they may be divided externally into two classes. There are some, he says, "who are so absorbed in the divine life, that they seem, even while they are in the flesh, to have no part in earth or in human nature; but to think, speak, and act under views, affections, and motives simply supernatural. . . . Such we may suppose to have been St. John; such St. Mary Magdalen; such the hermits of the desert; such many of the holy Virgins whose lives belong to the science of mystical theology."[65]

In contrast to such lives, in which there is an obvious sense of supernaturalized humanity participating in the divine nature in this life, Newman posits a second kind of saint, also "of the highest order of sanctity," "in whom the supernatural combines with nature, instead of superseding it, - invigorating it, elevating it, ennobling it."[66] Such figures "do not put away their natural endowments, but use them to the glory of the Giver; they do not act beside them, but through them; they do not eclipse them by the brightness of divine grace, but only transfigure them."[67] They are in the world and well-versed in the world, and they "have the thoughts, feelings, frames of mind, attractions, sympathies of other men, so far as these are not sinful, only they have these properties of human nature purified, sanctified, and exalted; and they are only made more eloquent, more poetical, more profound, more intellectual, by reason of their being more holy."[68] Newman suggests such saints include many of the early fathers: St. Chrysostom, St. Gregory Nazianzen, and St. Athanasius, as well as, above all, St. Paul.

Newman highlights that while it is to St. John that "the gift of the science of the saints" was given, no one had a more intimate communion with the Divine Majesty than St. Paul, who is gifted with a gift of being all things to all, "having the nature of man so strong within him, he is able to enter into human nature, and to sympathize with it,"[69] since "in him the fulness of divine gifts does not tend to destroy what is human in him, but to spiritualize and

---

65 Newman, *Sermons Preached on Various Occasions*, 91–92.

66 Newman, *Sermons Preached on Various Occasions*, 92.

67 Newman, *Sermons Preached on Various Occasions*, 92.

68 Newman, *Sermons Preached on Various Occasions*, 93.

69 Newman, *Sermons Preached on Various Occasions*, 96.

perfect it."[70] It is precisely this transformation and elevation of his nature by grace, Newman suggests, that give his teaching about sin—the "sin dwelling in him"—and grace its power; he "vividly apprehended," Newman says, "in that nature of his which grace had sanctified, what it was in its tendencies and results when deprived of grace."[71] In this way, St. Paul is both the special preacher of Divine Grace and "also the special friend and intimate of human nature." As such, St. Paul serves as a reminder of the possibility of the sanctification of ordinary men, that the vocation to holiness is for all, and further, that all areas of life may be sanctified.

It is notable that Newman doesn't include Mary within either of these two categories of saints. She is, of course, in a category of her own. Assumed into heaven, she is perfectly deified; immaculate and united with her son at the foot of the cross, she gave birth to us in the order of grace, is our spiritual mother, and is thus integral to our divinization. In concluding this examination of Newman and Ratzinger's thought on deification, I will reflect on the ways in which Newman and Ratzinger consider Mary in these terms, as both the model of deified humanity, our pattern of holiness, and as the agent of our deification, the mediatrix of all graces.

Among Newman's devotional writings are his *Meditations on the Litany of Loretto for the Month of May*, in which he reflects on her title within a thematic structure based on the Immaculate Conception, the Annunciation, Our Lady's Dolours, and the Assumption. Reflecting on Mary's holiness, Newman observes that our Lord "began His great work before she was born; before she could think, speak, or act, by making her *holy*, and thereby, while on earth, a citizen of heaven."[72] With regard to Mary as Mother of the Creator, he highlights "the wonderful promises that follow from this truth, that Mary is the Mother of God," included in which are that "if we live well, and die in the grace of God, . . . we shall be partakers of the Divine nature."[73] Newman nowhere describes Mary herself directly with the language of deification, but the theme of her personal purity and holiness, and exaltedness above all the saints, is characteristic of his overall perspective. Perhaps one may sum up this aspect of Newman's treatment of Mary with words that conclude his

---

70 Newman, *Sermons Preached on Various Occasions*, 95.

71 Newman, *Sermons Preached on Various Occasions*, 97.

72 John Henry Newman, *Prayers, Verses and Devotions* (San Francisco: Ignatius Press, 2000), 132.

73 Newman, *Prayers, Verses and Devotions*, 143.

discourse "On the Fitness of the Glories of Mary": "She is the personal type and representative image of that spiritual life and renovation in grace, 'without which no one shall see God.'"[74]

Newman's writing on Mary may be said to culminate in his *Letter to Pusey*, written in nine days prior to the Feast of the Immaculate Conception in 1865, a work that is undoubtedly "one of the most important Marian studies of the modern era."[75] In this sensitive and richly patristic exposition of Catholic Mariology, Newman highlights in particular evocation of Mary as the New Eve among the early fathers. From this typology, he vividly explains the dogma of the Immaculate Conception.[76] For our purposes, however, the key aspect of Newman's Mariology that pertains to deification is her intercessory power, which results from the fact that "the Blessed Mary is singularly dear to her Son and singularly exalted in sanctity and glory."[77] Indeed, once this is grasped, and the nature of the church as "one vast body in heaven and on earth" is understood, Newman suggests it is impossible

> not to perceive immediately, that her office above is one of perpetual intercession for the faithful militant, and that our very relation to her must be that of clients to a patron, and that, in the eternal enmity which exists between the woman and the serpent, while the serpent's strength lies in being the Tempter, the weapon of the Second Eve and Mother of God is prayer.[78]

Mary as perpetually interceding for us, and our relating to her as to one from whom we receive gifts—in this passage, Newman articulates very powerfully Mary's role as mediatrix of grace. For Newman, her intercessory power is integral to our sanctification and salvation.

Turning to the thought of Joseph Ratzinger with regard to Mary and deification, we can observe some striking developments. His early writings in the immediate postconciliar era evince a triumphant Marian minimalism

---

74 Newman, *Discourses Addressed to Mixed Congregations*, 376.

75 P. Andrej Mária Čaja, *La vergine Maria nella storia della salvezza: Sviluppo storico e significato teologico del titolo Mariano di "Corredentrice"* (Neuss: Familie Mariens, 2021), 120.

76 Philip Boyce, ed., *Mary: The Virgin Mary in the Life and Writings of John Henry Newman* (Leominster: Gracewing, 2001), 224–25.

77 Boyce, *Mary*, 261.

78 Boyce, *Mary*, 266–67.

that is quite extraordinary. He boldly states that "the idea of Mary as 'co-re-demptrix' is gone now, as is the idea of Mary as 'mediatrix of all graces,'" qualifying this statement a little by adding: "the text still retains a vestige of the latter title when it says that the custom has developed in the Church of addressing Mary as mediatrix as well as with other titles, but this undoubtedly is very different from saying that she is mediatrix of all graces."[79] Ratzinger sees the council as having largely supplanted the old systematic Mariology with a more positive and scriptural Mariology. Regarding Mary herself, not only are the above titles, once "under the protection of papal teaching," now gone but so, too, is any sense of her vastly superior holiness.[80] Mary, says Ratzinger, is now seen "as a member of the Church who does not, like Christ, stand before us, but rather has her place with us and among us before the Lord, as a representative faithful Christian in the world."[81] This emphasis on the ordinariness of Mary as "a representative faithful Christian" is followed a few years later by a statement in *Introduction to Christianity* that questions the necessity of Jesus having been conceived by the Holy Spirit and thus also calls in to question Mary's virginity. Ratzinger states that:

> According to the faith of the Church, the Divine Sonship of Jesus does not rest on the fact that Jesus had no human father; the doctrine of Jesus' divinity would not be affected if Jesus had been the product of a normal human marriage. For the Divine Sonship of which faith speaks is not a biological but an ontological fact, an event not in time but in God's eternity; God is always Father, Son, and Spirit; the conception of Jesus means, not that a new God-the-son comes into being, but that God as Son in the man Jesus draws the creature man to himself, so that he himself "is" man.[82]

The implications here are more than a denial of Mary's virginity and of a spousal relationship with the Holy Spirit. They also suggest a profoundly flawed Christology. As von Balthasar highlighted, in the context of Ratzinger's words that were "repeated eagerly everywhere," this position would ultimately mean

---

79 Joseph Ratzinger, *Theological Highlights of Vatican II*, trans. Henry Traub, SJ, Gerard C. Thormann, and Werner Barzel (New York: Paulist Press, 2009), 141.

80 Ratzinger, *Theological Highlights*, 143.

81 Ratzinger, *Theological Highlights*, 141.

82 Ratzinger, *Introduction to Christianity*, 274–75.

that Jesus would not "have any special ability to mediate his fellow men into a completely new relationship to their heavenly Father."[83]

In the 1970s, Ratzinger's writings about Mary shift quite dramatically. In *Daughter Zion*, he recognizes that "the appearance of a truly Marian awareness serves as the touchstone indicating whether or not the christological substance is fully present."[84] Furthermore, in a section on the theological meaning of Mary's virginity and motherhood, he explicitly affirms Mary's virginity and the validity of von Balthsar's criticisms: "The virgin birth is the necessary origin of him who is the Son and who as Son first endows the messianic hope with a permanent significance extending far beyond Israel."[85] *Daughter Zion* also offers brief but profound reflections on the Immaculate Conception and the Assumption that reveal more of the shift in Ratzinger's Mariology.

Indeed, Ratzinger considers both these dogmas in terms of perfection and sanctity, and the language, while not explicitly of deification, is akin to Newman's and certainly similar to the content of the doctrine of divinization by grace. For Ratzinger, the "correspondence of God's 'Yes' with Mary's being as 'Yes' is the freedom from original sin." This freedom from original sin is not simply a negative absence but an openness to God and plenitude: "Grace as dispossession becomes response as appropriation." Hence, Ratzinger adds, "the doctrine of the *Immaculata* reflects ultimately faith's certitude that there really is a holy Church—as a person and in a person."[86] The certainty of faith is also reflected in the Assumption, which was an act of Marian veneration that, Ratzinger explains, "by exalting the Mother to the highest degree, was intended to be a liturgy of faith." Moreover, he continues, "the dogma of the Assumption is simply the highest degree of canonization, in which the predicate 'saint' is recognized in the most strict sense, i.e., being wholly and undividedly in eschatological fulfilment."[87]

One of the ways in which Ratzinger's Mariology develops is through a deeper reflection of the place of Mariology within theology as a whole. In 1980,

---

83 Hans Urs von Balthasar and Joseph Cardinal Ratzinger, *Mary: The Church at the Source*, trans. Adrian Walker (San Francisco: Ignatius Press, 2005), 149.

84 Joseph Cardinal Ratzinger, *Daughter Zion: Meditations on the Church's Marian Belief*, trans. John M. McDermott, SJ (San Francisco: Ignatius Press, 1983), 35.

85 Ratzinger, *Daughter Zion*, 51. See n. 11 here for Ratzinger's statement about "the limits" of his "frequently cited observations" in *Introduction to Christianity* and von Balthasar's critique.

86 Ratzinger, *Daughter Zion*, 70.

87 Ratzinger, *Daughter Zion*, 74.

in a contribution to a joint volume with Hans Urs von Balthasar, Ratzinger returns to the question of whether "Mary's physical maternity still had any theological significance at all." The answer he gives is that it does, "as the ultimate personal concretisation of the Church." But it is also more than this because what her physical maternity brings about is "the true centre of all history, 'Christ and the Church.'" Particularly striking is the definition Ratzinger offers for the church in this context, namely the "Church here meaning the creature's fusion with its Lord in spousal love, in which its hope for divinization is fulfilled by way of faith."[88] As such, Ratzinger is arguing for a Mariology at the heart of faith, which "stands within the totality of the basic Christ-Church structure and is the most concrete expression of its inner coherence."[89]

Curiously, this language of salvation as deification, with Mary at the heart of it, isn't elaborated on. Yet, as we have seen elsewhere in Ratzinger's work, he does address the inverse phenomenon in the context of Mary, arguing for the importance of her feminine reality, as virgin and mother. For Ratzinger, in a profoundly powerful insight given our contemporary situation forty years later, Mary's concrete biological reality as female speaks directly into "today's anthropological program" that "hinges more radically than ever before on 'emancipation'" and "seeks a freedom whose goal is to 'be like God' (Gen 3:5)."[90] This goal is aspired to by modern man through the "treatment of 'biology' as a mere thing" that can be used and manipulated at will; in so doing, Ratzinger highlights, "humanity itself is negated."[91] It is "precisely as a woman" that 'Mary represents saved and liberated man';[92] similarly in the field of devotion, Marian piety, for Ratzinger, has the task to "awaken the heart and purify it in faith," and it can in this way work against "the misery of contemporary man" and "his increasing disintegration into *mere* bios and mere rationality."[93] Thus, the battle for man that Ratzinger highlighted in his review of Hans Küng's book, for which the Christian theology of deification is the only adequate answer, is one in which Mary is most intimately involved.

---

88 Von Balthasar and Ratzinger, *Mary: Church at Source*, 30.

89 Von Balthasar and Ratzinger, *Mary: Church at Source*, 30.

90 Von Balthasar and Ratzinger, *Mary: Church at Source*, 32.

91 Von Balthasar and Ratzinger, *Mary: Church at Source*, 32.

92 Von Balthasar and Ratzinger, *Mary: Church at Source*, 31.

93 Von Balthasar and Ratzinger, *Mary: Church at Source*, 36.

In conclusion, then, some distinct features emerge from this study of deification in the writings of Newman and Ratzinger. For Newman, the doctrine of deification is a strong theme of his writings in his post-evangelical Anglican days and reflects his deep grounding in the writings of the fathers, which would eventually lead him into full communion with the Catholic Church. While the theme of sanctity remains constant throughout, there is a shift in theological language evident in his Catholic writings, with a clear priority being given to the language of nature and grace. In contrast, Ratzinger appears somewhat reticent to offer a full articulation of the doctrine of deification in his early work, where a preference for the term "hominization" is apparent. By the late 1970s, however, partly in response to growing secularization and partly through a fuller engagement with patristic Christology, especially as developed by Maximus the Confessor, deification becomes an important and clear feature of Ratzinger's articulation of the faith. With regard to our Lady, both theologians' positions develop such as to clearly acknowledge Mary's role in the mediation of grace. While for Newman, this development is naturally bound up with his reception into the Catholic Church, for Ratzinger, the change runs parallel with his adoption of the language of deification in the 1970s. It is a striking testament to the further development of his Mariology that in some of his final words as pope, in sharp contrast to his views of the 1960s, he prays for "the intercession of the Blessed Virgin Mary Immaculate, Mediatrix of All Graces."[94]

---

94 Benedict XVI, "Letter Given to Sigismund Zimowski as an Extraordinary Mission for the Celebration of the 21st World Day of the Ill," 2013, https://www.vatican.va/content/benedict-xvi/la/letters/2013/documents/hf_ben-xvi_let_20130110_card-zimowski.html.

BIBLIOGRAPHY

Abraham, William J. "Reception of Newman on Divine Revelation." In *Receptions of Newman*, edited by Frederick D. Aquino and Benjamin J. King, 197–213. Oxford: Oxford University Press, 2015.

Agbaw-Ebai, Maurice Ashley. *Light of Reason, Light of Faith: Joseph Ratzinger and the German Enlightenment*. South Bend, IN: St. Augustine's Press, 2021.

Allchin, A. M. *Participation in God: A Forgotten Strand in the Anglican* Tradition. London: Darton, Longman, and Todd, 1988.

Allison, Dale C. "Matthew." In *The Oxford Bible Commentary*, edited by John Barton and John Muddiman, 844–65. Oxford: Oxford University Press, 2001.

Alsopp, Michael E. "Conscience, the Church and the Moral Truth: John Henry Newman, Vatican II, Today." *Irish Theological Quarterly* 3 (1992): 192–208.

Alston, William P. *Beyond "Justification": Dimensions of Epistemic Evaluation*. Ithaca, NY: Cornell University Press, 2005.

Amadasu, Idahosa. "Conscience and Holiness: Joseph Ratzinger/Pope Benedict XVI's Reception of John Henry Newman." In *Conscience, the Path to Holiness: Walking with Newman*, edited by Edward Jeremy Miller, 97–111. Newcastle upon Tyne: Cambridge Scholars, 2014.

Anatolios, Khaled. *Retrieving Nicaea: The Development and Meaning of Trinitarian* Doctrine. Grand Rapids, MI: Baker Academic, 2011.

Angielczyk, Kenneth. "What Do We Mean by 'Theory' in Science?" *Chicago Field Museum*, March 10, 2017. https://www.fieldmuseum.org/blog/what-do-we-mean-theory-science.

BIBLIOGRAPHY

Anton, Emil. "Ratzinger and Reformation Ruptures." In *The Oxford Handbook on Joseph Ratzinger*, edited by Francesca Murphy and Tracey Rowland. Oxford: Oxford University Press. Forthcoming.

Aquinas, Thomas. *Commentary on the Posterior Analytics*. Translated by Ralph McInerny. Notre Dame, IN: Dumb Ox Books, 2008.

———. *Summa Contra Gentiles: Book 3, Providence, Part 1*. Translated by Vernon Bourke. Notre Dame, IN: University of Notre Dame Press, 1975.

———. *Summa theologiae*. Translated by Fathers of the English Dominican Province. Westminster, MD: Christian Classics, 1981.

Aquino, Frederick D. *Communities of Informed Judgment: Newman and Accounts of Rationality*. Washington, DC: The Catholic University of America Press, 2004.

———. "An Educated Conscience: Perception and Reason in Newman's Account of Conscience." *Studies in the Literary Imagination* 49, no. 2 (2018): 63–80.

———. "Epistemology." In *The Oxford Handbook of John Henry Newman*, edited by Frederick D. Aquino and Benjamin J. King, 375–94. Oxford: Clarendon, 2018.

———. "Newman on the Grounds of Faith." *Quaestiones Disputatae* 8, no. 2 (2018): 5–18.

———. "Spiritual Formation, Authority, and Discernment." In *The Oxford Handbook of the Epistemology of Theology*, edited by Frederick D. Aquino and William J. Abraham, 157–72. Oxford: Clarendon, 2017.

Aquino, Frederick D., and Benjamin King. "Introduction." In *The Oxford Handbook of John Henry Newman*, 1–6. Oxford: Clarendon, 2017.

———., eds. *The Oxford Handbook of John Henry Newman*. Oxford: Clarendon, 2017.

Aquino, Frederick D., and Logan P. Gage. "Newman the Quasi-fideist: A Reply to Duncan Pritchard." *Heythrop Journal* 64, no. 5 (2023): 695–706.

———. "On the Epistemic Role of Our Passional Nature." *Newman Studies Journal* 17, no. 2 (2020): 41–58.

Arnold, Claus. "Newman's Reception in Germany: From Döllinger to Ratzinger." *Newman Studies Journal* 18 (2021): 5–23.

Arrupe, Pedro, SJ. *Jesuit Apostolates Today: An Anthology of Letters and Addresses III*. Edited by Jerome Aixala. Anand: Sahitya Prakash, 1981.

BIBLIOGRAPHY

Athanasius, *The Life of Antony and the Letter to Marcellinus*. Translated by Robert C. Gregg. Mahwah, NJ: Paulist Press, 1980.

——. *Traités contre les ariens*, 2 vols. Translated by Charles Kannengiesser and Adriana Bara. Sources chrétiennes 598–99. Paris: Cerf, 2019.

Arthur, James, and Guy Nicholls. *John Henry Newman*. London: Bloomsbury, 2007.

Attard, Fabio. *Conscience in the "Parochial and Plain Sermons" of John Henry Newman*. Valetta, Malta: Midseabooks, 2008.

Augustine. *The City of God*. Translated by R. W. Dyson. Cambridge: Cambridge University Press, 2015.

——. *Confessions*. Translated by Henry Chadwick. Oxford: Oxford University Press, 2008.

——. *The Literal Meaning of Genesis*. Translated by J. H. Taylor, Ancient Christian Writers 41. New York: Newman Press, 1982.

Austriaco, Nicanor et al., *Thomistic Evolution: A Catholic Approach to Understanding Evolution in the Light of Faith*, 2nd ed. Tacoma, WA: Cluny Media, 2019.

Baehr, Jason. *The Inquiring Mind: On Intellectual Virtues and Virtue Epistemology*. Oxford: Oxford University Press, 2011.

Baglow, Christopher. *Faith, Science, and Reason: Theology on the Cutting Edge*. Downers Grove, IL: Midwest Theological Forum, 2019.

Ballantyne, Nathan. *Knowing Our Limits*. Oxford: Oxford University Press, 2019.

von Balthasar, Hans Urs. *Nochmals Reinhold Schneider*. Einsiedeln: Johannes, 1991.

von Balthasar, Hans Urs, and Joseph Cardinal Ratzinger. *Mary: The Church at the Source*. Translated by Adrian Walker. San Francisco: Ignatius Press, 2005.

Barr, Colin. "Historical (Mis)understandings of The Idea of a University." In *Receptions of Newman*, edited by Frederick D. Aquino and Benjamin J. King, 114–33. Oxford: Oxford University Press, 2015.

Barth, Karl. *Church Dogmatics I: Part I, The Doctrine of the Word of God*. Translated by G. T. Thomson. Edinburgh: T&T Clark, 1936.

Bauerschmidt, Frederick Christian. "Augustine and Aquinas." In *T&T Clark Companion to Augustine and Modern Theology*, edited by C. C. Pecknold and Tarmo Toom, 113–30. London: Bloomsbury, 2013.

BIBLIOGRAPHY

Beattie, Tina. "*Humanae Vitae*—Nature, Sex, and Reason in Conflict." *Pastoral Review* 4, no. 4 (2008): 55–60.

Beaumont, Keith. "The Connection between Theology, Spirituality, and Morality." In *A Guide to John Henry Newman: His Life and Thought*, edited by Juan R. Vélez, 393–413. Washington, DC: The Catholic University of America Press, 2022.

——. *Dieu Intérieur: La théologie spirituelle de John Henry Newman*, Études Newmaniennes. Paris: Éditions Ad Solem, 2014.

Belcher, Kimberly Hope. "The Feast of Peace: The Eucharist as a Sacrifice and a Meal in Benedict XVI's Theology." In *Explorations in the Theology of Benedict XVI*, edited by John C. Cavadini, 254–75. Notre Dame, IN: University of Notre Dame Press, 2016.

Belleza, Jose Isidro. "Joseph Ratzinger, Student of Thomas." *Berkeley Journal of Religion and Theology* 5, no. 1 (2019): 94–120.

Benedict XVI, Pope. *See* Ratzinger, Joseph.

Benestad, J. Brian. "Doctrinal Perspectives on the Church in the Modern World." In *Vatican II: Renewal within Tradition*, edited by Matthew L. Lamb and Matthew Levering, 147–64. Oxford: Oxford University Press, 2008.

Berger, David. "Kommentar zur Enzyklika *Mystici Corporis*." *Einsicht: Römisch-Katholische Zeitschrift* 34, no. 2 (February 2004).

Berlin, Isaiah. *The Power of Ideas*, edited by Henry Hardy. Princeton, NJ: Princeton University Press, 2000.

Biemer, Günter. "Autonomie und Kirchenbindung: Gewissensfreiheit und Lehramt nach J. H. Newman." In *Sinnsuche und Lebenswenden: Gewissen als Praxis nach John Henry Newman. Internationale Cardinal-Newman-Studien XVI. Folge.* Frankfurt am Main: Verlag Peter Lang, 1998, 174–93.

Bischofsberger, Erwin. *Die sittlichen Voraussetzungen des Glaubens: Zur Fundamentalethik John Henry Newmans.* Mainz: Matthias Grünewald, 1974.

Bisson, Peter. "Breaking Open the Mysteries." In *Scrutinizing the Signs of the Times in the Light of the Gospel*, edited by Johan Verstraeten, 121–48. Bibliotheca Ephemeridum Theologicarum Lovaniensium 208. Leuven: Peeters, 2007.

Blanchard, Shaun. *The Synod of Pistoia and Vatican II: Jansenism and the Struggle for Catholic Reform.* Oxford: Oxford University Press, 2020.

BIBLIOGRAPHY

———. "*Traditionis Custodes* Was Never Merely about the Liturgy." *Church Life Journal*, August 2, 2021. https://churchlifejournal.nd.edu/articles/traditionis-custodes-was-never-merely-about-the-liturgy/.

Boeve, Lieven. "Conversion and Cognitive Dissonance: Evaluating the Theological-Ecclesial Program of Joseph Ratzinger/Pope Benedict XVI." *Horizons* 40, no. 2 (2013): 242–54.

———. "Europe in Crisis: A Question of Belief or Unbelief?" *Modern Theology* 23 (2007): 205–27.

———. "Thinking Sacramental Presence in a Postmodern Context." In *Sacramental Presence in a Postmodern Context: Contemporary Sacramental Contours of a God Incarnate; The Presence of Transcendence*, edited by Lieven Boeve and Lambert Leijssen, 3–37. Leuven: Leuven University Press, 2001.

Boeve, Lieven, and Gerard Mannion, eds. *The Ratzinger Reader*. London: T&T Clark, 2010.

Bonagura, David J., Jr. "The Relation of Revelation and Tradition in the Theology of John Henry Newman and Joseph Ratzinger." *New Blackfriars* 101, no. 1091 (2020): 67–84.

Borgman, Erik. *Want de plaats waarop je staat is heilige grond*. Meppel: Boom, 2008.

Boring, M. Eugene, and Fred B. Craddock. *The People's New Testament Commentary*. Louisville, KY: Westminster John Knox, 2009.

Bottone, Angelo. *The Philosophical Habit of Mind: Rhetoric and Person in John Henry Newman's Dublin Writings*. Bucharest: Zeta Books, 2010.

Bouyer, Louis. *L'Église de Dieu*. Paris: Cerf, 1970.

———. *Newman's Vision of Faith*. San Francisco: Ignatius Press, 1986.

Boyce, Philip, ed. *Mary: The Virgin Mary in the Life and Writings of John Henry Newman*. Leominster: Gracewing, 2001.

Bradford, Alina. "What Is a Scientific Theory?" *Live Science* July 29, 2017. https://www.livescience.com/21491-what-is-a-scientific-theory-definition-of-theory.html.

Brown, David. *God and Mystery in Words: Experience through Metaphor and Drama*. Oxford: Oxford University Press, 2008.

Brown, Stewart J., Peter Nockles, and James Pereiro, eds. *The Oxford Handbook of the Oxford Movement*. Oxford: Oxford University Press, 2017.

BIBLIOGRAPHY

Bullivant, Stephen. *Mass Exodus: Catholic Disaffiliation in Britain and America since Vatican II*. 2nd ed. Oxford: Oxford University Press, 2019.

Burtchaell, James Tunstead. *Catholic Theories of Biblical Inspiration since 1810: A Review and Critique*. Cambridge: Cambridge University Press, 1969.

Butler, Joseph. *The Analogy of Religion, Natural and Revealed, the Constitution and Course of Nature*. 2nd ed. Oxford: Knapton, 1736.

———. *Three Sermons upon Human Nature and Dissertation on Virtue*. London: S. Bell and Sons, 1914.

Čaja, P. Andrej Mária. *La vergine Maria nella storia della salvezza: Sviluppo storico e significato teologico del titolo Mariano di "Corredentrice."* Neuss, Germany: Familie Mariens, 2021.

Calderón, Álvaro. *Prometheus: The Religion of Man; An Essay on the Hermeneutics of the Second Vatican Council*. Translated by Inés de Erausquin. St. Marys, KS.: Angelus Press, 2021.

Capps, Donald. "A Biographical Footnote to Newman's *Lead, Kindly Light*." *Church History* 41, no. 4 (1972): 480–86.

Cardó, Daniel. *What Does It Mean to Believe? Faith in the Thought of Joseph Ratzinger*. Steubenville, OH: Emmaus Academic, 2020.

Carroll, Malachy. *The Mind and Heart of St. Paul: A Newman Anthology on St. Paul*. London: St. Paul Publications, 1959.

Cavadini, John C., ed. *Explorations in the Theology of Benedict XVI*. Notre Dame, IN: University of Notre Dame Press, 2016.

Chadwick, Owen. *From Bossuet to Newman*. 2nd ed. London: Cambridge University Press, 1987.

Chappell, Jonathan. "A Grammar of Descent: John Henry Newman and the Compatibility of Evolution with Christian Doctrine." *Science & Christian Belief* 27, no. 2 (2015): 180–206.

Chenu, M.-D., OP. "Les signes des temps." *Nouvelle revue théologique* 87, no. 1 (1965): 29–39.

Chesterton, G. K. *The Everlasting Man*, in *The Collected Works of G. K. Chesterton*. San Francisco: Ignatius Press, 1986.

Cicero, *Tusculanae disputationes*. Edited by Max Pohlenz. Leipzig: Bibliotheca Teubneriana, 1918.

———. *Vom rechten Handeln (De officiis)*. Translated and edited by Karl Büchner. 3rd ed. München: Artemis und Winkler, 1987.

Clark, Elizabeth A. "'Historical Development' and Early Christianity: George Tyrrell's Modernist Adaptation and Critique." In *Christians Shaping Identity from the Roman Empire to Byzantium: Studies Inspired by Pauline Allen*, edited by Geoffrey Dunn and Wendy Mayer, 454–77. Leiden: Brill, 2015.

Coakley, Sarah. "Dark Contemplation and Epistemic Transformation: The Analytic Theologian Re-Meets Teresa of Ávila." In *Analytic Theology: New Essays in the Philosophy of Theology*, edited by Oliver D. Crisp and Michael C. Rea, 280–312. Oxford: Oxford University Press, 2009.

Coleridge, John Taylor. *A Memoir of the Rev. John Keble*. 3rd ed. Oxford and London: James Parker and Co., 1870.

Collins, Christopher, SJ. *The Word Made Love: The Dialogical Theology of Joseph Ratzinger/Benedict XVI*. Collegeville, MN: Liturgical Press, 2013.

Collins, Paul M. *Partaking in Divine Nature: Deification and Communion*. London: T&T Clark, 2010.

Congar, Yves, OP. "Église et monde." *Esprit* 335 (1965): 337–59.

———. *Tradition and Traditions*. Translated by Michael Naseby and Thomas Rainborough. New York: Macmillan, 1967.

Congregation for the Doctrine of the Faith. *Instruction on Christian Freedom and Liberation*. 1986. https://www.vatican.va/roman_curia/congregations/cfaith/documents/rc_con_cfaith_doc_19860322_freedom-liberation_en.html.

Conn, Walter E. *Conscience & Conversion in Newman: A Developmental Study of Self in John Henry Newman*. Milwaukee: Marquette University Press, 2010.

———. "Newman on Conscience." *Newman Studies* 6, no. 2 (Fall 2009): 15–26.

Corkery, James. "Luther and the Theology of Pope Emeritus Benedict XVI." In *Remembering the Reformation: Martin Luther and Catholic Theology*, edited by Declan Marmion, Salvador Ryan, and Gesa E. Thiessen, 125–41. Minneapolis: Fortress, 2017.

Corona, Marial. *John Henry Newman and Pragmatism: A Comparison*. Washington, DC: The Catholic University of America Press, 2023.

Cottingham, John. *Philosophy of Religion: Towards A More Humane Approach*. New York: Cambridge University Press, 2014.

———. *The Spiritual Dimension: Religion, Philosophy, and Human Value*. Cambridge: Cambridge University Press, 2005.

Coulson, John and A. M. Allchin, eds. *The Rediscovery of Newman: An Oxford Symposium*. London: Sheed & Ward, 1967.

Coyne, Jerry. *Why Evolution Is True*. New York: Penguin Books, 2010.

Crosby, John. "Christliche Heiligkeit als Einheit von scheinbaren Gegensätzen: Die Lehre und das Zeugnis John Henry Newmans." In *Newman-Studien XII*, 207–18. Sigmaringendorf: Glock und Lutz, 1988.

———. "The 'Coincidentia Oppositorum,' in the Thought and in the Spirituality of John Henry Newman." *Anthropotes* 6, no. 2 (1990): 187–212.

———. "Newman on Mystery and Dogma." In *John Henry Newman. Lover of Truth. Academic Symposium and Celebration of the first Centenary of the Death of John Henry Newman*, edited by Margarete Binder and Maria Katharina Strolz. Rome: Pontificia Universitas Urbaniana, 1991.

———. *The Personalism of John Henry Newman*. Washington, DC: The Catholic University of America Press, 2014.

Culler, Dwight. *The Imperial Intellect*. New Haven, CT: Yale University Press, 1955.

Dahm, Brandon. "The Certainty of Faith: A Problem for Christian Fallibilists?" *Journal of Analytic Theology* 3 (2015): 130–46.

Daley, Brian E., SJ. "The Church Fathers." In *The Cambridge Companion to John Henry Newman*, edited by Ian Ker and Terrence Merrigan, 29–46. Cambridge: Cambridge University Press, 2009.

Dauphinais, Michael. "The Ratzinger Option: Introducing Christianity in a Postmodern Age." In *Ressourcement after Vatican II: Essays in Honor of Joseph Fessio, S. J.*, edited by Nicholas J. Healy and Matthew Levering, 112–38. San Francisco: Ignatius Press, 2019.

Dawkins, Richard. *The Greatest Show on Earth: The Evidence for Evolution*. New York: Free Press, 2009.

DeClue, Richard, Jr. "Joseph Ratzinger's Theology of Divine Revelation." STD diss. Catholic University of America, 2021.

De Gaál, Emery. *O Lord, I Seek Your Guidance: Explorations and Discoveries in Pope Benedict XVI's Theology*. Steubenville, OH: Emmaus Academic, 2018.

———. *The Theology of Pope Benedict XVI: The Christocentric Shift*. New York: Palgrave Macmillan, 2010.

Delfa, Rino La. *A Personal Church? The Foundation of Newman's Ecclesiological Thought*. Palermo: ILA Palma, 1997.

Delio, David P. *"An Aristocracy of Exalted Spirits": The Idea of the Church in Newman's Tamworth Reading Room*. Leominster: Gracewing, 2016.

BIBLIOGRAPHY

———. "Liberalism: Personal and Social Aspects in His Thoughts." In *A Guide to John Henry Newman: His Life and Thought*, edited by Juan R. Vélez, 489–508. Washington, DC: The Catholic University of America Press, 2022.

Democritus. *Die Fragmente der Vorsokratiker*, edited by Walther Diels and Herrmann Kranz. Hildesheim: Weidmann, 2004.

Dessain, Charles Stephen. "Cardinal Newman and the Doctrine of Uncreated Grace." *Clergy Review* 47 (1962): 207–25; 269–88.

———, et al., eds., *The Letters and Diaries of John Henry Newman*. Oxford: Oxford University Press, 1976.

———. "An Unpublished Paper by Cardinal Newman on the Development of Doctrine." *Journal of Theological Studies* 9 (1958): 324–35.

Dieter, Theodore. "Joseph Ratzinger." In *The Oxford Handbook of Ecclesiology*, edited by Paul Avis, 449–52. Oxford: Oxford University Press, 2022.

Dilthey, Wilhelm. *Selected Works IV: Hermeneutics and the Study of History*, edited by Rudolf A. Makkreel and Frithjof Rodi. Princeton, NJ: Princeton University Press, 1996.

Dive, Bernard. *John Henry Newman and the Imagination*. London: T&T Clark, 2018.

Drennan, D. A. *Privilege of Intellect: Conscience and Wisdom in Newman's Narrative*. Scranton, PA: University of Scranton Press, 2013.

Dubay, Thomas. *Faith and Certitude: Can We Be Sure of the Things That Matter Most to Us?* San Francisco: Ignatius Press, 1998.

Duffy, Eamon. "The Anglican Parish Sermons." In *Oxford Handbook of John Henry Newman*, 221–42. Oxford: Clarendon, 2017.

———. *John Henry Newman*. London: SPCK, 2019.

Dulles, Avery, SJ. "The Authority of Scripture: A Catholic Perspective." In *Scripture in the Jewish and Christian Traditions: Authority, Interpretation, Relevance*, edited by Frederick E. Greenspahn, 14–40. Nashville: Abingdon, 1982.

———. "On Ecclesiology." *Nova et Vetera* 15, no. 3 (2017): 779–93.

———. *The Resilient Church*. Garden City, NY: Doubleday, 1977.

———. "The Threefold Office in Newman's Ecclesiology." In *Newman after a Hundred Years*, edited by Ian Ker and Alan G. Hill, 375–99. Oxford: Clarendon, 1990.

BIBLIOGRAPHY

Durand, Michel. "Newman et la conscience dans son roman Callista et dans son sermon '"Ce qui dispose à la foi.'" *Cahiers victoriens et édourdiens* 70 (2009). Accessed at OpenEdition Journals. https://journals.openedition.org/cve/4778.

Ekeh, Ono. "John Henry Newman on Mystery as a Hermeneutical Problem." *New Blackfriars* 96, no. 1061 (2015): 74–89.

Elliott, Mark W., and Thomas C. Oden, eds. *Isaiah 40–66*. Ancient Christian Commentary on Scripture 11. Downers Grove, IL: IVP Academic, 2007.

Ernest, James D. "Athanasius of Alexandria: The Scope of Scripture in Polemical and Pastoral Context." *Vigiliae Christianae* 47 (1993): 341–62.

Evans, Bryce A. "Objective and Subjective Elements of Faith in John Henry Newman and Joseph Ratzinger." MA thesis, University of St. Thomas, 2017.

Fagan, Kevin Brendan. "A Toast to Conscience: Freedom of Conscience in John Henry Newman." PhD diss., University of Dallas, 1998.

Fagerberg, David W. *Liturgical Mysticism*. Steubenville, OH: Emmaus Academic, 2019.

Faggioli, Massimo. "The Battle over *Gaudium et Spes* Then and Now: Dialogue with the Modern World after Vatican II." *Origins* 42, no. 34 (2013): 545–51.

———. "Reading the Signs of the Times through a Hermeneutics of Recognition: *Gaudium et Spes* and Its Meaning for a Learning Church." *Horizons* 43 (2016): 332–50.

———. "Traditionalism, American-Style: A New Kind of Opposition to Rome." *Commonweal*, November 23, 2021. https://www.commonwealmagazine.org/traditionalism-american-style.

Farouq, Wael. "The Windows of Benedict XVI: Reason, Revelation, and Law." In *Pope Benedict XVI's Legal Thought: A Dialogue on the Foundation of Law*, edited by Marta Cartabia and Andrea Simoncini, 57–78. Cambridge: Cambridge University Press, 2015.

Finocchiaro, Maurice. *The Galileo Affair: A Documentary History*. Berkeley: University of California Press, 1989.

Fisher, Anthony, OP. "Conscience, Relativism, and Truth: The Witness of Saint John Henry Newman." *Nova et Vetera* 18 (2020): 337–53.

———. "Voice of God? Conscience, Relativism, and Truth." In *A Guide to John Henry Newman: His Life and Thought*, edited by Juan R. Vélez, 337–51. Washington, DC: The Catholic University of America Press, 2022.

BIBLIOGRAPHY

Frank, Joachim. "Die Rückkehr des 'Panzerkardinals.'" *Katholisch*, March 21, 2018. https://katholisch.de/artikel/16913-die-rueckkehr-des-panzerkardinals.

Franklin, Eric. "Luke." In *The Oxford Bible Commentary*, edited by John Barton and John Muddiman, 922–59. Oxford: Oxford University Press, 2001.

Fries, Heinrich, and Karl Rahner, SJ. *Unity of the Churches: An Actual Possibility*. Translated by Ruth C. L. Gritsch and Eric W. Gritsch. New York: Paulist Press, 1985.

Frings, Josef. "Das Konzil und die moderne Gedankenwelt." *Herder Korrespondenz* 16 (1961–62): 168–74.

Fuller, Robert C. *Spiritual, but Not Religious: Understanding Unchurched America*. Oxford: Oxford University Press, 2021.

Futuyma, Douglas. *Evolution*. Sunderland, MA: Sinauer, 2017.

Gabrielli, Timothy R. *One in Christ: Virgil Michel, Louis-Marie Chauvet, and Mystical Body Theology*. Collegeville, MN: Liturgical Press Academic, 2019.

Gagliardi, Mauro. *Revelation, Hermeneutics, and Doctrinal Development in Joseph Ratzinger*. Steubenville, OH: Emmaus Academic, 2024.

Galilei, Galileo. "Letter to the Grand Duchess Christina." In *The Galileo Affair: A Documentary History*, edited by Maurice Finocchiaro. Berkeley: University of California Press, 1989.

Gallois, Vincent. *Église et conscience chez John Henry Newman: Un commentaire de la Lettre au duc de Norfolk*. Paris: Artège, 2010.

Garrigou-Lagrange, Réginald, OP. *Thomistic Common Sense*. Translated by Matthew Minerd. Steubenville, OH: Emmaus Academic, 2021.

Geißler, Herrmann. "'Das Gewissen ist der ursprüngliche Statthalter Christi': Ein Blick auf Newmans Lehre über das Gewissen." *Internationale Zeitschrift Communio* 46, no. 5 (2017): 466–80.

———. *Gewissen und Wahrheit bei John Henry Kardinal Newman*. Bern: Lang, 1995.

———. "Gewissen und Wahrheit in den Schriften des seligen John Henry Newman." *Forum Katholische Theologie* 28 (2012): 185–200.

Ghose, Tia. "'Just a Theory': 7 Misused Science Words." *Scientific American*, April 2, 2013. https://www.scientificamerican.com/article/just-a-theory-7-misused-science-words/.

BIBLIOGRAPHY

Goins, Scott. "Newman: A Student and Tutor of Classics." In *A Guide to John Henry Newman: His Life and Thought*, edited by Juan R. Vélez, 140–57. Washington, DC: The Catholic University of America Press, 2022.

Goldie, Peter. "Emotion, Feeling, and Knowledge of the World." In *Thinking about Feeling: Contemporary Philosophers on Emotions*, edited by Robert C. Solomon, 91–106. Oxford: Oxford University Press, 2004.

———. *The Emotions: A Philosophical Exploration*. Oxford: Clarendon, 2000.

Goslee, David. *Romanticism and the Anglican Newman*. Athens: Ohio University Press, 1996.

Gourlay, Thomas V. "The Nuptial Character of the Relationship between Faith and Reason in the Thought of Joseph Ratzinger/Benedict XVI." *Heythrop Journal* 59 (2018): 265–76.

Graham, Donald. *From Eastertide to Ecclesia: John Henry Newman, the Holy Spirit and the Church*. Milwaukee: Marquette University Press, 2012.

Grave, Selwyn. *Conscience in Newman's Thought*. Oxford: Clarendon, 1989.

Gross, Jules. *The Divinization of the Christian according to the Greek Fathers*. Translated by Paul A. Onica. Anaheim, CA: A & C Press, 2002.

Gruber, Judith. "Conclusion: Dissent in the Roman Catholic Church; A Response." *Horizons* 45, no. 1 (2018): 155–59.

Guardini, Romano. *The Church and the Catholic*. Translated by Ada Lane. New York: Sheed & Ward, 1935.

———. *La Rosa Bianca*. Brescia: Morcelliana, 2007.

Guarino, Thomas G. "Tradition and Doctrinal Development: Can Vincent of Lérins Still Teach the Church?" *Theological Studies* 67 (2006): 34–72.

———. *Vincent of Lérins and the Development of Christian Doctrine*. Grand Rapids, MI: Baker Academic, 2013.

Hahn, Scott. "The Authority of Mystery: The Biblical Theology of Benedict XVI." *Letter & Spirit* 2 (2006): 97–140.

Hansen, Charlotte. "Newman, Conscience and Authority." *New Blackfriars* 3, no. 92 (2011): 209–23.

Harris, Harriet. "Does Analytical Philosophy Clip our Wings? Reformed Epistemology as a Test Case." In *Faith and Philosophical Analysis: The Impact of Analytical Philosophy on the Philosophy of Religion*, edited by Harriett A. Harris and Christopher J. Insole, 100–118. Aldershot: Ashgate, 2005.

BIBLIOGRAPHY

Harrold, Charles Frederick. *John Henry Newman: An Expository and Critical Study of His Mind, Thought, and Art*. New York: Longmans, Green, and Co., 1945.

Hart, David Bentley. *Tradition and Apocalypse: An Essay on the Future of Christian Belief*. Grand Rapids, MI: Baker Academic, 2022.

Healy, Nicholas. "Henri de Lubac on the Development of Doctrine." In *Ressourcement after Vatican II: Essays in Honor of Joseph Fessio, S. J.*, edited by Nicholas J. Healy and Matthew Levering, 346–66. San Francisco: Ignatius Press, 2019.

Heim, Maximilian Heinrich. *Joseph Ratzinger—Life in the Church and Living Theology: Fundamentals of Ecclesiology with Reference to Lumen Gentium*. Translated by Michael J. Miller. San Francisco: Ignatius Press, 2007.

Hemming, Lawrence Paul. *Benedict XVI: Fellow Worker for the Truth; An Introduction to His Life and Thought*. London: Continuum, 2005.

Hittinger, Russell. "*Quinquagesimo Ante:* Reflections on *Pacem in Terris* Fifty Years Later." *Pontifical Academy of Social Sciences* 18 (2013): 38–60.

Hollywood, Amy. "Spiritual but Not Religious: The Vital Interplay between Submission and Freedom." *Harvard Divinity Bulletin*, Winter/Spring 2010. https://bulletin.hds.harvard.edu/spiritual-but-not-religious/.

Holmes, J. Derek, ed. *The Theological Papers of John Henry Newman on Biblical Inspiration and Infallibility*. Oxford: Clarendon, 1979.

Holmes, J. Derek, and Robert Murray, eds. *On the Inspiration of Scripture: John Henry Newman*. Washington, DC: Corpus Books, 1967.

Honoré, Jean. *Newman: La fidelité d'une conscience*. Chambray-lés-Tours: CLD, 1986.

Horne, Brian. "Church and Nation: Newman and the Tractarians." *International Journal for the Study of the Christian Church* 5, no. 1 (2005): 25–40.

Huber, Werner. *Das Denken Joseph Ratzingers*. Paderborn: Schöningh, 2006.

Huddleston, Elizabeth. "To Witness the Unseen: A Portrait of Sanctity according to John Henry Newman and Wilfrid Ward." In *"Heart Speaks to Heart": Saint John Henry Newman and the Call to Holiness*, edited by Kevin J. O'Reilly, 69–92. Leominster: Gracewing, 2021.

Hughes, Gerard J. "Newman and the Particularity of Conscience." In *Newman and Faith*, edited by Ian Ker and Terrence Merrigan, 53–74. Louvain: Peeters, 2004.

BIBLIOGRAPHY

Hünermann, Peter. "Der Text: Werden—Gestalt—Bedeutung; Eine hermeneutische Reflexion." In *Herders theologischer Kommentar zum Zweiten Vatikanischen Konzil*, vol. 5, edited by Peter Hünermann and Bernd Jochen Hilberath, 7–101. Freiburg: Herder, 2006.

———. "Zu den Kategorien 'Konzil' und 'Konzilsentscheidung': Vorüberlegungen zur Interpretation des II. Vatikanums." In *Das II. Vatikanum: Christlicher Glaube im Horizont globaler Modernisierung*, edited by Peter Hünermann, 67–82. Paderborn: Ferdinand Schöningh, 1998.

Hütter, Reinhard. *John Henry Newman on Truth and Its Counterfeits: A Guide for Our Times*. Washington, DC: The Catholic University of America Press, 2020.

———. "Progress, Not Alteration of the Faith: Beyond Antiquarianism and Presentism; John Henry Newman, Vincent of Lérins, and the Criterion of Identity of the Development of Doctrine." *Nova et Vetera* 19 (2021): 333–91.

International Theological Commission. *Communion and Stewardship: Human Persons Created in the Image of God*. 2004. https://www.vatican.va/roman_curia/congregations/cfaith/cti_documents/rc_con_cfaith_doc_20040723_communion-stewardship_en.html.

Jaki, Stanley. *Newman's Challenge*. Grand Rapids, MI: Eerdmans, 2000.

Jameson, Frederic. "Postmodernism, or The Cultural Logic of Late Capitalism." In *Postmodernism: A Reader*, edited by Thomas Docherty, 62–92. New York: Columbia University Press, 1992.

Jennings, Peter, ed. *Benedict XVI and Cardinal Newman*. Oxford: Family Publications, 2005.

John XXIII, Pope. *Gaudet Mater Ecclesia*. October 11, 1962. In *Acta Apostolicae Sedis* 54 (1962): 786–96; English translation in *The Documents of Vatican II*, edited by Walter M. Abbott. New York: Crossroad, 1989.

———. *Humanae Salutis*. 1861. Translated by Joseph Komonchak. https://jakomonchak.files.wordpress.com/2011/12/humanae-salutis.pdf.

John of the Cross. *Dark Night of the Soul*. Edited and translated by E. Allison Peers. New York: Image Books, 1959.

John Paul II, Pope. *Discorso di Giovanni Paolo II nel XXX Anniversario della proclamazione della Costituzione pastorale 'Gaudium et Spes.'* November 8, 1995. https://www.vatican.va/content/john-paul-ii/it/speeches/1995/november/documents/hf_jp-ii_spe_19951108_anniv-gaudium.html.

BIBLIOGRAPHY

———. *Fides et Ratio*. September 14, 1998. https://www.vatican.va/content/john-paul-ii/en/encyclicals/documents/hf_jp-ii_enc_14091998_fides-et-ratio.html.

———. "Message to the Pontifical Academy of Sciences on Evolution." October 22, 1996.

———. *Ut Unum Sint*. May 25, 1995. https://www.vatican.va/content/john-paul-ii/en/encyclicals/documents/hf_jp-ii_enc_25051995_ut-unum-sint.html.

Jones, Richard. *Mystery 101: An Introduction to the Big Questions and the Limits of Human Knowledge*. Albany: SUNY Press, 2018.

Kabala, Florence Abala. "Conscience as the Capacity for the Truth of Love: A Comparative Analysis between John Henry Newman and Joseph Ratzinger." STL thesis, Pontifical Lateran University, 2013.

Kaiser, F. James. *The Concept of Conscience according to John Henry Newman*. Washington, DC: The Catholic University of America Press, 1958.

Kalthoff, Mark. "A Different Voice from the Eve of *The Origin*: Reconsidering John Henry Newman on Christianity, Science, and Intelligent Design." *Perspectives in Science and Christian Belief* 53 (2001): 14–23.

Kant, Immanuel. *Groundwork to the Metaphysics of Morals*. Translated by Allen Wood. New Haven, CT: Yale University Press, 2018.

Kaplan, Grant. "Vatican II as a Constitutional Text of Faith." *Horizons* 41, no. 1 (2014): 1–21.

Kasper, Walter. *Dogma unter dem Wort Gottes*. Mainz: Matthias-Grünewald, 1965.

Keating, James. "Newman: Conscience and Mission." *Irish Theological Quarterly* 67 (2002): 99–112.

———. "Theology as Thinking in Prayer." *Chicago Studies* 53, no. 1 (2014): 70–83.

Ker, Ian. *Healing the Wound of Humanity: The Spirituality of John Henry Newman*. London: Darton, Longman and Todd, 1993.

———. *John Henry Newman: A Biography*. Oxford: Oxford University Press, 2010.

———. *Newman and Vatican II*. Oxford: Oxford University Press, 2014.

———. "Newman Can Lead Us out of Our Post-Vatican II Turmoil." *Catholic Herald*, July 10, 2009.

———. *On Being a Christian*. London: Harper Collins, 1992.

BIBLIOGRAPHY

Kerr, Fergus. *Twentieth-Century Catholic Theologians: From Neoscholasticism to Nuptial Mysticism*. Malden, MA: Blackwell, 2007.

King, Benjamin. *Newman and the Alexandrian Fathers: Shaping Doctrine in Nineteenth-Century England*. Changing Paradigms in Historical and Systematic Theology. Oxford: Oxford University Press, 2009.

Knab, Jakob. *Ich schweige nicht: Hans Scholl und die Weisse Rose*. Darmstadt: WBG Theiss, 2018.

Koepcke, Cordula. *Reinhold Schneider: Eine Biographie*. Würzburg: Echter, 1993.

Komonchak, Joseph. "The Church in Crisis: Pope Benedict's Theological Vision." *Commonweal*, June 3, 2005. https://www.commonwealmagazine.org/church-crisis-pope-benedicts-theological-vision.

———. "'A Postmodern Augustinian Thomism'?" In *Augustine and Postmodern Thought: A New Alliance against Modernity?* edited by L. Boeve, M. Lamberigts, and M. Wisse, 123–46. Bibliotheca Ephemeridum Theologicarum Lovaniensium 219. Leuven: Peeters, 2009.

———. "Returning from Exile: Catholic Theology in the 1930's." In *The Twentieth Century: A Theological Overview*, edited by Gregory Baum, 35–48. Maryknoll, NY: Orbis Books, 1999.

———. Review of *Henri de Lubac et le Concile Vatican II (1960–1965)*, by Loïc Figoureux. *Cristianesimo nella storia* 40 (2019): 739–50.

———. "Le valutazioni sulla *Gaudium et spes*: Chenu, Dossetti, Ratzinger." In *Volti di fine Concilio: Studi di storia e teologia sulla conclusione del Vaticano II*, edited by Joseph Doré and Alberto Melloni, 115–53. Bologna: Il Mulino, 2000.

Küng, Hans. "Pour le théologien Hans Küng, l'Eglise 'risque de devenir une secte.'" By Nicolas Bourcier and Stéphanie Le Bars. *Le Monde*, February 24, 2009. https://www.lemonde.fr/europe/article/2009/02/24/pour-le-theologien-hans-kung-l-eglise-risque-de-devenir-une-secte_1159626_3214.html.

Kwasniewski, Peter, ed. *From Benedict's Peace to Francis's War: Catholics Respond to the* Motu Proprio Traditionis Custodes *on the Latin Mass*. New York: Angelico, 2021.

Läpple, Alfred. *Der Einzelne in der Kirche: Wesenszüge einer Theologie des Einzelnen nach John Henry Kardinal Newman*. Munich: Zink, 1952.

BIBLIOGRAPHY

———. "That New Beginning That Bloomed among the Ruins." Interview with Alfred Läpple. *30Days*, February 1, 2006. https://www.30giorni.it/articoli_id_10125_l3.htm.

Lash, Nicholas. Introduction. In *An Essay in Aid of a Grammar of Assent*, by John Henry Newman, 1–24. Notre Dame, IN: University of Notre Dame Press, 1992.

Lattier, Daniel. "John Henry Newman and Georges Florovsky: An Orthodox-Catholic Dialogue on the Development of Doctrine." PhD diss., Duquesne University, 2012.

Ledek, Ronald. *The Nature of Conscience and Its Religious Significance with a Special Reference to John Henry Newman*. Bethesda, MD: International Scholars Publications, 1995.

Lenormant, Francois. *Les origins de l'histoire d'après la Bible et les traditions des peuples orientaux*. Paris: Maisonneuve & Cie., 1880–84.

Leo XIII, Pope. *Providentissimus Deus*. 1893. https://www.vatican.va/content/leo-xiii/en/encyclicals/documents/hf_l-xiii_enc_18111893_providentissimus-deus.html.

Levering, Matthew. *The Abuse of Conscience: A Century of Catholic Moral Theology*. Grand Rapids, MI: Eerdmans, 2021.

———. *Engaging the Doctrine of Revelation: The Mediation of the Gospel through Church and Scripture*. Grand Rapids, MI: Baker Academic, 2014.

———. *An Introduction to Vatican II as an Ongoing Theological Event*. Washington, DC: The Catholic University of America Press, 2017.

———. *Newman on Doctrinal Corruption*. Park Ridge, IL: Word on Fire Academic, 2022.

Libaud, Frédéric. *Voir l'invisible: Le monde surnaturel chez John Henry Newman*. Paris: Saint-Léger Éditions, 2016.

Liddell, Henry, Robert Scott, and Henry Stuart Jones. *A Greek-English Lexicon*. 9th ed. Oxford: Oxford University Press, 1940.

Lienhard, Joseph T., SJ. "From Gwatkin Onwards: A Guide through a Century and a Quarter of Studies on Arianism." *Augustinian Studies* 44, no. 2 (2013): 265–85.

Lloyd, Alexander, and Jakob Knab, eds. *The White Rose: Reading, Writing, Resistance*. Oxford: Taylor Institution Library, 2019.

BIBLIOGRAPHY

Locke, John. *"Some Thoughts concerning Education" and "Of the Conduct of the Understanding."* Edited by Ruth W. Grant and Nathan Tarcov. Indianapolis, IN: Hackett, 1996.

Louth, Andrew. "Manhood into God: The Oxford Movement, the Fathers and the Deification of Man." In *Essays Catholic and Radical: A Jubilee Group Symposium for the 150th Anniversary of the Beginning of the Oxford Movement*, edited by Kenneth Leech and Rowan Williams, 70–80. London: Bowerdean Press, 1983.

de Lubac, Henri, SJ. *A Brief Catechesis on Nature and Grace*. Translated by Richard Arnandez. San Francisco: Ignatius Press, 1984.

Lynch, T., ed. "The Newman-Perrone Paper on Development." *Gregorianum* 16 (1935): 402–47.

Maas-Ewerd, Theodor. *Die Krise der liturgischen Bewegung in Deutschland und Österreich: Zu den Auseinandersetzungen um die "liturgische Frage" in den Jahren 1939 bis 1944*. Regensburg: Pustet, 1981.

Maceri, Francesco. *La Formazione della Coscienza del Credente: Una Proposta educativa alla Luce dei Parochial and Plain Sermons di John Henry Newman*. Rome: Gregorian University Press, 2002.

MacIntyre, Alasdair. *Whose Justice? Which Rationality?* Notre Dame, IN: University of Notre Dame Press, 1988.

Maher, Daniel P. "Pope Benedict XVI on Faith and Reason." *Nova et Vetera* 7, no. 3 (2009): 625–52.

Mahieu, Éric. Introduction to *My Journal of the Council*, by Yves Congar. Collegeville, MN: Liturgical Press, 2012.

de Mallerais, Bernard Tissier. *L'Étrange Théologie de Benoît XVI: Herméneutique de continuité ou rupture?* Avrillé: Editions du Sel, 2010.

Mansini, Guy, OSB. "The Historicity of Dogma and Common Sense." *Nova et Vetera* 18 (2020): 111–38.

Marion, Jean-Luc. *Givenness and Revelation*. Translated by Stephen E. Lewis. Oxford: Oxford University Press, 2016.

Maritain, Jacques. *The Degrees of Knowledge*. London: Geoffrey Bles, 1937.

———. *On the Church of Christ*. Translated by Joseph W. Evans. Notre Dame, IN: University of Notre Dame Press, 1973.

Marr, Ryan. "Infallibility." In *Oxford Handbook of John Henry Newman*, 346–49. Oxford: Clarendon, 2017.

———. *To Be Perfect Is to Have Changed Often: The Development of John Henry Newman's Ecclesiological Outlook, 1845–1877*. Lanham, MD: Fortress Academic, 2018.

Marschler, Thomas. "Signs of the Times as a New Locus Theologicus?" *Church Life Journal*, August 18, 2022. https://churchlifejournal.nd.edu/articles/signs-of-the-times-as-a-new-locus-theologicus/#_ftnref53.

Martin, Brian. *John Henry Newman: His Life and Work*. New York: Oxford University Press, 1982.

Martinez, Javier. "Address to the Youth of the Archdiocese of Melbourne." May 12, 2014.

Mattox, Mickey L. "The Luther the Cardinal Did Not Know: Occasional Notes on the Luther of Recent Research." In *Joseph Ratzinger and the Healing of the Reformation-Era Divisions*, edited by Emery de Gaál and Matthew Levering, 169–91. Steubenville, OH: Emmaus Academic, 2019.

Maximus the Confessor. *On the Cosmic Mystery of Christ*. Translated by Paul M. Blowers and Robert Louis Wilken. New York: St. Vladimir's Seminary Press, 2003.

McKnight, Scot, and Dennis Venema. *Adam and the Genome: Reading Scripture after Genetic Science*. Grand Rapids, MI: Brazos Press, 2017.

Meconi, David Vincent, SJ. "The Mystical Body in the *Nouvelle Théologie*." In *Ressourcement after Vatican II: Essays in Honor of Joseph Fessio, S. J.*, edited by Nicholas J. Healy and Matthew Levering, 26–56. San Francisco: Ignatius Press, 2019.

Merrigan, Terrence. "Conscience and Selfhood: Thomas More, John Henry Newman, and the Crisis of the Postmodern Subject." *Theological Studies* 73 (2012): 841–60.

Mersch, Émile, SJ. *The Whole Christ: The Historical Development of the Doctrine of the Mystical Body in Scripture and Tradition*. Translated by John R. Kelly. Milwaukee: Bruce Publishing, 1938; originally published in French as *Le corps mystique du Christ: Études de théologie historique*. 2 vols. Brussels: L'Edition Universelle, S.A., 1936.

Merton, Thomas. *The Ascent to Truth: A Study of St. John of the Cross*. New York: Harcourt and Brace, 1951.

Meszaros, Andrew. *The Prophetic Church: History and Doctrinal Development in John Henry Newman and Yves Congar*. Oxford: Oxford University Press, 2016.

BIBLIOGRAPHY

Milbank, John. *Word Made Strange: Theology, Language, and Culture*. London: Blackwell, 1997.

Miller, Edward Jeremy. *John Henry Newman: On the Idea of the Church*. Shepherdstown, W.V.: Patmos, 1987.

Mitchell, Basil. "Newman as a Philosopher." In *Newman after a Hundred Years*, edited by Ian T. Ker and Alan G. Hill, 223–46. Oxford: Clarendon, 1990.

Mobbs, Frank. "Newman's Doctrine of Conscience." *Irish Theological Quarterly* 57 (1991): 311–16.

Moeller, Charles. "Preface and Introductory Statement." In *Commentary on the Documents of Vatican II*, edited by Herbert Vorgrimler, 91–92. New York: Herder & Herder, 1969.

Möhler, Johann Adam. *Unity in the Church, or the Principle of Catholicism Presented in the Spirit of the Church Fathers of the First Three Centuries*. Translated by Peter C. Erb. Washington, DC: The Catholic University of America Press, 2015.

Moran, Valentine G. "Loisy's Theological Development." *Theological Studies* 40, no. 3 (September 1989): 411–52.

Morerod, Charles, OP. "La conscience, voie vers Dieu et l'Église selon John Henry Newman." *Nova et Vetera* 86 (2011): 29–57.

Moritz, Berta. "A Patron Saint of Evolution?" *Church Life Journal*, October 16, 2019. https://churchlifejournal.nd.edu/articles/a-patron-saint-of-evolution/.

Morris, Jeremy. "Pope Benedict XVI on Faith and Reason in Western Europe." *Pro Ecclesia* 17, no. 3 (2008): 326–42.

Morris-Chapman, D. J. Pratt. "The Philosophical Legacy of John Henry Newman: A. Neglected Chapter in Newman Research." *New Blackfriars* 98 (November 2017): 722–50.

Moser, Paul. "Philosophy and Spiritual Formation: From Christian Faith to Christian Philosophy." *Journal of Spiritual Formation and Soul Care* 7 (2014): 258–69.

———. *The Severity of God: Religion and Philosophy Reconceived*. Cambridge: Cambridge University Press, 2013.

Müller, Gerhard. *John Henry Newman begegnen*. Augsburg: Sankt Ulrich Verlag, 2000.

———. *The Power of Truth*. San Francisco: Ignatius Press, 2019.

BIBLIOGRAPHY

Murphy, Francesca Aran. "De Lubac, Ratzinger and von Balthasar: A Communal Adventure in Ecclesiology." In *Ecumenism Today: The Universal Church in the 21st Century*, edited by Francesca Aran Murphy and Christopher Asprey, 45–80. London: Routledge, 2008.

———. "Papal Ecclesiology." In *Explorations in the Theology of Benedict XVI*, edited by John C. Cavadini, 215–35. Notre Dame, IN: University of Notre Dame Press, 2016.

Mushi, Edward. "Benedict XVI's Hermeneutics of Reform and Its Implication for the Renewal of the Church." *Pacifica: Australasian Theological Studies*, no. 26 (2013): 279–94.

Neuhaus, Richard John, ed. *Biblical Interpretation in Crisis: The Ratzinger Conference on Bible and Church*. Grand Rapids, MI: Eerdmans, 1989.

Newman, John Henry. *Apologia Pro Vita Sua*. Melbourne: E.W. Cole, 1920.

———. *The Arians of the Fourth Century*. London: E. Lumley, 1871; reprint, Notre Dame, IN: University of Notre Dame Press, 2001.

———. *Autobiographical* Writings. London: Sheed & Ward, 1956.

———. *Callista: A Tale of the Third Century*. London: Longmans, Green, and Co., 1890.

———. *Certain Difficulties Felt by Anglicans in Catholic Teaching*. London: Burns and Oates, 1879.

———. *Discourses on the Scope and Nature of University Education Addressed to the Catholics of Dublin*. Dublin: James Duffy, 1852.

———. *Discourses Addressed to Mixed Congregations*. 1849; Leominster: Gracewing, 2002.

———. *Discussions and Arguments on Various Subjects*. New York: Longmans, Greens, and Co., 1907.

———. *Essays Critical and Historical*. London: Longmans, Green, and Co., 1907.

———. *An Essay in Aid of a Grammar of Assent*. Edited by Ian T. Ker. Oxford: Clarendon, 1985.

———. *An Essay on the Development of Christian Doctrine*. Notre Dame, IN: University of Notre Dame Press, 1989.

———. *Fifteen Sermons Preached before the University of Oxford: Between A. D. 1826 and 1843*. Edited by James David Earnest and Gerard Tracey. Oxford: Clarendon, 2006.

BIBLIOGRAPHY

——. *The Greek Devotions of Bishop Andrewes, Translated and Arranged.* London: J. G. & F. Rivington, 1840.

——. *Lectures on Justification.* London: J. G. & F. Rivington, 1838.

——. "On Consulting the Faithful in Matters of Doctrine." *The Rambler* (July 1859): 198–230.

——. *Parochial and Plain Sermons.* San Francisco: Ignatius Press, 1987.

——. *Prayers, Verses and Devotions.* San Francisco: Ignatius Press, 2019.

——. *Roman Catholic Writings on Doctrinal Development.* Edited and translated by James Gaffney. Kansas City, MO: Sheed & Ward, 1997.

——. *Selected Treatises of Saint Athanasius in Controversy with the Arians.* London: Longmans, Green, and Co., 1895.

——. *The Theological Papers of John Henry Newman on Faith and Certainty.* Edited by Derek Holmes. Oxford: Clarendon, 1976.

——. *The Via Media of the Anglican Church.* Vol. 1, *On the Prophetical Office of the Church.* London: Basil Montagu Pickering, 1877.

——. *Verses on Various Occasions.* London: Longmans, Green, and Co., 1903.

Nichols, Aidan, OP. *The Conversation of Faith and Reason: Modern Catholic Thought from Hermes to Benedict XVI.* Chicago: Hillenbrand Books, 2009.

——. *A Grammar of Consent: The Existence of God in Christian Tradition.* Notre Dame, IN: University of Notre Dame Press, 1991.

——. *The Thought of Pope Benedict XVI: An Introduction to the Theology of Joseph Ratzinger.* London: Burns & Oates, 2007.

Nichols, David, and Fergus Kerr, OP, eds. *John Henry Newman: Reason, Rhetoric and Romanticism.* Carbondale: Southern Illinois University Press, 1991.

Niebuhr, H. Richard. *Christ and Culture.* London: Harper Collins, 2002.

Nockles, Peter B. "The Oxford Movement." In *The Oxford Handbook of John Henry Newman*, edited by Frederick D. Aquino and Benjamin J. King, 7–27. Oxford: Clarendon, 2018.

——. *The Oxford Movement in Context: Anglican High Churchmanship, 1760–1857.* Cambridge: Cambridge University Press, 1994.

Noonan, John T. *A Church That Can and Cannot Change: The Development of Catholic Moral Teaching.* Notre Dame, IN: University of Notre Dame Press, 2006.

BIBLIOGRAPHY

Norris, Thomas J. "The Role of Conscience in the Adventure of Holiness according to Blessed John Henry Newman." In *Conscience: The Path to Holiness; Walking with John Henry Newman*, edited by Edward Jeremy Miller, 15–30. Newcastle: Cambridge Scholars, 2014.

Nussbaum, Martha. *Upheavals of Thoughts: The Intelligence of Emotions*. Cambridge: Cambridge University Press, 2001.

O'Collins, Gerald, SJ. *Fundamental Theology*. Eugene, OR: Wipf & Stock, 2001.

O'Connell, Marvin R., CSC. *The Oxford Conspirators: A History of the Oxford Movement, 1833–1845*. New York: University Press of America, 1991.

O'Donnell, Robert A. "The Two Worlds of John Henry Newman." *New Oxford Review* 78, no. 7 (September 2011): 36–38.

O'Malley, Frank. "The Thinker in the Church: The Spirit of Newman." *Review of Politics* 21, no. 1 (1959): 5–23.

O'Malley, John, SJ. "'The Hermeneutic of Reform': A Historical Analysis." *Theological Studies* 73, no. 3 (September 2012): 517–46.

———. *What Happened at Vatican II?* Cambridge, MA: The Belknap Press of Harvard University Press, 2008.

O'Malley, Timothy P. "Joseph Ratzinger Is Not a Platonist." *Church Life Journal*, October 16, 2018. https://churchlifejournal.nd.edu/articles/joseph-ratzinger-is-not-a-platonist/.

O'Regan, Cyril. "John Henry Newman." In *The Oxford Handbook of the Epistemology of Theology*, edited by Frederick D. Aquino and William J. Abraham, 511–22. Oxford: Clarendon, 2017.

Pahls, Michael. "Development in the Service of Rectification: John Henry Newman's Understanding of the *Schola Theologorum*." In *Authority, Dogma, and History: The Role of the Oxford Movement Converts in the Papal Infallibility Debates*, edited by Kenneth L. Parker and Michael J. G. Pahls, 195–211. Bethesda, MD: Academica Press, 2009.

———. "School of the Prophets: John Henry Newman's Anglican *Schola* and the Ecclesial Vocation of Theology." PhD diss., St. Louis University, 2015.

Parker, Kenneth L., and C. Michael Shea. "The Roman Catholic Reception of the *Essay on Development*." In *Receptions of Newman*, edited by Frederick D. Aquino and Benjamin J. King, 30–49. Oxford: Oxford University Press, 2015.

Paul VI, Pope. *Ecclesiam Suam*. August 6, 1964. https://www.vatican.va/content/paul-vi/en/encyclicals/documents/hf_p-vi_enc_06081964_ecclesiam.html.

BIBLIOGRAPHY

———. "Una luce sul cammino dell'anno Santo il pensiero del Cardinale Newman." In *Insegnamenti di Paolo VI*, 13. Vatican City: Tipografia Poliglotta Vaticana, 1976. 276–78.

Pedraza, Brian. "Signs of the Times: Origin and Meaning." *Church Life Journal*, November 8, 2022. https://churchlifejournal.nd.edu/articles/signs-of-the-times-origin-and-meaning/#_ftnref19.

Pelikan, Jaroslav. *The Christian Tradition: A History of the Development of Doctrine*. Vol. 2, *The Spirit of Eastern Christendom (600–1700)*. Chicago: University of Chicago Press, 1974.

Pelton, Robert S. "CELAM and the Emerging Reception of the 'Bridge Theology' of Pope Francis: From Marcos Gregorio McGrath to the Latin American Church Today." *Horizonte* 16 (2018): 454–81.

Penaskovic, Richard. "Two Classical Western Theologians." *Augustinian Studies* 13 (1982): 67–79.

Pereiro, James. *"Ethos" and the Oxford Movement: At the Heart of Tractarianism*. Oxford: Oxford University Press, 2008.

Peterson, Brandon. "Critical Voices: The Reactions of Rahner and Ratzinger to 'Schema XIII' (*Gaudium et Spes*)." *Modern Theology* 31, no. 1 (2015): 1–26.

Phillips, Jacob. "After Etsi Veluti Si Deus Daretur: Joseph Ratzinger and Cardinal Robert Sarah." In *Joseph Ratzinger and the Promise of African Theology*, edited by Matthew Levering and Maurice Ashley Agbaw-Ebai, 98–121. Eugene, OR: Pickwick, 2021.

———. *Human Subjectivity in Christ in Dietrich Bonhoeffer's Theology: Simplicity and Wisdom*. London: Bloomsbury, 2019.

———. "John Henry Newman and the English Sensibility." *Logos* 24, no. 3 (Summer 2021): 108–29.

———. *John Henry Newman and the English Sensibility: Distant Scene*. London: Bloomsbury, 2023.

———. "Lumen Gentium: The Church as Mystical Body and the Communion of the Faithful." In *The Oxford Handbook of Joseph Ratzinger*, edited by Tracey Rowland and Francesca Aran Murphy. Oxford: Oxford University Press. Forthcoming.

———. *Mary, Star of Evangelization*. Mahwah, NJ: Paulist Press, 2018.

———. "My Enemy's Enemy Is My Friend: Martin Luther and Joseph Ratzinger on the Bi-Dimensionality of Conscience." *Heythrop Journal* 61 (2020): 317–26.

BIBLIOGRAPHY

Philo of Alexandria. *De Fuga et Inventione*. Translated and edited by E. Starobinski-Safran. Les Oeuvres de Philon d'Alexandrie 17. Paris: Cerf, 1970.

Pidel, Aaron, SJ. "*Christi Opera Proficiunt*: Ratzinger's Neo-Bonaventurian Model of Social Inspiration." *Nova et Vetera* 13, no. 3 (2015): 693–711.

———. *The Inspiration and Truth of Scripture: Testing the Ratzinger Paradigm*. Washington, DC: The Catholic University of America Press, 2023.

———. "Joseph Ratzinger on Biblical Inerrancy." *Nova et Vetera* 12, no. 1 (2014): 307–30.

Pieper, Josef. *The Four Cardinal Virtues*. Notre Dame, IN: University of Notre Dame Press, 1965.

———. *In Defense of Philosophy*. San Francisco: Ignatius Press, 1992.

Pilch, Jeremy. *"Breathing the Spirit with Both Lungs": Deification in the Work of Vladimir Solov'ev*. Leuven: Peeters, 2018.

Pius XII, Pope. *Mystici Corporis Christi*. June 29, 1943. https://www.vatican.va/content/pius-xii/en/encyclicals/documents/hf_p-xii_enc_29061943_mystici-corporis-christi.html.

Porter, Steve. "Philosophy and Spiritual Formation: A Call to Philosophy and Spiritual Formation." *Journal of Spiritual Formation and Soul Care* 7 (2014): 248–57.

Powell, Jouett Lynn. "Cardinal Newman on Faith and Doubt: The Role of Conscience." *Downside Review* 99 (1981): 137–48.

Prickett, Stephen. *Words and the Word: Language, Poetics, and Biblical Interpretation*. Cambridge: Cambridge University Press, 1986.

Pritchard, Duncan. "Wittgenstein on Faith and Reason: The Influence of Newman." In *God, Truth, and Other Enigmas*, edited by Miroslaw Szatkowski, 197–216. Berlin: de Gruyter, 2015.

Przywara, Erich. "Kierkegaard-Newman." *Newman Studien* 1 (1948): 77–101.

———. "Newman möglicher Heiliger und Kirchenlehrer der neuen Zeit?" *Newman Studien* 3 (1957): 28–36. Available in English as "Newman: Saint and Modern Doctor of the Church?" Translated by Christopher M. Wojtulewicz. *Church Life Journal*, October 11, 2019. https://churchlifejournal.nd.edu/articles/newman-possible-saint-and-modern-doctor-of-the-church/.

BIBLIOGRAPHY

Pseudo-Dionysius. *Pseudo-Dionysius: The Complete Works.* Translated by Colm Lubheid and Paul Rorem. Classics of Western Spirituality. New York: Paulist Press, 1987. Original text available in *Corpus Dionysiacum.* 2 vols. Edited by Beate Regina Suchla, Günter Heil, and Adolf Martin Ritter. Patristische Texte und Studien 36 (Berlin: de Gruyter, 1990–91).

Quy, Joseph Lam Cong. "Der Einfluss des Augustinus auf die Theologie des Papstes Benedikt XVI." *Augustiniana* 56, no. 3/4 (2006): 411–32.

Rahner, Karl, SJ. *Foundations of Christian Faith: An Introduction to the Idea of Christianity.* New York: Crossroad, 1986.

———. "Yesterday's History of Dogma and Theology for Tomorrow." In *Theological Investigations,* vol. 18, *God and Revelation.* Translated by Edward Quinn, 3–34. New York: Crossroad, 1983.

Rahner, Karl, SJ, and K. Lehmann. "Geschichtlichkeit der Vermittlung." In *Mysterium Salutis* I, edited by J. Feiner and M. Löhrer, 727–87. Einsiedeln: Oxford Academic, 1965.

Ramage, Matthew J. *The Experiment of Faith: Pope Benedict XVI on Living the Theological Virtues in a Secular Age.* Washington, DC: The Catholic University of America Press, 2020.

———. *Jesus, Interpreted: Benedict XVI, Bart Ehrman, and the Historical Truth of the Gospels.* Washington, DC: The Catholic University of America Press, 2017.

Ratzinger, Joseph. "Address of His Holiness Benedict XVI to Participants at a Congress on 'The Heritage of the Magisterium of Pius XII and the Second Vatican Council' Promoted by the Pontifical Lateran University and the Pontifical Gregorian University." November 8, 2008. https://www.vatican.va/content/benedict-xvi/en/speeches/2008/november/documents/hf_ben-xvi_spe_20081108_congresso-pioxii.html.

———. "Address on the Occasion of Christmas Greetings to the Roman Curia." Clementine Hall. December 21, 2012. https://www.vatican.va/content/benedict-xvi/en/speeches/2012/december/documents/hf_ben-xvi_spe_20121221_auguri-curia.html.

———. "Angesichts der Welt von heute: Überlegungen zur Konfrontation mit der Kirche im Schema XIII." *Wort und Wahrheit* 20 (1965): 493–504.

———. *Behold the Pierced One: An Approach to a Spiritual Christology.* Translated by Graham Harrison. San Francisco: Ignatius Press, 1986.

———. *Called to Communion: Understanding the Church Today.* Translated by Adrian Walker. San Francisco: Ignatius Press, 1991.

BIBLIOGRAPHY

———. "Catholicism after the Council." *The Furrow* 18, no. 1 (1967): 3–23.

———. "Christ, Faith and the Challenge of Cultures: Meeting with the Doctrinal Commissions in Asia." Hong Kong. March 3, 1993. https://www.vatican.va/roman_curia//congregations/cfaith/incontri/rc_con_cfaith_19930303_hong-kong-ratzinger_en.html.

———. "Le christianisme sans peine—*Etre chrétien* de Hans Küng." *Communio* (September–October 1978): 84–95.

———. "Christmas Greetings to the Members of the Roman Curia and Prelature." December 22, 2005. https://www.vatican.va/content/benedict-xvi/en/speeches/2005/december/documents/hf_ben_xvi_spe_20051222_roman-curia.html.

———. *Church, Ecumenism and Politics*. San Francisco: Ignatius Press, 2008.

———. *Collected Works*. Vol. 11. *Theology of the Liturgy: The Sacramental Foundation of Christian Existence*. Translated by John Saward, Kenneth Baker, Henry Taylor et al. San Francisco: Ignatius Press, 2014.

———. *Commentary on the Documents of Vatican II*. 5 vols. Edited by Herbert Vorgrimler. New York: Herder, 1967–69.

———. "Conscience and Truth." In *Crisis of Conscience*, edited by John M. Haas, 1–20. New York: Crossroad, 1996.

———. "Conscience in Time." Translated by W. J. O'Hara. In *Joseph Ratzinger in Communio*, vol. 2, *Anthropology and Culture*, edited by David Schindler and Nicholas J. Healy, 17–27. Grand Rapids, MI: Eerdmans, 2013.

———. *Co-Workers of the Truth*. San Francisco: Ignatius Press, 1992.

———. "Culture and Truth: Reflections on *Fides et Ratio*." St. Patrick's Seminary, New York. February 13, 1999. https://www.ratzinger.us/Some-Reflections-on-the-Encyclical-Letter-Fides-et-Ratio/.

———. *Daughter Zion: Meditations on the Church's Marian Belief*. Translated by John M. McDermott, SJ. San Francisco: Ignatius Press, 1983.

———. *Deus Caritas Est*. December 25, 2005. https://www.vatican.va/content/benedict-xvi/en/encyclicals/documents/hf_ben-xvi_enc_20051225_deus-caritas-est.html.

———, and Jürgen Habermas. *The Dialectics of Secularization: On Reason and Religion*. San Francisco: Ignatius Press, 2005.

———. *Dogma and Preaching: Applying Christian Doctrine to Daily Life*. San Francisco: Ignatius Press, 2005.

———. "Die Ekklesiologie des Zweiten Vatikanums." *Internationale katholische Zeitschrift: Communio* 15, no. 1 (January 1986): 41–52. Published in English as "The Ecclesiology of the Second Vatican Council." *Communio: International Catholic Review* 13, no. 3 (Fall 1986): 239–52.

———. "Faith, Reason and the University: Memories and Reflections." Regensburg. September 12, 2006.

———. "Freiheit und Befreiung: Die anthropologische Vision der Instruktion 'Libertatis conscientiae.'" *Communio* [German] 15 (1986): 409–24.

———. "General Audience Address." August 27, 2008. https://www.vatican.va/content/benedict-xvi/en/audiences/2008/documents/hf_ben-xvi_aud_20080827.html.

———. *God Is Near Us; The Eucharist; The Heart of the World.* San Francisco: Ignatius Press, 2003.

———. *God's Word: Scripture—Tradition—Office.* Translated by Henry Taylor. Edited by Peter Hünermann and Thomas Söding. San Francisco: Ignatius Press, 2008.

———. "Herkunft und Sinn der Civitas-Lehre Augustins." In *Augustinus Magister, Congrès International Augustinien, Paris, 21–24 Septembre 1954.* 3 vols. Paris: Études Augustiniennes, 2:965–79.

———. *In the Beginning: A Catholic Understanding of the Story of Creation and the Fall.* Grand Rapids, MI: Eerdmans, 1995.

———. *Introduction to Christianity.* San Francisco: Ignatius Press, 2004.

———. *Jesus of Nazareth: From the Baptism in the Jordan to the Transfiguration.* New York: Doubleday, 2007.

———, and Peter Seewald. *Last Testament.* Translated by Jacob Phillips. London: Bloomsbury, 2016.

———. "Letter Given to Sigismund Zimowski as an Extraordinary Mission for the Celebration of the 21st World Day of the Ill." 2013. https://www.vatican.va/content/benedict-xvi/la/letters/2013/documents/hf_ben-xvi_let_20130110_card-zimowski.html.

———. "Mass 'Pro Eligendo Romano Pontifice,' Homily of His Eminence Cardinal Joseph Ratzinger, Dean of the College of Cardinals." April 18, 2005. http://www.vatican.va/gpII/documents/homily-pro-eligendo-pontifice_20050418_en.html.

BIBLIOGRAPHY

———. "Mass with the Beatification of Venerable Cardinal John Henry Newman." September 19, 2010. www.vatican.va/content/benedict-xvi/en/homilies/2010/documents/hf_ben-xvi_hom_20100919_beatif-newman.html.

———. "The Meaning of Sacrament." *FCS Quarterly* (Spring 2011): 28–35.

———. "Meeting with Clergy of the Dioceses of Belluno-Feltre and Treviso." July 24, 2007.

———. *Milestones: Memoirs, 1927–1977.* San Francisco: Ignatius Press, 1998.

———. "The New Pagans and the Church." Translated by Kenneth Baker, SJ. *Homiletic and Pastoral Review*, January 30, 2017. https://www.hprweb.com/2017/01/the-new-pagans-and-the-church/. Originally published in German as "Die neuen Heiden und die Kirche." *Hochland* 51 (1958–59): 1–11.

———. *Das Offenbarungsverständnis und die Geschichtstheologie Bonaventuras: Habilitationsschrift und Bonaventura-Studien.* In *Gesammelte Schriften*, band 2, edited by Gerhard Ludwig Müller. Freiburg: Herder, 2009. A portion of this was published in English as *The Theology of History in St. Bonaventure.* Translated by Zachary Hayes. Chicago: Franciscan Herald Press, 1971.

———. *On Conscience: Two Essays.* San Francisco: Ignatius Press, 2007.

———. *Pilgrim Fellowship of Faith: The Church as Communion.* Translated by Henry Taylor. San Francisco: Ignatius Press, 2002.

———. Preface. In *Evolutionismus und Christentum*, edited by Robert Spaemann, R. Löw, and P. Koslowski, vii–ix. Weinheim: Acta Humaniora, 1986.

———. Preface. In *The Organic Development of the Liturgy: The Principles of Liturgical Reform and Their Relation to the Twentieth-Century Liturgical Movement Prior to the Second Vatican Council*, by Dom Alcuin Reid. San Francisco: Ignatius Press, 2005.

———. "Presentation of His Eminence Joseph Cardinal Ratzinger on the Occasion of the First Centenary of the Death of Cardinal John Henry Newman." Rome. April 28, 1990. www.vatican.va/roman_curia/congregations/cfaith/documents/rc_con_cfaith_doc_19900428_ratzinger-newman_en.html.

———. *Priester aus innerstem Herzen.* Munich: Klerusblatt, 2007.

———. *Principles of Catholic Theology: Building Stones for a Fundamental Theology.* Translated by Mary Frances McCarthy. San Francisco: Ignatius Press, 1982.

———. *Das Problem der Dogmengeschichte in der Sicht der katholischen Theologie.* Cologne: Westdeutscher Verlag, 1966.

BIBLIOGRAPHY

———, and Vittorio Messori. *The Ratzinger Report: An Exclusive Interview on the State of the Church*. Translated by Salvator Attanasio and Graham Harrison. San Francisco: Ignatius Press, 1985.

———. *A Reason Open to God: On Universities, Education, and Culture*. Washington, DC: The Catholic University of America Press, 2013.

———, and William Congdon. *The Sabbath of History*. Translated by Susan S. Cesaritti and John Rock. Washington, DC: WGC Foundation, 2006. Originally published in German as *Meditationen Zur Karwoche*. Freising: Meitinger Kleinschriften, 1969.

———. *Salt of the Earth*. San Francisco: Ignatius Press, 1997.

———. "Soy Negra Pero Hermosa." In *El Nuevo Pueblo de Dios*, translated by Daniel Ruiz Bueno, 285–90. Barcelona: Herder, 1972.

———. *Storia e dogma*. Milan: Jaca Book, 1971.

———. *Theological Highlights of Vatican II*. New York: Paulist Press, 1966.

———. *Truth and Tolerance: Christian Belief and World Religions*. San Francisco: Ignatius Press, 2003.

———. *The Unity of the Nations: A Vision of the Church Fathers*. Translated by Boniface Ramsey. Washington, DC: The Catholic University of America Press, 2015.

———. *Values in a Time of Upheaval*. San Francisco: Ignatius Press, 2006.

———. *Volk und Haus Gottes in Augustins Lehre von der Kirche*. In *Gesammelte Schriften*, band 1. Freiburg: Herder, 2011.

———. *Vom Wiederauffinden der Mitte: Grundorientierungen*. Freiburg: Herder, 1997.

———. *Western Culture Today and Tomorrow*. Translated by Michael J. Miller. San Francisco: Ignatius Press, 2007.

———. *What It Means to Be a Christian*. Translated by Henry Taylor. San Francisco: Ignatius Press, 2006.

———. *The Yes of Jesus Christ: Spiritual Exercises in Faith, Hope and Love*. Translated by Robert Nowell. New York: Crossroad, 1991.

Rickabaugh, Brandon L. "Eternal Life as Knowledge of God: An Epistemology of Knowledge by Acquaintance and Spiritual Formation." *Journal of Spiritual Formation and Soul Care* 6 (2013): 204–28.

Rickaby, Joseph. *Index to the Works of John Henry Cardinal Newman*. London: Longmans, Green, and Co., 1914.

Roberts, Robert C. *Emotions: An Essay in Aid of Moral Psychology*. Cambridge: Cambridge University Press, 2003.

Roberts, Robert C., and W. Jay Wood. *Intellectual Virtues: An Essay in Regulative Epistemology*. Oxford: Clarendon, 2007.

Robinson, Denis. "Preaching." In *The Cambridge Companion to John Henry Newman*, edited by Ian Ker and Terrence Merrigan, 241–54. Cambridge: Cambridge University Press, 2009.

Römer, Thomas. "The Revelation of the Divine Name to Moses and the Construction of a Memory about the Origins of the Encounter between Yhwh and Israel." In *Israel's Exodus in Transdisciplinary Perspective*, edited by Thomas Levy, Thomas Schneider, and William Propp, 305–16. New York: Springer, 2015.

Rule, Philip C. *Coleridge and Newman: The Centrality of Conscience*. New York: Fordham University Press, 2004.

Rulla, Luigi M., Franco Imoda, and Sr. Joyce Ridick. "Anthropology of the Christian Vocation: Conciliar and Postconciliar Aspects." In *Vatican II: Assessment and Perspectives; Twenty-Five Years After (1962–1987)*, edited by René Latourelle, 2:402–59. 3 vols. New York: Paulist Press.

Rumayor, Miguel. "Notas sobre la Formacíon de la Conciencia en John Henry Newman." *Scripta Theologica* 51 (2019): 801–23.

Rowell, Geoffrey. "The Ecclesiology of the Oxford Movement." In *Oxford Handbook of the Oxford Movement*, 216–30. Oxford: Oxford University Press, 2017.

Rowland, Tracey. *Beyond Kant and Nietzsche: The Munich Defence of Christian Humanism*. London: Bloomsbury, 2021.

———. *Catholic Theology*. London: T&T Clark, 2017.

———. *The Culture of the Incarnation: Essays in Catholic Theology*. Steubenville, OH: Emmaus Academic, 2017.

———. "Karl Marx y el marxismo: El problema de la primacía de la praxis." In *Ratzinger y Los Filosofos: De Platón a Vattimo*, edited by Alejandro Sada, Tracey Rowland, y Rudy Albino de Assunção, 191–209. Madrid: Encuentro, 2023.

BIBLIOGRAPHY

———. *Ratzinger's Faith: The Theology of Pope Benedict XVI*. Oxford: Oxford University Press, 2008.

———. "The World in the Theology of Joseph Ratzinger/Benedict XVI." *Journal of Moral Theology* 2, no. 2 (2013): 109–32.

Rowland, Tracey, and Francesca Aran Murphy, eds. *The Oxford Handbook on Joseph Ratzinger*. Oxford: Oxford University Press, forthcoming.

Russell, Norman. *The Doctrine of Deification in the Greek Patristic Tradition*. Oxford: Oxford University Press, 2004.

Saldarini, Anthony J. "Matthew." In *Eerdmans Commentary on the Bible*, edited by James D. G. Dunn. Grand Rapids, MI: Eerdmans, 2003.

Sander, Hans-Joachim. "Theologischer Kommentar zur Pastoralkonstitution über die Kirche in der Welt von heute." In *Herders theologischer Kommentar zum Zweiten Vatikanischen Konzil*, edited by Bernd Jochen Hilberath and Peter Hünermann, 4:581–886. Freiburg: Herder, 2005.

Sanford, Johnathan J. "Newman and the Virtue of Philosophy." *Expositions* 9, no. 1 (2015): 41–55.

San Martín, Inés. "Experts Debate Meaning of 'Synodality' for Global Church." *Crux*, June 13, 2022. https://cruxnow.com/church-in-the-americas/2022/06/experts-debate-meaning-of-synodality-for-global-church.

Sanz, Santiago. "Joseph Ratzinger y la doctrina de la creación: Los apuntes de Münster de 1964 (y III)." *Revista Española de Teología* 74 (2014): 453–96.

Sarto, Pablo Blanco. "Fe, razon y amor: Los discursos de Ratisbona." *Scripta Theologia* 39, no. 3 (2007): 767–82.

———. "*Logos* and *Dia-Logos*: Faith, Reason, (and Love) according to Joseph Ratzinger." *Anglican Theological Review* 92, no. 3 (2010): 499–509.

Scally, Derek. "Roots in Traumatic German History." *Irish Times*, April 21, 2005. https://www.irishtimes.com/news/roots-in-traumatic-german-history-1.433886.

Schall, James, SJ. *The Regensburg Lecture*. South Bend, IN: St. Augustine's Press, 2007.

Schenk, Richard. "Officium Signa Temporum Perscrutandi: New Encounters of Gospel and Culture in the Context of the New Evangelization." In *Scrutinizing the Signs of the Times in the Light of the Gospel*, edited by Johan Verstraeten, 167–203. Bibliotheca Ephemeridum Theologicarum Lovaniensium 208. Leuven: Peeters, 2007.

BIBLIOGRAPHY

Schlier, Heinrich. *Besinnung auf das Neue Testament.* Freiburg: Herder, 1964.

——. *Die Zeit der Kirche: Exegetische Aufsätze und Vorträge.* Freiburg: Herder, 1966.

Schlögl, Manuel. "Platón: Dios, conciencia y verdad." In *Ratzinger y Los Filosofos,* 29–40.

Schweiker, William. "Theology of Culture and its Future." In *The Cambridge Companion to Paul Tillich,* edited by Russell Manning, 138–51. Cambridge: Cambridge University Press, 2009.

Second Vatican Council. *Ad gentes. Decree on the Mission Activity of the Church.* December 7, 1965. https://www.vatican.va/archive/hist_councils/ii_vatican_council/documents/vat-ii_decree_19651207_ad-gentes_en.html.

——. *Apostolicam Actuasitatem. Decree on the Apostolate of the Laity.* November 18, 1965. https://www.vatican.va/archive/hist_councils/ii_vatican_council/documents/vat-ii_decree_19651118_apostolicam-actuositatem_en.html.

——. *Dei verbum. Dogmatic Constitution on Divine Revelation.* November 18, 1965. https://www.vatican.va/archive/hist_councils/ii_vatican_council/documents/vat-ii_const_19651118_dei-verbum_en.html.

——. *Dignitatis Humanae. Declaration on Religious Freedom.* December 7, 1965. https://www.vatican.va/archive/hist_councils/ii_vatican_council/documents/vat-ii_decl_19651207_dignitatis-humanae_en.html.

——. *Gaudium et spes. Pastoral Constitution on the Church in the Modern World.* December 7, 1965. https://www.vatican.va/archive/hist_councils/ii_vatican_council/documents/vat-ii_const_19651207_gaudium-et-spes_en.html.

——. *Lumen gentium. Dogmatic Constitution on the Church.* November 21, 1964.

——. *Sacrosanctum concilium. Constitution on the Sacred Liturgy.* December 4, 1963. https://www.vatican.va/archive/hist_councils/ii_vatican_council/documents/vat-ii_const_19631204_sacrosanctum-concilium_en.html.

Seewald, Michael. *Theories of Doctrinal Development in the Catholic Church.* Translated by David West. Cambridge: Cambridge University Press, 2023.

Seneca. *De Otio, De Brevitate Vitae.* Edited by G. D. Williams. Cambridge: Cambridge University Press, 2008.

Seynaeve, Jaack. *Cardinal Newman's Doctrine on Holy Scripture according to His Published Works and Unedited Manuscripts.* Universitas Catholica Lovaniensis Series II, tomus 5. Leuven: Publications Universitaires de Louvain, 1953.

BIBLIOGRAPHY

Shea, C. Michael "Development." In *The Oxford Handbook of John Henry Newman*, edited by Frederick D. Aquino and Benjamin J. King, 284–303. Oxford: Clarendon, 2018.

——. *Newman's Early Roman Catholic Legacy, 1845–1854*. Oxford: Oxford University Press, 2017.

Sheridan, Thomas L. "Justification." In *The Cambridge Companion to John Henry Newman*, edited by Ian Ker and Terrence Merrigan, 98–117. Cambridge: Cambridge University Press, 2009.

Shrimpton, Paul. *Conscience before Conformity: Hans and Sophie Scholl and the White Rose Resistance in Nazi Germany*. Leominster: Gracewing, 2018.

——. *The Making of Men: The Idea and Reality of Newman's University in Oxford and Dublin*. Leominster: Gracewing, 2011.

Shusterman, Richard. "Fallibilism and Faith." In *A "Dictatorship of Relativism?" Symposium in Response to Cardinal Ratzinger's Last Homily*, edited by Jeffrey M. Perl, 379–84. Durham, NC: Duke University Press, 2007.

Sieben, Hermann-Josef. *Manna in deserto: Studien zum Schriftgebrauch der Kirchenväter*. Edition Cardo 92. Cologne: Koinonia-Oriens, 2002.

Sillem, Edward, ed. *The Philosophical Notebook of John Henry Newman*. Leuven: Nauwelaerts, 1969.

deSilva, David A. *Introducing the Apocrypha: Message, Context, and Significance*. 2nd ed. Grand Rapids, MI: Baker Academic, 2018.

Simpson, W. J. Sparrow. *Roman Catholic Opposition to Papal Infallibility*. London: John Murray, 1909.

Söhngen, Gottlieb. *Humanität und Christentum*. Essen: Verlagsgesellschaft Augustin Wibbelt, 1946.

——. *Kardinal Newman: Sein Gottesgedanke und seine Denkergestalt*. Bonn: Verlag Götz Schwippert, 1946.

——. *Symbol und Wirklichkeit im Kultmysterium*. Bonn: Peter Hanstein, 1937.

Sokolowski, Robert. "God's Word and Human Speech." *Nova et Vetera* 11 (2013): 187–210.

Solomon, Robert. *The Passions: Emotions and the Meaning of Life*. Indianapolis, IN: Hackett, 1993.

Sonderegger, Katherine. "Writing Theology in a Secular Age: Joseph Ratzinger on Theological Method." In *The Theology of Benedict XVI: A Protestant Appreciation*, edited by Tim Perry, 28–45. Bellingham, WA: Lexham, 2019.

BIBLIOGRAPHY

de Sousa, Ronald. *Emotional Truth*. Oxford: Oxford University Press, 2011.

Spadaro, Antonio. "A Big Heart Open to God: An Interview with Pope Francis." *America Magazine*, September 30, 2013. https://www.americamagazine.org/faith/2013/09/30/big-heart-open-god-interview-pope-francis.

Spicq, Ceslas, OP. "Gewissen." In *Bibeltheologisches Wörterbuch*, edited by Johannes B. Bauer. Graz: Styria, 1994.

Starčević, Mirko. "John Henry Newman and the Oxford Movement: A Poet of the Church." *English Language Overseas Perspectives and Enquiries* 12, no. 2 (November 2015): 129–45.

Steinbüchel, Theodor. *Friedrich Nietzsche: Eine christliche Besinnung*. Stuttgart: Deutsche Verlags-Anstalt, 1946.

Steiner, George. *Real Presences*. London: Faber and Faber, 1989.

Stelzenberger, Johannes. *Conscientia bei Augustinus: Studie zur Geschichte der Moraltheologie*. Paderborn: Schöningh, 1959.

Stewart, Kenneth J. "The Tractarian Critique of the Evangelical Invisible: Tracts 2, 11, 20 and 47 in Historical Context." *Churchman* 121, no. 4 (Winter 2007): 349–62.

Van Stichel, Ellen, and Yves De Maeseneer. "*Gaudium et Spes*: Impulses of the Spirit for an Age of Globalisation." *Louvain Studies* 39 (2015–2016): 63–73.

Strange, Roderick. *Newman and the Gospel of Christ*. Oxford: Oxford University Press, 1981.

———. "Newman and the Mystery of Christ." In *Newman after a Hundred Years*, edited by Ian Ker and Alan Hill, 323–36. Oxford: Oxford University Press, 1990.

Tabaczek, Mariusz. "What Do God and Creatures Really Do in an Evolutionary Change? Divine Concurrence and Transformism from the Thomistic Perspective." *American Catholic Philosophical Quarterly* 93 (2019): 445–82.

Tanner, Kathryn. *Theories of Culture: A New Agenda for Theology*. Minneapolis: Augsburg Fortress, 1997.

Terlinden, Luc. "The Originality of Newman's Teaching on Conscience." *Irish Theological Quarterly* 73 (2008): 294–306.

von Teuffenbach, Alexandra. *Pius XII: Neue Erkenntnisse über sein Leben und Wirken*. Aachen: MM Verlag, 2010.

Thérèse of Lisieux. *Story of a Soul*. Translated by John Clarke. Washington, DC: ICS Publications, 1996.

BIBLIOGRAPHY

Thiel, John E. "The New Donatism: An Old Controversy Illuminates the Bishops' Biden Gambit." *Commonweal*, July 5, 2021. https://www.commonwealmagazine.org/new-donatism.

Thomas à Kempis. *The Imitation of Christ*. Edited by Mary Lea Hill. Translated by Mary Nazarene Prestofillipo. Boston: Pauline Books & Media, 2015.

Thomas, Stephen. *Newman and Heresy*. Cambridge: Cambridge University Press, 1991.

Tillich, Paul. *Theology of Culture*. Oxford: Oxford University Press, 1959.

——. *Über die Idee einer Theologie der Kultur*. Berlin: Reuther & Reichard, 1919.

Tillman, Mary Katherine. "Economies of Reason: Newman and the *Phronesis* Tradition." In *Discourse and Context: An Interdisciplinary Study of John Henry Newman*, edited by Gerard Magill, 45–53. Carbondale: Southern Illinois University Press, 1993.

——. *John Henry Newman: Man of Letters*. Milwaukee: Marquette University Press, 2015.

Trocholepczy, Bernd. "Gewissen: Befähigung und Herausforderung zur Conversio Continua." In *Sinnsuche und Lebenswenden: Gewissen als Praxis nach John Henry Newman*, edited by Günter Biemer, Lothar Kuld, and Roman Siebenrock, 51–64. Bern: Lang, 1998.

Tromp, Sebastian, SJ. "Annotations ad enc. *Mystici Corporis*." *Periodica de re morali, canonica, liturgica* 32 (1943): 377–401.

Trower, Philip. *Turmoil and Truth: The Historical Roots of the Modern Crisis in the Catholic Church*. San Francisco: Ignatius Press, 2003.

Tuckett, C. M. "Mark." In *The Oxford Bible Commentary*, edited by John Barton and John Muddiman, 886–921. Oxford: Oxford University Press, 2001.

Twomey, D. Vincent. *Pope Benedict XVI, The Conscience of Our Age: A Theological Portrait*. San Francisco: Ignatius Press, 2007.

Tyrrell, George. *Through Scylla and Charybdis, or The Old Theology and the New*. London: Longmans, Green, and Co., 1907.

Vélez, Juan. *Holiness in a Secular Age: The Witness of Cardinal Newman*. New York: Scepter, 2017.

Vilbig, Ryan. "John Henry Newman's View of the 'Darwin Theory.'" *Newman Studies Journal* 8, no. 2 (2011): 52–61.

Viviano, Benedict T., OP. "The Gospel according to Matthew." In *The New Jerome Biblical Commentary*, edited by Raymond E. Brown, Joseph A. Fitzmyer, and Roland E. Murphy. Englewood Cliffs, NJ: Prentice Hall, 1968.

——. "The Reception of the Second Vatican Council in Light of Its Prehistory and the Discernment of the Signs of the Times." *Verba theologica* 2 (2013): 5–19.

Wainwright, William J. *Reason and the Heart: A Prolegomenon to a Critique of Passional Reason*. Ithaca, NY: Cornell University Press, 1995.

Wallis, Richard T. "The Idea of Conscience in Philo of Alexandria." *Studia Philonica* 3 (1974/1975): 27–40.

Ward, Wilfred. *The Life of John Henry Cardinal Newman: Based on His Private Journals and Correspondence*. Vol. 2. London: Longmans, 1912.

Webb, Hillary S. "Coincidentia Oppositorum." In *Encyclopedia of Psychology and Religion*, edited by David A. Leeming, Kathryn Madden, and Stanton Marlan, 157–59. Boston: Springer, 2010.

Whitaker, Charles. "Clouds (Part One): A Really Special Cloud." *Forerunner Magazine* 30, no. 2 (2021).

White, James Emery. *Rise of the Nones: Understanding and Reaching the Religiously Unaffiliated*. Grand Rapids, MI: Baker Books, 2014.

White, Thomas Joseph, OP. *"Gaudium et Spes."* In *The Reception of Vatican II*, edited by Matthew L. Lamb and Matthew Levering, 113–43. Oxford: Oxford University Press, 2017.

——. *The Incarnate Lord*. Washington, DC: The Catholic University of America Press, 2015.

Wicks, Jared, SJ. "Another Text by Joseph Ratzinger as *Peritus* at Vatican II." *Gregorianum* 101 (2020): 233–49.

——. *Investigating Vatican II: Its Theologians, Ecumenical Turn, and Biblical Commitment*. Washington, DC: The Catholic University of America Press, 2018.

——. "Six Texts by Prof. Ratzinger as *Peritus* before and during Vatican Council II." *Gregorianum* 89 (2008): 233–311.

——. "Vatican II on Revelation—From behind the Scenes." *Theological Studies* 71, no. 3 (September 2010): 637–50.

Wiles, Maurice. *Archetypal Heresy: Arianism through the Ages*. Oxford: Clarendon, 1996.

BIBLIOGRAPHY

Williams, Rowan. *Arius: Heresy and Tradition*. 2nd ed. London: SCM, 2001.

Wolterstorff, Nicholas. *John Locke and The Ethics of Belief*. Cambridge: Cambridge University Press, 1996.

Wood, Susan. "Continuity and Development in Roman Catholic Ecclesiology." *Ecclesiology* 7, no. 2 (May 2011): 149–50.

Worner, Tod. "When Father Ratzinger Predicted the Future of the Church." *Aleteia*, June 13, 2016. https://aleteia.org/2016/06/13/when-cardinal-joseph-ratzinger-predicted-the-future-of-the-church/.

Wynn, Mark. "The Relationship of Religion and Ethics: A Comparison of Newman and Contemporary Philosophy of Religion." *Heythrop Journal* 46, no. 4 (2005): 435–49.

Zuijdwegt, Geertjan. *An Evangelical Adrift: The Making of John Henry Newman's Theology*. Washington, DC: The Catholic University of America Press, 2023.

———. "Richard Whately's Influence on John Henry Newman's Oxford University Sermons on Faith and Reason (1839–1840)." *Newman Studies Journal* 10, no. 1 (2013): 82–95.

INDEX

acculturation, 202

Adam (Biblical), 16, 116, 178, 260n14, 263, 286, 291–93, 300

Adam, Karl, 1

aggiornamento, 148–49, 157, 212

Albert the Great, St., 33

Alexandria, Cyril of, St., 98n2, 284

Alexandrian: Christology, 16; city, 175; exegesis, 80; Alexandrian Church, 207

Allison, Dale C., 166

Ambrose, St., 25

analogia entis, 5, 22

analogia fidei, 22

anamnesis, 138–39, 141

anarchy, 136, 235

angel(s), 113, 117, 128n52, 173, 207, 297–98

Anglican Church, 10, 205–6, 212n3, 216, 217n26, 298

Anglicanism, 22, 205–6, 212n3

Anglo-Catholic movement, 205

Anglo-Catholic teaching, 206

Anthony of Egypt, St., 284

anthropology, 13, 16–17, 19, 26, 28, 160n53, 161, 185, 197, 225, 266, 292–93

antihumanism, 161

Antiochene School, 80

apologetics, 256

apostle(s), 10, 38, 41, 78, 83n31, 86, 183n147, 222, 228–29, 234, 237, 253, 297

Apostles' Creed, 288

Apostolic Church, 216

Apostolicam Actuositatem, 149

Appleton, Charles, 274

Aquinas, Thomas (*Doctor Angelicus*), 4, 19–20, 23, 33, 115, 151, 195, 256, 262n22, 268–69, 271n43, 293

arete, 10

Arianism (Arian(s), Arius), 77–78, 79n11, 80–82, 175–76, 206–7, 241, 284

Aristotle, 9, 14, 136, 268–69, 276n58, 277, 277n61

Arrupe, Pedro, 195–97, 201, 203

INDEX

Arthur, James, 10

Ascension, 111–12, 292

assent. *See* complex ascent (CA); simple assent (SA)

Assumption (Mary's), 302, 305

Assyria, 175

Athanasius, St., 26, 77–80, 82–84, 86, 88, 90, 94, 284, 286–87, 301

atheism, 21–24, 30, 34, 146, 160, 180, 294

Augustine of Hippo, St., 23–24, 26–27, 44, 45n35, 120, 123, 129n52, 142, 151, 161–63, 171, 178–79, 186, 190, 223n46, 235n7, 256n1

authoritarianism, 235

Bacon, Francis, 52, 126, 128

baptism, 117, 177, 216–17, 219, 230, 286

Barberi, Dominic, 124

Barth, Karl, 5, 22, 41, 151

Basil, St., 24, 138

Bellarmine, Cardinal Robert, 236n12, 264

Benedict XVI, Pope. *See* Ratzinger, Joseph Cardinal

biblical inerrancy, 83, 94. *See also* senses of Scripture

biblical literalism, 263, 270, 280

Birmingham Oratory, 3

Bloch, Ernst, 294

Body of Christ (Mystical Body), 6, 104n17, 162–63, 186, 211–13, 215–23, 225–31, 233, 235–38, 247, 253, 254, 291–92

Boeve, Lieven, 186n157, 190–92

Boisen, Anton, 115

Bonaventure (*Doctor Seraphicus*), 35, 37, 40, 42, 48, 52, 77, 86–90, 91n58, 94, 115

Borgman, Erik, 156–57

Bornkamm, Günther, 39

Bouyer, Louis, 129, 212n5

Bride (of Christ), 108n34, 183n148, 223

Bridegroom, 223

Brunner, Emil, 22

Butler, Joseph, 31, 56n3, 122–24

Calvinism, 22, 31

canon law, 85

canonization, 202, 209, 284, 305

catechesis, 172, 294

Catholic University of Dublin, 111

catholicum, 191

causality, 257, 262, 264

Chalcedon, 289, 294

charity, 72, 156, 172, 231, 288

Charles I, King, 133

Chenu, Marie-Dominique, 154–57, 164, 179–81, 184–85

Christ the King, 296

Christendom, 230, 246

Christological foundations, 225

Christology, 16, 40, 284, 288–90, 292, 294–95, 304, 307

Cicero, 9–10, 12, 119–20, 126, 137

circumincession, 49, 53

Claudel, Paul, 15

Clement, St., 51, 123

Codex Koridethianus, 135

coincidentia oppositorum, 103, 109

Coleridge, John Taylor, 215

INDEX

Cologne, 8, 11

colonized peoples, 155

Communio, 34, 131, 135, 212, 224–30, 250n71, 289, 294

community, 2n3, 30, 47, 118, 162, 198, 217, 221, 227, 249, 270–71, 277n61

complex assent (CA), 60

conciliar documents, 225, 245; Newman's influence on, 145n1

Concilium, 224–25, 230

confession(s), 124, 166, 242

Congregation for the Doctrine of the Faith (CDF), 5n13, 134, 189, 233

conquistadores, 132

conscientia, 119–20, 131–32, 134, 137

conscientiousness, 147, 177

consciousness, 33, 41, 59, 155, 193, 206, 226, 287

Constantinople III, 243, 295

contemplation, 297

contradiction, 99n6, 110, 137, 159, 185, 259

contrition, 116, 187

conversion, 124, 133, 141, 160, 169, 176, 180, 187–88, 207–8, 209n70, 213n6, 214, 215n14, 237–38, 273, 283, 297

corpus mysticum, 226

Coulson, John, 216

council fathers, 148n8, 149, 151, 241, 244, 250, 299

Council of Jerusalem, 224

Council of Trent, 36, 42, 84

Craddock, Fred, 166

creation, 18–19, 21, 28, 37n9, 76, 91–93, 97, 104n17, 119, 129n52, 136, 140, 147, 155, 178, 196,

222n42, 258, 260n14, 261–65, 267–68, 279

Critical Theory, 132, 134, 136, 141

Crosby, John, 103–5, 109, 112

Cross (Christ's cross), 48, 135, 160–61, 165n84, 167, 185, 188, 289, 293, 302

crucifixion, 44, 164, 292

Darwin, Charles, 75, 213n8, 256–59, 265, 267–68, 279

Darwinian cosmology, 76

Darwinism, 128

De fontibus revelationis, 36, 48, 89–90

de Lubac, Henri, 50, 153, 212n5, 236, 289, 294, 299

de Mallerais, Bernard Tissier, 292

De voluntate Dei erga hominem, 36, 48, 90

Dei Filius, 14, 38, 261n17

Dei Verbum (Constitution on Divine Revelation), 2, 41–42, 47n43, 94–95, 183n148, 239n22, 240, 244

deification, vi, 6, 30–31, 283–89, 291, 293–97, 299–303, 305–7

deism, 124

Democritus, 118

deposit of faith, 3, 6, 220n36, 237, 239, 241, 252, 281

Descartes, René, 69, 102n11, 123

desolation, 127, 147

despair, 30

Dessain, Stephen, 283

development of doctrine (doctrinal development(s)), 2–3, 5, 50, 55n2, 82n27, 86, 203, 204n57, 204–6, 213n8, 214, 234, 239, 243–44, 280

349

INDEX

Dignitatis Humanae, 149

disciplina arcani, 207

divine causality, 262

Divine Nature, 286–87, 297, 301–2

Divine Redeemer, 222

Divine Sonship, 304

divine word, 54, 151

divinity, 78, 83, 97n2, 228, 294, 304

divinization, 283, 287, 291, 302, 305–6

Divino Afflante Spiritu, 223

dogma(s), 6, 23, 25, 27, 36–38, 43, 47–50, 53–54, 104, 109–10, 112, 122–23, 142, 242, 248, 259, 303, 305

dogmatic authority, 251

dogmatic formula(s) (dogmatic formulae), 41, 45, 241

dogmatic principle, 105, 204, 206

dogmatic theology, 43–44

Dulles, Avery, 46, 219n35, 223n46, 247

Eastern fathers (Fathers of the Eastern Church), 151, 284–85

Eastern Orthodox, 246

ecclesial authority, 6, 131, 233–34, 246, 252–54

Ecclesiam Suam, 148–49, 154

ecclesiology (ecclesiologies), 6, 19, 21, 186, 212, 213n6, 215, 218n33, 219–20, 223, 225–30, 233–35, 236, 238, 240, 246–47, 249n63, 250n71, 252, 254, 295

Eco, Umberto, 198

efficient causes, 257

Ekeh, Ono, 102, 105n22, 107n30, 111n43

empiricism, 206, 208

enemies of Christ, 177

Enlightenment, 102n11, 190

epistemic goods, 69, 72n87

epistemology, 13, 23, 56n3, 69–70, 72, 120n25, 255, 264, 266, 270

Eucharist, 108, 137, 227, 229, 231, 295

Evangelii Nuntiandi, 196, 201

evangelization, 31, 154, 158, 181–82, 245, 283

evangelize, 155–56, 251, 299

evil(s), 107, 117–19, 125, 127, 139, 167–68, 178–79, 181, 207, 222, 258n10, 297

evolution, 86, 255–59, 260n14, 261, 262, 264–76, 279–80. *See also* Darwinism

evolutionary history, 255, 266, 270, 281

evolutionary theory, 6, 255–56, 258, 261, 262n21, 263–67, 271–74, 280–81

ex cathedra, 243, 246

existentialism, 289, 292

Faggioli, Massimo, 157–58

fallen man, 15, 178

fideism, 55, 73

Fides et Ratio, 202

First Vatican Council (Vatican I), 1, 14, 38, 84, 220n38, 241–46, 248–49, 261n17

Flanagan, J. S., 86

Francis, Pope, 13, 231

Franzelin, Johann Baptist, 1

INDEX

freedom, 17, 45, 100, 117, 131–32, 134–36, 149, 153, 164, 230n76, 241, 248, 257, 292, 295, 305–6

Freising (Seminary), 23, 130, 141, 233

French Revolution, 125, 296

Frings, Cardinal, 35, 89

fundamental theology, 6, 7n1, 9n8, 19, 34, 39, 50, 296n46

Galileo, 256n1, 259, 264

Gaudium et Spes, 11n12, 13, 15–16, 19, 23, 48, 125, 138, 145–46, 148–49, 151–54, 157, 160–62, 164, 169, 171, 181–82, 184–85, 187–88, 196–97, 202, 244, 261n17, 292, 296n46, 299

geocentrism, 259, 264

German Idealism, 24

Gestalt, 78

Gethsemane, 295

global consciousness, 193

glory, 97, 108, 160, 161, 301, 303

Gnosticism, 42

Goppel, Alfons, 136

Good Samaritan, 182

Görres, Albert, 137

government, 135, 177, 178

grace(s), 13, 18, 32, 47, 126, 128, 129n52, 155, 156n37, 157, 160–61, 179–80, 183n147, 187, 216–17, 221, 284–85, 291, 294, 296–305, 307

Great Britain, 275

great pestilence, 173

Greek Fathers, 10, 286

Gregory the Great, St., 10, 72

Guardini, Romano, 1, 4, 17, 136, 225–26, 238

Günther, Anton, 38

Haecker, Theodor, 4, 9, 10, 18, 34

Hamann, Johann Georg, 198

Harnack, Adolf von, 39, 202n50

Hegel, Georg, 135–36

Heidegger, Martin, 23, 292

Heim, Maximilian, 237

hermeneutic: of continuity, 224n50, 240; of discontinuity, 240–41, 245; of reform, 224, 240–41, 245–46; of rupture, 2, 224, 241

hierarchology, 238

hierarchy, 91n58, 233–34, 247, 253

higher criticism, 75

historical-critical, 48, 82

historical criticism, 76, 92

historical Jesus, 39, 76

historicism, 160

historicity, 36, 38–44, 46–47, 50, 53–54, 156

Hitler, 132–33, 137, 222n42

Hittinger, Russell, 148

Hobbes, 126, 128

holiness, 9, 28, 108n34, 120, 122, 129, 175, 187, 283, 285, 302, 304

Holy Spirit (Holy Ghost), 16, 29, 41, 43, 47, 77–78, 86, 94, 95, 116–17, 119, 123, 134–35, 153, 162, 184n148, 215, 221, 223, 226, 236, 269, 285–86, 298–99, 304

homines bonae voluntatis, 161

hominization, 290–92, 294, 307

homoousion, 81

Honorius, Pope, 243

351

Hugh of St. Victor, 52

human condition, 178, 193

human nature, 14, 45, 99n6, 180, 196–97, 202, 206, 221, 288, 298, 300–302

Humanae Salutis, 146, 148, 164

Humanae Vitae, 19

humanism, 9, 11, 13, 16, 23, 30, 34, 288, 293

Humanistic Gymnasium, 11

Humanitas, 9, 147n3, 161, 186

humanities, 125, 200

humanoid, 266

humanum, 15–16

humility, 72, 83, 171, 175, 189, 231, 300

Hütter, Reinhard, 4, 53n67, 99n7, 130, 239n23

hypostatization, 32

idea of Christianity, 203, 253

identity theology, 38

illative sense, 27, 71, 207, 276–78, 280

image of Christ, 28, 217

imagination, 10, 25, 112, 166, 214n13, 215–16, 218, 230

Immaculata, 305

Immaculate Conception, 242, 244n44, 302–3, 305

Incarnation, 11, 13, 30, 44, 49, 53–54, 77, 97n2, 104–5, 136, 151, 170, 184–85, 196, 228, 286–90, 292–93, 300

Incarnationalism, 185

Incarnationalists, 152

Inculturation, 191–92, 195–96, 199, 202–3, 205

indicia temporum, 148–49

indifference, 294, 296

infallibility, 6, 17, 21, 70, 177n114, 242, 245, 251, 269

infidelity, 160, 180

informal inference, 273, 277

inner tribunal, 115

inspiratio, 87

instrumental causality, 257, 262

intellect, 18, 24–27, 71, 88, 99n7, 102, 110n41, 111, 122, 125, 127, 130

intelligibility, 37n9, 63, 64n43, 184

international collaboration, 155

International Theological Commission, 262

Irenaeus, 51, 293

Israel, 37n9, 104n17, 105, 106n28, 107, 116, 305

Jaspers, Karl, 23, 292

Jerusalem, 108, 165, 174, 224, 253

Jesus, 11n12, 29, 33, 39, 40, 76, 89–90, 92–93, 101n10, 104, 109, 117, 134–35, 139–40, 142, 146, 163–69, 173, 183, 186, 188, 195, 201, 215, 229, 237, 239, 291, 297, 304–5

John XXIII, Pope, 146–48, 150, 152, 154–55, 159n51, 164, 169, 181, 183, 220n38, 245, 252, 281

John Paul II, Pope (Karol Wojtyła), 16, 21, 185, 202, 251, 261, 266, 281

Joint Declaration on the Doctrine of Justification, 22

Jonah, 116, 167–68, 174, 186n154

INDEX

Judaism, 155

judgments of God, 173

Jüngel, Eberhard, 33

justice, 56, 135, 156, 187n157, 195, 297

justification, 22, 58, 60, 85, 285–86

Kant, 24, 62, 128, 133, 140

Kasper, Walter, 1, 11, 44n34, 203n57

Keble, John, 31, 215, 285

Ker, Ian, 145n1, 241n28, 283

Kerr, Fergus, 235

King, Benjamin, 80n14, 81, 82n25, 83n33

kingdom of God, 90, 156

kingdom of heaven, 111, 168, 256n1

kingdoms, 166–67

Kleutgen, Josef, 1

Knoepfler, Maria, 4

knowledge, 7, 12–13, 37, 50, 52, 57–58, 66, 68–71, 75, 83, 98, 99n7, 105, 107n30, 108, 123, 138, 145n1, 177, 179–80, 202, 207, 214n13, 222n42, 237, 256, 258, 262n21, 265, 268, 271–72, 275, 277

Koch, Wilhelm, 4

Komonchak, Joseph, 153n24, 162n65, 164

Küng, Hans, 189, 190n3, 294, 306

Lamentabili, 38

Landgraf, A., 39

Läpple, Alfred, 3, 7n1, 26, 33–34, 130, 236

Laros, Matthias, 4

las Casas, Bartolomé de, 133

Latitudinarian, 81

law: divine law, 128n52, 129n52, 130, 134; eternal law, 128n52, 129n52, 130; moral law, 176

laws, 3, 62, 117, 133–35, 219, 257–58, 264, 271n43

legislator, 18

Lenormant, François, 85

Leo II, Pope, 243

Leo XII, Pope, 52

Leo XIII, Pope, 85, 220n37

Leonine Thomism, 24, 26

Lérins, Vincent of, 38, 213n8

Leyes Nuevas, 133

liberalism: doctrinal liberalism, 125, 141; Malthus and Manchester liberalism, 124; religious liberalism, 22

liberation, 131, 134–36, 153, 295

liberation theology, 134, 153

Libertatis Conscientiae, 134

Liebfrauenkirche, 91

Locke, 67n59, 69–70, 126, 128

locus theologicus, 157

Logos, 17, 63, 65, 67n61, 139

Löhrer, Magnus, 45n37, 48

Louth, Andrew, 285

love, 24, 28, 33, 46, 48, 67, 69, 72, 75, 103n17, 107n32, 108, 110, 117, 125, 130, 135–36, 138, 140, 162, 171, 185, 188, 228, 254, 288, 306

Lumen Fidei, 13

Lumen Gentium, 227, 238

Lutheran, 22, 227

Magisterium, 2n3, 5, 141, 219, 248

Manning, Cardinal, 10

manualist tradition, 235

Mariology, 303–7

marriage(s), 172, 174, 190, 304

Marx, Karl, 135–36; Marxism, 293; Marxist, 132, 294, 296

Mary: Blessed Virgin, 298, 307; Mary, 5, 79, 302–7; mediatrix of (all) grace(s), 303–4, 307; Our Lady, 283, 302, 307

materialism, 160

Maximus the Confessor, 288, 295, 307

McGrath, Mark, 148, 182

Mediator Dei, 223

mercy, 17, 122, 128, 166, 297

merit(s), 1, 16, 145, 161, 178, 286, 289, 298, 300

Messiah, 156

messianic times, 155

Metz, Johann Baptist, 1, 19

Middle Ages, 41, 155

Milbank, John, 197–99

miracle, 92, 167, 298

Modernist Crisis, 213n8, 219–20

Möhler, Johann Adam, 1, 6, 159, 213n8

Monophysite controversy, 206

monothelitism, 243

moral relativism, 160

moral theology, 19, 21, 23, 34

Mount Tabor, 297

multiculturality, 190

Munich, 5n13, 7, 17, 19, 91, 223n46, 233, 236

Murphy, Francesca Aran, 227–29

mysterium, 33

Mystical Body. *See* Body of Christ.

Mystici Corporis, 212n2, 220–21, 222n42, 223, 227n62, 292

nationalism, 6n16, 194, 197n32

naturalism, 299

Nazi, 17, 21, 132, 137, 222n42; Nazism, 4

Neoplatonic philosophy, 80

neoscholasticism, 41, 44, 141, 208, 235

neothomism, 236

Newman, John Henry, writings
   Apologia Pro Vita Sua, 14, 17, 21, 273n47
   Arians of the Fourth Century, 80, 207, 241
   Callista, 130, 171–74
   Certain Difficulties, 128
   "The Communion of Saints," 216
   De quarta oratione s. Athanasii contra Arianos, 80
   Difficulties of Anglicans, 205
   Discourses Addressed to Mixed Congregations, 52, 296
   An Essay on the Development of Christian Doctrine, 2–3, 36, 50, 58n13, 71, 110, 124, 192, 203, 205, 212, 213n8, 214, 239n23, 243, 290
   "Further Illustrations," 83–84
   Grammar of Assent, 7, 9, 13, 17, 25, 27, 56n3, 58n11, 59, 60n24, 71, 123, 128, 206, 214n13, 269, 273, 275–76, 277n61
   "Holiness necessary for future Blessedness," 129
   The Idea of a University, 3, 10, 12, 52–53, 70, 172, 256
   "The Invisible World," 212n4, 218

INDEX

"Lead Kindly Light," 100, 137

Idea of a University, 3, 10, 12, 52–53, 70, 112n45, 172, 256

"Inspiration in its Relation to Revelation," 83–84

Letters on Justification, 285

Letter to the Duke of Norfolk, 20, 127, 138

Letter to Pusey, 284, 303

Meditations on the Litany of Loretto for the Month of May, 302

"Nature and Grace," 299, 300

Oxford University Sermons, 82

Parochial and Plain Sermons, 30, 104, 215n14

Parochial Sermons, 236

Philosophical Notebook, 123

"The Pillar of the Cloud," 100

The Present Position of Catholics in England, 4

Rambler, 253

"The Rise and Progress of Universities," 173

"Saintliness the Standard of Christian Principle," 297

"The Salvation of the Hearer, the Motive of the Preacher," 297

"The Secrecy and Suddenness of Divine Visitations," 174

Select Treatises of St. Athanasius, 83

Sermons Preached on Various Occasion, 296, 300

Tract 73, 103, 109

Tracts for the Times, 218

two posterior sermons, 103

"The Unity of Church," 217

University Sermon(s), 58n13, 60n24, 65n47, 70–71, 82

Newman Week, 8

Nicholls, Guy, 10

Nichols, Aidan, 278

Niebuhr, H. Richard, 195–97

Nietzsche, Friedrich, 22–23, 30

Noonan, John T., 252

Norris, Thomas, 129

obedience, 17, 47, 125, 127, 129n52, 142, 166, 170, 175, 234, 250, 253–54

obediential potency, 155

Ockham's Razor, 268

O'Collins, Gerald, 159n50, 169, 183–84

O'Malley, Frank, 29

O'Malley, John, 149n9, 151–52, 164

O'Malley, Timothy P., 33

Oriel College, 122–23, 215

Origen, 77–78, 135

original sin, 305

orthodoxy, 199, 237, 284

Oxford Movement, 22, 31, 80, 101, 205, 212–15, 216n19, 230, 285

Pacem in Terris, 147, 149, 155

paganism, 171, 194, 204

paideia, 10

Panzerkardinal, 189

papacy, 5, 20–21, 187n157, 209n70, 248, 252

papal authority, 131, 138, 234, 251

papal centralism, 249–50

Parker, Kenneth, 3

Parousia, 165

INDEX

Passion(s), 10, 164, 180, 292, 294

Pastor Aeternus, 246, 248

pastoral realism, 177

patristic doctrine, 283, 285

patristic tradition, 235

Paul VI, Pope, 145n1, 148, 197, 294

peace, 75, 120, 122, 124, 135, 147, 171, 178, 259

Pelagianism, 28, 30

penance, 174, 297

Pentecost, 186

periti / peritus, 145n1, 150, 159, 224, 240, 244n45, 261n16

Personalism, 19, 131

personalist approach, 15, 34

personalist vision, 234

Petrine authority, 51

Petrine office, 20, 251

Pharisee(s), 139, 166–68, 173

Philip Neri, St., 297

Philo, 117

phronesis, 276–77

physiognomy, 200

Pieper, Josef, 280

pierres d'attente, 155, 164

piety, 27, 306

pilgrimage, 100, 179, 295; pilgrims, 178

Pius IX, Pope (Pio Nono), 6n16, 208, 244, 246, 248

Pius X, Pope, 38, 220n37, 244n46, 249n59, 299

Pius XII, Pope, 212n2, 220–23, 292

Plato, 14n25, 118, 119n11, 126, 136

Polemo (character), 130

political theology, 163

positivism, 53, 55

postmodernity, 142, 198, 230

Preparatory Commission, 89

primordial sacrament, 141

prophecies, 149, 174

Protestant(s), 22, 36, 38–39, 43, 54, 159, 192, 207, 227, 289, 298; Protestantism, 4, 22–23, 206, 208, 299

Providentissimus Deus, 85, 220n37

prudence, 29, 276

Przywara, Erich, 1, 4–5, 8, 22, 128, 213n7

Pusey, E. B., 75n1, 258, 285

Quanta cura, 244

Queen of Sheba, 168

Queen of the South, 168

Rademacher, Arnold, 9–10

Rahner, Karl, 1, 5, 44n34, 153n25, 224, 240

Rahnerian system, 153

rationalism, 55, 61, 105, 124, 222n42, 254; hyperrationalism, 73; irrationalism, 27

rationality, 56, 61–62, 64–66, 110n41, 116, 190, 306

Ratzinger, Joseph Cardinal
    Behold the Pierced One, 289, 295
    Called to Communion, 254
    Christmas Address to the Roman Curia, 98, 240
    "The Church as the Mystery of Faith," 237
    Church, Ecumenism, and Politics, 238

INDEX

"Communion: Eucharist–Fellowship–Mission," 229

"Conscience and Truth," 141

"Conscience in its Time," 131

The Conscience of Our Age, 115

Das Problem der Dogmengeschichte (Das Problem), 35n1, 41, 47, 49

Daughter Zion, 305

De voluntate Dei erga hominem, 36, 48, 90

"The Ecclesiology of the Second Vatican Council," 225

"Freiheit und Befreiung. Die anthropologische Vision der Instruktion '*Libertatis Conscientia*'," 131

Habilitationsschrift, 7n1, 13, 40–41, 47n43, 86, 90

In the Beginning, 76, 91–92, 93n65

Instruction on Christian Freedom and Liberation, 131

Introduction to Christianity, 13, 15, 103, 105, 108, 200n46, 235, 265, 288–89, 292–93, 304, 305n85

The Meaning of Christian Brotherhood, 291

"The Meaning of Sacrament," 33

Milestones, 11, 47n43, 55n2, 87n46, 118n6

Offenbarungsverständnis und Geschichtstheologie Bonaventuras, 86

Principles of Catholic Theology, 17

"The Problem of the History of Dogma from a Catholic Viewpoint," 35–36

"The Question of the Concept of Tradition," 49

"Reflections on Europe," 296

Regensburg Address, 11, 13, 260

The Spirit of the Liturgy, 295

Theological Highlights of Vatican II, 179n126, 240, 248

"The Unity of the Nations," 163

Vom Auffinden der Mitte, 137

Vom Wiederauffinden der Mitte, 132

Western Culture Today and Tomorrow, 296

What It Means to Be a Christian, 287

Rauschning, Herrmann, 132

Realpolitik, 175

reconciliation, 95, 127, 151, 160n53, 296n46

redemption, 136, 174, 292

reductio in historiam, 37, 43, 46–47, 49–50, 53

reductio in theologiam, 37, 43, 47, 49–50, 53

Reformation, 8, 213, 236, 285, 289

Reformers, 216

Regula Fidei, 79

Reid, Dom Alcuin, 250

relativism, 24, 99–100, 142, 160, 200–201, 208

religious zeal, 175

Renan, Ernest, 83

renewal, 6, 8, 225, 240–41, 244, 280, 285

repentance, 139–40, 166, 168–69, 172–76, 182, 187; repent, 174–76

Ressourcement, 95, 212–13, 289

Resurrection, 39, 41, 44, 47–48, 168, 256n1, 292–93

revelatio, 87, 94

Risen One, 229

Robinson, Denis, 102, 112

INDEX

Roman Empire, 156

Roman rite, 250

Roman School, 1, 299

Romanism, 206; Romanists, 216

Romanticism, 8, 216n19, 220

Rome, 1, 4, 10, 13, 25, 136, 141, 163, 177n114, 206, 208, 220n38, 231n77, 251, 253

Rowland, Tracey, 3–4, 6–7, 161n64, 162n65, 224–25, 236

rupture. *See* hermeneutic

Russian Orthodox ecclesiology, 227

sacrament(s), 31–33, 117, 136, 141, 160n53, 186, 216–17, 219, 229, 249

sacramental economy, 33

sacramentality, 31–34, 249

sacramental participation, 162

Sacred Congregation of Studies, 52

Sacrosanctum Concilium, 250

Sadducee(s), 166–68, 173

salvation, 13–14, 21, 25, 30, 32, 54, 88–89, 92, 94–96, 128, 159, 179, 183, 186, 229, 236, 287, 291, 297, 303, 306

sanctification, 30–31, 192, 208, 227n62, 284–85, 302–3

Santa Maria Consolatrice, 136

Scheeben, Matthias Joseph, 1

Schema 13, 152, 159

Schenk, Richard, 153

Schillebeeckx, Edward, 156, 294

Schlier, Heinrich, 46–48

Schneider, Reinhold, 131–33

schola theologorum, 242–43, 247

scholasticism, 14, 25, 39, 235

Scott, Thomas, 122, 124

second coming, 166, 170. *See also* Parousia

Second Quest. *See* historical Jesus

Second Spring of English Catholicism, 208

Second Vatican Council (Vatican II), 1, 5, 31n90, 34–35, 39n11, 44, 131, 145–46, 149, 184, 196, 212, 220, 223–26, 230, 234, 237n17, 239–41, 243–45, 248–50, 252, 294, 297, 299; spirit of the council, 169, 245

Seeberg, Reinhold, 39

Seewald, Michael, 2–3

semen evangelii, 157

seminarian, 19, 26, 33, 130

seminary, 3–4, 6, 7n1, 23, 55n2, 130, 141, 191n9, 236

Seneca, 120, 124

senses of Scripture: literal sense, 78; spiritual senses, 78

sensus fidei, 141

Shea, Michael, 3, 244n44

Sicca, 171–74

sign from heaven, 167, 172

Signa temporum, 147–48, 150

simple assent (SA), 59

sin, 14, 30, 108, 119, 125, 129, 134, 139–40, 151, 153, 160–61, 175, 178–79, 187, 292, 300, 302, 305

skepticism, 22, 100, 125, 153

skopos, 77–80, 82n25, 83–86, 89–95

social conformism, 137

socialization, 155, 178

societas perfecta, 236–37

Socrates, 118–19, 119n11, 137

Söhngen, Gottlieb, 4–16, 18, 21–28, 31–34, 299

Solomon, 168–69

Son of Man, 165–66, 186n154, 229
Sonderegger, Katherine, 5
Sophists, 137
Spicq, Ceslas, 117
spiritual life, 177, 193, 296, 303
spirituality, 72, 87, 103, 112, 159n51, 230, 285, 292
Stein, Edith, 4
Steinbüchel, Theodore, 23
Stoa, 119
Strange, Roderick, 102n14, 103, 104n20, 105, 110n39
Suarez, Francisco, 41
suffering(s), 107, 133, 141, 179, 221, 291–92
symbolism, 33
syneidesis, 116
synteresis, 137, 139

Tanner, Kathryn, 196–99
technological progress, 155, 179
Temple, 164, 165n81, 174, 286
temptations, 162, 178, 247, 254, 286, 294
theological loci, 154
theology (theologies) of culture, 191–95, 197–200, 204
theology of history, 35, 152
Third Reich, 133, 194
Thomas, Stephen, 81
Tillich, Paul, 193–95, 197, 199
Tillman, Mary Katherine, 276, 278n61
totalitarianism, 132
Tractarian, 207, 215, 215n14, 216, 218n33, 219

tradition(s), 3, 10, 17, 22, 24–25, 36, 38–39, 42–43, 49, 55n2, 56n3, 82, 92, 128, 154, 157n42, 158, 165n84, 170, 190, 198, 207, 216, 234–37, 241, 246, 250–54, 257, 271–72, 276, 278n61, 285n6
Transcendence, 63, 198
Tricoranutum, 11
Tübingen School of Theology, 3
tutorial office, 215
Twomey, Vincent, 27, 115

una mystica persona, 222
unbelievers, 170, 177, 187
unity, 1, 9, 24, 49, 52, 67, 79n11, 88, 124, 138, 163, 186, 213n8, 216–17, 222, 229, 249, 251, 253, 279, 291, 295
universalism, 195
universality, 12, 191–95, 197–99, 201–4, 208
University Church of St. Mary the Virgin in Oxford, 215
University of Munich, 5n13, 17, 19, 223n46
University of Tübingen, 103
Urerinnerung, 138
Utilitarianism, 128

vera philosophia, 191–92
Veritatis Splendor, 21
Victorian England, 66n52, 192, 209, 220
Victorian era, 215
vigilance, 169–70
virgin, 79, 215, 216n25, 298, 301, 305–7

virginity, 304–5

virtue(s), 16, 20, 72, 117, 155, 176, 187, 192, 207–8, 260, 291

Vischer, Lukas, 153, 159

Viviano, Benedict, 152

vocation, 134, 235n6, 239, 247, 250–51, 254, 302

von Balthasar, Hans Urs, 1, 212n5, 288–89, 304, 305n85, 306

von Döllinger, Ignaz, 6

von Drey, Johann Sebastian, 1

Vorgrimler, Herbert, 240

Ward, Wilfred, 274

White Rose martyrs, 17–18, 128n51

White, Thomas Joseph, 152n22, 202

Wicks, Jared, 48, 244n46

Wiles, Maurice, 81

Williams, Rowan, 80–81

wisdom, 3, 65–66, 69–72, 79, 92–93, 130, 139, 168–69, 175, 221, 258, 264, 280

Wissenschaft, 13, 45

Wojtyła, Karol. *See* John Paul II

Wolterstorff, Nicholas, 69

women, 103, 147, 155, 229

working classes, 155

World War I (First World War), 8, 193, 220n37

World War II (Second World War), 3–4, 130, 132, 220

worship, 23, 69, 112, 117, 123, 136, 162, 172, 190, 203, 222n42, 231, 253n76

wounds, 128, 231

Xenophon, 118